Introducing
Windows Server® 2008

Mitch Tulloch with the
Microsoft® Windows Server Team

01/17/08
Birdy

PUBLISHED BY
Microsoft Press
A Division of Microsoft Corporation
One Microsoft Way
Redmond, Washington 98052-6399

Library of Congress Control Number: 2007924650

Printed and bound in the United States of America.

2 3 4 5 6 7 8 9   QWT   2 1 0 9 8 7

Distributed in Canada by H.B. Fenn and Company Ltd.

A CIP catalogue record for this book is available from the British Library.

Microsoft Press books are available through booksellers and distributors worldwide. For further information about international editions, contact your local Microsoft Corporation office or contact Microsoft Press International directly at fax (425) 936-7329. Visit our Web site at www.microsoft.com/mspress. Send comments to tkinput@microsoft.com.

Acquisitions Editor: Martin DelRe
Developmental Editor: Karen Szall
Project Editor: Denise Bankaitis

Body Part No. X13-72717

Contents at a Glance

1   Introduction. 1

2   Usage Scenarios. 9

3   Windows Server Virtualization 17

4   Managing Windows Server 2008 39

5   Managing Server Roles 71

6   Windows Server Core. 109

7   Active Directory Enhancements 149

8   Terminal Services Enhancements 189

9   Clustering Enhancements 251

10 Network Access Protection 285

11 Internet Information Services 7.0. 341

12 Other Features and Enhancements 377

13 Deploying Windows Server 2008. 421

14 Additional Resources 441

Table of Contents

Preface xiii

1   Introduction. 1

    What's Between the Sheets 3

    Acknowledgments. 4

    One Last Thing—Humor 7

2   Usage Scenarios. 9

    Providing an Identity and Access Infrastructure. 10

    Ensuring Security and Policy Enforcement 10

    Easing Deployment Headaches. 11

    Making Servers Easier to Manage 12

    Supporting the Branch Office 13

    Providing Centralized Application Access. 13

    Deploying Web Applications and Services 14

    Ensuring High Availability 14

    Ensuring Secure and Reliable Storage 15

    Leveraging Virtualization. 16

    Conclusion 16

3   Windows Server Virtualization 17

    Why Enterprises Love Virtualization. 17

        Server Consolidation. 18

        Business Continuity 18

        Testing and Development 19

        Application Compatibility 19

        Virtualization in the Datacenter 19

What do you think of this book? We want to hear from you!

Microsoft is interested in hearing your feedback so we can continually improve our books and learning resources for you. To participate in a brief online survey, please visit:

www.microsoft.com/learning/booksurvey/

Virtualization Today 20
    Monolithic Hypervisor 22
    Microkernelized Hypervisor 22
Understanding Virtualization in Windows Server 2008 24
    Partition 1: Parent 25
    Partition 2: Child with Enlightened Guest 26
    Partition 3: Child with Legacy Guest 27
    Partition 4: Child with Guest Running Linux 28
Features of Windows Server Virtualization 28
Managing Virtual Machines in Windows Server 2008 29
System Center Virtual Machine Manager 2007 36
SoftGrid Application Virtualization 36
Conclusion 37
Additional Reading 37

4   Managing Windows Server 2008 39
Performing Initial Configuration Tasks 39
Using Server Manager 42
    Managing Server Roles 44
    ServerManagerCmd.exe 50
    Remote Server Administration Tools 53
Other Management Tools 56
    Group Policy 56
    Windows Management Instrumentation 59
    Windows PowerShell 64
    Microsoft System Center 68
Conclusion 69
Additional Resources 69

5   Managing Server Roles 71
Understanding Roles, Role Services, and Features 71
    Available Roles and Role Services 72
    Available Features 83

Adding Roles and Features 95

Using Initial Configuration Tasks. 97

Using Server Manager 104

From the Command Line 105

Conclusion 108

Additional Reading 108

6   Windows Server Core 109

What Is a Windows Server Core Installation? 109

Understanding Windows Server Core 111

The Rationale for Windows Server Core 115

Performing Initial Configuration of a Windows Server Core Server 118

Performing Initial Configuration from the Command Line 118

Managing a Windows Server Core Server 130

Local Management from the Command Line. 130

Remote Management Using Terminal Services 137

Remote Management Using the Remote Server Administration Tools. 140

Remote Administration Using Group Policy 141

Remote Management Using WinRM/WinRS. 142

Windows Server Core Installation Tips and Tricks 143

Conclusion 147

Additional Resources 147

7   Active Directory Enhancements 149

Understanding Identity and Access in Windows Server 2008 149

Understanding Identity and Access 149

Identity and Access in Windows 2000 Server 150

Identity and Access in Windows Server 2003 151

Identity and Access in Windows Server 2003 R2 152

Identity and Access in Windows Server 2008 153

Active Directory Domain Services 158

AD DS Auditing Enhancements. 158

Read-Only Domain Controllers 164

Restartable AD DS 168

Granular Password and Account Lockout Policies 169

Active Directory Lightweight Directory Services 172

Active Directory Certificate Services 176

    Certificate Web Enrollment Improvements 176

    Network Device Enrollment Service Support 177

    Online Certificate Status Protocol Support 177

    Enterprise PKI and CAPI2 Diagnostics 179

    Other AD CS Enhancements 180

Active Directory Federation Services 182

Active Directory Rights Management Services 186

Conclusion 187

Additional Resources 187

8 Terminal Services Enhancements 189

Core Enhancements to Terminal Services 190

    Remote Desktop Connection 6.0 191

    Single Sign-On for Domain-joined Clients 200

    Other Core Enhancements 201

    Installing and Managing Terminal Services 209

Terminal Services RemoteApp 216

    Using TS RemoteApp 217

    Benefits of TS RemoteApp 225

Terminal Services Web Access 226

    Using TS Web Access 227

    Benefits of TS Web Access 232

Terminal Services Gateway 232

    Implementing TS Gateway 235

    Benefits of TS Gateway 237

Terminal Services Licensing 238

Other Terminal Services Enhancements 243

    Terminal Services WMI Provider 243

    Windows System Resource Manager 246

    Terminal Services Session Broker 247

Conclusion 249

Additional Resources 250

9   Clustering Enhancements **251**

    Failover Clustering Enhancements 252

        Goals of Clustering Improvements 253

        Understanding the New Quorum Model......................... 254

        Understanding Storage Enhancements 256

        Understanding Networking and Security Enhancements.............. 259

        Other Security Improvements 261

        Validating a Clustering Solution 261

        Tips for Validating Clustering Solutions........................ 266

        Setting Up and Managing a Cluster........................... 267

        Creating a Highly Available File Server 269

        Performing Other Cluster Management Tasks 273

    Network Load Balancing Enhancements............................ 278

    Conclusion 283

    Additional Resources 283

10   Network Access Protection **285**

    The Need for Network Access Protection 286

    Understanding Network Access Protection 287

        What NAP Does... 288

        NAP Enforcement Methods................................. 289

    Understanding the NAP Architecture 297

    A Walkthrough of How NAP Works 299

    Implementing NAP 301

        Choosing Enforcement Methods 302

        Phased Implementation 303

        Configuring the Network Policy Server 307

        Configuring NAP Clients 317

    Troubleshooting NAP 319

    Conclusion 339

    Additional Resources 340

11 Internet Information Services 7.0 . . . . **341**

Understanding IIS 7.0 Enhancements 341

Security and Patching 342

Administration Tools 351

Configuration and Deployment 360

Diagnostics 365

Extensibility 368

What's New in IIS 7.0 in Windows Server 2008 370

The Application Server Role 371

Conclusion 374

Additional Resources 375

12 Other Features and Enhancements **377**

Storage Improvements 378

File Server Role 378

Windows Server Backup 381

Storage Explorer 384

SMB 2.0 386

Multipath I/O 387

iSCSI Initiator 390

iSCSI Remote Boot 397

iSNS Server 401

Networking Improvements 402

Security Improvements 407

Other Improvements 414

Conclusion 419

Additional Resources 419

13 Deploying Windows Server 2008 . . . . **421**

Getting Windows Server 2008 421

Installing Windows Server 2008 422

Manual Installation 422

Unattended Installation 423

Using Windows Deployment Services 423

Multicast Deployment 424

TFTP Windowing 427

EFI x64 Network Boot Support 430

Solution Accelerator for Windows Server Deployment. 431

Understanding Volume Activation 2.0 432

Conclusion 439

Additional Resources 440

14   Additional Resources 441

Product Home Page 441

Microsoft Windows Server TechCenter 442

Microsoft Download Center 442

Microsoft Connect. 443

Microsoft TechNet. 445

Beta Central 445

TechNet Events. 446

TechNet Virtual Labs. 448

TechNet Community Resources 448

TechNet Columns. 451

TechNet Magazine. 451

TechNet Flash Newsletter. 451

MSDN 451

Blogs 452

Blogs by MVPs. 453

Channel 9 454

Microsoft Press Books. 454

Conclusion 455

Index. 457

What do you think of this book? We want to hear from you!

Microsoft is interested in hearing your feedback so we can continually improve our books and learning resources for you. To participate in a brief online survey, please visit:

www.microsoft.com/learning/booksurvey/

Preface

OK, let's begin with the standard boilerplate text that a title like this is always supposed to open with. My editors demanded that I add this, so in deference to their absolute power over me, I obediently give you, Dear Reader, the following Preface...

What Is This Book About?

Introducing Windows Server 2008 is the first title from Microsoft Press to present Windows Server 2008 (formerly called Windows Server Code Name "Longhorn"), the latest version of the Windows Server operating system. This book provides a comprehensive overview of Windows Server 2008 at the Beta 3 milestone. Because Beta 3 is a pre-release version of the platform, some features will likely change before release to manufacturing (RTM) occurs. So the descriptions of these features in this book might not be completely accurate. However, please be assured that the author, working together with the Windows Server 2008 product team at Microsoft, has tried very hard to ensure that the information presented in this book will still be as accurate as possible even after RTM.

Who Is This Book For?

The target audience for this book is IT professionals who plan on deploying Windows Server 2008 in enterprise environments, and who might therefore be testing pre-release versions of Windows Server 2008 prior to rolling it out on their production networks. The book will be distributed widely at TechEd 2007 and other Microsoft events, but it will also be available through the usual commercial channels (bookstores) for IT pros who can't make these events and who therefore might want to purchase it.

How Is This Book Organized?

The book is organized into 14 chapters, which start with a brief introduction followed by an overview of different usage scenarios for Windows Server 2008. After the intro and overview, the chapter text describes in technical detail the new features and enhancements of Windows Server 2008 and also the tools for managing these features. The book concludes with a final chapter that lists additional resources for those who want to learn more about the platform.

Conventions Used in This Book

Apart from the main narrative discussion contained in the text, the main style element IT pro readers will be interested in is the frequent "From The Expert" sidebars. These sidebars have been contributed by individuals on (or working closely with) the Windows Server 2008 product team at Microsoft, and they provide readers with technical insights, recommendations, and tips that only those who are creating Windows Server 2008 can supply.

Support Policy

As indicated previously, this book is based on Beta 3 of Windows Server 2008, so features and user interface elements are subject to change between the time of writing and RTM. Microsoft therefore makes no guarantees that the information presented in this book will still be accurate when Windows Server 2008 RTM's.

If you have feedback for Microsoft Press concerning this title, you can submit it as follows:

Postal mail:

Microsoft Press
Attn: Editor, Introducing Windows Server Longhorn
One Microsoft Way
Redmond, WA 98052-6399

Email: mspinput@microsoft.com

Please note that product support is *not* offered through the above e-mail address. For support information, please visit the Microsoft Web site at *http://www.microsoft.com/support.*

The Show Begins

Whew! Now that we've got all that dreadful boilerplate stuff out of the way, turn the page and let's go to the *real* introduction to this title. Enjoy!

–Mitch Tulloch, MVP

Chapter 1
Introduction

Well, you've made it past the table of contents and have arrived at the Introduction, so I guess I better start introducing this book to you and explaining what it's about. This is the first book about Microsoft Windows Server 2008 published by Microsoft Press, and let me be straight with you right from the beginning. What? A book about Windows Server 2008 is being published when the product is only in Beta 3? Won't it have inaccuracies? (Sure.) Aren't features still subject to change? (Yup.) Doesn't that make this a "throwaway" book? (Not on your life, you'll see.) And why would Microsoft Press publish a book about a product that's not even finished yet?

The short answer to that final question is that Microsoft Press has always done this sort of thing. Remember *Introducing Windows Vista* by William Stanek? Or *Introducing Microsoft Windows Server 2003* by Jerry Honeycutt? Or *Introducing Microsoft .NET* by David S. Platt? See? I told you. Why does Microsoft Press do this? To get you excited about what's coming down the product pipeline from Microsoft. To help you become familiar with new products while they're still in the development stage. And, of course, to get you ready to buy other books from them once the final version of the product is released. After all, you know what it's like. You have a business and have to make money—so do they.

But isn't a book that's based on a pre-release version (in this case, close to Beta 3) going to be full of inaccuracies and not reflect the final feature lineup in the RTM version of the product? Well, not really, for several reasons. First, I've had the pleasure (sometimes the intense pleasure) of interacting daily with dozens of individuals on the Windows Server 2008 product team at Microsoft during the course of writing this book. And they've been generous (sometimes too generous) in supplying me with insights, specifications, pre-release documentation, and answers to my many, many questions—the answers to some of which I was actually able to understand (sometimes). It's been quite an experience interacting with the product team like this; they're proud of the features they're developing and they have good reason to be. And all this interaction with the product group should mean that a lot of technical errors and inaccuracies will have been avoided for many descriptions of features in this book.

In addition, the product team has generously given their time (occasionally after repeated, badgering e-mails on my part) to review my chapters in draft and to make comments and suggestions (sometimes a lot of suggestions). This, too, should result in a lot of technical gaffs being weeded out. To understand what it means for these individuals to have given their time like this to poring over my chapter drafts, you've got to understand something about the stress of developing a product like Windows Server 2008 and getting it out the door as bug-free as possible and into customers' hands while working under heavy time constraints. After all, the market won't stand still if a product like Windows Server 2008 is delayed. There are competitors—we won't mention their names here, but they're out there and you know about them.

Another reason this book has a high degree of technical accuracy (especially for a pre-release title) is because a lot of it is actually written by the product team themselves! You'll find scattered throughout most of the chapters almost a hundred sidebars (95 at last count) whose titles are prefixed "From the Experts." These sidebars are a unique feature of this book (and especially for a pre-release book), and they provide valuable "under the hood" insights concerning how different Windows Server 2008 features work, recommendations and best practices for deploying and configuring features, and tips on troubleshooting features. These sidebars range from a couple of paragraphs to several pages in length, and most of them were written by members of the Windows Server 2008 product team at Microsoft. A few were written by members of other teams at Microsoft, while a couple were contributed by contractors and vendors who work closely with Microsoft. And more than anything else, the depth of expertise provided by these sidebars makes this book a "keeper" instead of a "throwaway," as most pre-release books usually are.

I'll get you a list of all the names of these sidebar writers in a minute to acknowledge them, but maybe I better show you what a sidebar actually looks like if you've never seen one before (or if you've seen them in other titles but didn't know what they were called). Here's an example of a sidebar:

From the Experts: Important Disclaimer!

The contents of this book are based on a pre-release version of Windows Server 2008 and are subject to change. The new features and enhancements described in the chapters that follow might get pulled at the last minute, modified (especially the GUI), tweaked, twisted, altered, adjusted, amended—press Shift+F7 in Microsoft Office Word for more. Nothing written here is written in stone, and the product group (and myself) have tried not to promise anything or describe features that might not make it into RTM. So while we've made our best effort to ensure this book is a technically accurate description of Windows Server 2008 at the Beta 3 milestone (and hopefully well beyond), we disclaim and deny and renounce and repudiate and whatever (Shift+F7 again) any and all responsibility for anything in this book that is no longer accurate once the final release of Windows Server 2008 occurs. Thanks for understanding.

—*Mitch Tulloch with the Windows Server Team at Microsoft*

That's what a sidebar looks like. Sure hope you've read it!

And having a disclaimer like that shouldn't be a problem, right? For example, if the UI changes for some feature between now and RTM, that shouldn't decrease the technical value of this book much, should it? After all, you're IT pros, so you're pretty smart and can figure out a UI, right? And if a feature has to be dropped at the last minute or changed to make it meet some emerging standard, interoperate better with products from other vendors, or simply to ensure the highest possible stability of the final product, you'll understand, won't you? I mean, you're IT pros, so you know all about how the software development process works, right?

Thanks for cutting us some slack on this. I'm sure you won't be disappointed by what you find between these covers. And whatever flaws or errors or gaps you do happen to find, feel free to fill them in yourself with extra reading and hands-on experimenting with the product. You have the power—you're IT pros. You rock. You rule.

What's Between the Sheets

I guess I should have said "what's between the covers," but sheets are pages, right? Lame attempt at humor there, but I guess you want to know what I'm going to be covering in this book. Well, I could start talking about the "three pillars of Windows Server 2008," which are (Warning! The Marketing Police insist on Init Caps here!) More Control, Increased Protection, and Greater Flexibility. But if I started talking like that you'd probably clap your hands tightly over your ears and start shouting, "Augh! Marketing fluff! Shut it off! Shut it off!!" and run away screaming madly to the server room.

I know that's not being fair to those who work in marketing (poor souls), but we all need to pick on somebody sometimes, don't we? And since you are an IT pro (the target audience of this book), what you want is technical "meat," not marketing "fluff"—and that's exactly what we (myself together with the product team at Microsoft) have tried to bring you. So instead of talking about "pillars," we're going to focus on "features" and "enhancements" (changes to features found on previous Windows Server platforms) so that you can derive the utmost benefit from reading this book.

Windows Server 2008 has a lot of new features and a ton of enhancements to existing ones. Unfortunately, in a book this size (there's no point writing a 1500-page book about pre-release software) this means some features have to get more prominence than others. So some features and enhancements have their own separate chapters, while others get unceremoniously lumped together for coverage. Don't read more into this than is intended, however, as some features simply interest me more than others and some are closer to being finished at the time of writing this than others. Features closer to being finished generally have more internal documentation (the raw source material for much of this book) available and that documentation is usually in near-finished condition.

Anyway, for personal reasons or otherwise, the following new features and enhancements have been chosen by me (and me alone) to be showcased within their own separate chapters:

- The Windows server core installation option of Windows Server 2008
- New and improved server management tools
- Identity and Access (IDA) enhancements to Active Directory
- Clustering enhancements
- Terminal Services enhancements
- Network Access Protection (NAP)
- Internet Information Services 7.0
- Deployment tools

These features all got their own chapters, while most everything else has been lumped together into Chapter 12, "Other Features and Enhancements"—not because they're any less important, but simply for reasons of my personal interest in things, limited time and resources, and convenience.

I'll also talk briefly in Chapter 2, "Usage Scenarios" about why you *will* (the Marketing Police insisted on my using italics there) want to deploy Windows Server 2008 in your enterprise. Thus, Chapter 2 will briefly talk about various scenarios where the new features and enhancements found in Windows Server 2008 can bring your enterprise tangible benefits. So there's a bit of marketing content in that chapter, but it's important for reasons of planning and design. Otherwise, the rest of the book is pure geek stuff.

Acknowledgments

Anyway, before I jump in and start describing all the new features and enhancements found in Windows Server 2008, I'd first like to say "Hats off" to all those working inside Microsoft and others who contributed their valuable time and expertise. Their efforts in writing sidebars for this book, reviewing chapters in their draft form, answering questions, and providing me with access to internal documentation and specifications made this book the quality technical resource that I'm sure you'll find it to be. In fact, let me acknowledge them by name now. I'll omit their titles, as these can be found in the credits at the end of each sidebar. I know the compositor (the person who transforms my manuscript into pages) will probably hate this, but I'm going to put everyone's name on a separate line to call them out and recognize them better for their invaluable contribution to this book. Here goes:

Aaron J. Smith

Ahmed Bisht

Ajay Kumar

Alain Lissoir

Alex Balcanquall

Amit Date

Amith Krishnan

Andrew Mason

Aruna Somendra

Asad Yaqoob

Aurash Behbahani

Avi Ben-Menahem

Bill Staples

Brett Hill

Chandra Nukala

Chris Edson

Chuck Timon

Claudia Lake

Craig Liebendorfer

Dan Harman

David Lowe

Dino Chiesa

Donovan Follette

Eduardo Melo

Elden Christensen

Emily Langworthy

Eric Deily

Eric Fitzgerald

Eric Holk

Eric Woersching

George Menzel

Harini Muralidharan

Harish Kumar Poongan Shanmugam

Isaac Roybal

Jason Olson

Jeff Woolsey

Jeffrey Snover

Jez Sadler

Joel Sloss

John Morello

Kadirvel C. Vanniarajan

Kalpesh Patel

Kapil Jain

Kevin London

Kevin Rhodes

Kevin Sullivan

Kurt Friedrich

Lu Zhao

Mahesh Lotlikar

Manish Kalra

Marcelo Mas

Mike Schutz

Mike Wilenzick

Moon Majumdar

Nick Pierson

Nils Dussart

Nisha Victor

Nitin T Bhat

Oded Shekel

Paul Mayfield

Peter Waxman

Piyush Lumba

Rahul Prasad

Rajiv Arunkundram

Reagan Templin

Samim Erdogan

Samir Jain

Santosh Chandwani

Satyajit Nath

Scott Dickens

Scott Turnbull

Siddhartha Sen

Somesh Goel

Soo Kuan Teo

Sriram Sampath

Suryanarayana Shastri

Suzanne Morgan

Tad Brockway

Thom Robbins

Tim Elhajj

Tobin Titus

Tolga Acar

Tom Kelnar

Tony Ureche

Tres Hill

Ulf B. Simon-Weidner

Vijay Gajjala

Wai-O Hui

Ward Ralston

Yogesh Mehta

Zardosht Kasheff

I hope I haven't missed anyone in the above list of reviewers, sidebar contributors, and other experts. If I have, I'm really sorry—e-mail me and I'll see that you get a free copy of my book!

And since we're acknowledging people here, let me also give credit to the editorial staff at Microsoft Press who helped bring this project to fruition. Thank you, Martin DelRe, Karen Szall, and Denise Bankaitis for your advice, patience, and prodding to help me get this book completed on time for TechEd '07. And thank you, Roger LeBlanc, for your skill and restraint in copyediting my writing and weeding out dangling participles, nested colons, and other grammatical horrors while maintaining my natural voice and rambling style of writing. Thank you to Waypoint Press for their editorial and production services. And thanks especially to Ingrid, my wife and business partner, who contributed many hours of research gathering and organizing material for this book and helped in many other ways every step of the way. She deserves to have her name on a separate page all by herself, but the compositor would probably choke if I tried this, so I'll just give her a whole line to herself, like this:

Thank you, Ingrid!

One Last Thing—Humor

You've probably noticed by now that this chapter is written with a fairly light tone. After all, I'm a geek, so my wife usually doesn't find the jokes I tell to be funny, right? (I'm being ironic actually and using "my wife" as a literary device here, but please don't tell her in case she's offended by this usage.) (More irony.)

OK, so maybe I'm not the most slapstick kind of guy. And why add humor, anyway, to a serious book about a serious product developed by a serious company like Microsoft? Well, apart from the fact that Microsoft can poke fun at itself sometimes (search the Internet for the "Microsoft IPod" video and you'll see what I mean), the main reason I've tried to use humor is to better engage you, the reader. Yes, you're an IT pro, a geek, and you read manuals all day long and get your kick out of finding errors in them. Well I am too—my father used to tell me a story about how, when I was in high school, he came down to see me in my room one evening and found me "reading a calculus textbook and chuckling in a superior way" about something I was reading. I can't remember that particular incident, but I do recall getting a laugh over some of the textbooks I had to read in university. Such is the curse of being a geek.

And, hopefully, that describes you as well—because if you're the totally wound-up and straight-laced type, you're probably in the wrong business if you're an IT pro. Software doesn't always do what it's supposed to do, and it's usually best just to laugh about it and find a workaround instead of taking it out on the vendor.

Anyway, I'm telling you all this just so that you're aware that I'll be adding the occasional joke or giving lighthearted treatment to some of the features and enhancements discussed in this book. In fact, at one point I even thought of trying to add a Dilbert cartoon at the start of each chapter to set the stage for what I wanted to tell you concerning each feature. Unfortunately, I eventually abandoned this plan for three reasons:

- Reason #1: I had to write this book in a hurry so that it could be published in time for TechEd while still being based on builds as near to Beta 3 as possible. So, unfortunately, there was no time to wade through the red tape that Microsoft Legal would probably have required to make this happen.

- Reason #2: My project manager didn't have the kind of budget to pay the level of royalties that United Feature Syndicate, Inc., would probably have demanded for doing this kind of thing.

- Reason #3: Scott Adams probably uses a Mac.

Chapter 2
Usage Scenarios

In this chapter:

Providing an Identity and Access Infrastructure. 10

Ensuring Security and Policy Enforcement 10

Easing Deployment Headaches. 11

Making Servers Easier to Manage. 12

Supporting the Branch Office 13

Providing Centralized Application Access 13

Deploying Web Applications and Services 14

Ensuring High Availability 14

Ensuring Secure and Reliable Storage 15

Leveraging Virtualization 16

Conclusion 16

Before we jump into the technical stuff, let's pause and make a business case for deploying Microsoft Windows Server 2008 in your organization. Sure, there's a marketing element in doing this, and as a techie you'd rather get to the real stuff right away. However, reality for most IT pros means preparing RFPs for bosses, presenting slide decks showing ROI from planned implementations of products, and generally trying to work within the constraints of a meager budget created by pointy-headed executives who can't seem to understand how cool technology is and why they need it for their business.

So let's look briefly at how Windows Server 2008 can benefit your enterprise. I'm assuming you already know a few basic things about the new features and enhancements of the platform (otherwise, you wouldn't be going to TechEd '07 and similar events where this book is being distributed), but you might also want to give this chapter a re-read once you've finished the rest of the book. This will give you a better idea of what Windows Server 2008 is and what it's capable of.

Anyway, let's ask the sixty-four-dollar questions: Who needs Windows Server 2008? And why do I need it?

Oh yeah, I forgot:

```
<marketing jargon=ON>
```

Providing an Identity and Access Infrastructure

At the core of any mid- or large-sized organization are controls—controls concerning who is allowed to access your organization's information resources, how you verify someone's identity, what they're allowed to do, how you enforce controls, and how you keep records for auditing and for increasing efficiency.

An umbrella name for all this is *Identity and Access Management*, or IDA. Organizations need an IDA solution that provides services for managing information about users and computers, making information resources available and controlling access to them, simplifying access using single sign-on, ensuring sensitive business information is adequately protected, and safeguarding your information resources as you communicate and exchange information with customers and business partners.

Why is Windows Server 2008 an ideal platform for building your IDA solution? Because it both leverages the basic functionality of Active Directory found in previous Windows Server platforms and includes new features and enhancements to Active Directory in Windows Server 2008. For example, you can now use Active Directory Domain Services (AD DS) auditing to maintain a detailed record of changes made to directory objects that records both the new value of an attribute that was changed and its original value. You can leverage the new support for Online Certificate Status Protocol in Active Directory Certificate Services (AD CS) to streamline the process of managing and distributing revocation status information across your enterprise. You can use several enhancements in Active Directory Rights Management Services (AD RMS) together with RMS-enabled applications to help you safeguard your company's digital information from unauthorized use more easily than was possible using RMS on previous Windows Server platforms. And you can use the integrated Active Directory Federation Services (AD FS) role to leverage the industry-supported Web Services (WS-*) protocols to securely exchange information with business partners and provide a single sign-on (SSO) authentication experience for users and applications over the life of an online session.

Want to find out more about these enhancements? Turn to Chapter 7, "Active Directory Enhancements," to learn about all this and more. And with Windows Vista on the client side, you have added benefits such as an integrated RMS client, improved smart card support, and better integration with SSO and other Active Directory enhancements in Windows Server 2008.

Ensuring Security and Policy Enforcement

Do users and computers connecting to your network comply with your company's security policy requirements? Is there any way to enforce that this is indeed the case? Yes, there is. In addition to standard policy enforcement mechanisms such as Group Policy and Active Directory authentication, Windows Server 2008 also includes the new Network Access Protection (NAP) platform. NAP provides a platform that helps ensure that client computers trying to connect to your network meet administrator-defined requirements for system health as laid out in your security policy. For example, NAP can ensure that computers connecting to your network to access resources on it have all critical security updates, antivirus software, the latest signature files, a functioning host-based firewall that's properly configured, and so on. And if NAP determines that a client computer doesn't meet all these health requirements, it can quarantine the computer on an isolated network until remediation can be performed or it can deny access entirely to the network. By using the power of NAP, you can enforce compliance with your network health requirements and mitigate the risk of having improperly configured client computers that might have been exposed to worms and other malware.

Want to find out more about NAP? Turn to Chapter 10, "Implementing Network Access Protection," where I have a comprehensive description of the platform and how it's implemented using Windows Server 2008 together with Windows Vista.

And if you *really* want to enhance the security of your servers, try deploying the Windows server core installation option of Windows Server 2008 instead of the full installation option. The Windows server core installation option has a significantly smaller attack surface because all nonessential components and functionality have been removed. Want to learn about this installation option? Turn to Chapter 6, "Windows Server Core," for a detailed walkthrough of its capabilities and tasks related to its management.

Easing Deployment Headaches

Do you currently use third-party, image-based deployment tools to deploy your Windows servers? I'm not surprised—until Microsoft released the Windows Automated Installation Kit (Windows AIK), you were pretty much limited to either deploying Windows using third-party imaging tools or using Sysprep and answer files. The Windows AIK deploys Windows Vista based on Vista's new componentized, modular architecture and Windows image (.wim) file-based installation media format. Windows Vista and the Windows AIK has changed everything, and now Microsoft has finally come on strong in the deployment tools arena. And with the release of the Microsoft Solution Accelerator for Business Desktop Deployment (BDD) 2007 customers now have a best-practice set of comprehensive guidance and tools from Microsoft that they can use to easily deploy Windows Vista and the 2007 Office system across an enterprise.

So deploying Windows clients is a snap now, but what about deploying Windows servers? Windows Server 2008 includes huge improvements in this area with its new Windows Deployment Services role, an updated and redesigned version of the Remote Installation Services (RIS) feature found in Windows Server 2003 and Windows 2000 Server. Windows Deployment Services enables enterprises to rapidly deploy Windows operating systems using network-based installation, a process that doesn't require you to be physically present at each target computer or to install directly from DVD media.

And if you liked BDD 2007, you'll like the similar set of guidance and tools that Microsoft is currently developing for deploying Windows Server 2008 machines. This new set of tools and best practices will be called the *Solution Accelerator for Windows Server Deployment* and it will integrate the capabilities of Windows AIK, ImageX, Windows Deployment Services, and other deployment tools to provide a point-and-click, drag-and-drop deployment experience similar to what you've experienced with BDD 2007 if you've had a chance to play with it already.

Deploying systems is a headache sometimes, but managing licensing and activation of these machines can bring on a migraine. Instead of taking two pills and going to bed, however, you'll find that the enhancements made to Volume Activation 2.0 in Windows Server 2008 take the pain away. This improved feature will also help you sleep at night, knowing that your machines are in compliance with licensing requirements.

Want to read more about all these improvements? Crack open Chapter 13, "Deploying Windows Server 2008," and you'll find everything you need to get you started in this area.

Making Servers Easier to Manage

I usually don't get excited about tools—they're designed to get the job done and nothing more. Sure, some people might buy a new compound miter saw, show it to all their neighbors, and go "Ooh, aah." Not me—maybe it's because I'm a geek and I get excited about quad-core processors instead! Still, you've gotta love tools when they make life easier, and Windows Server 2008 includes a slate of new and improved tools for managing Windows Server 2008 machines throughout your enterprise.

There's Server Manager, an integrated MMC console that provides a single source for managing your server's roles and features and for monitoring your server's status. Server Manager even comes in a command-line version called ServerManagerCmd.exe, which you can use to quickly add role services and features or perform "what if" scenarios such as, "What components would get installed if I added the Web Server role on my system?"

Then there's Windows PowerShell, a command-line shell and scripting language that includes more than 130 *cmdlets*, plus an intuitive scripting language specifically designed for IT pros like you. As of the Beta 3 release of Windows Server 2008, PowerShell is now included as an optional component you can install. PowerShell is a powerful tool for performing administration tasks on Windows Server 2008, such as managing services, processes, and storage. And PowerShell can also be used to manage aspects of certain server roles such as Internet Information Services (IIS) 7.0, Terminal Services, and Active Directory Domain Services.

Then there's the Windows Remote Shell (WinRS) and Windows Remote Management (WinRM) components first included in Windows Vista; enhancements to Windows Management Instrumentation (WMI), also introduced in Windows Vista; improvements in how Group Policy works, including both changes in Windows Vista and in Windows Server 2008; and more.

Where can you learn more about these different tools? Try Chapter 4, "Managing Windows Server 2008" for a start. Then turn to Chapter 6 and to Chapter 11, "Internet Information Services 7.0," for more examples of seeing these tools at work. Managing your Windows servers has never been easier than using what the Windows Server 2008 platform provides for you to do this.

Supporting the Branch Office

It would be nice if all your servers were set up in a single location so that you could keep an eye on them, wouldn't it? Unfortunately, today's enterprise often consists of a corporate head-quarters and a bunch of remote branch offices, sometimes scattered all around the globe. What's worse, you might be the main IT person stuck there at headquarters, while people who don't know a router from a switch have hands-on physical access to your servers, which just happen to be located out there in remote sites instead of being safe under your watchful eye. What can you do to maintain control? "My precioussss! gollum..."

Windows Server 2008 has several technologies that help you keep control and be Lord of the Servers in your enterprise. Read-Only Domain Controllers (RODCs) are a new type of domain controller that hosts a read-only replica of your Active Directory database. If you combine RODCs with the BitLocker Drive Encryption feature first introduced in Windows Vista, you no longer have to worry about thieves (or silly employees) walking off with one of your domain controllers and all your goodies. Restartable Active Directory Domain Services lets you stop Active Directory services on your domain controllers so that updates can be applied or offline defragmentation of the database can be performed, and it can do this without requiring you to reboot your machine. This is a big improvement that not only reduces down-time, but makes your domain controllers easier to manage, which is a plus when they're located at a remote site. Other improvements—such as delegation improvements, the new SMB 2.0 protocol, and the enhanced DFSR introduced in Windows Server 2003 R2—help make Windows Server 2008 an ideal platform for domain controllers that need to be located at branch offices.

Want to find out more about these improvements? Chapter 7 covers RODC and Restartable AD DS, while various other improvements can be found in Chapter 12, "Other Features and Enhancements."

Providing Centralized Application Access

Mobile users can be a pain to support. Although virtual private network (VPN) technologies have made remote access simpler, giving remote users full access to your internal network from over the Internet is often not the best solution. With the improvements to Terminal

Services in Windows Server 2008, however, users (both remote and on the network) can securely access business applications running on your Terminal Servers and have the same kind of experience as if these applications were installed locally on their machines.

Terminal Services Gateway (TS Gateway) lets remote users securely punch through your perimeter firewall and access Terminal Servers running on your corpnet. Terminal Services RemoteApp enables remoting of individual application windows instead of the whole desktop so that an application that is actually running on a Terminal Server looks and feels to the user as if it were running on her own desktop. And Terminal Services Web Access makes application deployment a snap—the user visits a Web site, clicks on a link or icon, and launches an application on a Terminal Server located somewhere in a galaxy far, far away.

Interested in learning more about these new features and enhancements to Terminal Services in Windows Server 2008? Flip to Chapter 8, "Terminal Services Enhancements," and you'll find a ton of information on the subject.

Deploying Web Applications and Services

Does your organization rely on providing Web applications and Web services to customers? Is the Web a way of life for your business? The new features and enhancements found in Internet Information Services 7.0 are going to excite you if that's the case.

Hosting companies will benefit from xcopy deployment, which copies both a site's content and its configuration to the Web server in one single action. The new modular architecture of IIS 7.0 will make a difference in datacenters because it enables you to deploy Web servers that have a low footprint and minimal attack surface.

Enterprises that build B2B and B2C solutions that rely on the .NET Framework 3.0 can use the Application Server role of Windows Server 2008 to leverage industry-standard Web Services (WS-*) protocols for building these solutions on top of IIS 7.0. And Windows System Resource Manager and other components can help you make efficient use of your hardware resources and ensure a consistent end-user experience.

Want to learn more about IIS 7.0 and the Application Server role? Turn to Chapter 11 for a whirlwind tour of these topics.

Ensuring High Availability

I get miffed when I try to buy a book online from some bookstore and have to wait more than five seconds for the check-out page to appear, or if the site temporarily seems to go down. What's wrong with these guys? Don't they understand high availability? What, are they running their entire store on a single box? Don't they know *single point of failure*?

Whatever applications are critical to the operation of your business, you need to use some form of clustering to make sure they never go down or become inaccessible to customers. Windows Server 2008 includes two enhancements in the area of high availability. First, server clusters (now called *failover clusters*) have been significantly improved to make them simple to set up and configure, easier to manage, more secure, and more stable. Improvements have been made in the way the cluster communicates with storage, which can increase performance for both storage area network (SAN) and direct attached storage (DAS). Failover clusters also offer new configuration options that can eliminate the quorum resource from being a single point of failure.

Network Load Balancing (NLB) has also been improved in Windows Server 2008 to include support for IPv6 and the NDIS 6.0 specification. And the WMI provider has been enhanced with new functionality to make NLB solutions more manageable.

Has this piqued your interest? Check out Chapter 9, "Clustering Enhancements," and find out more.

Ensuring Secure and Reliable Storage

I used to think file servers were boring until I learned about the new storage features and enhancements in Windows Server 2008. Not any more. The Share And Storage Management snap-in provided by the File Server role makes managing volumes and shares easier than ever before with its two new wizards. The Provision Storage Wizard provides an integrated storage provisioning experience for performing tasks like creating a new LUN, specifying the LUN type, unmasking a LUN, and creating and formatting a volume. The wizard also supports multiple protocols—including Fibre Channel, iSCSI, and SAS—and it requires only a VDS 1.1 hardware provider. The Provision A Shared Folder Wizard provides an integrated file-share provisioning experience that lets you easily configure permissions, quotas, file screens, and other settings for SMB shares, and it supports NFS shares also.

Then there's Storage Explorer, a new MMC snap-in that provides a tree-structured view of detailed information concerning all the components of your Fibre Channel or iSCSI SAN, including Fabrics, Platforms, Storage Devices, and LUNs. And it provides integrated support for Microsoft Multipath IO (MPIO), which enables software and hardware vendors to develop multipathing solutions that work effectively with solutions built using Windows Server 2008 and vendor-supplied storage hardware devices. And the built-in iSCSI Initiator lets you configure a target iSCSI storage device, plug your server and storage device into a Gigabit Ethernet switch, and—presto!—you've now got high-speed block storage over IP. And there's iSCSI Boot, which lets you install Windows Server 2008 directly to an iSCSI volume on a SAN. The enhanced Windows Server Backup uses the same block-level, image-based (.vhd) backup technology that is used by the CompletePC Backup And Recovery feature of Windows Vista.

How's all that for your lowly, much-maligned file server? Find out more about storage improvements and lots more in Chapter 12.

Leveraging Virtualization

Last but not least (in fact, so *not* least that we'll be covering this topic in our very next chapter), there's Windows Server Virtualization, which will change (once it's released after Windows Server 2008 is released) the entire architecture of Windows servers in fundamental ways. And even though Windows Server Virtualization is still in an early stage of development at the time of writing this book, IT pros like you already know the power virtualization technologies have to affect today's enterprises through server consolidation, business continuity management, development and testing environments, application compatibility, and datacenter workload decoupling.

I won't go into more details about Windows Server Virtualization here—turn to Chapter 3, "Windows Server Virtualization," and get a preview.

Conclusion

```
<marketing jargon=OFF>
```

Whew, that's a relief! That's not the hat I usually wear, because I'm a geek and not a hawker of wares and potions. I'm glad that's over with because now we can get to the technical stuff that we IT pros love to talk about. But, in point of fact, I respect the marketing professionals for what they have to do. If they don't get the news out there about Windows Server 2008, who's going to buy it? And if people don't buy it, how can Microsoft stay in business? And if Microsoft goes out of business, how can I write about their products, make money, and feed my family?

Anyway, now that all that's out of the way, let's dig into the technical stuff and get down and geeky.

Chapter 3
Windows Server Virtualization

In this chapter:

Why Enterprises Love Virtualization 17

Virtualization Today 20

Understanding Virtualization in Windows Server 2008. .24

Features of Windows Server Virtualization 28

Managing Virtual Machines in Windows Server 2008. 29

System Center Virtual Machine Manager 2007. 36

SoftGrid Application Virtualization. 36

Conclusion 37

Additional Reading 37

Now that we've examined some possible usage scenarios for Microsoft Windows Server 2008, it's time to start digging deep into the features of the platform. But there are a *lot* of new features and enhancements in Windows Server 2008–why begin with virtualization?

Customer-facing answer? Need.

Technical answer for us IT pros? Architecture.

Why Enterprises Love Virtualization

Virtualization has been around in computing since the mainframe days of the late '60s. Those of us who are old enough to remember punch cards (carrying boxes of them around was a great way of getting exercise) might remember the IBM 360 mainframe system and the CP/CMS time-sharing operating system, which simulated the effect of each user having a full, standalone IBM mainframe at their fingertips. Each user's "virtual machine" was fully independent of those belonging to other users, so if you ran an application that crashed "your" machine, other users weren't affected.

PCs changed this paradigm in the '80s, and eventually gave users' *physical* machines that today are far more powerful than the mainframes of the '60s and '70s. But as desktop PCs began to proliferate, so did servers in the back rooms of most businesses. Soon you'd have two domain controllers, a mail server running Microsoft Exchange, a couple of file servers, a database server, a Web server for your intranet, and so on. Larger companies might have dozens or even hundreds of servers, some running multiple roles such as AD, DNS, DHCP, or more.

Managing all these separate boxes can be a headache, and restoring them from backup after a disaster can involve costly downtime for your business. But even worse from a business standpoint is that many of them are underutilized. How does virtualization for x86/x64 platforms solve these issues?

Server Consolidation

In a production environment, having a server that averages only 5 percent CPU utilization doesn't make sense. A typical example would be a DHCP server in an enterprise environment that leases addresses to several thousand clients. One solution to such underutilization is to consolidate several roles on one box. For example, instead of just using the box as a DHCP server, you could also use it as a DNS server, file server, and print server. The problem is that as more roles are installed on a box, the uncertainty in their peak usage requirements increases, making it difficult to ensure that the machine doesn't become a bottleneck. In addition, the attack surface of the machine increases because more ports have to be open so that it can listen for client requests for all these services. Patching also becomes more complicated when updates for one of the running service need to be applied—if the update causes a secondary issue, several essential network services could go down instead of one.

Using virtualization, however, you can consolidate multiple server roles as separate virtual machines running on a single physical machine. This approach lets you reduce "server sprawl" and maximize the utilization of your current hardware, and each role can run in its own isolated virtual environment for greater security and easier management. And by consolidating multiple (possibly dozens of) virtual machines onto enterprise-class server hardware that has fault-tolerant RAID hardware and hot-swappable components, you can reduce downtime and make the most efficient use of your hardware. The process of migrating server roles from separate physical boxes onto virtual machines is known as *server consolidation*, and this is probably the number one driver behind the growing popularity of virtualization in enterprise environments. After all, budgets are limited nowadays!

Business Continuity

Being able to ensure business continuity in the event of a disaster is another big driver toward virtualization. Restoring a critical server role from tape backup when one of your boxes starts emitting smoke can be a long and painful process, especially when your CEO is standing over you wringing his hands waiting for you to finish. Having hot-spare servers waiting in the closet is, of course, a great solution, but it costs money, both in terms of the extra hardware and the licensing costs.

That's another reason why virtualization is so compelling. Because *guest* operating systems, which run inside virtual machines (VMs), are generally independent of the hardware on which the *host* operating system runs, you can easily restore a backed-up virtual server to a system that has different hardware than the original system that died. And using virtual machines, you can reduce both scheduled and unscheduled downtime by simplifying the restore process to ensure the availability of essential services for your network.

Testing and Development

IT pros like us are always in learn mode because of the steady flow (or flood) of new technologies arriving on our doorstep. I remember when I had to set up a test network to evaluate Exchange 5.5. I had eight boxes sitting on a bench just so I could try out the various features of the new messaging platform. These included an Exchange 5.0 server, an Exchange 4.0 server, and an MS Mail 3.0 server so that I could test migration from these platforms. Plus I had several different clients running on different boxes. The heat alone from these systems could have kept me warm during a Winnipeg winter.

Testing new platforms is a lot easier today because of virtualization. I can run a half dozen virtual machines easily on a single low-end server, and I can even set up a routed network without having to learn IOS by enabling IP routing on a virtual Microsoft Windows XP machine with two virtual NICs. Architects can benefit from virtualization by being able to create virtual test networks on a single server that mimic closely the complexity of large enterprise environments. Developers benefit too by being able to test their applications in isolated environments, where they can roll back their virtual machines when needed instead of having to install everything from scratch. The whole IT life cycle becomes easier to manage because virtualization reduces the time it takes to move new software from a development environment to test and then production.

Application Compatibility

Another popular use of virtualization today is to ensure application compatibility. Suppose you upgrade the version of Windows you have running on your desktop and find that a critical LOB application won't run properly on the new version. You can try several ways to resolve this problem. You can run the program in application compatibility mode, using the Application Compatibility Toolkit to shim the application so that it works on the new platform. Or you can contact the vendor for an updated version of the application. Another alternative, however, is virtualization: install Microsoft Virtual PC 2007 on each desktop computer where the user needs to use the problem application, install the old version of Windows as a guest OS, and then run the application from there.

Virtualization in the Datacenter

Virtualization also has a special place in the datacenter, as it lets you decouple workloads from hardware to make the best use of your resources. You can rapidly provision workloads as they are needed so that your solutions can both scale up and scale out easily. Virtualization also simplifies automating complex solutions, though current virtualization products are limited in this regard. But that's where Windows Server 2008 comes in.

Virtualization Today

Virtualization today on Windows platforms basically takes one of two forms: Type 2 or Hybrid. A typical example of Type 2 virtualization is the Java virtual machine, while another example is the common language runtime (CLR) of the .NET Framework. In both examples, you start with the host operating system—that is, the operating system installed directly onto the physical hardware. On top of the host OS runs a Virtual Machine Monitor (VMM), whose role is to create and manage virtual machines, dole out resources to these machines, and keep these machines isolated from each other. In other words, the VMM is the virtualization layer in this scenario. Then on top of the VMM you have the guests that are running, which in this case are Java or .NET applications. Figure 3-1 shows this arrangement, and because the guests have to access the hardware by going through both the VMM and the host OS, performance is generally not at its best in this scenario.

Figure 3-1   Architecture of Type 2 VMM

More familiar probably to most IT pros is the Hybrid form of virtualization shown in Figure 3-2. Here both the host OS and the VMM essentially run directly on the hardware (though with different levels of access to different hardware components), whereas the guest OSs run on top of the virtualization layer. Well, that's not exactly what's happening here. A more accurate depiction of things is that the VMM in this configuration still must go through the host OS to access hardware. However, the host OS and VMM are both running in kernel mode and so they are essentially playing tug o' war with the CPU. The host gets CPU cycles when it needs them in the host context and then passes cycles back to the VMM and the VMM services then provide cycles to the guest OSs. And so it goes, back and forth. The reason why the Hybrid model is faster is that the VMM is running in kernel mode as opposed to the Type 2 model where the VMM generally runs in User mode.

Anyway, the Hybrid VMM approach is used today in two popular virtualization solutions from Microsoft, namely Microsoft Virtual PC 2007 and Microsoft Virtual Server 2005 R2.

The performance of Hybrid VMM is better than that of Type 2 VMM, but it's still not as good as having separate physical machines.

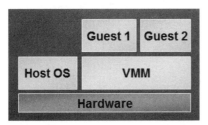

Figure 3-2   Architecture of Hybrid VMM

> **Note**   Another way of distinguishing between Type 2 and Hybrid VMMs is that Type 2 VMMs are *process virtual machines* because they isolate processes (services or applications) as separate guests on the physical system, while Hybrid VMMs are *system virtual machines* because they isolate entire operating systems, such as Windows or Linux, as separate guests.

A third type of virtualization technology available today is Type 1 VMM, or hypervisor technology. A *hypervisor* is a layer of software that sits just above the hardware and beneath one or more operating systems. Its primary purpose is to provide isolated execution environments, called *partitions*, within which virtual machines containing guest OSs can run. Each partition is provided with its own set of hardware resources—such as memory, CPU cycles, and devices—and the hypervisor is responsible for controlling and arbitrating access to the underlying hardware.

Figure 3-3 shows a simple form of Type 1 VMM in which the VMM (the hypervisor) is running directly on the bare metal (the underlying hardware) and several guest OSs are running on top of the VMM.

Figure 3-3   Architecture of Type 1 VMM

Going forward, hypervisor-based virtualization has the greatest performance potential, and in a moment we'll see how this will be implemented in Windows Server 2008. But first let's compare two variations of Type 1 VMM: monolithic and microkernelized.

Monolithic Hypervisor

In the monolithic model, the hypervisor has its own drivers for accessing the hardware beneath it. (See Figure 3-4.) Guest OSs run in VMs on top of the hypervisor, and when a guest needs to access hardware it does so through the hypervisor and its driver model. Typically, one of these guest OSs is the administrator or console OS within which you run the tools that provision, manage, and monitor all guest OSs running on the system.

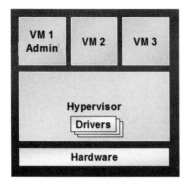

Figure 3-4   Monolithic hypervisor

The monolithic hypervisor model provides excellent performance, but it can have weaknesses in the areas of security and stability. This is because this model inherently has a greater attack surface and much greater potential for security concerns due to the fact that drivers (and even sometimes third-party code) runs in this very sensitive area. For example, if malware were downloaded onto the system, it could install a keystroke logger masquerading as a device driver in the hypervisor. If this happened, every guest OS running on the system would be compromised, which obviously isn't good. Even worse, once you've been "hyperjacked" there's no way the operating systems running above can tell because the hypervisor is invisible to the OSs above and can be lied to by the hypervisor!

The other problem is stability—if a driver were updated in the hypervisor and the new driver had a bug in it, the whole system would be affected, including all its virtual machines. Driver stability is thus a critical issue for this model, and introducing any third-party code has the potential to cause problems. And given the evolving nature of server hardware, the frequent need for new and updated drivers increases the chances of something bad happening. You can think of the monolithic model as a "fat hypervisor" model because of all the drivers the hypervisor needs to support.

Microkernelized Hypervisor

Now contrast the monolithic approach just mentioned with the microkernelized model. (See Figure 3-5.) Here you have a truly "thin" hypervisor that has no drivers running within it. Yes, that's right—the hypervisor has *no drivers at all*. Instead, drivers are run in each partition so that each guest OS running within a virtual machine can access the hardware through the hypervisor. This arrangement makes each virtual machine a completely separate partition for greater security and reliability.

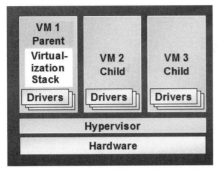

Figure 3-5   Microkernelized hypervisor

In the microkernelized model, which is used in Windows Server virtualization in Windows Server 2008, one VM is the parent partition while the others are child partitions. A partition is the basic unit of isolation supported by the hypervisor. A partition is made up of a physical address space together with one or more virtual processors, and you can assign specific hardware resources—such as CPU cycles, memory and devices—to the partition. The *parent partition* is the partition that creates and manages the *child partitions*, and it contains a virtualization stack that is used to control these child partitions. The parent partition is generally also the *root partition* because it is the partition that is created first and owns all resources not owned by the hypervisor. And being the default owner of all hardware resources means the root partition (that is, the parent) is also in charge of power management, plug and play, managing hardware failure events, and even loading and booting the hypervisor.

Within the parent partition is the virtualization stack, a collection of software components that work in conjunction with and sit on top of the hypervisor and that work together to support the virtual machines running on the system. The virtualization stack talks with the hypervisor and performs any virtualization functions not directory supplied by the hypervisor. Most of these functions are centered around the creation and management of child partitions and the resources (CPU, memory, and devices) they need.

The virtualization stack also exposes a management interface, which in Windows Server 2008 is a WMI provider whose APIs will be made publicly known. This means that not only will the tools for managing virtual machines running on Windows Server 2008 use these APIs, but third-party system management vendors will also be able to code new tools for managing, configuring, and monitoring VMs running on Windows Server 2008.

The advantage of the microkernelized approach used by Windows Server virtualization over the monolithic approach is that the drivers needed between the parent partition and the physical server don't require any changes to the driver model. In other words, existing drivers just work. Microsoft chose this route because requiring new drivers would have been a showstopper. And as for the guest OSs, Microsoft will provide the necessary facilities so that these OSs just work either through emulation or through new synthetic devices.

On the other hand, one could argue that the microkernelized approach does suffer a slight performance hit compared with the monolithic model. However, security is paramount nowadays, so sacrificing a percentage point or two of performance for a reduced attack surface and greater stability is a no-brainer in most enterprises.

> **Tip**   What's the difference between a virtual machine and a partition? Think of a virtual machine as comprising a partition together with its state.

Understanding Virtualization in Windows Server 2008

Before I get you too excited, however, you need to know that what I'm going to describe now is not yet present in Windows Server 2008 Beta 3, the platform that this book covers. It's coming soon, however. Within 180 days of the release of Windows Server 2008, you should be able to download and install the bits for Windows Server virtualization that will make possible everything that I've talked about in the previous section and am going to describe now. In fact, if you're in a hotel after a long day at TechEd and you're reading this book for relaxation (that is, you're a typical geek), you can probably already download tools for your current prerelease build of Windows Server 2008 that might let you test some of these Windows Server virtualization technologies by creating and managing virtual machines on your latest Windows Server 2008 build.

I said *might* let you test these new technologies. Why? First, Windows Server virtualization is an x64 Editions technology only and can't be installed on x86 builds of Windows Server 2008. Second, it requires hardware processors with hardware-assisted virtualization support, which currently includes AMD-V and Intel VT processors only. These extensions are needed because the hypervisor runs out of context (effectively in ring 1), which means that the code and data for the hypervisor are not mapped into the address space of the guest. As a result, the hypervisor has to rely on the processor to support various intercepts, which are provided by these extensions. And finally, for security reasons it requires processor support for hardware-enabled Data Execution Prevention (DEP), which Intel describes as XD (eXecute Disable) and AMD describes as NX (No eXecute). So if you have suitable hardware and lots of memory, you should be able to start testing Windows Server virtualization as it becomes available in prerelease form for Windows Server 2008.

Let's dig deeper into the architecture of Windows Server virtualization running on Windows Server 2008. Remember, what we're looking at won't be available until after Windows Server 2008 RTMs—today in Beta 3, there is no hypervisor in Windows Server 2008, and the operating system basically runs on top of the metal the same way Windows Server 2003 does. So we're temporarily time-shifting into the future here, and assuming that when we try and add the Windows Virtualization role to our current Windows Server 2008 build that it actually does something!

Figure 3-6 shows the big picture of what the architecture of Windows Server 2008 looks like with the virtualization bits installed.

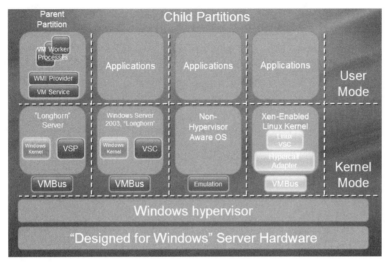

Figure 3-6   Detailed architecture of Windows Server virtualization

Partition 1: Parent

Let's unpack this diagram one piece at a time. First, note that we've got one parent partition (at the left) together with three child partitions, all running on top of the Windows hypervisor. In the parent partition, running in kernel mode, there must be a guest OS, which must be Windows Server 2008 but can be either a full installation of Windows Server 2008 or a Windows server core installation. Being able to run a Windows server core installation in the parent partition is significant because it means we can minimize the footprint and attack surface of our system when we use it as a platform for hosting virtual machines.

Running within the guest OS is the Virtualization Service Provider (VSP), a "server" component that runs within the parent partition (or any other partition that owns hardware). The VSP talks to the device drivers and acts as a kind of multiplexer, offering hardware services to whoever requests them (for example, in response to I/O requests). The VSP can pass on such requests either directly to a physical device through a driver running in kernel or user mode, or to a native service such as the file system to handle.

The VSP plays a key role in how device virtualization works. Previous Microsoft virtualization solutions such as Virtual PC and Virtual Server use emulation to enable guest OSs to access hardware. Virtual PC, for example, emulates a 1997-era motherboard, video card, network card, and storage for its guest OSs. This is done for compatibility reasons to allow the greatest possible number of different guest OSs to run within VMs on Virtual PC. (Something like over 1,000 different operating systems and versions can run as guests on Virtual PC.) Device emulation is great for compatibility purposes, but generally speaking it's lousy for performance. VSPs avoid the emulation problem, however, as we'll see in a moment.

In the user-mode portion of the parent partition are the Virtual Machine Service (VM Service), which provides facilities to manage virtual machines and their worker processes; a Virtual Machine Worker Process, which is a process within the virtualization stack that represents and services a specific virtual machine running on the system (there is one VM Worker Process for each VM running on the system); and a WMI Provider that provides a set of interfaces for managing virtualization on the system. As mentioned previously, these WMI Providers will be publicly documented on MSDN, so you'll be able to automate virtualization tasks using scripts if you know how. Together, these various components make up the user-mode portion of the virtualization stack.

Finally, at the bottom of the kernel portion of the parent partition is the VMBus, which represents a system for sending requests and data between virtual machines running on the system.

Partition 2: Child with Enlightened Guest

The second partition from the left in Figure 3-6 shows an "enlightened" guest OS running within a child partition. An *enlightened guest* is an operating system that is aware that it is running on top of the hypervisor. As a result, the guest uses an optimized virtual machine interface. A guest that is fully enlightened has no need of an emulator; one that is partially enlightened might need emulation for some types of hardware devices. Windows Server 2008 is an example of a fully enlightened guest and is shown in partition 2 in the figure. (Windows Vista is another possible example of a fully enlightened guest.) The Windows Server 2003 guest OS shown in this partition, however, is only a partially enlightened, or "driver-enlightened," guest OS.)

By contrast, a *legacy guest* is an operating system that was written to run on a specific type of physical machine and therefore has no knowledge or understanding that it is running within a virtualized environment. To run within a VM hosted by Windows Server virtualization, a legacy guest requires substantial infrastructure, including a system BIOS and a wide variety of emulated devices. This infrastructure is not provided by the hypervisor but by an external monitor that we'll discuss shortly.

Running in kernel mode within the enlightened guest OS is the Virtualization Service Client (VSC), a "client" component that runs within a child partition and consumes services. The key thing here is that there is one VSP/VSC pair for each device type. For example, say a user-mode application running in partition 2 (the child partition second from the left) wants to write something to a hard drive, which is server hardware. The process works like this:

1. The application calls the appropriate file system driver running in kernel mode in the child partition.

2. The file system driver notifies the VSC that it needs access to hardware.

3. The VSC passes the request over the VMBus to the corresponding VSP in partition 1 (the parent partition) using shared memory and hypervisor IPC messages. (You can think of the VMBus as a protocol with a supporting library for transferring data between different partitions through a ring buffer. If that's too confusing, think of it as a pipe. Also, while the diagram makes it look as though traffic goes through all the child partitions, this is not really the case—the VMBus is actually a point-to-point inter-partition bus.)

4. The VSP then writes to the hard drive through the storage stack and the appropriate port driver.

Microsoft plans on providing VSP/VSC pairs for storage, networking, video, and input devices for Windows Server virtualization. Third-party IHVs will likely provide additional VSP/VSC pairs to support additional hardware.

Speaking of writing things to disk, let's pause a moment before we go on and explain how pass-through disk access works in Windows Server virtualization. Pass-through disk access represents an entire physical disk as a virtual disk within the guest. The data and commands are thus "passed through" to the physical disk via the partition's native storage stack without any intervening processing by the virtual storage stack. This process contrasts with a virtual disk, where the virtual storage stack relies on its parser component to make the underlying storage (which could be a .vhd or an .iso image) look like a physical disk to the guest. Pass-through disk access is totally independent of the underlying physical connection involved. For example, the disk might be direct-attached storage (IDE disk, USB flash disk, FireWire disk) or it might be on a storage area network (SAN).

Now let's resume our discussion concerning the architecture of Windows Server virtualization and describe the third and fourth partitions shown in Figure 3-6 above.

Partition 3: Child with Legacy Guest

In the third partition from the left is a legacy guest OS such as MS-DOS. Yes, there are still a few places (such as banks) that run DOS for certain purposes. Hopefully, they've thrown out all their 286 PCs though. The thing to understand here is that basically this child partition works like Virtual Server. In other words, it uses emulation to provide DOS with a simulated hardware environment that it can understand. As a result, there is no VSC component here running in kernel mode.

Partition 4: Child with Guest Running Linux

Finally, in the fourth partition on the right is Linux running as a guest OS in a child partition. Microsoft recognizes the importance of interoperability in today's enterprises. More specifically, Microsoft knows that their customers want to be able to run *any* OS on top of the hypervisor that Windows Server virtualization provides, and therefore it can't relegate Linux (or any other OS) to second-class status by forcing it to have to run on emulated hardware. That's why Microsoft has decided to partner with XenSource to build VSCs for Linux, which will enable Linux to run as an enlightened guest within a child partition on Windows Server 2008. I knew those FOSS guys would finally see the light one day...

Features of Windows Server Virtualization

Now that we understand something about how virtualization works (or will work) on Windows Server 2008, let's look at what it can actually do. Here's a quick summary:

■ Creates and manage child partitions for both 32-bit (x86) and 64-bit (x64) operating systems.

■ Creates VMs that can use SMP to access 2, 4, or even 8 cores.

■ Creates VMs that use up to 1 TB of physical memory. Windows Server virtualization can do this because it's built on 64-bit from the ground up. That means 64-bit HV, 64-bit virtualization stack, and so on.

■ Supports direct pass-through disk access for VMs to provide enhanced read/write performance. Storage is often a bottleneck for physical machines, and with virtual disks it can be even more of a bottleneck. Windows Server virtualization overcomes this issue.

■ Supports hot-add access to any form of storage. This means you can create virtual storage workloads and manage them dynamically.

■ Supports dynamic addition of virtual NICs and can take advantage of underlying virtual LAN (VLAN) security.

■ Includes tools for migrating Virtual Server workloads to Windows Server virtualization. This means your current investment in Virtual Server won't go down the drain.

■ Supports Windows Server 2008 Core as the parent OS for increased security. I said this earlier, but it bears repeating here because it's important.

■ Supports NAT and network quarantine for VMs, role-based security, Group Policy, utilization counters, non-Microsoft guests, virtual machine snapshots using Volume Shadow Copy Service (VSS), resource control using Windows System Resource Manager (WSRM), clustering, and a whole bunch of other things.

To put this all in perspective, take a look at Table 3-1, which provides a comparison between Virtual Server 2005 R2 and Windows Server virtualization.

Table 3-1   Comparison of Virtual Server 2005 R2 and Windows Server Virtualization Features

Feature	Virtual Server 2005 R2	Windows Server Virtualization
32-bit VMs	Yes	Yes
64-bit VMs	No	Yes
SMP VMs	No	Up to 8 core virtual machines
Hot-add memory	No	Yes
Hot-add processors	No	Yes
Hot-add storage	No	Yes
Hot-add networking	No	Yes
Max memory per VM	3.6 GM	> 32 GB
Cluster support	Yes	Yes
Scripting support	Using COM	Using WMI
Max number of VMs	64	No limit—depends only on hardware
Management tool	Web UI	MMC snap-in
Live migration support	No	Yes
Works with System Center Virtual Machine Manager	Yes	Yes

Note   Virtual Server 2005 R2 Service Pack 1 will support Intel VT and AMD-V technologies, as well as VSS.

Managing Virtual Machines in Windows Server 2008

At the time of this writing, the MMC snap-in for managing virtual machines that is provided with Windows Server virtualization is still evolving, but I wanted to give you a quick preview here. Figure 3-7 shows the Windows Virtualization Management console for a near-Beta 3 build of Windows Server 2008. The console tree on the left displays the name of the server, while the Details pane in the middle shows a number of virtual machines, most of them in an Off state and two in a Saved state. The Actions pane on the right lets you manage virtualization settings, import virtual machines, connect to a virtual machine, and perform other tasks.

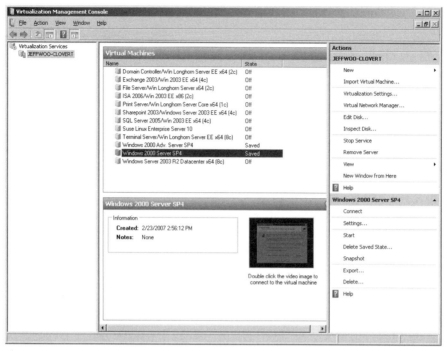

Figure 3-7   Windows Virtualization Management console

So that's a very brief preview of what's in store for virtualization in Windows Server 2008 in terms of managing virtual machines. Fortunately we also have some experts on the product team at Microsoft who provide us with some more information concerning this feature and especially the planning issues surrounding implementing Windows Server virtualization in your environment.

First, here's one of our experts talking about using Windows Server virtualization in conjunction with the Windows server core installation option of Windows Server 2008:

From the Experts: Windows Server Virtualization and a Windows Server Core Installation

The Windows server core installation option of Windows Server 2008 and Windows Server virtualization are two new features of Windows Server 2008 that go hand in hand. The Windows server core installation option is a new minimal GUI shell-less installation option for Window Server 2008 Standard, Enterprise and Datacenter Editions that reduces the management and maintenance required by an administrator. The Windows server core installation option provides key advantages over a full installation of Windows Server 2008 and is the perfect complement to Windows Server virtualization. Here are a couple of reasons why.

■ **Reduced attack surface**   A Windows server core installation provides a greatly reduced attack surface because it is tailored to provide only what a role requires. By providing a minimal parent partition, this reduces the need to patch the parent partition. In the past with one workload running per server, if you needed to reboot the server for a patch, it wasn't ideal, but generally one workload was affected. With Windows Server virtualization, you're not just running a single workload. You could be running dozens (even hundreds) of workloads in their own virtual machine. If the virtualization server requires a reboot for a patch (and you don't have a high availability solution in place), the result could be significant downtime.

- **Reduced resource consumption**   With the parent partition requiring only a fraction of the memory resources for a Windows server core installation as opposed to a full installation of Windows Server 2008, you can use that memory to run more virtual machines.

In short, it is *highly recommended* that you use Windows Server virtualization in conjunction with a Windows server core installation.

–Jeffrey Woolsey
Lead Program Manager, Windows Virtualization

Next, let's hear another of our experts on the virtualization team at Microsoft share about how to identify what should be virtualized in your environment and what maybe shouldn't:

From the Experts: Virtualization Sizing

It is very important to understand how to roll out virtualization in your organization and what makes the most sense for your environment and business conditions. So often, some enthusiastic users and organizations start either attempting to virtualize every-thing or start with their most complex middleware environments. There are no right or wrong first candidates for virtualization but you need to ensure that you have fully thought about the impact of using virtualization in your environment and for the work-loads in question.

As you think about what to virtualize and how to go about picking the right workloads, the order of deployment, and what hardware capabilities you need, find a model or a set of models that help you conceptualize the end solution. The System Center family of products provides you a set of tools that help simplify some of these issues, and other solutions from vendors like HP provide you tools to help size the deployment environment once you have figured out the candidates and the rollout process.

The next few paragraphs help identify some of the best practices in sizing your virtualization environment. Think of the following as a set of steps that will help you identify what workloads to virtualize and what the deployment schedule should look like.

1. **Assessment**   As with any project, the first step is to fully know about where you are today and what capabilities you already have in your environment. The last thing you want to do is to sit and re-create the wheel and invest in things you already have in your environment. As you think about assessment, think about assessing all the components you have in your infrastructure, the types of workloads, and interdependencies of the various workloads. Also evaluate all the management assets you already have in your infrastructure and identify the functions that these are performing, such as monitoring, deployment, data protection, security, and so on. These are the easier items to assess, but the more critical one to assess will be the overall process discipline that exists in your organization and how you deal with change in today's world. While this is a hard factor to quantify, this is critical in evaluating what capacity you have to deploy virtualization. To help you make this assessment from a holistic perspective, there are tools available such as Microsoft's Infrastructure Optimization Model or Gartner's IT Maturity Model that you can choose to use. There is one thing a customer once told me that I will never forget–"If someone tells you they have a solution for your problems when you have not identified or told them what your problems are, most likely they are giving you something you already have in a different package–that is, if you are lucky."

2. **Solution Target**   Once you have identified and assessed your current environment, find out where you can use virtualization today. All server virtualization solutions today provide these usage scenarios:

   ❑ Production Server Consolidation, which encompasses all forms of consolidation of systems in existing or new environments.

   ❑ Test and Development Environments, which addresses the use of virtualization for optimizing the test and dev cycles and not only enables you to leverage the cost saving from hardware needs but also enables easy creation and modification of the environments.

   ❑ Business Continuance, where your primary motivator is to leverage the fact that virtualization transforms your IT infrastructure to files (in Microsoft's case a VHD file) to enable new and interesting continuance and disaster recovery solutions.

❑ Dynamic Datacenter, which is a new set of capabilities unleashed by virtualization to now enable you to not only create and manage your environment more efficiently, but provide a new level of capability to be able to dynamically modify the characteristics of the environments for workloads based on usage. The dynamic resource manipulation enables you to take the consolidation benefits and translate it to now making your IT a more agile environment.

❑ Branch Office, which while not being a core solution, is one usage scenario where virtualization helps change how IT systems are deployed, monitored, and managed and helps extend the capabilities of the branch environment to bring in legacy and new application environments under one common infrastructure umbrella.

As you are trying to decide which solution area or areas to target for your virtualization solution, do keep in mind the level of complexity of the solutions and the need for increasing levels of management tools and process discipline. Test and dev environments are the easiest to virtualize and usually can manage to take some downtime in case of hiccups–hence this is a natural start for everyone. Server Consolidation is another area that you can start using virtualization in today. The initial cost savings here are in the hardware consolidation benefits–but the true value of consolidation is seen only when you have figured out how to use a unified management infrastructure. Business continuance and branch scenarios need you to have a management infrastructure in place to help orchestrate these solutions and again to see the true value – you will need to have a certain level of processes outlined. Dynamic datacenter is a complex solution for most customers to fully deploy and this usually applies to a certain subset of the org's infrastructure–select the workloads that need this type of solution more carefully as adding the SLAs to maintain such a solution should mean that the workload is really critical to the organization.

3. **Consolidation Candidates**   Most users today are deploying virtualization to help consolidate workloads and bring in legacy systems into a unified management umbrella. In this light, it becomes important to identify which workloads are the most logical ones to consolidate today and what makes sense in the future. There are some workloads that sound attractive for virtualization, but might not be ideal at any stretch because of certain I/O characteristics or purely because they are so big and critical that they easily scale up to or beyond the capabilities of the hardware being thrown at them. Operations Manager or Virtual Machine Manager has a report that is generated called the virtualization candidates report that helps scan your entire IT org and tell you exactly what workloads are ideal for virtualization based on a number of thresholds such as CPU utilization, I/O intensity, network usage, size of the workload, and so on. Based on this report and knowing the

interdependencies identified during the assessment phase, you can make intelligent decisions on what workloads to virtualization and when.

4. **Infrastructure Planning**   This is where the rubber meets the road so to speak. Once you have identified the candidates to virtualize, you need a place to host the virtualized workloads. Tools from companies such as HP (HP Virtualization Sizing Guide) help you identify the type of servers you will need in your environment to host the virtualization solution that you have identified in the previous step. There is one fundamental rule to consider as you are selecting the infrastructure for virtualization–the two biggest limiting factors for virtualization are memory and I/O throughput–so always ensure that you select a x64 platform for your hardware to ensure a large memory access, and always try to get the best disk subsystem either into the system for DAS or good SAN devices.

5. **Placement**   This is not so much an area that is going to affect the sizing of your environment, but has the potential to impact your sizing decisions in the long run. Here we are referring to the act of taking one of the virtualization candidates and actually deploying it to one of the selected virtualization host systems. The knowledge of interdependencies of the various workloads affects some of how this placement occurs but from a high level, this is more about optimizing the placement for a few selected variables. Virtual Machine Manager has an intelligent placement tool that helps you optimize either to a load balancing algorithm or to a maximizing utilization algorithm. You can alternatively also tweak individual parameters to help optimize your environment based on your business weights of the different parameters.

As you size your virtualization environment, also keep in mind the overall manageability factor and how you can scale your management apps to help cover the new environment. Now that you have seen how to size your virtualization environments, keep two things in mind–virtualization is a great technology that can help in multiple levels and scenarios but is still not the panacea for all problems so do take the time to identify your true problems and also remember that you need to look at deploying and managing virtualized environments over a long period of time and hence the need to think about virtualization as a 3-year solution at least.

Virtualization is primarily a consolidation technology that abstracts resources and aids aggregation of workloads, so think carefully about how this affects your environment and what steps you need to have in place to avoid disasters and plan for them early.

–Rajiv Arunkundram
  Senior Product Manager, Server Virtualization

Finally, an important planning item for any software deployment is licensing. Here's one of our experts explaining the current licensing plan for Windows virtualization:

From the Experts: Virtualization Licensing

One of the most talked about and often most confused areas for virtualization is licensing. Some of this is primarily caused due to the lack of one industry standard way of dealing with licensing and the other cause is that virtualization is a disruptive technology in how companies operate and hence not clear to customers on what the various policies mean in this new world.

Microsoft's licensing goals are to provide customers and partners cost-effective, flexible, and simplified licensing for our products that will be applicable across all server virtualization products, regardless of vendor. To this effect, several changes were put in place in late 2005 to help accelerate virtualization deployments across vendors:

- Windows server licensing was changed from installation-based licensing to instance-based licensing for server products.

- Microsoft changed licensing to allow customers to run up to 1 physical and 4 virtual instances with a single license of Windows Server 2003 Enterprise Edition on the licensed device; and 1 physical and unlimited virtual instances with Windows Server 2003 Datacenter Edition on the licensed device.

- With the release of SQL Server 2005 SP2, Microsoft announced expanded virtualization use rights to allow unlimited virtual instances on servers that are fully licensed for SQL Server 2005 Enterprise Edition.

With all these changes, you can now easily acquire and license Windows Server and other technologies in a much more efficient process. Virtualization also adds another level of complexity for licensing with the ability to easily move the images or instances around between machines. This is where licensing from the old era makes it tricky. The simple way to remember and ensure that you are fully licensed is to look at the host systems as the primary license holders with the instances being the deployment front. So if you want to move a workload to a system that has Windows Server Enterprise Edition running and already has 4 instances running, you will need an additional license; if it is lower than 4, you will not need an additional license to make the move happen.

Do note that the licensing policies for these apply across virtualization products in the same manner across all server virtualization platforms.

—Rajiv Arunkundram
Senior Product Manager, Server Virtualization

System Center Virtual Machine Manager 2007

The Virtualization Management Console snap-in that is included with Windows Server virtualization is limited in several ways, and it's mainly intended for managing virtual machines on a few servers at a time. Large enterprises want infrastructure solutions, however, and not just point tools. System Center Virtual Machine Manager fills this gap and will enable you to centralize management of a large enterprise's entire virtual machine infrastructure, rapidly provision new virtual machines as needed, and efficiently manage physical server utilization. Plus it's fully integrated with the Microsoft System Center family of products, so you can leverage your existing skill sets as you migrate your network infrastructure to Windows Server 2008.

System Center Virtual Machine Manager runs as a standalone server application, and it can be used to manage a virtualized datacenter that contains hundreds or even thousands of virtual machines in an Active Directory environment. System Center Virtual Machine Manager will be able to manage virtual machines running on both Microsoft Virtual Server 2005 R2 and Windows 2008 Server with Windows Server virtualization installed. You can even deploy System Center Virtual Machine Manager in a fiber-channel SAN environment for performing tasks such as the following:

- Deploying VMs from your SAN library to a host
- Transferring VMs from a host to your library
- Migrating VMs from one host to another host

The administrator console for System Center Virtual Machine Manager is built upon Windows PowerShell, and you can use it to add and manage host machines, create and manage virtual machines, monitor tasks, and even migrate physical machines to virtual ones (something called P2V).

System Center Virtual Machine Manager also includes a self-service Web portal that enables users to independently create and manage their own virtual machines. The way this works is that the administrator predetermines who can create virtual machines, which hosts these machines can run on, and which actions users can perform on their virtual machines.

At the time of this writing, System Center Virtual Machine Manager is in Beta 1 and supports managing only virtual machines hosted on Virtual Server 2005 R2.

SoftGrid Application Virtualization

Finally, another upcoming virtualization technology you should know about is SoftGrid Application Virtualization, which Microsoft took ownership of when it acquired Softricity in July 2006. SoftGrid provides a different kind of virtualization than we've been discussing here—instead of virtualizing an entire operating system, it virtualizes only an application. This functionality makes SoftGrid a more fine-grained virtualization technology than Windows

Server virtualization. Also, it's designed not for the server end but for deploying applications to desktops easily and updating them as necessary.

Essentially, what SoftGrid can do using its streaming delivery mechanism is to transform any Windows program into a dynamic service that then follows users wherever they might go. These services can then be integrated into Microsoft's management infrastructure so that they can be configured and managed using standard policy-based methods. At this point, SoftGrid isn't directly associated with Windows 2008 Server or Windows Server virtualization, but it's a new Microsoft technology you should be aware of as the virtualization landscape continues to evolve.

Conclusion

It would have been nice to have looked in greater depth at how Windows Server virtualization in Windows Server 2008 works. Unfortunately, at the time of this writing the bits aren't there yet. Still, you have to admit that this is one of the hottest features of Windows Server 2008, both from the perspective of the day-to-day needs of IT professionals and as a prime selling point for Windows Server 2008. I've tried to give you a taste of how this new technology will work and a glimpse of what it looks like, but I hope you're not satisfied with that—I'm not. I can't wait till all this comes together, and the plain truth of the matter is that in only a few years virtualization will be inexpensive and ubiquitous. So get ready for it now.

Bring back the mainframe!!

Additional Reading

If you want to find out more about the underlying processor enhancements from Intel and AMD that will support and be required by Windows Server virtualization, check out the following sources:

- See *http://www.intel.com/technology/virtualization/index.htm* for information concerning Intel VT technology
- See *http://www.amd.com/us-en/Processors/ProductInformation/ 0,,30_118_8826_14287,00.html* for information about AMD-V technology

For information on how Microsoft and XenSource are collaborating to support running Linux on Windows Server 2008, read the following article on Microsoft PressPass: *http://www.microsoft.com/presspass/press/2006/jul06/07-17MSXenSourcePR.mspx*.

The starting point for finding out more about current (and future) Microsoft virtualization products is *http://www.microsoft.com/windowsserversystem/virtualserver/default.mspx* on Microsoft.com.

For more information about System Center Virtual Machine Manager and how you can join the beta program for this product, see *http://www.microsoft.com/windowsserversystem/ virtualization/default.mspx* on the Microsoft Web site. From there, you can jump to pages describing Virtual Server 2005 R2, Virtual PC 2007, System Center Virtual Machine Manager, and most likely Windows Server virtualization on Windows Server 2008 in the near future as well.

If you're interested in finding out more about SoftGrid Application Virtualization, see *http://www.softricity.com/index.asp*, although the Softricity Web site will probably be folded soon into Microsoft.com.

Finally, be sure to turn to Chapter 14, "Additional Resources," if you want to find more resources about Windows Server virtualization in Windows Server 2008. In that chapter, you'll find links to webcasts, whitepapers, blogs, newsgroups, and other sources of information on this feature and other Microsoft virtualization technologies.

Chapter 4
Managing Windows Server 2008

In this chapter:

Performing Initial Configuration Tasks. 39

Using Server Manager. 42

Other Management Tools. 56

Conclusion 69

Additional Resources. 69

I was kidding, of course, when I said we should bring back the mainframe. After all, remember how much fun it was managing those machines? Sitting at a green screen all day long, dropping armfuls of punch cards into the hopper...what fun! At least running an IBM System/360 could be more fun than operating a PDP-11. When I was a university student years ago (decades actually), I worked one summer for the physics department, where there was a PDP-11 in the sub-sub-basement where the Cyclotron was located. I remember sitting there alone one night around 3 a.m. while an experiment was running, watching the lights blink on the PDP and flipping a switch from time to time to read a paper tape. And that was my introduction to the tools used for managing state-of-the-art computers in those days—specifically, lights, switches, and paper tape.

Computers have come a long way since then. Besides being a lot more powerful, they're also a lot easier to manage. So before we examine other new and exciting features of Microsoft Windows Server 2008, let's look at the new and enhanced tools you can use to manage the platform. These tools range from user interface (UI) tools for configuring and managing servers to a new command-line tool for installing roles and features, tools for remote administration, Windows Management Instrumentation (WMI) enhancements for improved scripted management, Group Policy enhancements, and more.

Performing Initial Configuration Tasks

The first thing you'll notice when you install Windows Server 2008 is the Initial Configuration Tasks screen (shown in Figure 4-1).

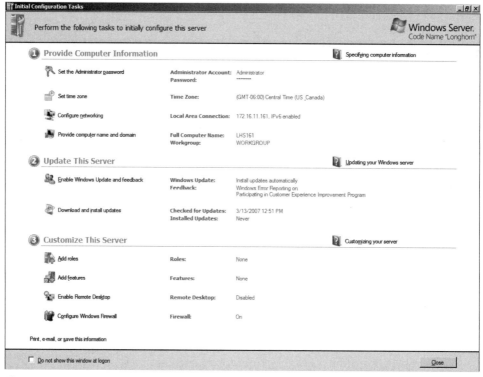

Figure 4-1 The Initial Configuration Tasks screen

Remember for a moment how you perform your initial configuration of a machine running Windows Server 2003 Service Pack 1 or later, where you do this in three stages:

1. During Setup, when you specify your administrator password, network settings, domain membership, and so on

2. Immediately after Setup, when a screen appears asking if you want to download the latest updates from Windows Update and turn on Automatic Updates before the server can receive inbound traffic

3. After you've allowed inbound traffic to your server, when you can use Manage Your Server to install roles on your server to make it a print server, file server, domain controller, and so on

Windows Server 2008, however, consolidates these various server configuration tasks by consolidating during- and post-Setup tasks together and presenting them to you in a single screen called Initial Configuration Tasks (ICT). Using the ICT you can

- Specify key information, including the administrator password, time zone, network settings, and server name. You can also join your server to a domain. For example, clicking the Provide Computer Name And Domain link opens System Properties with the Computer Named tab selected.

- Search Windows Update for available software updates, and enable one or more of the following: Automatic Updates, Windows Error Reporting (WER), and participation in the Customer Experience Improvement Program.

- Configure Windows Firewall on your machine, and enable Remote Desktop so that the server can be remotely managed using Terminal Services.

- Add roles and features to your server—for example, to make it a DNS server or domain controller.

In addition to providing a user interface where you can perform these tasks, ICT also displays status information for each task. For example, if a task has already been performed, the link for the task changes color from blue to purple just like an ordinary hyperlink. And if WER has been turned on, the message "Windows Error Reporting on" is displayed next to the corresponding task item.

Once you've performed the initial configuration of your server, you can click the Print, E-mail Or Save This Information link at the bottom. This opens Internet Explorer and displays a results page showing the settings you've configured.

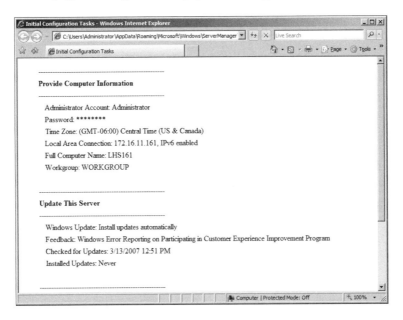

This results page can be found at %systemdrive%\users\<username>\AppData\ Roaming\Microsoft\Windows\ServerManager\InitialConfigurationTasks.html, and it can be saved or e-mailed for reporting purposes.

A few more notes concerning Initial Configuration Tasks:

■ Performing some tasks requires that you log off or reboot your machine. For example, by default when you install Windows Server 2008, the built-in Administrator account is enabled and has no password. If you use ICT to change the name of this account or specify a password, you must log off and then on again for this change to take effect.

■ If Windows Server 2008 detects that it is deployed on a restricted network (that is, quarantined by NAP) when you first log on, the Update This Server section of the ICT displays a new link named Restore Network Access. Clicking this link allows you to review current network access restrictions and restore full network access for your server, and until you do this your server is in quarantine and has only limited network access. The reason that the other two items in this section (Enable Windows Update And Feedback and Download And Install Updates) are not displayed in this situation is that machines in quarantine cannot access Windows Update directly and must receive their updates from a remediation server. For more information about this, see Chapter 10, "Network Access Protection."

■ OEMs can customize the ICT screen so that it displays an additional section at the bottom that can include an OEM logo, a description, and task links that can launch EXEs, DLLs, and scripts provided by the OEM. Note that OEM task links cannot display status information, however.

■ The ICT is not displayed if you upgrade to Windows Server 2008 from a previous version of Windows Server.

■ The ICT is also not displayed if the following Group Policy setting is configured:

Computer Configuration\Administrative Templates\System\Server Manager\Do Not Open Initial Configuration Tasks Windows At Logon

Using Server Manager

OK, you've installed your server, performed the initial configuration tasks, and maybe installed a role or two—such as file server and DHCP server—on your machine as well. Now what? Once you close ICT, another new tool automatically opens—namely, Server Manager (shown in Figure 4-2). I like to think of Server Manager as "Computer Management on steroids," as it can do everything compmgmt.msc can do plus a whole lot more. (Look at the console tree on the left in this figure and you'll see why I said this.)

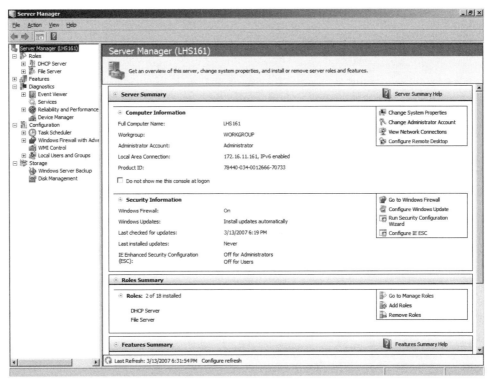

Figure 4-2   Main page of Server Manager

The goal of Server Manager is to provide a straightforward way of installing roles and features on your server so that it can function within your business networking environment. As a tool, Server Manager is primarily targeted toward the IT generalist who works at medium-sized organizations. IT specialists who work at large enterprises might want to use additional tools to configure their newly installed servers, however—for example, by performing some initial configuration tasks during unattended setup by using Windows Deployment Services (WDS) together with unattend.xml answer files. See Chapter 13, "Deploying Windows Server 2008," for more information on using WDS to deploy Windows Server 2008.

Server Manager also enables you to modify any of the settings you specified previously using the Initial Configuration Tasks screen. For example, in Figure 4-2 you can see that you can enable Remote Desktop by clicking the Configure Remote Desktop link found on the right side of the Server Summary tile. In fact, Server Manager lets you configure additional advanced settings that are not exposed in the ICT screen, such as enabling or disabling the Internet Explorer Enhanced Security Configuration (IE ESC) or running the Security Configuration Wizard (SCW) on your machine.

Managing Server Roles

Let's dig a bit deeper into Server Manager. Near the bottom of Figure 4-2, you can see that we've already installed two roles on our server using the ICT screen. We'll learn more about the various roles, role services, and features you can install on Windows Server 2008 later in Chapter 5, "Managing Server Roles." For now, let's see what we can do with these two roles that have already been installed.

Clicking the Go To Manage Roles link changes the focus from the root node (Server Manager) to the Roles node beneath it. (See Figure 4-3.) This page displays a list of roles installed on the server and the status of each of these roles, including any role services that were installed together with them. (Role services will be explained later in Chapter 5.)

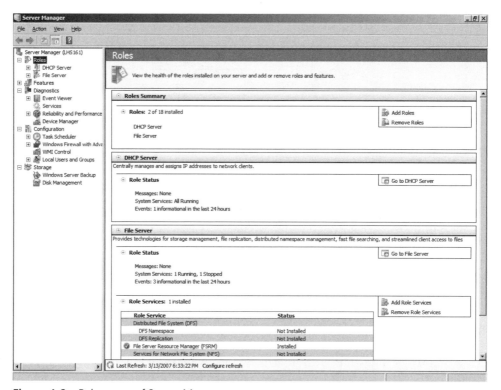

Figure 4-3   Roles page of Server Manager

The status of this page is updated in real time at periodic intervals, and if you look carefully at these figures you'll see a link at the bottom of each page that says "Configure refresh." If you click this link, you can specify how often Server Manager refreshes the currently displayed page. By default, the refresh interval is two minutes.

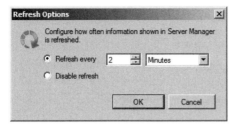

Selecting the node for the File Server role in the console tree (or clicking the Go To File Server link on the Roles page) displays more information about how this role is configured on the machine (as shown in Figure 4-4). Using this page, you can manage the following aspects of your file server:

- View events relevant to this role (by double-clicking on an event to display its details).

- View system services for this role, and stop, start, pause, or resume these services.

- View role services installed for this role, and add or remove role services.

- Get help on how to perform role-related tasks.

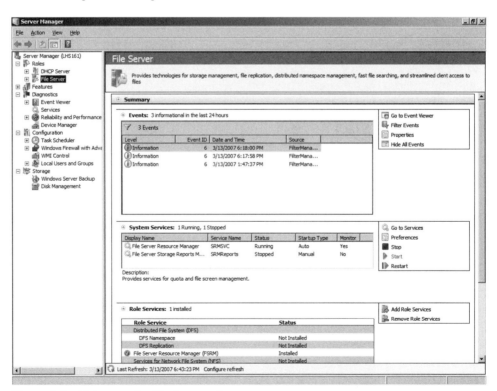

Figure 4-4   Main page for File Server role

Note the check mark in the green circle beside File Server Resource Manager (FSRM) under Role Services. This means that FSRM, an optional component or "role service" for the File

Server role, has been installed on this server. You probably remember FSRM from Windows Server 2003 R2—it's a terrific tool for managing file servers and can be used to configure volume and folder quotas, file screens, and reporting. But in Windows Server 2003 R2, you had to launch FSRM as a separate administrative tool—not so in Windows Server 2008. What's cool about Server Manager is that it is implemented as a managed, user-mode MMC 3.0 snap-in that can host other MMC snap-ins and dynamically show or hide them inline based on whether a particular role or feature has been installed on the server.

What this means here is that we can expand our File Server node, and underneath it you'll find two other snap-ins—namely, File Server Resource Manager (which we chose to install as an additional role service when we installed the File Server role on our machine) and Shared Folders (which is installed by default whenever you add the file server role to a machine.) And underneath the FSRM node, you'll find the same subnodes you should already be familiar with in FSRM on Windows Server 2003 R2. (See Figure 4-5.) And anything you can do with FSRM in R2, you do pretty much the same way in Windows Server 2008. For example, to configure an SMTP server for sending notification e-mails when quotas are exceeded, right-click on the File Server Resource Manager node and select Properties. (In addition to hosting the FSRM snap-in within Server Manager, adding the FSRM role service also adds the FSRM console to Administrative Tools.)

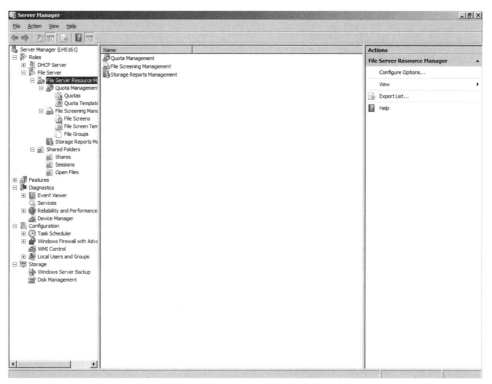

Figure 4-5   File Server role showing hosted snap-ins for File Server Resource Manager and Shared Folders

Here are a few more important things to know about Server Manager. First, Server Manager is designed to be a single, all-in-one tool for managing your server. In that light, it replaces both Manage Your Server (for adding roles) and the Add/Remove Windows Components portion of Add Or Remove Programs found on previous versions of Windows Server. In fact, if you go to Control Panel and open Programs And Features (which replaced Add Or Remove Programs in Windows Vista), you'll see a link called Turn Windows Features On And Off. If you click that link, Server Manager opens and you can use the Roles or Features node to add or remove roles, role services, and features. (See Chapter 5 for how this is done.)

Also, when Server Manager is used to install a role such as File Server on your server, it makes sure that this role is *secure by default*. (That is, the only components that are installed and ports that are opened are those that are absolutely necessary for that role to function.) In Windows Server 2003 Service Pack 1 or later, you needed to run the Security Configuration Wizard (SCW) to ensure a server role was installed securely. Windows Server 2008 still includes the SCW, but the tool is intended for use by IT specialists working in large enterprises. For medium-sized organizations, however, IT generalists can use Server Manager to install roles securely, and it's much easier to do than using SCW. In addition, while Server Manager can be used for installing new roles using *smart defaults*, SCW is mainly designed as a post-deployment tool for creating security policies that can then be applied to multiple servers to harden them by reducing their attack surface. (You can also compare policies created by SCW against the current state of a server for auditing reasons to ensure compliance with your corporate security policy.) Finally, while Server Manager can only be used to add the default Windows roles (or out-of-band roles made available later, as mentioned in the extensibility discussion a bit later), SCW can also be used for securing nondefault roles such as Exchange Server and SQL Server. But the main takeaway for this chapter concerning Server Manager vs. SCW is that when you run Server Manager to install a new role on your server, you don't need to run SCW afterward to lock down the role, as Server Manager ensures the role is already secure by default.

Server Manager relies upon something called Component Based Servicing (CBS) to discover what roles and services are installed on a machine and to install additional roles or services or remove them. For those of you who might be interested in how this works, there's a sidebar in the next section that discusses it in more detail. Server Manager is also designed to be extensible. This means when new features become available (such as Windows Server Virtualization, which we talked about in Chapter 3, "Windows Server Virtualization"), you'll be able to use Server Manager to download these roles from Microsoft and install them on your server.

Server Manager is designed to manage one server only (the local server) and cannot be used to manage multiple servers at once. If you need a tool to manage multiple servers simultaneously, use Microsoft System Center. You can find out more about System Center products and their capabilities at *http://www.microsoft.com/systemcenter/*, and it will be well worth your time to do so. In addition, the status information displayed by Server Manager is limited to event information and whether role services are running. So if you need more detailed information concerning the status of your servers, again be sure to check out System Center, the next generation of the SMS and MOM platforms.

Unlike using Computer Management, you can't use Server Manager to remotely connect to another server and manage it. For example, if you right-click on the root node in Server Manager, the context menu that is displayed does not display a Connect To A Different Computer option. However, this is not really a significant limitation of the tool because most admins will simply enable Remote Desktop on their servers and use Terminal Services to remotely manage them. For example, you can create a Remote Desktop Connection on a Windows Vista computer, use it to connect to the console session on a Windows Server 2008 machine, and then run Server Manager within the remote console session. And speaking of Computer Management, guess what happens if you click Start, right-click on Computer, and select Manage? In previous versions of Windows, doing this opened Computer Management—what tool do you think opens if you do this in Windows Server 2008?

Finally, a few more quick points you can make note of:

- Server Manager cannot be used to manage servers running previous versions of the Windows Server operating system.

- Server Manager cannot be installed on Windows Vista or previous versions of Microsoft Windows.

- Server Manager is not available on a Windows server core installation of Windows Server 2008 because the supporting components (.NET Framework 2.0 and MMC 3.0) are not available on that platform.

- You can configure the refresh interval for Server Manager and also whether the tool is automatically opened at logon by configuring the following Group Policy settings:

  Computer Configuration\Administrative Templates\System\Server Manager\Do Not Open Server Manager Automatically At Logon

  Computer Configuration\Administrative Templates\System\Server Manager\ Configure The Refresh Interval For Server Manager

From the Experts: The Security Configuration Wizard in Windows Server 2008

The Security Configuration Wizard (SCW) reduces the attack surface of Windows Servers by asking the user a series of questions designed to identify the functional requirements of a server. Functionality not required by the roles the server is performing is then disabled. In addition to being a fundamental security best practice, SCW reduces the number of systems that need to be immediately patched when a vulnerability is exposed. Specifically, SCW:

- Disables unneeded services.

- Creates required firewall rules.

- Removes unneeded firewall rules.

- Allows further address or security restrictions for firewall rules.

- Reduces protocol exposure to server message block (SMB), LanMan, and Lightweight Directory Access Protocol (LDAP).

SCW guides you through the process of creating, editing, applying, or rolling back a security policy based on the selected roles of the server. The security policies that are created with SCW are XML files that, when applied, configure services, Windows Firewall rules, specific registry values, and audit policy. Those security policies can be applied to an individual machine or can be transformed into a group policy object and then linked to an Organizational Unit in Active Directory.

With Windows Server 2008 some important improvements have been made to SCW:

- On Windows Server 2003, SCW was an optional component that had to be manually installed by administrators. SCW is now a default component of Windows Server 2008 which means Administrators won't have to perform extra steps to install or deploy the tool to leverage it.

- Windows Server 2008 will introduce a lot of new and exciting functionality in Windows Firewall. To support that functionality, SCW has been improved to store, process, and apply firewall rules with the same degree of precision that the Windows Firewall does. This was an important requirement since on Windows Server 2008 the Windows Firewall will be on by default.

- The SCW leverages a large XML database that consists of every service, firewall rule and administration option from every feature or component available on Windows Server 2008. This database has been totally reviewed and updated for Windows Server 2008. Existing roles have been updated, new roles have been added to the database, and all firewall rules have been updated to support the new Windows Firewall.

- SCW now validates all XML files in its database files using a set of XSD files that contains the SCW XML schema. This will help administrators or developers extend the SCW database by creating new SCW roles base on their own requirements or applications. Those XSD files are available under the SCW directory.

- All SCW reports have been updated to reflect the changes made to the SCW schema regarding support for the new Window Firewall. Those reports include the Configuration Database report, the Security Policy report and the Analysis report that will compare the current configuration of Windows Server 2008 against an SCW security policy.

SCW provides an end to end solution to reduce the attack surface of Windows Server 2008 machines by providing a possible configuration of default components, roles, features, and any third-party applications that provide an SCW role.

SCW is not responsible for installing or removing any roles, features, or third-party applications from Windows Server 2008. Instead, Administrators should use Server Manager if they need to install roles and features, or use the setup provided with any third party application. The installation of roles and features via Server Manager is made based on security best practices.

While SCW complements well Server Manager, its main value is in the configuration of the core operating system and third-party applications that provide an SCW role. SCW should be used every time the configuration of a default component on Windows Server 2008 needs to be modified or when a third-party application is added or removed. In some specific scenarios, like for remote administration, running SCW after using Server Manager might provide some added value to some specific roles or features. Using SCW after modifying a role or feature through Server Manager is not a requirement, however.

–Nils Dussart
  Program Manager for the Security Configuration Wizard (SCW), Windows Core Operating System Division

ServerManagerCmd.exe

In addition to the Server Manager user interface, there is also a command-line version of Server Manager called ServerManagerCmd.exe that was first introduced in the IDS_2 build of Windows Server 2008 (that is, the February CTP build). This command-line tool, which is found in the %windir%\system32 folder, can be used to perform the following tasks:

- Display a list of roles and features already installed on a machine.

- Display a list of role services and features that would be installed *if* you chose to install a given role.

- Add a role or feature to your server using the default settings of that role or feature.

- Add several roles/features at once by providing an XML answer file listing the roles/features to be installed.

- Remote roles or features from your server.

  What ServerManagerCmd.exe *can't* do includes the following:

- Install a role or feature, and change its default settings.

- Reconfigure a role or feature already installed on the machine.

- Connect to a remote machine, and manage roles/features on that machine.

- Manage roles/features on machines running a Windows server core installation of Windows Server 2008.

- Manage non-OOB roles/features—such as Exchange Server or SQL Server.

Let's take a look at the **servermanagercmd -query** command, which displays the list of roles and features currently available on the computer, along with their command-line names (values that should be used to install or remove the role or feature from the command line). When you run this command, something called *discovery* runs to determine the different roles and features already installed.

After discovery completes (which may take a short period of time), the command generates output displaying installed roles/features in green and marked with "X".

You can also type **servermanagercmd –query results.xml** to send the output of this command to an XML file. This is handy if you want to save and programmatically parse the output of this command.

Let's now learn more about ServerManagerCmd.exe from one of our experts at Microsoft:

From the Experts: Automating Common Deployment Tasks with ServerManagerCmd.exe

Rolling out a new internal application or service within an organization frequently means setting up roles and features on multiple servers. Some of these servers might need to be set up with exactly the same configuration, and others might reside in remote locations that are not readily accessible by full-time IT staff. For these reasons, you might want to write scripts to automate the deployment process from the command line.

One of the tools that can facilitate server deployment from the command line is ServerManagerCmd.exe. This tool is the command-line counterpart to the graphical Server Manager console, which is used to install and configure server roles and features. The graphical and command-line versions of Server Manager are built on the same synchronization platform that determines what roles and features are installed and applies user-specified configurations to the server.

ServerManagerCmd.exe provides a set of command-line switches that enable you to automate many common deployment tasks as follows:

View the List of Installable Roles and Features

You can use the –query command to see a list of roles and features available for installation and find out what's currently installed. You can also use –query to look up the command-line names of roles and features. These are listed in square brackets [] after the display name.

Install and Uninstall Roles and Features

You can use the –install and –remove commands to install and uninstall roles and features. One issue to be aware of is that ServerManagerCmd.exe enables you only to install and uninstall. Apart from a few notable exceptions for required settings, you cannot specify configuration settings as you can with the graphical Server Manager console. You need to use other role-specific tools, such as MMC snap-ins and command-line utilities, to specify configuration settings after installing roles and features using ServerManagerCmd.exe.

Run in "What-If" Mode

After you create a script to set up the server with ServerManagerCmd.exe, you might want to check that the script will perform as expected. Or you might want to see what will happen if you type a specific command with ServerManagerCmd.exe. For these scenarios, you can supply the –whatif switch. This switch tells you exactly what would be installed and removed by a command or answer file, based on the current server configuration, without performing the actual operations.

Specify Input Parameters via an Answer File

ServerManagerCmd.exe can operate in an interactive mode, or it can be automated using an answer file. The answer file is specified using the −inputPath <answer.xml> switch, where <answer.xml> is the name of an XML file with the list of input parameters. The schema for creating answer files can be found in the ServerManagerCmd.exe documentation.

Redirect Output to a Results File

It is usually a good practice to keep a history of configuration changes to your servers in case you need to troubleshoot a problem, migrate the settings of an existing server to a new server, or recover from a disaster or failure. To assist with record keeping, you can use the resultPath <results.xml> switch to save the results of an installation or removal to a file, where <results.xml> is the name of the file where you want the output to be saved.

−Dan Harman
  Program Manager, Windows Server, Windows Enterprise Management Division

You'll learn more about using ServerManagerCmd.exe for adding roles and features in Chapter 5, but for now let's move on and look at more tools for managing Windows Server 2008.

Remote Server Administration Tools

What if you want to manage our file server running Windows Server 2008 remotely from another machine? We already saw one way you could do this—enable Remote Desktop on the file server, and use Terminal Services to run our management tools remotely on the server. Once we have a Remote Desktop Connection session with the remote server, we can run tools such as Server Manager or File Server Resource Manager as if we were sitting at the remote machine's console.

In Windows Server 2003, you can also manage remote servers this way. But you can also manage them another way by installing the Windows Server 2003 Administration Tools Pack (Adminpak.msi) on a different Windows Server 2003 machine, or even on an admin workstation running Windows XP Service Pack 2. And once the Tools Pack is installed, you can open any of these tools, connect to your remote server, and manage roles and features on the server (provided the roles and features are installed).

Is there an Adminpak for Windows Server 2008? Well, there's an equivalent called the Remote Server Administration Tools (RSAT), which you can use to install selected management tools on your server even when the binaries for the roles/features those tools will manage are not installed on your server. In fact, the RSAT does Adminpak one better because Adminpak installs all the administrative tools, whereas the RSAT lets you install only those tools you need. (Actually, you can just install one tool from Adminpak if you want to, though it takes a bit of work to do this—see article 314978 in the Microsoft Knowledge Base for details.)

What features or roles can you manage using the RSAT? As of Beta 3, you can install management tools for the following roles and features using the RSAT:

- Roles
    - Active Directory Domain Services
    - Active Directory Certificate Services
    - Active Directory Lightweight Directory Services
    - Active Directory Rights Management Services
    - DNS Server
    - Fax Server
    - File Server
    - Network Policy and Access Services
    - Print Services
    - Terminal Services
    - Web Server (IIS)
    - Windows Deployment Services
- Features:
    - BitLocker Drive Encryption
    - BITS Server Extensions
    - Failover Clustering
    - Network Load Balancing
    - Simple SAN Management
    - SMTP Server
    - Windows System Resource Management (WSRM)
    - WINS Server

How do you install individual management tools using the RSAT? With Windows Server 2008, it's easy—just start the Add Feature Wizard, and select the RSAT management tools you want to install, such as the Terminal Services Gateway management tool. (See Figure 4-6. Note that installing some RSAT management tools might require that you also install additional features. For example, if you choose to install the Web Server (IIS) management tool from the

RSAT, you must also install the Configuration APIs component of the Windows Process Activation Service [WPAS] feature.)

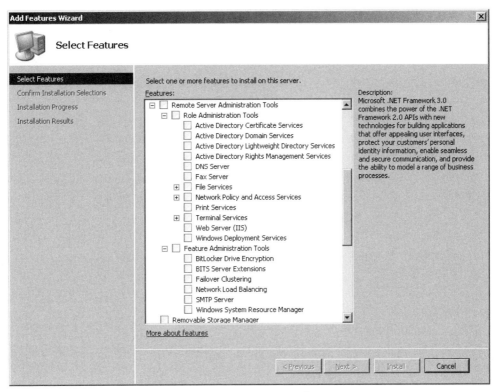

Figure 4-6   Installing a management tool using the RSAT feature

The actual steps for installing features on Windows Server 2008 are explained in Chapter 5. For now, just note that when you install an RSAT subfeature such as TS Gateway, what this does is add a new shortcut under Administrative Tools called TS Gateway. Then if you click Start, then Administrative Tools, then TS Gateway, the TS Gateway Manager console opens. In the console, you can right-click on the root node, select Connect To TS Gateway Server, and manage a remote Windows Server 2008 terminal server with the TS Gateway role service installed on it without having to enable Remote Desktop on the terminal server.

Finally, the Windows Server 2003 Adminpak can be installed on a Windows XP SP2 workstation, which lets you administer your servers from a workstation. Can the RSAT be installed on a Windows Vista machine so that you can manage your Windows Server 2008 machines from there?

As of Beta 3, the answer is "not yet." Plans for how RSAT will be made available for Windows Vista are uncertain at this moment, but it's likely we can expect something that can do this around or shortly after Windows Vista Service Pack 1. We'll just have to wait and see.

Other Management Tools

There are other ways you can manage Windows Server 2008 besides the tools we've discussed so far. Let's examine these now. Specifically, we're going to look at the following items:

- Group Policy
- Windows Management Instrumentation (WMI)
- Windows PowerShell
- Microsoft System Center

Group Policy

Group Policy in Windows Vista and Windows Server 2008 has been enhanced in several ways, including:

- Several new areas of policy management, including configuring Power Management settings, blocking installation of devices, assigning printers based on location, and more.
- A new format for Administrative Templates files called *ADMX* that is XML-based and replaces the proprietary-syntax ADM files used in previous versions of Windows.
- Network Location Awareness to enable Group Policy to better respond to changing network conditions and remove the need for relying on ICMP for policy processing.
- The ability to use local group policy objects, the capability of reducing SYSVOL bloat by placing ADMX files in a central store, and several other new features and enhancements.

A good source of information about Group Policy in Windows Vista (and therefore also in Windows Server 2008, because the platforms were designed to fit together) is Chapter 13, "Managing the Desktop Environment," in the *Windows Vista Resource Kit* from Microsoft Press. Meanwhile, while your assistant is running out to buy a couple of copies of that title (I was lead author for that title and my retirement plans are closely tied to the royalties I earn from sales, so please go buy a dozen or so copies), let's kick back and listen to one of our experts at Microsoft telling us more about post-Vista enhancements to Group Policy found in Windows Server 2008:

From the Experts: What's New in Group Policy in Windows Server 2008

The following is a description of some of the Group Policy enhancements found in Windows Server 2008.

Server Manager Integration

The first noticeable change in Windows Server 2008 is how the Group Policy tools are presented. In past operating systems, other than Windows Vista, an admin would have to go to the Microsoft Web site to download the Group Policy Management Console (GPMC) and install it on every administrative workstation where Group Policy management is performed. In Windows Server 2008, the installation bits are delivered with the operating system. No more downloads, no more wondering where the installation media is—it is just there.

A difference in this new environment is how optional Windows components are installed. Windows Server 2008 introduces a new management console for servers called Server Manager. This is the tool that is used to install server roles, as well as optional Windows components. If you choose to go the old-school route and add Windows components from the Add/Remove Control Panel, it will launch Server Manager.

Not only do you use Server Manager to install the optional components, but the GPMC console itself is hosted within the Server Manager console. This means all of your administrative tools are kept in one place and are easily discoverable. Of course, you will still be able to find the tools in the common locations, such as Administrative Tools.

Search/Filters, Comments, and Starter GPOs

These features really enhance the administrative experience around managing and authoring policy. They are, technically, multiple features, but they work well when described as a "feature set," as they all address the same business problem—difficulty in authoring policy. As you are probably aware, in the Windows Vista/Windows Server 2008 wave of operating systems there are hundreds of new settings to be managed. This means the total number of settings approaches 3000. That is a lot of manageable settings. Even though this provides a ton of value to the IT Professional, it increases the complexity when it comes to actually locating the setting or policy item that you are trying to manage. Microsoft has provided a "settings" spreadsheet that contains all the Group Policy settings in one relatively easy-to-use document, but it really doesn't solve the problem. Microsoft has received feedback from many IT pros that there needs to be a method within the Group Policy tool itself to make finding the right settings easier.

Now with Search and Filters, when you are authoring a policy right in the editor you have a great mechanism to locate the setting you are looking for. You will see a new Filter button in the toolbar, and if you right-click on the Administrative Templates node in the editor you will see a menu item called Filter Options. Filter Options allows you to set the criteria that you are looking to search on. For example, you can narrow your view to only *configured* items, specific key words, or the system requirements (for example, Internet Explorer 6.0 settings). Filter Options provides a very intuitive interface and has great flexibility to help in locating the settings that you are looking for. Once you set Filter Options and turn on the Filter (global setting), the editor displays only settings that you are targeting. The Group Policy team is really excited to bring these features to you because we know it will reduce some of the administrative burden of what is otherwise a fantastic management technology.

You can also filter for settings that have Comments. This is also a new feature introduced in Windows Server 2008. You can now place a comment on any setting that you want. This means when admins are authoring policy, they can document their intentions at author time and other administrators can use that Comment as a search criteria. This feature is incredible at helping Group Policy administrators communicate to themselves, or other administrators, why specific settings are being managed and what the impact of those settings is.

The last piece of this feature set is called Starter GPOs. Starter GPOs are a starting point for administration. When a GPO is created, you can still create a blank GPO, or you can choose to create your GPO from one of the pre-existing Starter GPOs. Starter GPOs are a collection of preconfigured Administrative Template settings, complete with comments. You will see a node in the Group Policy Management Console (GPMC) called Starter GPOs. Simply right-click on this node and choose New. You will have a Starter GPO that is available to edit. There is delegation available on the Starter GPO container to ensure that only specific administrators can modify it..

This feature set—Search/Filters, Comments, and Starter GPOs—comes together to greatly enhance the authoring and management experience around Group Policy. It provides ease of authoring and discovering settings, inline documentation of Group Policy settings, and baseline configurations for starting the process.

ADMX/ADML

ADMX/AMDL files were introduced in Windows Vista to replace the legacy data format of the ADM files that we have become used to. ADMX files are XML files that contain the same type of information that we have become familiar with to build the administrative experience around Administrative Template settings. Using XML makes the whole process more efficient and standardized. ADML files are language-specific files that are critical in a multilanguage enterprise. In the past, all localization was done right within each ADM file. This caused some confusing version control issues when multiple administrators were managing settings in a GPO from workstations using different languages. With ADMX/ADML, all administrators work off of the same GPOs and simply call the appropriate ADML file to populate the editor.

Another value associated with ADML/ADMX files is that GPOs no longer contain the ADM files themselves. Prior to Windows Vista/Windows Server 2008, each GPO created would contain all the ADM files. This was about 4 MB by default. This was a contributing factor in SYSVOL bloat.

Take a look at *http://www.microsoft.com/GroupPolicy* to read more on ADMX/ADML. You can also find the ADMX migration utility to help in moving to this new environment at *http://technet2.microsoft.com/windowsserver/en/technologies/featured/gp/default.mspx.* Just a note that ADM and ADMX can coexist; read up on it on one of the sites just referenced.

Central Store

Related to ADMX files is the Central Store. As was previously stated, ADM files used to be stored in the GPO itself. That is no longer the case. Now the GPO contains only the data that the client needs for processing Group Policy. In Windows Vista/Windows Server 2008, the default behavior for editing is that the editor pulls the ADMX files from the local workstation. This is great for smaller environments with few administrators managing Group Policy, but in larger, more complex environments or environments that need a bit more control, a Central Store has been introduced. The Central Store provides a single instance in SYSVOL that holds all of the ADMX/ADML files that are required. Once the Central Store is set up, all administrators load the appropriate files from the Central Store instead of the local machine. Check out one of the Group Policy MVP's Central Store Creation Utility at *http://www.gpoguy.com/cssu.htm.* You can also find more information on the Central Store at *http://www.microsoft.com/grouppolicy.*

Summary

Windows Server 2008 and Windows Vista have introduced a lot of new functionality for Group Policy. Administrators will find that these new features for management, along with the around 700 new settings to manage, will increase the ease of use of Group Policy and expand the number of areas that can be managed with policy.

−Kevin Sullivan
  Lead Program Manager for Group Policy, Windows Enterprise Management Division

Pretty cool enhancements, eh? Sorry, that's the Canadian coming out of me, or through me, or channeling through me—whatever.

Windows Management Instrumentation

WMI is a core Windows management technology that administrators can use to write scripts to perform administrative tasks on both local and remote computers. There are no specific enhancements to WMI in Windows Server 2008 beyond those included in Windows Vista, but it's important to know about the Windows Vista enhancements since these apply to Windows Server 2008 also. Here are a few of the more significant changes to WMI in Windows Vista and Windows Server 2008:

- **Improved tracing and logging**   The WMI service now uses Event Tracing for Windows (ETW) instead of the legacy WMI log files used on previous Windows platforms, and this makes WMI events available through Event Viewer or by using the Wevtutil.exe command-line tool.

- **Enhanced WMI namespace security**   The NamespaceSecuritySDDL qualifier can now be used to secure any namespace by setting WMI namespace security in the Managed Object Format (MOF) file

- **WMI namespace security auditing**   WMI now uses the namespaces system access control lists (SACL) to audit namespace activity and report events to the Security event log.

- **Get and Set security descriptor methods for securable objects**   new scriptable methods to get and set security descriptors have been added to Win32_Printer, Win32_Service, StdRegProv, Win32_DCOMApplicationSetting, and __SystemSecurity.

- **Manipulate security descriptors using scripts**   The Win32_SecurityDescriptorHelper class now has methods that allow scripts to convert binary security descriptors on securable objects into Win32_SecurityDescriptor objects or Security Descriptor Definition Language (SDDL) strings.

- **User Account Control**   User Account Control (UAC) affects what WMI data is returned, how WMI is remotely accessed, and how scripts must be run.

What all this basically means is that WMI is more secure and more consistent in how it works in Windows Server 2008, which is good news for administrators who like to write WMI scripts to manage various aspects of their Windows-based networks.

Still, from personal experience, I know that writing WMI scripts isn't always easy, especially if you're trying to get them to run properly against remote machines. Windows Vista and Windows Server 2008 complicate things in this regard because of their numerous security improvements, including User Account Control (UAC). So it's instructive if we sit back and listen now to one of our experts at Microsoft, who will address this very issue in detail (this sidebar is worth its weight in gold):

From the Experts: WMI Remote Connection

Talking about management obviously implies the need to connect remotely to the Windows systems you want to manage. Speaking about remote connection immediately implies security. Management and security are not always easy to combine. It is not rare to see situations where management represents a breach of security, or the other way around; it is not rare either to see security settings preventing the proper management of a system. In this respect, WMI is not different from any other technologies; it provides remote management capabilities involving some security considerations.

Windows Vista and Windows Server 2008 come with a series of new security features. The most important one is called User Account Control (UAC). It is very likely that every administrator in the world will be challenged by the presence of UAC, especially if you use the Local Accounts part of the Administrator group to perform remote access. This is because any token account used in this context is automatically filtered and finally acts as a normal user in the remote system. Therefore, it is wise to consider the various security aspects to properly and securely manage your remote systems.

Before looking at the UAC aspects, let step back and look at the requirements to call WMI remotely. This applies to any Windows platform since Windows 2000. We will examine the Windows Vista and Windows Server 2008 aspects next.

To connect remotely, four conditions must be met:

1. **Firewall**   Introduced with Windows XP, the Windows Firewall must be properly set up to enable connectivity for the WMI RPC traffic. Usually, you get an "RPC connection failure" if the Windows Firewall is enabled and RPC is disallowed. If you get an "access denied" message, the firewall is not the root cause of the issue. Keep in mind that the firewall is the key component to go through before anything else happens. Before Windows Vista and Windows Server 2008, RPC traffic must be enabled to allow the WMI traffic to go through. With Windows Vista and Windows Server 2008, a dedicated set of Firewall WMI rules is available to enable only WMI traffic. (This can be done with the FW.MSC MMC snap-in, Group Policies, Scripting, or NETSH.EXE.) Note that if you use WMIDiag (available on Microsoft Download Center), it will tell you which NETSH.EXE command to use to configure your firewall properly.

2. **DCOM**   Once the firewall gate is passed, it is time to consider the DCOM security. The user issuing the remote call must have the right to "Launch and Activate" (which can be viewed and changed with DCOMCNFG.EXE) for both the My Computer and Windows Management and Instrumentation objects. By default, only users who are part of the Administrators group of the remote machine have the right to remotely "Launch and Activate" these DCOM objects.

3. **WMI namespace**   Once the DCOM security is verified, WMI namespace security comes next. In this case, the user connecting to a remote WMI namespace must have at the minimum the Enable Remote and Enable Account rights granted for the given namespace. By default, only users who are part of the Administrators group of the remote machine have the Enable Remote right granted. (This can be updated with WMIMGMT.MSC.)

4. **Manageable entity**   Last but not least, once WMI has accepted the remote request, it is actually executed against the manageable entity (which could be a Windows Service or a Terminal Server configuration setting, for instance). This last step must also succeed for the WMI operation to succeed. WMI does not add any privilege that the user does not have when issuing the WMI request. (By default, WMI impersonates the calls, which means it issues the call within the security context of the remote user.) So, depending on the WMI operation requested and the rights granted to the remote user, the call might succeed or fail at the level of the manageable entity. For instance, if you try to stop a Windows service remotely, the Service Control Manager requires the user to be an Administrator by default. If you are not, the WMI request performing this operation will fail.

This describes the behavior of WMI since Windows 2000. In the light of Windows Vista and Windows Server 2008, things can be slightly different because UAC is enabled by default on both platforms and everything depends on whether you use a local account or a domain account. If you use a local user of the remote machine who is a member of the Local Administrators group, the Administrators membership of the user is always filtered. In this context, DCOM, WMI, and the manageable entity are applying the security restrictions with respect to the filtered token presented. Therefore, with respect to the UAC behavior, the token is a user token, not an administrative token! As a consequence, the Local User is actually acting as a plain user on that remote machine even if it is part of the Local Administrators group. By default, a user does not have the rights to pass the security gates defined earlier (in step 2, 3, and 4).

Now that the scene is set, how do you manage a remote Windows Vista machine or 2008 server while respecting the Firewall, UAC, DCOM, WMI, and manageable entity security enforcements?

This challenge must be looked at in two different ways:

1. **The remote machine is part of a domain.**   If the remote machine is part of a domain, it is highly recommended that you use a Domain User part of the Local Administrators group of the remote machine (and *not* a Local User part of the Local Administrators group). By doing so, you will be a plain Administrator because UAC does *not* filter users out of the Local Administrators group when the user is a Domain User. UAC only filters Local Users out of the Local Administrators group.

2. **Your machine is a workgroup machine.**   If your machine is in a workgroup environment, you are forced to use a Local User part of the Local Administrators group to connect remotely. Obviously, because of the UAC behavior, that user is filtered and acts as a plain user. The first approach if you are in a large enterprise infrastructure is to consider the possibility of making this machine part of a domain to use a

Domain User. If this is not possible because you must keep the machine as part of a workgroup, from this point you have two choices:

☐ You decide to keep UAC active. In this case, you must adjust the security settings of DCOM and WMI to ensure that the Local User has the explicit rights to get remote access. Don't forget that a best practice is to use a dedicated Local Group and make this Local User a member of that group. In this context, the WMI requests against the manageable entity might work or not depending on the manageable entity security requirements (discussed in step 3). If the manageable entity does not allow a plain user to perform the task requested, you might be forced to change the security at the manageable entity level to explicitly grant permissions to your Local User or Group as well. Note that this is not always possible because it heavily depends on the manageable entity security requirements and security management capabilities of the manageable entity. For the Windows Services example, this can be done with the SC.EXE command via an SDDL string, the *Win32_Service* WMI class (with the *Get/SetSecurityDescriptor* methods implemented in Windows Vista and Windows Server 2008), or Group Policies (GPEDIT.MSC). By updating the security at these three levels, you will be able to gracefully pass the DCOM and WMI security gates and stop a Windows Service as a plain user. Note that this customization represents clearly the steps for a granular delegation of the management. Only the service you changed the security for can be stopped by that dedicated user (or group). In this case, you actually define a very granular security model for a specific task. (You can watch the "Running Scripts Securely While Handling Passwords and Security Contexts Properly" webcast at *http://go.microsoft.com/fwlink/?LinkId=39643* to understand this scenario better.) Now it is possible that some manageable entities only require the user to be an Admin (typical for most devices) because there is no possibility to update the security descriptor. In such a case, for a workgroup scenario, only the second option (discussed next) becomes possible. Last but not least, keep in mind that these steps are also applicable in a domain environment to delegate some management capabilities to a group of domain users.

☐ You decide to disable the UAC filtering for remote access. This must be the last-resort solution. It is not an option you should consider right away if you want to maintain your workgroup system with a high level of security. So consider it only after investigating the possibility of making your system part of a domain or after reviewing the security wherever needed. If making your system part of a domain is not possible, you can consider this option. In this case, you must set the registry key in the reference shown below to ZERO on the remote system. Note that you must be an administrator to change that registry key. So you need to do this locally once, before any remote access is made. Note that this configuration setting disables the filtering on Local Accounts only; it does not disable UAC as a whole.

```
[HKLM\SOFTWARE\Microsoft\Windows\CurrentVersion\Policies\System]"Local
AccountTokenFilterPolicy"=dword:00000001
```

Once set, the registry key is created and set to ONE, and the Local User remotely accessing the machine will be an administrator (if the user is a member of the Local Administrators group).Therefore, by default, the user will pass the security gates defined in steps 2, 3, and 4. Note that it is required to reboot the machine to get this change activated.

–Alain Lissoir
Senior Program Manager, Windows Enterprise Management Division (WEMD)
Check out Alain's Web site at http://www.lissware.net.

Windows PowerShell

Another powerful tool for automating administrative tasks in Windows Server 2008 is Windows PowerShell, a command-line shell and scripting language. PowerShell includes more than 130 command-line tools (called *cmdlets*), has consistent syntax and naming conventions, and uses simplified navigation for managing data such as the registry and certificate store. PowerShell also includes an intuitive scripting language specifically designed for IT administration. As of Beta 3, PowerShell is included as an optional feature you can install on Windows Server 2008.

PowerShell can be used to efficiently perform Windows Server 2008 administration tasks, including managing services, processes, and storage. PowerShell can also be used to manage aspects of server roles, such as Internet Information Services (IIS) 7.0, Terminal Services, and Active Directory Domain Services. Some of the things you can do with PowerShell on Windows Server 2008 include

- Managing command-line services, processes, the registry, and WMI data using the get-service, get-process, and get-wmiobject cmdlets.

- Automating Terminal Services configuration, and comparing configurations across a Terminal Server farm.

- Deploying and configuring Internet Information Services 7.0 across a Web farm.

- Creating objects in Active Directory, and listing information about the current domain.

For example, let's look at the third item in this list—managing IIS 7.0 using PowerShell. But rather than have me explain this, why don't we listen to one of our experts at Microsoft concerning this?

From the Experts: PowerShell Rocks!

Of all the new Microsoft technology coming down the pipe, PowerShell has got to be one of the most exciting (after IIS 7.0 of course). You might wonder why I am so excited about the new scripting shell for Windows. Even if PowerShell is better than Command Prompt on steroids, what does this have to do with my main passion, Web servers and Web applications? Check out the Channel9 video I did with Jeffrey Snover, architect of PowerShell, to get an idea of how cool PowerShell really is (see *http://channel9. msdn.com/Showpost.aspx?postid=256994*). In the video, we show off a demo we put together for Bob Muglia's keynote article in TechEd IT Forum this week, which appears to have gone very, very well. Well done, Jeffrey.

A long, long, long time ago, when I was in school and even after that, before I came to Microsoft and joined the IIS team, I used Linux and spent my days in BASH and ZSH getting work done. Until now, we sadly never really had the productive power of an interactive shell on Windows. So as a previously heavy user of shells, I have to tell you what I really like about this new shell interface on its own, and then I'll explain the many ways PowerShell can make work simpler for IIS administrators.

OK, first off, in PowerShell you input commands on objects, not text, and PowerShell returns objects and not text. So you can easily pipe commands together in one line. This allows me to input in just one line complicated commands like this one:

```
PS C:\Windows\System32> Get-ChildItem -Path G:\ -Recurse -Include
  *.mp3 | Where-Object -FilterScript {($_.LastWriteTime -gt
  "2006-10-01") -and ($_.Name -match "pearl jam")}| Copy
  -Destination C:\User\bills\Desktop\New_PJ_MP3s
```

which recursively looks through my entire external hard drive (G:), collects all the "Pearl Jam" mp3s that were recently added, and copies them into a folder on my desktop. Never was I given a text output listing all the mp3s, and I didn't have to use the Copy command over and over. I just piped all the items to Copy once.

Another thing I like so much about PowerShell is how consistent PowerShell commands are. In the preceding example, I used only one Get-ChildItem command, but rest assured if I wanted to get anything else, the command for that would start with Get. Similarly, if we want to stop a process or an application or anything, we always use the Stop command, not kill, not terminate, not halt, just stop.

Finally, I love that PowerShell is extensible. I love this because it means my team can produce a whole set of IIS PowerShell cmdlets to help you manage IIS 6.0, IIS 7.0, and future versions of IIS. You will also be able to submit your IIS PowerShell scriptlets to this community area (coming very soon).

Now that I've listed my favorite things about this new shell, I'd like to give you a few ways that PowerShell can and will make IIS administration simpler than ever before. The top 5...

1. IIS 7.0 has a new WMI Provider for quickly starting, stopping, creating, removing, and configuring sites and applications. Now use PowerShell to give a list of applications sorted by a particular configuration setting. Then pipe apps with the particular setting into the tasks you were performing before with the WMI Provider. My colleague Sergei Antonov wrote and just published a fantastic article, titled "Writing PowerShell Command-lets for IIS 7.0," that describes how to write PowerShell cmdlets using our WMI provider.

2. 2. Because IIS 7.0 has a distributed file-based configuration store, you can store your application's IIS configurations in a *web.config* file in the application's directory next to its code and content. Use PowerShell to rapidly XCopy deploy the application to an entire Web farm in one step.

3. IIS 7.0's new Web.Administration API allows admins to write short programs in .NET to programmatically tackle frequent IIS 7.0 management tasks. Then, because PowerShell completely supports the .NET Framework, use it to pipe IIS objects in and out of these handy bits of code.

4. With IIS 7.0, you can use the new Runtime Status and Control API to monitor the performance of your Web applications. Use PowerShell to monitor performance information at a regular interval of every five minutes, and then have this valuable runtime information displayed to the console or sent to a log file whenever CPU is above 80%.

5. Take advantage of IIS 7.0's extensibility by writing your own custom request processing module with its own configuration and IIS Manager plug-in. Then write a PowerShell cmdlet to serve as a management interface to expose your custom IIS configuration to the command line and to power your IIS Manager plug-in.

For more information on managing IIS 7.0 using PowerShell, see "An Introduction to Windows PowerShell and IIS 7.0," found at *http://www.iis.net/default.aspx?tabid=2& subtabid=25&i=1212.*

−*Bill Staples*
Product Unit Manager, IIS

Like WMI discussed earlier, Windows PowerShell is a work in progress and is still evolving. For example, Windows PowerShell version 1.0 doesn't yet have any cmdlets for managing Active Directory, but by using the .NET Framework 2.0 together with PowerShell, you can manage Active Directory even so.

Chapter 14, "Additional Resources," has lots of pointers to where you can find more information about using PowerShell to manage Windows Server 2008. But before you flip ahead to look there, listen to what another expert at Microsoft has to say concerning the *raison d'être* behind PowerShell:

From the Experts: The Soul of Automation

"Civilization advances by extending the number of important operations which we can perform without thinking about them."

Alfred North Whitehead, "Introduction to Mathematics" (1911)
English mathematician & philosopher (1861 - 1947)

I really understood Whitehead's point during the great windstorm of 2006 when we lost power in my area for six days. During this time, we were without the benefits of most of the things I took for granted. I was struck by how much time it took to do things that previously I performed without thinking about them. Washing the dishes in the sink by hand took a lot more time than using the dishwasher. There were dozens of things like this. I didn't mind terribly, but I found myself resenting that I didn't have time to do as much reading as I usually do.

Whitehead's point is *not* that civilization advances by us becoming non-thinking idiots. Rather, by increasing the number of things that we don't have to think about, we free up time to think about *new* things and solve *new* problems, and then transform those things into things that we no longer have to think about. And so on and so on. Because I spent time doing dishes means that I didn't have time to read, which meant that I didn't get more educated, which would have made it easier to move the ball forward.

This is the essence of PowerShell and the soul of automation. In our world, there is no end of interesting and hard problems to think about, and the degree that our tools continue to make us think about the low-level junk is the degree to which we reduce the time that we have to think about the interesting problems. The ball gets moved forward as we adopt better and better tools that do what we want them to do without us having to tell them, and by our getting in the habit of using automation for repeating operations and sharing that automation with others.

Huge advances come from the accumulation of small deltas. In *David Copperfield*, Charles Dickens wrote, "Annual income twenty pounds, annual expenditure nineteen pounds six, result happiness. Annual income twenty pounds, annual expenditure twenty ought and size, result misery." Einstein said it this way, "The most powerful force in the universe is compound interest." So the next time you find yourself thinking about

---

how to do something that you've done before, you should take it as an opportunity to invest a little bit and automate the activity so that you don't have to think about it again. Give the function a good long name so that you can remember it, find it, and recognize it when you see it; then give it an alias so that you can minimize your typing (for example, Get-FileVersionInfo and gfvi).

Last but not least, SHARE. Put your script out on a blog or newsgroup or Web site so that others can benefit from your thinking. Newton might have figured out gravity, but if he didn't share his thoughts with others, he would not have moved the ball forward. OK, so your script is not in the same league as "F=ma," but share it anyway because "huge advances come from the accumulation of small deltas."

Enjoy!

–Jeffrey Snover
  Partner Architect, Windows Management

Microsoft System Center

Finally, the Microsoft System Center family of enterprise management solutions will be supporting management of Windows Server 2008, though at the time of this writing, the date for such support has not been made known to me. System Center is a collection of products that evolved from the earlier Microsoft Systems Management Server (SMS) and Microsoft Operations Manager (MOM) platforms. The plan for the System Center family currently includes the following products:

- System Center Operations Manager (the next generation of MOM)
- System Center Configuration Manager (the next generation of SMS)
- System Center Data Protection Manager
- System Center Essentials
- System Center Virtual Machine Manager
- System Center Capacity Planner

Keep your eye on these products as Microsoft announces its support for Windows Server 2008. You can find out more about System Center at *http://www.microsoft.com/systemcenter*.

Conclusion

Windows Server 2008 can be managed using a number of in-box and out-of-band tools. If you only need to manage a single server, use Initial Configuration Tasks and Server Manager. If you need to do this remotely, enable Remote Desktop on your server. If you need to manage multiple servers roles on different machines, install the Remote Server Administration Tools (RSAT) and use each tool to manage multiple instances of a particular role. And if you need to automate the administration of Windows Server 2008 machines, use ServerManagerCmd.exe, WMI, Windows PowerShell, or some combination of the three.

Additional Resources

TechNet has a level 300 webcast called "Installing, Configuring, and Managing Server Roles in Windows Server 2008" that you can download from *http://msevents.microsoft.com/cui/Web-CastEventDetails.aspx?EventID=1032294712&EventCategory=5&culture=en-US&CountryCode=US* (registration required).

If you have access to the Windows Server 2008 beta on Microsoft Connect (*https://connect.microsoft.com/*), you can download the following items:

- Microsoft Windows Server 2008 Server Manager Lab Companion
- Microsoft Windows Server 2008 Initial Configuration Tasks Step-By-Step Guide
- Live Meeting on Server Manager

If you don't have access to beta builds of Windows Server 2008, you can still test drive Server Manager online using the Microsoft Windows Server 2008 Server Manager Virtual Lab, available at *http://msevents.microsoft.com/CUI/WebCastEventDetails.aspx?EventID=1032314461&EventCategory=3&culture=en-IN&CountryCode=IN*.

A good starting point for exploring the potential of using Windows PowerShell to manage Windows Server 2008 is *http://www.microsoft.com/windowsserver/2008/powershell.mspx*.

Information about Group Policy enhancements in Windows Vista and Windows Server 2008 can be found at *http://technet2.microsoft.com/WindowsVista/en/library/a8366c42-6373-48cd-9d11-2510580e48171033.mspx?mfr=true*.

More information about WMI enhancements in Windows Vista and Windows Server 2008 can be found on MSDN at *http://msdn2.microsoft.com/en-gb/library/aa394053.aspx*.

And if you want to find out more about Microsoft System Center, see *http://www.microsoft.com/systemcenter/*.

Finally, be sure to turn to Chapter 14 for more information on the topics in this chapter and also for webcasts, whitepapers, blogs, newsgroups, and other sources of information about all aspects of Windows Server 2008.

Chapter 5

Managing Server Roles

In this chapter:

Understanding Roles, Role Services, and Features 71

Adding Roles and Features 95

Conclusion 108

Additional Reading 108

Now that you've seen some of the tools you can use to manage Microsoft Windows Server 2008, let's give them a test drive. Key to managing Windows Server 2008 is understanding the difference between roles, role services, and features. This chapter starts by explaining these differences and then looks at how you can add or remove roles from Windows Server 2008 using some of the tools discussed in the previous chapter.

Understanding Roles, Role Services, and Features

A server role (or simply *role*) is a specific function that your server performs on your network. Examples of roles you can deploy on Windows Server 2008 include File Server, Print Services, Terminal Services, and so on. Many of these roles will be familiar to administrators who work with Windows Server 2003 R2, but a few are new—such as Windows Deployment Services (WDS) and Network Policy and Access Services (NAP/NPS).

Most server roles are supported by one or more *role services*, which provide different kinds of functionality to that role. A good example here is the File Server role, which is supported by the following role services:

- Distributed File System (DFS)
- File Server Resource Manager (FSRM)
- Services for Network File System (NFS)
- Single Instance Store (SIS)
- Windows Search Service
- Windows Server 2003 File Services

These role services are optional for the File Server role and can be added to provide enhanced functionality for that role. For example, by adding the File Server Resource Manager role service, you gain access to a console (fsrm.msc) that lets you configure file and volume quotas, implement file screens, and generate reports. The File Server Resource Manager console was first included in Windows Server 2003 R2, and it has basically the same functionality in Windows 2008 Server as it did on the previous platform. We'll look at how to install this tool later in this chapter.

Note also that some role services are supported by additional role services. For example, the Distributed File System role service is supported by these two other services:

- DFS Namespace
- DFS Replication

When you choose to install the Distributed File System, Windows Server 2008 automatically selects both of these other services for installation as well, though can you choose to deselect either one of these services if they are not needed on your server.

Finally, in addition to roles and roles services, there are things called *features* that you can install on Windows Server 2008. Features are usually optional, although some roles might require that certain features be installed, in which case you'll be prompted to install these features if they're not already installed when you add the role. Optional features are usually Windows services or groups of services that provide additional functionality you might need on your server. Examples of features range from foundational components such as the .NET Framework 3.0 (which contains some sub-features also) to management essentials such as the Remote Server Administration Tools (which we talked about in Chapter 4, "Managing Windows Server 2008") to legacy roles such as the WINS Server (yes it's still around if you need it) to Failover Clustering (clustering is a feature, not a role—see Chapter 9, "Clustering Enhancements," to find out why) and lots of other stuff.

In a moment, we'll look at how to add (install) roles, role services, and features. But first let's summarize what's on the menu.

Available Roles and Role Services

First let's look at a list of the different roles you can install on Windows Server 2008, along with brief descriptions of what these roles do and which optional role services are available for each role. We'll list these server roles in alphabetical order together with the various role services available (or needed) by each role.

Note that some role services might be required for a particular role, while other services are optional and should be added only if their functionality is required. The cool thing about Windows Server 2008 is that so little functionality is installed by default. This is intentional, as it increases the security of the platform. For example, if the DHCP Server role is not installed, the bits for the DHCP Server service are not present, which means the server can't be compromised by malware attempting to access the server on UDP port 67 or attempting to compromise the DHCP Server service. For even greater protection, a Windows server core installation has even less functionality by default than a full installation of Windows Server 2008, and also has a more limited set of roles you can install—see Chapter 6, "Windows Server Core," for more details.

Anyway, let's look now at each available role you can install, together with its role services.

Active Directory Certificate Services

Active Directory Certificate Services enables creation and management of digital certificates for users, computers, and organizations as part of a public key infrastructure. The following role services are available when you install this role:

- **Certification Authority**   Certification Authority (CA) issues and manages digital certificates for users, computers, and organizations. Multiple CAs can be linked to form a public key infrastructure.

- **Certification Authority Web Enrollment**   Web Enrollment allows you to request certificates, retrieve certificate revocation lists, and perform smart card certificate enrollment using a Web browser.

- **Online Certificate Status Protocol**   Online Certificate Status Protocol (OCSP) Support enables clients to determine certificate revocation status using OCSP as an alternative to using certificate revocation lists.

- **Microsoft Simple Certificate Enrollment Protocol**   Microsoft Simple Certificate Enrollment Protocol (MSCEP) Support allows routers and other network devices to obtain certificates.

For more information concerning the Active Directory Certificate Services role, see Chapter 7, "Active Directory Enhancements."

Active Directory Domain Services

Active Directory Domain Services (AD DS) stores information about objects on the network and makes this information available to users and network administrators. AD DS uses domain controllers to give network users access to permitted resources anywhere on the network. The following role services are available when you install this role (note that the Identity Management for UNIX role service is not available for installation until after you have installed the Active Directory Domain Controller role service):

- **Active Directory Domain Controller**   Active Directory Domain Controller enables a server to store directory data and manage communication between users and domains, including user logon processes, authentication, and directory searches.

- **Identity Management for UNIX**   Identity Management for UNIX integrates computers running Windows into an existing UNIX environment and has the following sub-components.

   ❏ **Server for Network Information Service** Integrates Windows and NIS networks by exporting NIS domain maps to Active Directory entries, giving an Active Directory domain controller the ability to act as a master NIS server.

   ❏ **Password Synchronization** Automatically changes a user password on the UNIX network when the user changes his or her Windows password, and vice versa. This allows users to maintain just one password for both networks.

   ❏ **Administration Tools** Used for administering this feature.

For more information concerning the Active Directory Domain Services role, see Chapter 7.

Active Directory Federation Services

Active Directory Federation Services (AD FS) provides simplified, secured identity federation and Web single sign-on (SSO). The following role services are available when you install this role:

- **Federation Service**   Federation Service provides security tokens to client applications in response to requests for access to resources.

- **Federation Service Proxy**   Federation Service Proxy collects user credentials from browser clients and Web applications and forwards the credentials to the federation service on their behalf.

- **AD FS Web Agents**   AD FS Web Agents validate security tokens and allow authenticated access to Web resources from browser clients and Web applications. There are two types of agents you can install:

   ❏ **Claims-Aware Agent** Enables authentication for applications that use claims directly for authentication.

   ❏ **Windows Token-Based Agent** Enables authentication for applications that use traditional Windows security token-based authentication.

For more information concerning the Active Directory Federation Services role, see Chapter 7.

Active Directory Lightweight Directory Services

Active Directory Lightweight Directory Services (AD LDS) provides a store for application-specific data. For more information concerning this role, see Chapter 7.

Active Directory Rights Management Services

Active Directory Rights Management Services (AD RMS) helps protect information from unauthorized use. AD RMS includes a certification service that establishes the identity of users, a licensing service that provides authorized users with licenses for protected information, and a logging service to monitor and troubleshoot AD RMS. Note that the server must be joined to a domain before you can install this role on it. The following role services are available when you install this role:

- **Active Directory Rights Management Server**   Rights Management Server helps protect information from unauthorized use.

- **Identity Federation Support**   AD RMS can use an existing federated trust relationship between your organization and another organization to establish user identities and provide access to protected information created by either organization. For example, a trust established by Active Directory Federation Services can be used to establish user identities for AD RMS.

For more information concerning the Active Directory Rights Management Services role, see Chapter 7.

Application Server

Application Server supports running distributed applications, such as those built with the Windows Communication Foundation or COM+. The following role services are available when you install this role:

- **Application Server Core**   Application Server Core provides technologies for deploying and managing .NET Framework 3.0 applications.

- **Web Server (IIS) Support**   Web Server (IIS) Support enables Application Server to host internal or external Web sites and Web services that communicate over HTTP.

- **COM+ Network Access**   COM+ Network Access enables Application Server to host and allow remote invocation of applications built with COM+ or Enterprise Services components.

- **TCP Port Sharing**   TCP Port Sharing allows multiple net.tcp applications to share a single TCP port so that they can exist on the same physical computer in separate, isolated processes while sharing the network infrastructure required to send and receive traffic over a TCP port such as port 80.

- **Windows Process Activation Service Support**   Windows Process Activation Service Support enables Application Server to invoke applications remotely over the network using protocols such as HTTP, Message Queuing, TCP, and named pipes. Subcomponents of this role service include:

  - ❑ **HTTP Activation** Supports process activation via HTTP.

  - ❑ **Message Queuing Activation** Supports process activation via Message Queuing.

  - ❑ **TCP Activation** Supports process activation via TCP.

  - ❑ **Named Pipes Activation** Supports process activation via named pipes.

- **Distributed Transactions**   Distributed Transactions provides services that help ensure complete and successful transactions over multiple databases hosted on multiple computers on the network. Subcomponents of this role service include:

  - ❑ **Incoming Remote Transactions** Provides distributed transaction support for applications that enlist in remote transactions.

  - ❑ **Outgoing Remote Transactions** Provides distributed transaction support for propagating transactions that an application generates.

  - ❑ **WS-Atomic Transactions** Provides distributed transaction support for applications that use two-phase commit transactions with exchanges based upon the Simple Object Access Protocol (SOAP).

Note that installing this server role also requires that you install the Windows Process Activation Service (WPAS) and .NET Framework 3.0 features, together with some of their subcomponents.

For more information concerning the Application Server role, see Chapter 12, "Other Features and Enhancements."

DHCP Server

Dynamic Host Configuration Protocol (DHCP) Server enables the central provisioning, configuration, and management of temporary IP addresses and related information for client computers. For more information concerning this role, see Chapter 12.

DNS Server

Domain Name System (DNS) Server translates domain and computer DNS names to IP addresses. DNS is easier to manage when it is installed on the same server as Active Directory Domain Services. If you select the Active Directory Domain Services role, you can install and configure DNS Server and Active Directory Domain Services to work together. For more information concerning this role, see Chapter 7.

Fax Server

Fax Server sends and receives faxes and allows you to manage fax resources such as jobs, settings, reports, and fax devices on this computer or on the network. For more information concerning this role, see Chapter 12.

File Services

File Services provides technologies for storage management, file replication, distributed namespace management, fast file searching, and streamlined client access to files. The following role services are available when you install this role:

- **Distributed File System** Distributed File System (DFS) provides tools and services for DFS Namespace and DFS Replication. Subcomponents of this role service include:

    - ❑ **DFS Namespace** Aggregates the files from multiple file servers into a single, global namespace for users.

    - ❑ **DFS Replication** Enables configuration, management, monitoring, and replication of large quantities of data over the WAN in a scalable and highly efficient manner.

- **File Server Resource Manager** File Server Resource Manager (FSRM) generates storage reports, configures quotas, and defines file-screening policies.

- **Services for Network File System** Services for Network File System (NFS) permits UNIX clients to access files on a server running a Windows operating system.

- **Single Instance Store** Single Instance Store (SIS) reduces the amount of storage required on your server by consolidating files that have the same content into one master copy.

- **Windows Search Service** Windows Search Engine enables fast file searches on this server from Windows Search-compatible clients.

- **Windows Server 2003 File Services** Provides file services for Windows Server 2003. Subcomponents of this role service include:

    - ❑ **File Replication Service (FRS)** Supports legacy distributed file environments. If you're running your server in an environment with Windows 2003 replication and you want to use this server to support that, select this option. If you want to enable the latest replication technology, select DFS Replication instead.

    - ❑ **Indexing Service** Catalogs contents and properties of files on local and remote computers, and provides rapid access to files through a flexible query language.

For more information concerning the File Services role, see Chapter 12.

Network Policy and Access Services

Network Access Services provides support for routing LAN and WAN network traffic, creating and enforcing network access policies, and accessing network resources over VPN and dial-up connections. The following role services are available when you install this role:

- **Network Policy Server** Network Policy Server (NPS) creates and enforces organization-wide network access policies for client health, connection request authentication, and network authorization. In addition, you can use NPS as a RADIUS proxy to forward connection requests to NPS or other RADIUS servers that you configure in remote RADIUS server groups.

- **Routing and Remote Access Services**   Routing and Remote Access Services (RRAS) provide remote users access to resources on your private network over virtual private network (VPN) or dial-up connections. Servers configured with Routing and Remote Access Services can provide LAN and WAN routing services to connect network segments within a small office or to connect two private networks over the Internet. Subcomponents of this role service include:

  - ❑ **Remote Access Service** Enables remote or mobile workers to access private office networks through VPN or dial-up connections.

  - ❑ **Routing** Provides support for NAT Routers, LAN Routers running RIP, and multi-cast-capable routers (IGMP Proxy).

- **Health Registration Authority**   Health Registration Authority validates client requests for health certificates used in Network Access Protection.

- **Host Credential Authorization Protocol**   Host Credential Authorization Protocol (HCAP) behaves as a connection point between Cisco Access Control Server and the Microsoft Network Policy Server, allowing the Microsoft Network Policy Server to validate the machine's posture in a Cisco 802.1X environment.

For more information concerning the Network Access Services role, see Chapter 10, "Network Access Protection."

Print Services

Print Services manages and provides access to network printers and printer drivers. The following role services are available when you install this role:

- **Print Server**   Print Server manages and provides access to network printers and printer drivers.

- **Internet Printing**   Internet Printing enables Web-based printer management and allows printing to shared printers via HTTP.

- **LPD Service**   Line Printer Daemon (LPD) Service provides print services for UNIX-based computers.

For more information concerning the Print Services role, see Chapter 12.

Terminal Services

Terminal Services provides technologies that enable access to a server running Windows-based programs or the full Windows desktop. Users can connect to a terminal server to run programs, save files, and use network resources on that server. The following role services are available when you install this role:

- **Terminal Server**   Terminal Server enables sharing of Windows-based programs or the full Windows desktop. Users can connect to a terminal server to run programs, save files, and use network resources on that server.

- **TS Licensing**   TS Licensing manages the Terminal Server client access licenses (TS CALs) that are required to connect to a terminal server. You use TS Licensing to install, issue, and monitor the availability of TS CALs.

- **TS Session Broker**   TS Session Broker supports reconnection to an existing session on a terminal server that is a member of a load-balanced TS farm.

- **TS Gateway**   TS Gateway provides access to Terminal Servers inside a corporate network from the outside via HTTP.

- **TS Web Access**   TS Web Access provides access to Terminal Servers via the Web.

For more information concerning the Terminal Services role, see Chapter 8, "Terminal Services Enhancements."

UDDI Services

Universal Description, Discovery, and Integration (UDDI) Services organizes and catalogs Web services and other programmatic resources. A UDDI Services site consists of a UDDI Web Application connected to a UDDI Database. The following role services are available when you install this role:

- **UDDI Services Database**   UDDI Database provides a store for the UDDI Services catalog and configuration data.

- **UDDI Services Web Application**   UDDI Web Application provides a Web site where users and Web applications can search and discover Web services in the UDDI Services catalog.

Web Server (IIS)

Web Server provides a reliable, manageable, and scalable Web application infrastructure. Because this particular role has a whole lot of role services you can optionally enable, let's start with the three main ones and then examine additional services that depend on these three services:

- **Web Server**   Internet Information Services provides support for HTML Web sites and, optionally, support for ASP.NET, classic ASP, and Web server extensions.

- **Management Tools**   Web Server Management Tools enable administration of Web servers and Web sites.

- **FTP Publishing Service**   File Transfer Protocol (FTP) Publishing Service provides support for hosting and managing FTP sites.

Now let's take a closer look at each of these role services with their optional subcomponents.

Web Server Role Service   When you choose to install the Web Server role service, the following subcomponents are available for installation as well:

- **Common HTTP Features**   Common HTTP Features provides support for static Web server content such as HTML and image files. Subcomponents of this role service include:

    - **Static Content** Serves .htm, .html, and image files from a Web site.

    - **Default Document** Permits a specified default file to be loaded when users do not specify a file in a request URL.

    - **Directory Browsing** Allows clients to see the contents of a directory hosted on a Web site.

    - **HTTP Errors** Allows you to customize the error messages returned to clients.

    - **HTTP Redirection** Provides support to redirect client requests to a specific destination.

- **Application Development**   Web Application Support provides infrastructure for hosting applications developed using ASP.NET, classic ASP, CGI, and ISAPI extensions. Subcomponents of this role service include:

    - **ASP.NET** Hosts .NET Web applications built using ASP.NET.

    - **.NET Extensibility** Provides support for hosting .NET Framework managed module extensions.

    - **Active Server Pages (ASP)** Provides support for hosting traditional Web applications built using ASP.

    - **Common Gateway Interface (CGI)** Provides support for executing scripts such as Perl and Python.

❑ **Internet Server Application Programming Interface (ISAPI) Extensions**
Provides support for developing dynamic Web content using ISAPI extensions. An ISAPI extension runs when requested just like any other static HTML file or dynamic ASP file.

❑ **Internet Server Application Programming Interface (ISAPI) Filters** Provides support for Web applications developed using ISAPI filters. ISAPI filters are files that can be used to modify and enhance the functionality provided by IIS.

❑ **Server Side Includes** Serves .stm, .shtm, and .shtml files from a Web site.

■ **Health and Diagnostics**   Health and Diagnostics enables you to monitor and manage server, site, and application health. Subcomponents of this role service include:

❑ **HTTP Logging** Enables logging of Web site activity on this server.

❑ **Logging Tools** Enables you to manage Web activity logs and automate common logging tasks.

❑ **Request Monitor** Shows server, site, and application health.

❑ **Tracing** Enables tracing for ASP.NET applications and failed requests.

❑ **Custom Logging** Enables support for custom logging for Web servers, sites, and applications.

❑ **ODBC Logging** Enables support for logging to an ODBC-compliant database.

■ **Security**   Security Services provides support for securing servers, sites, applications, virtual directories, and files. Subcomponents of this role service include:

❑ **Basic Authentication** Provides support for requiring a valid Windows user name and password to connect to resources.

❑ **Windows Authentication** Provides support for authenticating clients using NTLM or Kerberos authentication.

❑ **Digest Authentication** Provides support for authenticating clients by sending a password hash to a Windows domain controller.

❑ **Client Certificate Mapping Authentication** Provides support for authenticating client certificates with Directory Service accounts.

❑ **IIS Client Certificate Mapping Authentication** Provides support for mapping client certificates to a Windows user account.

❑ **URL Authorization** Provides support for authorizing client access to the URLs that compose a Web application.

❑ **Request Filtering** Provides support for configuring rules to block selected client requests.

❑ **IP and Domain Restrictions** Provide support for allowing or denying content access based on IP address or domain name.

- **Performance** Performance Services compress content before returning it to a client. Subcomponents of this role service include:

  - ❑ **Static Content Compression** Compresses static content before returning it to a client.

  - ❑ **Dynamic Content Compression** Compresses dynamic content before returning it to a client.

Management Tools When you choose to install the Management Tools role service, the following subcomponents are available for installation as well:

- **IIS Management Console** IIS Management Console enables local and remote administration of Web servers using a Web-based management console.

- **IIS Management Scripts and Tools** IIS Management Scripts and Tools enables managing Web servers from the command line and automating common administrative tasks.

- **Management Service** Management Service allows this Web server to be managed remotely from another computer using the Web Server Management Console.

- **IIS 6 Management Compatibility** IIS 6 Management Compatibility allows you to use existing IIS 6 interfaces and scripts to manage this IIS 7 Web server. Subcomponents of this role service include:

  - ❑ **IIS 6 Metabase Compatibility** Translates IIS 6 metabase changes to the new IIS 7 configuration store.

  - ❑ **IIS 6 WMI Compatibility** Provides support for IIS 6 WMI scripting interfaces.

  - ❑ **IIS 6 Scripting Tools** Streamlines common administrative tasks for IIS 6 Web servers.

  - ❑ **IIS 6 Management Console** Provides support for administering remote IIS 6 Web servers from this computer.

FTP Publishing Service When you choose to install the FTP Publishing Service role service, the following subcomponents are available for installation as well:

- **FTP Server** File Transfer Protocol (FTP) Server provides support for hosting FTP sites and transferring files using FTP.

- **FTP Management Console** File Transfer Protocol (FTP) Management Console enables administration of local and remote FTP servers.

Note that adding the Web Server (IIS) role requires that you also add the Windows Process Activation Service (WPAS) feature together with these three subcomponents of this feature:

- Process Model

- .NET Environment

- Configuration APIs

For more information concerning this role, see Chapter 11, "Internet Information Services 7.0."

Windows Deployment Services

Windows Deployment Services (WDS) provides a simplified, secure means of rapidly deploying Windows to computers via network-based installation, without the administrator visiting each computer directly or installing Windows from physical media.

- **Deployment Server**   Deployment Server provides the full functionality of WDS, which you can use to configure and remotely install Windows operating systems. With Windows Deployment Server, you can create and customize images and then use them to reimage computers. Deployment Server is dependent on the core parts of Transport Server.

- **Transport Server**   Transport Server provides a subset of the functionality of WDS services. It contains only the core networking parts, which you can use to transmit data using multicasting on a standalone server. You should use this role service if you want to transmit data using multicasting but do not want to implement all of WDS services.

For more information concerning the Windows Deployment Services role, see Chapter 12.

Windows SharePoint Services

Windows SharePoint Services helps organizations increase productivity by creating Web sites where users can collaborate on documents, tasks, and events and easily share contacts and other information. Note that installing this server role also requires that you install the Web Server role and some of its role services, and also the Windows Process Activation Service (WPAS) and .NET Framework 3.0 features together with some of their subcomponents.

Remember, of course, that this book is based on a prerelease version (Beta 3) of Windows Server 2008, so there might be changes to the aforementioned list of roles and role services in RTM.

Available Features

Now that we've summarized the various roles and role services you can install on Windows Server 2008, let's examine the different features you can install. Once we've done this, we'll look at how to add roles, role services, and features on a server.

.NET Framework 3.0

Microsoft .NET Framework 3.0 combines the power of the .NET Framework 2.0 APIs with new technologies for building applications that offer appealing user interfaces, protect your customers' personal identity information, enable seamless and secure communication, and provide the ability to model a range of business processes. The following are subcomponents of this feature:

- **.NET Framework 3.0 Features** Microsoft .NET Framework 3.0 combines the power of the .NET Framework 2.0 APIs with new technologies for building applications that offer appealing user interfaces, protect your customers' personal identity information, enable seamless and secure communication, and provide the ability to model a range of business processes.

- **XPS Viewer** An XML Paper Specification (XPS) document is electronic paper that provides a high-fidelity reading and printing experience. The XPS Viewer allows for the viewing, signing, and protecting of XPS documents.

- **Windows Communication Foundation Activation Components** Windows Communication Foundation (WCF) Activation Components use Windows Process Activation Service (WPAS) Support to invoke applications remotely over the network. It does this by using protocols such as HTTP, Message Queuing, TCP, and named pipes. Consequently, applications can start and stop dynamically in response to incoming work items, resulting in application hosting that is more robust, manageable, and efficient. Subcomponents of this component include:

  - **HTTP Activation** Supports process activation via HTTP. Applications that use HTTP Activation can start and stop dynamically in response to work items that arrive over the network via HTTP.

  - **Non-HTTP Activation** Supports process activation via Message Queuing, TCP, and named pipes. Applications that use Non-HTTP Activation can start and stop dynamically in response to work items that arrive over the network via Message Queuing, TCP, and named pipes.

Before we continue our look at the various optional features we can install on Windows Server 2008, let's pause a moment and dig deeper into the improvements of the feature we just mentioned, namely the .NET Framework 3.0. Let's hear what an expert at Microsoft has to say concerning this:

From the Experts: .NET Framework 101

The .NET Framework is an application development and execution environment that includes programming languages and libraries designed to work together to create Windows client and Internet-based applications that are easier to build, manage, deploy, and integrate with other networked systems. The .NET Framework 3.0 is installed by default on Windows Vista. On Microsoft Windows Server 2008, you can install the .NET Framework 3.0 as a Windows feature using the Roles Management tools.

The .NET Framework is composed of several abstraction layers. At the bottom is the common language runtime (CLR). The CLR contains a set of components that implement language integration, garbage collection, security, and memory management. Programs written for the .NET Framework execute in a software environment that manages the program's runtime requirements. The CLR provides the appearance of an application virtual machine so that programmers don't have to consider the capabilities of the specific CPU that will execute the program. The CLR also provides other important services, such as security mechanisms, memory management, and exception handling.

At runtime, the output of application code compiled within the CLR is Microsoft Intermediate Language (MIL). MIL is a language-neutral byte code that operates within the managed environment of the CLR. For developers, the CLR provides lifetime management services and structured exception handling. An object's lifetime within the .NET Framework is determined by the garbage collector (GC), which is responsible for checking every object to evaluate and determine its current status. The GC traverses the memory tree, and any objects that it encounters are marked as alive. During a second pass, any object not marked is destroyed and the associated resources are freed. Finally, to prevent memory fragmentation and increase application performance, the entire memory heap is compacted. This process automatically prevents memory leaks and ensures that developers don't have to write code that deals with low-level system resources.

On top of the CLR is a layer of class libraries that contain the interface and classes that are used within the framework abstraction layers. This Base Class Library (BCL) is a set of interfaces that define things such as data types, data access, and I/O methods. The BCL is then inherited into the upper layers to provide services for Windows, Web Forms, and Web Services. For example, all the base controls that are used to design forms are inherited from classes that are defined within the BCL. At the core of the BCL is the XML enablement classes that are inherited and used within the entire framework and provide a variety of additional services that include data access. Layered on top of the data access and XML layers and inheriting all of their features is the visual presentation layer of Windows Forms and Web Forms.

Residing at the top level of the .NET Framework is the Common Language Specification (CLS), which provides the basic set of language features. The CLS is responsible for defining a subset of the common type system that provides a set of rules that define how language types are declared, managed, and used in the runtime environment. This ensures language interoperability by defining a set of feature requirements that are common in all languages. Because of this, any language that exposes CLS interfaces is guaranteed to be accessible from any other language that supports the CLS. This layer is responsible for guaranteeing that the Framework is language agnostic for any CLS-compliant language. For example, both Microsoft Visual Basic .NET and C# are CLS compliant and therefore interoperable.

.NET Framework 3.0 is an extension of the existing .NET Framework 2.0 CLR and runtime environment. Designed to leverage the extensibility of the .NET Framework 2.0, it contains several new features but no breaking changes to existing applications.

Windows CardSpace (CardSpace)

Windows CardSpace is a new feature of Microsoft Windows and the .NET Framework 3.0 that enables application users to safely manage and control the exchange of their personal information online. By design, Windows CardSpace puts the user at the center of controlling his online identities. Windows CardSpace simplifies the online experience by allowing users to identify themselves. Users do this by submitting cryptographically strong information tokens rather than having to remember and manually type their details into Web sites. This approach leverages what is known as an *identity selector*: when a user needs to authenticate to a Web site, CardSpace provides a special security-hardened UI with a set of information "cards" for the user to choose from.

CardSpace visually represents a user's identity information as an information card. Each information card is controlled by the user and represents one or more *claims* about their identity. Claims are a set of named values that the issuer of the information card asserts is related to a particular individual. Windows CardSpace supports two types of information cards: personal cards and managed cards. *Personal cards* are created by the user, and *managed cards* are obtained from trusted third parties such as the user's bank, employer, insurance company, hotel chain, and so on. To protect any type of personal information, all information cards are stored on the local computer in a secure encrypted store that is unique to the user login. Each file is encrypted twice to prevent malicious access. Managed cards provide an additional layer of protection, as no personal data is stored on the user's machine; instead, it is stored by a trusted provider like your bank or credit card provider and is released only as an encrypted and signed token on demand.

Windows Presentation Foundation (WPF)

Windows Presentation Foundation (WPF) is the next-generation presentation subsystem for Windows. It provides developers and designers with a unified programming model for building rich Windows smart client user experiences that incorporate UI, media, and documents. WPF is designed to build applications for client-side application development and provide either a richer Windows Forms application or a Rich Internet Application (RIA) that is designed to run on the application client workstation.

Windows Workflow Foundation

Windows Workflow Foundation (WF) is a part of the .NET Framework 3.0 that enables developers to create workflow-enabled applications. Activities are the building blocks of workflow. They are a unit of work that needs to be executed. They can be created by either using code or composing them from other activities.

Microsoft Visual Studio contains a set of activities that mainly provide structure—such as parallel execution, if/else, and call Web service. Visual Studio also contains the Workflow Designer that allows for the graphical composition of workflows by placing activities within the workflow model. For developers, this feature of the designer can be rehosted within any Windows Forms or ASP.NET application. WF also contains a rules engine. This engine enables declarative, rule-based development for workflows and any .NET application to use.

Finally, there is the Workflow Runtime. This is a lightweight and extensible engine that executes the activities that make up a workflow. The runtime is hosted within any .NET process, enabling developers to bring workflow to anything from a Windows Forms application to an ASP.NET Web site or a Windows Service. WF provides a common UI and API for application developers and is used within Microsoft's own products, such as SharePoint Portal Server 2007.

Windows Communication Foundation

Modern distributed systems are based on the principles of Service Oriented Architecture (SOA). This type of application architecture is based on loosely coupled and interoperable services. The global acceptance of Web Services has changed how these application components are defined and built. The widespread acceptance has been fueled by vendor agreements on standards and proven interoperability. This combination has helped set Web Services apart from other integration technologies. Windows Communication Foundation (WCF) is Microsoft's unified framework for building reliable, secure, transacted, and interoperable distributed applications. WCF was completely designed with service orientation in mind. It is primarily implemented as a set of classes on top of the .NET Framework CLR.

SOA is an architectural pattern that has many styles. To support this, WCF provides a layered architecture. At the bottom layer, WCF exposes a channel architecture that provides asynchronous, untyped messages. Built on top of this are protocol facilities for secure reliable, transacted data exchange and a broad choice of transport and encoding options. Although WCF introduces a new development environment for distributed applications, it is designed to interoperate with applications that are not WCF based. There are two important aspects to WCF interoperability: interoperability with other platforms, and interoperability with the Microsoft technologies that preceded WCF.

The typed programming model or service model exposed by WCF is designed to ease the development of distributed applications and provide developers with experience in using the ASP.NET Web service. .NET Remoting and Enterprise Services are a familiar development experience with WCF. The service model features a straightforward mapping of Web service concepts to the types of the .NET Framework CLR. This includes a flexible and extensible mapping of messages to the service implementation found in the .NET languages. WCF also provides serialization facilities that enable loose coupling and versioning, while at the same time providing integration and interoperability with existing .NET technologies such as MSMQ, COM+, and others. The result of this technology unification is greater flexibility and significantly reduced development complexity.

To allow more than just basic communication, WCF implements Web services technologies defined by the WS-* specifications. These specifications address several areas, including basic messaging, security, reliability, transactions, and working with a service's metadata. Support for the WS-* protocols means that Web services can easily take advantage of interoperable security, reliability, and transaction support required by businesses today. Developers can now focus on business logic and leave the underlying plumbing to WCF. Windows Communication Foundation also provides opportunities for new messaging scenarios with support for additional transports such as TCP and named pipes and new channels such as the Peer Channel. More flexibility is also available with regard to hosting Web services. Windows Forms applications, ASP.NET applications, console applications, Windows services, and COM+ services can all easily host Web service endpoints on any protocol. WCF also has many options for digitally signing and encrypting messages, including support for Kerberos and X.509.

−Thom Robbins
Director of .NET Platform Product Management

BitLocker Drive Encryption

BitLocker Drive Encryption helps to protect data on lost, stolen, or inappropriately decommissioned computers by encrypting the entire volume and checking the integrity of early boot components. Data is decrypted only if those components are successfully verified and the encrypted drive is located in the original computer. Integrity checking requires a compatible trusted platform module.

BITS Server Extensions

Background Intelligent Transfer Service (BITS) Server Extensions allow a server to receive files uploaded by clients using BITS. BITS allows client computers to transfer files in the foreground or background asynchronously, preserve the responsiveness of other network applications, and resume file transfers after network failures and computer restarts.

Connection Manager Administration Kit

Connection Manager Administration Kit (CMAK) generates Connection Manager profiles using a wizard that guides you through the process of building service profiles that exactly meet your business needs.

Desktop Experience

Desktop Experience includes features of Windows Vista, such as Windows Media Player, desktop themes, and photo management. Desktop Experience does not enable any of the Windows Vista features; you must manually enable them.

Failover Clustering

Failover Clustering allows multiple servers to work together to provide high availability of services and applications. Failover Clustering is often used for file and print services, as well as database and mail applications.

Internet Printing Client

Internet Printing Client allows you to use HTTP to connect to and use printers that are on Web print servers. Internet printing enables connections between users and printers that are not on the same domain or network. Examples of uses include enabling a traveling employee at a remote office site or in a coffee shop equipped with Wi-Fi access to send documents to a printer located at her main office.

Internet Storage Naming Server

Internet Storage Naming Server (iSNS) processes registration requests, de-registration requests, and queries from iSCSI devices.

LPR Port Monitor

Line Printer Remote (LPR) Port Monitor allows users who have access to UNIX-based computers to print on devices attached to them.

Message Queuing

Message Queuing provides guaranteed message delivery, efficient routing, security, and priority-based messaging between applications. Message Queuing also accommodates message delivery between applications that run on different operating systems, use dissimilar network infrastructures, are temporarily offline, or that are running at different times to communicate across heterogeneous networks and systems that might be temporarily offline. MSMQ provides guaranteed message delivery, efficient routing, security, and priority. The following subcomponents are available when you install this feature:

- **Message Queuing Services** Message Queuing Services enable applications running at different times to communicate across heterogeneous networks and systems that may be temporarily offline. Message Queuing provides guaranteed message delivery, efficient routing, security, and priority-based messaging between applications. Subcomponents of this component include:

    - ❑ **MSMQ Server** Provides guaranteed message delivery, efficient routing, security, and priority-based messaging. It can be used to implement solutions for both asynchronous and synchronous messaging scenarios.

- ❑ **Directory Service Integration** Enables publishing of queue properties to the directory, out-of-the-box authentication and encryption of messages using certificates registered in the directory, and routing of messages across Windows sites.

- ❑ **Message Queuing Triggers** Enables the invocation of a COM component or an executable, depending on the filters that you define for the incoming messages in a given queue.

- ❑ **HTTP Support** Enables the sending of messages over HTTP.

- ❑ **Multicasting Support** Enables queuing and sending of multicast messages to a multicast IP address.

- ❑ **Routing Service** Routes messages between different sites and within a site.

- ■ **Windows 2000 Client Support**   Windows 2000 Client Support is required for Message Queuing clients on Windows 2000 computers in the domain.

- ■ **Message Queuing DCOM Proxy**   Message Queuing DCOM Proxy enables the computer to act as a DCOM client of a remote MSMQ server.

Multipath I/O

Microsoft Multipath I/O (MPIO), along with the Microsoft Device Specific Module (DSM) or a third-party DSM, provides support for using multiple data paths to a storage device on Microsoft Windows.

Network Load Balancing

Network Load Balancing (NLB) distributes traffic across several servers, using the TCP/IP networking protocol. NLB is particularly useful for ensuring that stateless applications, such as a Web server running Internet Information Services (IIS), are scalable by adding additional servers as the load increases.

Peer Name Resolution Protocol

Peer Name Resolution Protocol (PNRP) allows applications to register on and resolve names from your computer so that other computers can communicate with these applications.

Remote Assistance

Remote Assistance enables you (or a support person) to offer assistance to users with computer issues or questions. Remote Assistance allows you to view and share control of the user's desktop to troubleshoot and fix the issues. Users can also ask for help from friends or co-workers.

Remote Server Administration Tools

Remote Server Administration Tools (RSAT) enable role and feature management tools on a computer so that you can target them at another 2008 Server machine for remote administration. This feature will not set up the core binaries for the selected components but only their administration tools. Note that the following list of Remote Server Administration Tools is based on the Beta 3 milestone of Windows Server 2008 and that additional tools for managing roles and features may be provided in Release Candidate builds:

- **Role Administration Tools**   Role administration tools that are not installed by default in 2008 Server computers. The following role administration tools are available for installation:

  - Active Directory Certificate Services
  - Active Directory Domain Services
  - Active Directory Lightweight Directory Services
  - Active Directory Rights Management Services
  - DNS Server
  - Fax Server
  - File Services
  - Network Policy and Access Services
  - Print Services
  - Terminal Services.
  - Web Server (IIS)
  - Windows Deployment Services

- **Feature Administration Tools**   Feature administration tools that are not installed by default in 2008 Server computers. The following feature administration tools are available for installation:

  - BitLocker Drive Encryption
  - BITS Server
  - Failover Clustering.
  - Network Load Balancing
  - SMTP Server
  - Simple SAN Management
  - Windows System Resource Management (WSRM)
  - WINS Server

Removable Storage Manager

Removable Storage Manager (RSM) manages and catalogs removable media and operates automated removable media devices.

RPC Over HTTP Proxy

RPC Over HTTP Proxy is a proxy that is used by objects that receive remote procedure calls (RPC) over Hypertext Transfer Protocol (HTTP). This proxy allows clients to discover these objects even if the objects are moved between servers or if they exist in discrete areas of the network for security or other reasons.

Simple TCP/IP Services

Simple TCP/IP Services supports the following TCP/IP services: Character Generator, Daytime, Discard, Echo, and Quote of the Day. Simple TCP/IP Services is provided for backward compatibility and should not be installed unless it is required.

SMTP Server

SMTP Server supports the transfer of e-mail messages between e-mail systems.

SNMP Services

Simple Network Management Protocol (SNMP) Services includes the SNMP Service and SNMP WMI Provider. The following subcomponents are available when you install this feature:

- **SNMP Service**   SNMP Service includes agents that monitor the activity in network devices and report to the network console workstation.

- **SNMP WMI Provider**   SNMP Windows Management Instrumentation (WMI) Provider enables WMI client scripts and applications to get access to SNMP information. Clients can use WMI C++ interfaces and scripting objects to communicate with network devices that use the SNMP protocol and can receive SNMP traps as WMI events.

Storage Manager for SANs

Storage Manager for Storage Area Networks (SANs) helps you create and manage logical unit numbers (LUNs) on Fibre Channel and iSCSI disk drive subsystems that support Virtual Disk Service (VDS) in your SAN.

Subsystem for UNIX-based Applications

Subsystem for UNIX-based Applications (SUA), along with a package of support utilities available for download from the Microsoft Web site, enables you to run UNIX-based programs, and compile and run custom UNIX-based applications in the Windows environment.

Telnet Client

Telnet Client uses the Telnet protocol to connect to a remote telnet server and run applications on that server.

Telnet Server

Telnet Server allows remote users, including those running UNIX-based operating systems, to perform command-line administration tasks and run programs by using a telnet client.

TFTP Client

Trivial File Transfer Protocol (TFTP) Client is used to read files from, or write files to, a remote TFTP server. TFTP is primarily used by embedded devices or systems that retrieve firmware, configuration information, or a system image during the boot process from a TFTP server.

Windows Internal Database

Windows Internal Database is a relational data store that can be used only by Windows roles and features, such as UDDI Services, Active Directory Rights Management Services, Windows SharePoint Services, Windows Server Update Services, and Windows System Resource Manager.

Windows Process Activation Service

Windows Process Activation Service generalizes the IIS process model, removing the dependency on HTTP. All the features of IIS that were previously available only to HTTP applications are now available to applications hosting Windows Communication Foundation (WCF) services, using non-HTTP protocols. IIS 7.0 also uses Windows Process Activation Service for message-based activation over HTTP. The following subcomponents are available when you install this feature:

- **Process Model**   The process model hosts Web and WCF services. Introduced with IIS 6.0, the process model is a new architecture that features rapid failure protection, health monitoring, and recycling. Windows Process Activation Service Process Model removes the dependency on HTTP.

- **.NET Environment**   .NET Environment supports managed code activation in the process model.

■ **Configuration APIs**   Configuration APIs enable applications that are built using the .NET Framework to configure Windows Process Activation Service programmatically. This lets the application developer automatically configure Windows Process Activation Service settings when the application runs instead of requiring the administrator to manually configure these settings.

Windows Server Backup

Windows Server Backup allows you to back up and recover your operating system, applications, and data. You can schedule backups to run once a day or more often, and you can protect the entire server or specific volumes.

Windows System Resource Manager

Windows System Resource Manager (WSRM) is a Windows Server operating system administrative tool that can control how CPU and memory resources are allocated. Managing resource allocation improves system performance and reduces the risk that applications, services, or processes will interfere with each other to reduce server efficiency and system response.

WINS Server

Windows Internet Name Service (WINS) provides a distributed database for registering and querying dynamic mappings of NetBIOS names for computers and groups used on your network. WINS maps NetBIOS names to IP addresses and solves the problems arising from NetBIOS name resolution in routed environments.

Wireless Networking

Wireless Networking configures and starts the WLAN AutoConfig service, regardless of whether the computer has any wireless adapters. WLAN AutoConfig enumerates wireless adapters and manages both wireless connections and the wireless profiles that contain the settings required to configure a wireless client to connect to a wireless network.

Again, please remember that this book is based on a prerelease version (Beta 3) of Windows Server 2008, so there might be changes to the preceding list of features in RTM. For example, in the build that this particular chapter is based on (IDS_2, also known as February 2007 Community Technology Preview), the Group Policy Management Console (GPMC) is not present and there are no RSAT tools present for managing certain roles such as File Server, Network Policy and Access Services, Windows Deployment Services, and so on.

Adding Roles and Features

Now that we've looked at the various roles, role services, and features that are available in Windows Server 2008, let's look at how to install them on a server. There are basically three ways to do this:

- From the Initial Configuration Tasks (ICT) screen
- Using Server Manager
- From the command line

What about installing roles and features during setup? Can you configure an unattend.xml file so that a role such as File Server or Network Policy and Access Services is automatically installed after setup finishes? I asked this question of someone on the product team while writing this chapter. The answer I got was "Yes and no," meaning that it might be possible but would involve "stitching" a lot of things together to make it happen. To understand why this is so, we need to understand a bit about how roles and features are defined "under the hood" in Windows Server 2008, and this involves understanding something called CBS Updates. And no, this has nothing to do with late-breaking news on television...

Let's pause again for a moment and listen to an expert at Microsoft explain the architecture behind roles and features in Windows Server 2008:

From the Experts: Component Based Servicing

Windows Vista and Windows Server 2008 have a new architecture, called Component Based Servicing (CBS), to capture all the dependencies across binaries, system integrity information per resource, and any customized commands that were needed for servicing to occur. The new architecture provides a unified platform for OS installation and optional component installation and servicing. CBS allows Microsoft to build new SKUs in a more agile way, and the Windows server core installation of Windows Server 2008 is a direct result of moving Microsoft Windows to this new architecture.

The flip side of providing this level of componentization is that now there are many more optional components that you can install on Windows Server since fewer components are now installed by default. Another factor that adds complexity is the number of dependencies between these different optional components. Finally, while most of the optional components in Windows Server use the CBS technology, there are a couple of exceptions (such as SharePoint and the Windows Internal Database) that use MSI as their installer technology instead. One can get a glimpse of this complexity by using

---

tools such as pkgmgr.exe and OCSetup.exe to install optional components. The command to perform a complete install of the Web Server role looks like this:

```
start /w pkgmgr /iu:IIS-WebServerRole;IIS-WebServer;IIS-
CommonHttpFeatures;IIS-StaticContent;IIS-DefaultDocument;IIS-
DirectoryBrowsing;IIS-HttpErrors;IIS-HttpRedirect;IIS-
ApplicationDevelopment;IIS-ASPNET;IIS-NetFxExtensibility;IIS-ASP;IIS-CGI;IIS-
ISAPIExtensions;IIS-ISAPIFilter;IIS-ServerSideIncludes;IIS-
HealthAndDiagnostics;IIS-HttpLogging;IIS-LoggingLibraries;
IIS-RequestMonitor;IIS-HttpTracing;IIS-CustomLogging;IIS-ODBCLogging;IIS-
Security;IIS-BasicAuthentication;IIS-WindowsAuthentication;IIS-
DigestAuthentication;IIS-ClientCertificateMappingAuthentication;
IIS-IISCertificateMappingAuthentication;IIS-URLAuthorization;IIS-
RequestFiltering;IIS-IPSecurity;IIS-Performance;IIS-HttpCompressionStatic;IIS-
HttpCompressionDynamic;IIS-WebServerManagementTools;IIS-ManagementConsole;IIS-
ManagementScriptingTools;IIS-ManagementService;IIS-IS6ManagementCompatibility;
IIS-Metabase;IIS-WMICompatibility;IIS-LegacyScripts;IIS-LegacySnapIn;IIS-
FTPPublishingService;IIS-FTPServer;IIS-FTPManagement;WAS-
WindowsActivationService;WAS-ProcessModel;WAS-NetFxEnvironment;WAS-
ConfigurationAPI
```

Server Manager reduces these complexities by grouping optional components into Roles and Features, which are collections of optional components that together address a particular need. Server Manager also automatically handles dependencies between optional components, so that you don't need to worry about creating a command that is more than a dozen lines long! The different installer technologies are also handled uniformly by Server Manager. Thus, you don't need to worry about which command to use to install roles and features based on which installer technology they use.

Finally, which command do you like better? The one above or this one:

```
servermanagercmd -install Web-Server -allsubfeatures
```

For more on the Server Manager command-line interface (CLI), see my second sidebar later in this chapter.

–Eduardo Melo
Lead Program Manager, Windows Enterprise Management Division

Using Initial Configuration Tasks

The most obvious way of adding roles and features is to do so from the Initial Configuration Tasks (ICT) screen that is presented to you the first time you log on to Windows Server 2008. We looked at this tool in the previous chapter; now let's try using it—first to add a role and then to add a feature.

We'll begin by adding the File Server role. Here's the ICT screen again:

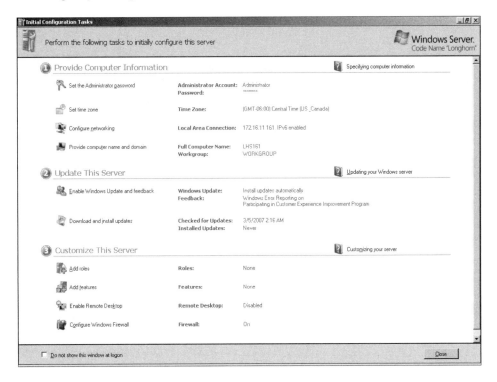

Note that next to "Roles," it says "None." This means that we haven't installed any roles yet on this particular machine. Let's click the Add Roles link. This starts the Add Roles Wizard (ARW), a simple-to-use tool that walks us through the steps for installing roles on our server. The initial ARW screen looks like this:

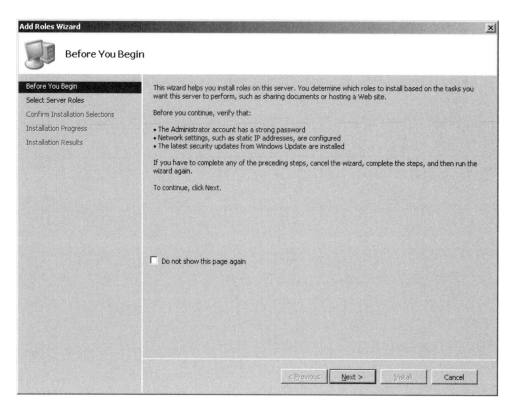

Notice that the initial screen of the wizard reminds us to make sure we've completed certain precautionary steps before adding roles to our wizard. Clicking Next displays the different roles we can now choose to install:

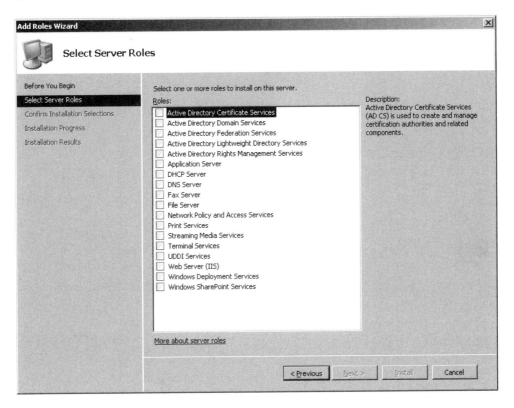

A big improvement of Windows Server 2008 over previous versions of Windows Server is that you can now choose to install multiple roles at once. Remember the Manage Your Server Wizard in Windows Server 2003? If you wanted to configure your server as both a file server and a print server, you had to walk through the wizard twice to do this. With Windows Server 2008, however, you can multiselect the roles you want to install and you need to walk through the wizard only once. Of course, this might not be 100 percent true because certain roles can have dependencies on other roles—I have to confess that I haven't tried all 262,143 ($2^{18}-1$) possible combinations of roles in this wizard, so I can't confirm or deny whether this might be an issue or not. Perhaps the technical reviewer for this book can test this matter thoroughly, provided he feels that Microsoft Press is paying him enough for all the effort involved!

Anyway, let's select the check box for the File Server role and click Next. When we do this, a screen gives us a short description of the role we selected. We'll skip this screen and click Next again to display a list of role services we can install together with this role:

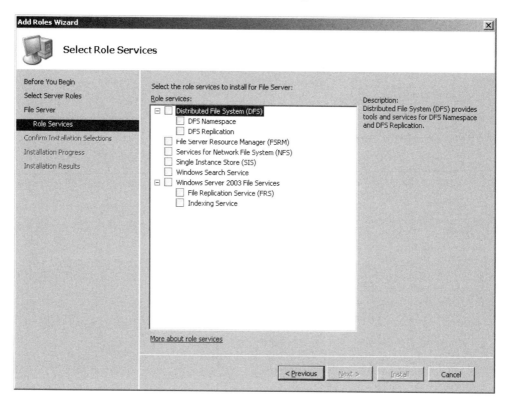

Because there are no check boxes preselected on this screen, all the role services available here are optional. So if we wanted to install only the File Server role and nothing else, we could just click Next and finish the wizard. Let's choose one of these role services, however—namely, the File Server Resource Manager (FSRM) console, a tool for managing file servers that was first introduced in Windows Server 2003 R2.

After we select to install this additional role service to our role, we click Next and get a confirmation screen telling us which role(s) and role service(s) we're going to install:

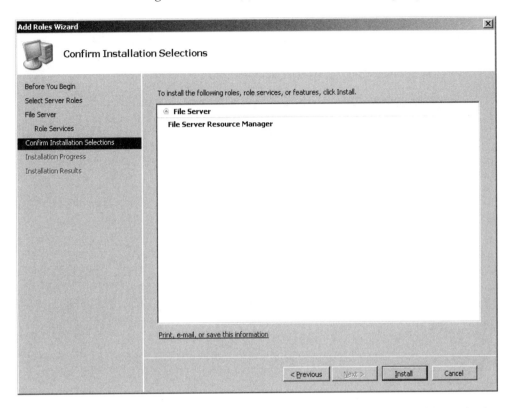

What if we decide we want to add another role service, or maybe even an additional role? The nice thing about this wizard is that you can jump to any screen of the wizard simply by selecting its link from the left.

But we want to install only one role and one additional service. To do this we click Install and wait awhile for the selected components to install. (This takes some time because we're dealing with a beta version of the platform.) Note that we aren't prompted for the source files, which is a nice touch—when you install Windows Server 2008, everything you need to install additional components later is already there on your server.

Once the File Server role has been successfully installed, the wizard displays confirmation of this. When you close the wizard and return to the Initial Configuration Tasks screen, the added role is displayed where before it said "None." (See the first screen shot of this section.) And sure enough, if you select Administrative Tools from the Start menu, you'll see a shortcut there for launching the File Server Resource Management console.

Adding features is a very similar process, and it uses an Add Feature Wizard (AFW) that you can launch by clicking the Add Features link in the Initial Configuration Tasks screen. The AFW wizard displays a list of optional features you can add to your server:

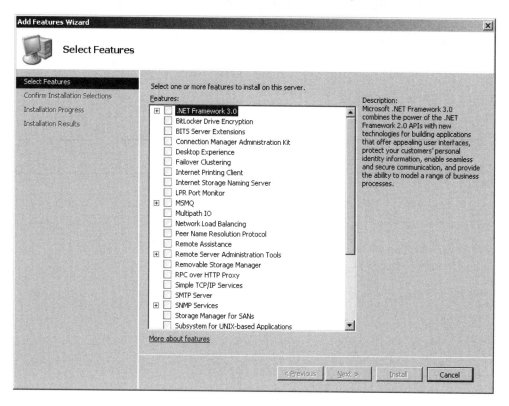

I won't bother walking you through this second wizard, as you're an IT pro, you're smart—you get wizards. If you do want to try adding a feature, however, you might start by installing Windows Server Backup. Why that feature in particular? Because backups are important—duh!

There is one more thing you might be wondering, however, if you've played around with adding roles using ICT. If you click Add Roles once more in ICT to run the ARW again and display the list of roles, you'll see that the File Server role is grayed out:

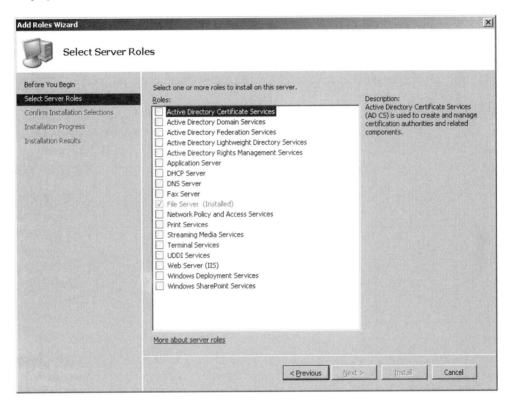

In other words, you can't deselect the File Server role to uninstall it should you want to do this. Why can't you do this? Well, it's not called the *Add* Roles Wizard for nothing! Anyway, we'll see how to remove roles in a moment, but first let's move on to another tool for managing roles: Server Manager.

Using Server Manager

Adding roles and features using Server Manager is a no-brainer. But before we do this, let's open Server Manager and view the results of the procedure we just completed, where we added the File Server role and File Server Resource Management console to our server:

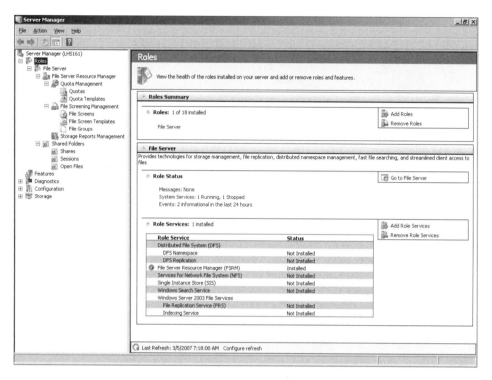

Now to add a new role to your server, simply right-click the Roles node (which is selected in the preceding screen shot) and choose Add Roles to launch the Add Roles Wizard. You can also remove roles easily by right-clicking the Roles node and selecting Remove Roles, which launches the (you guessed it) Remove Roles Wizard.

In a similar way, you can add or remove role services for a particular role by right-clicking a role (such as File Server displayed here) and choosing either Add Role Services or Remove Role Services from the context menu. And you can add or remove features by right-clicking the Features node and choosing the appropriate option. Finally, by right-clicking the root node (Server Manager), you can add or remove both features and roles. I told you it was a no-brainer.

From the Command Line

Something neat that was added in IDS_2, also known as February 2007 Community Technology Preview, is the ability to add or remove roles and features from the command line. This can be done using the ServerManagerCmd.exe command that we talked about in the previous chapter. As we saw, ServerManagerCmd.exe is a powerful tool both for installing and removing roles and also for previewing what components would be installed *if* you actually decide to add a particular role. I showed you some basic examples of how to use this command in the previous chapter, so here I'm just going to provide you with a few more examples of what this powerful command can do:

- **servermanagercmd –install Web-Server –whatif**   This command analyzes which specific roles, role services, and features would be installed as part of installing the Web Server role. It compares the list of roles, role services, and features that we know are part of the Web-server role with the list of roles, role services, and features that are already installed on the computer. Only the ones currently not installed are identified as applicable for installation on that particular computer. This functionality really helps you understand the full list of actions that will be performed with the command, without actually making changes to the computer.

- **servermanagercmd –install Web-Server**   This command is the same as the previous command without the **–whatif** flag. So this time it actually installs the Web Server role.

- **servermanagercmd –install Terminal-Services –restart**   This command installs the Terminal Services role. Given that the installation of this role requires a reboot to complete, the **–restart** flag is used to automatically restart the machine to complete the role installation. If **–restart** is not used, you need to restart the computer manually to complete the role installation.

- **servermanagercmd –remove Web-Server**   This command removes the Web Server role (assuming it is already installed on the computer). Note that if roles and features that depend on Web Server are installed on the computer (for example, Windows SharePoint Services), they will also be removed from the computer.

- **servermanagercmd –remove Web-Server –resultPath results.xml**   This command is the same as the previous command, with the addition of the **–resultPath** flag. Using this flag, ServerManagerCmd.exe will save the results of the removal operation in an XML file that can then be programmatically parsed.

- **servermanagercmd –inputPath input.xml**   If you want to install (or remove) multiple roles, role services, and features, a more expedient way to do this is by using the **–inputPath** option instead of using **–install** or **–remove**. This is because these two flags accept only one role, role service, or feature at a time, whereas you can specify as many items as needed in the *input*.xml file. Here's an example of an *input*.xml file (which can be named anything else if you like) that installs a whole bunch of features (also called OCs for Optional Components) in a single step:

```xml
<?xml version="1.0" encoding="utf-8" ?>
<ServerManagerConfiguration Action="Install"
  xmlns="http://schemas.microsoft.com/sdm/Windows/ServerManager/Configuration
  /2007/1" xmlns:xs="http://www.w3.org/2001/XMLSchema">

    <Feature Id="NLB"                    InstallAllSubFeatures="true"/>
    <Feature Id="Desktop-Experience"     InstallAllSubFeatures="true"/>
    <Feature Id="NET-Framework"          InstallAllSubFeatures="true"/>
    <Feature Id="WSRM"                   InstallAllSubFeatures="true"/>
    <Feature Id="Wireless-Networking"    InstallAllSubFeatures="true"/>
    <Feature Id="Backup"                 InstallAllSubFeatures="true"/>
    <Feature Id="WINS-Server"            InstallAllSubFeatures="true"/>
    <Feature Id="Remote-Assistance"      InstallAllSubFeatures="true"/>
    <Feature Id="Simple-TCPIP"           InstallAllSubFeatures="true"/>
    <Feature Id="Telnet-Client"          InstallAllSubFeatures="true"/>
    <Feature Id="Telnet-Server"          InstallAllSubFeatures="true"/>
    <Feature Id="Subsystem-UNIX-Apps"    InstallAllSubFeatures="true"/>
    <Feature Id="RPC-over-HTTP-Proxy"    InstallAllSubFeatures="true"/>
    <Feature Id="SMTP-Server"            InstallAllSubFeatures="true"/>
    <Feature Id="LPR-Port-Monitor"       InstallAllSubFeatures="true"/>
    <Feature Id="Storage-Mgr-SANs"       InstallAllSubFeatures="true"/>
    <Feature Id="BITS"                   InstallAllSubFeatures="true"/>
    <Feature Id="MSMQ"/>
    <Feature Id="MSMQ-Services"/>
    <Feature Id="MSMQ-DCOM"/>
    <Feature Id="WPAS"                   InstallAllSubFeatures="true"/>
    <Feature Id="Windows-Internal-DB"    InstallAllSubFeatures="true"/>
    <Feature Id="BitLocker"              InstallAllSubFeatures="true"/>
    <Feature Id="Multipath-IO"           InstallAllSubFeatures="true"/>
    <Feature Id="ISNS"                   InstallAllSubFeatures="true"/>
    <Feature Id="Removable-Storage"      InstallAllSubFeatures="true"/>
    <Feature Id="TFTP-Client"            InstallAllSubFeatures="true"/>
    <Feature Id="SNMP-Service"           InstallAllSubFeatures="true"/>
    <Feature Id="Internet-Print-Client"  InstallAllSubFeatures="true"/>
    <Feature Id="PNRP"                   InstallAllSubFeatures="true"/>
    <Feature Id="CMAK"                   InstallAllSubFeatures="true"/>

</ServerManagerConfiguration>
```

Finally, here's one more example that's a bit unique. Normally, you use ServerManagerCmd.exe to install the bits and files associated with a particular role or feature in Windows Server 2008, while any configuration settings associated with that role or feature can be specified later using role-specific or feature-specific tools. But Windows SharePoint Services (WSS) is an exception to this because there are two settings that must be specified as part of the role installation. These two settings determine whether WSS should be installed as a single server deployment or as part of a server farm, and which language should be used for the SharePoint administration Web site. Here's how you install the WSS role on your server using ServerManagerCmd.exe and configure these two settings:

servermanagercmd -install Windows-SharePoint −setting InstallAsPartOfServerFarm= false−setting Language=de-de

Finally, a few words from one of our experts on the product team concerning ServerManagerCmd.exe and its usefulness for adding and removing roles from the command line:

From the Experts: The Server Manager CLI

The Server Manager command-line interface (CLI) is one of my favorite features in Server Manager. The Server Manager GUI (console and wizards) provides a consolidated view of the server, including information about server configuration, status of installed roles, and links for adding and removing roles and features. The CLI makes the key pieces of functionality from the Server Manager GUI also available from the command-line prompt, which allows the user to perform tasks such as installing a role and verifying which roles are currently installed on the machine from the command prompt or via scripts.

Using remoting technologies such as Windows Management Instrumentation (WMI) and Windows Remote Management (WinRM), you can now start taking advantage of the CLI from a remote machine (your Windows Vista desktop, for example) or manage multiple servers at the same time. Additionally, the CLI takes input and produces output in XML format, which makes it much easier to programmatically "control" the CLI.

You might be asking where I am going with this. Well, here is what I want to do: create a lightweight application that I can run on my Windows Vista machine and that allows me to remotely connect (via WMI or WinRM) to my Windows Server 2008 server in my office. After connected to the server, my application would remotely run the CLI with the −query flag and get the list of available roles and features back in an XML file. It would then parse the results from the XML and list back to me the roles and features available on my server, including which roles and features are currently installed on the server. My application GUI would then allow me to select roles and features that I want to install (or remote). After making my selections, the application would again remotely run the CLI (this time using the −install, −remove or most likely the −inputPath flag) so that the roles and features that I specified can be remotely installed (or removed) on my Windows Server 2008 machine.

Now I just need to find some spare time to build this application!

−Eduardo Melo
  Lead Program Manager, Windows Enterprise Management Division

Conclusion

Adding and removing roles and features is easier and more efficient in Windows Server 2008 than in previous versions of Windows Server. For instance, you can now add or remove roles from the command line, and you can add or remove multiple roles in one step. What goes on underneath the hood is quite complex, but the wizards you can launch from Server Manager and Initial Configuration Tasks make adding and configuring new roles on your server a snap.

Additional Reading

The TechNet Webcast titled "Installing, Configuring, and Managing Server Roles in Windows Server 2008" is a good demonstration of how to add roles and features to Windows Server 2008. This Webcast can be downloaded for replay from *http://msevents.microsoft.com/cui/WebCastEventDetails.aspx?EventID=1032294712& EventCategory=5&culture=en-US&CountryCode=US*. (Registration is required.)

By registering for the TechNet Virtual Lab, "Microsoft Windows Server 2008 Beta 2 Server Manager Virtual Lab," which can be found at *http://msevents.microsoft.com/CUI/ WebCastEventDetails.aspx?EventID=1032314461&EventCategory=3&culture=en-IN& CountryCode=IN*, you can gain some hands-on experience adding and removing roles using Server Manager. TechNet Virtual Labs are designed to allow IT pros to evaluate and test new server technologies from Microsoft using a series of guided, hands-on labs that can be completed in 90 minutes or less. TechNet Virtual Labs can be accessed online and are free to use. You can find general information concerning them at *http://www.microsoft.com/technet/ traincert/virtuallab/default.mspx*.

Finally, be sure to turn to Chapter 14, "Additional Resources," for more information on the topics in this chapter and also for webcasts, whitepapers, blogs, newsgroups, and other sources of information about all aspects of Windows Server 2008.

Chapter 6

Windows Server Core

In this chapter:

What Is a Windows Server Core Installation? 109

Performing Initial Configuration of a Windows Server Core Server 118

Managing a Windows Server Core Server 130

Windows Server Core Installation Tips and Tricks 143

Conclusion 147

Additional Resources. 147

When you try to install Microsoft Windows Server 2008 manually from media on a system, you're presented with two installation options to choose from:

- A full installation of the Microsoft Windows Server 2008 operating system

- A Windows server core installation of the Windows Server 2008 operating system

Selecting the first option means you get the type of Windows server you're used to, with its full slate of GUI tools, support for the .NET Framework, and support for a wide range of possible roles and features you can install on your machine. But what if you select the second option? What's a Windows server core installation of Windows Server 2008? And how does this differ from a full installation of the product? Well, that's what this chapter is all about–read on!

What Is a Windows Server Core Installation?

The best way of learning about the Windows server core installation option is to simply install it and log on. Here's what you see when you first log on to a Windows server core server.

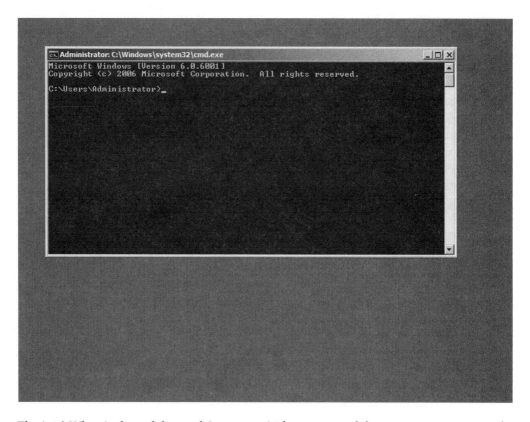

That's it? Where's the task bar and Start menu? There is no task bar or Start menu. How do you start Windows Explorer then? You can't–the tool is not available in a Windows server core installation. Where's the Initial Configuration Tasks screen? It's not there. How can I open Server Manager to add roles and features? Sorry, Server Manager is unavailable on a Windows server core installation. Well, what can I do with this thing then? Am I stuck with only a command prompt to work with?

You can do a lot with a Windows server core installation, as we'll see in a moment. And no, you're not just stuck with a command prompt. But if you were, would it be bad? Ever hear a Unix admin complain about "being stuck" with having to use the command line to administer a server? Isn't command-line administration of servers a *good* thing because it means you can automate complex management tasks using batch files and scripts and there is no graphical UI taking resources away from server tasks?

And that's one of the things that a Windows server core installation is all about–scripted administration of Windows servers in enterprise (and especially datacenter) environments. But why remove the desktop and all the GUI management tools? Doesn't that cripple the server? Not at all–in fact, just the opposite!

Understanding Windows Server Core

Windows server core is a "minimal" installation option for Windows Server 2008. What this means is that when you choose this option during setup (or when using unattended setup), Windows Server 2008 installs a minimum set of components on your machine that will allow you to run certain (but not all) server roles. In other words, selecting the Windows server core installation option installs only a subset of the binaries that are installed when you choose the full installation option for Windows Server 2008.

Here are some of the Windows Server 2008 components that are *not* installed when you specify the Windows server core installation option during setup:

- No desktop shell (which means no glass, wallpaper, or screen savers either)

- No Windows Explorer or My Computer (we already said no desktop shell, right?)

- No .NET Framework or CLR (which means no support for managed code, which also means no PowerShell support)

- No MMC console or snap-ins (so no Administrative tools on the Start menu—whoops! I forgot, no Start menu!)

- No Control Panel applets (with a few small exceptions)

- No Internet Explorer or Windows Mail or WordPad or Paint or Search window (no Windows Explorer!) or GUI Help and Support or even a Run box.

Wow, that sounds like a lot of stuff that's missing in a Windows server core installation of Windows Server 2008! Actually though, it's not—compare the preceding list to the following list of components that *are* available on a Windows server core server.

First, you've still got the kernel. You always need the kernel.

Then you've got hardware support components such as the Hardware Abstraction Layer (HAL) and device drivers. But it's only a limited set of device drivers that supports disks, network cards, basic video support, and some other stuff. A lot of in-box drivers have been removed from the Windows server core installation option, however—though there is a way to install out-of-box drivers if you need to, as we'll see later in this chapter.

Next, you've still got all the core subsystems that are needed by Windows Server 2008 in order to function. That means you've got the security subsystem and Winlogon, the networking subsystem, the file system, RPC and DCOM, SNMP support, and so on. Without these subsystems, your server simply wouldn't be able to do anything at all, so they're a necessity for a Windows server core installation.

Then you've got various components you need to configure different aspects of your server. For example, you have components that let you create user accounts and change passwords, enable DHCP or assign a static IP address, rename your server or join a domain, configure Windows Firewall, enable Automatic Updates, choose a keyboard layout, set the time and date, enable Remote Desktop, and so on. Many of these configuration tasks can be performed using various command-line tools included in a Windows server core installation (more about tools in a moment), but a few of them use scripts or expose minimal UI.

There are some additional infrastructure components present as well on a Windows server core installation. For instance, you still have the event logs plus a command-line tool for viewing, configuring, and forwarding them using Windows eventing. You've got performance counters and a command-line tool for collecting performance information about your server. You have the Licensing service, so you can activate and use your server as a fully licensed machine. You've got IPSec support, so your server can securely communicate on the network. You've got NAP client support, so your server can participate in a NAP deployment. And you've got support for Group Policy of course.

Then there are various tools and infrastructure items to enable you to manage your Windows server core server. As we saw in our screen shot earlier, you've got the command prompt cmd.exe, so you can log on locally to your server and run various commands from a command-prompt window. In fact, as we saw, a command-prompt window is already open for you when you first log on to a Windows server core server. What happens, though, if you accidentally close this window? Fortunately, a Windows server core installation still includes Task Manager, so if you close your command window you can start another by doing the following:

1. Press CTRL+SHIFT+ESC, to open Task Manager.

2. On the Applications tab, click New Task.

3. Type **cmd** and click OK.

In addition to the command prompt, of course, there are dozens (probably over a hundred, and more when different roles and features are installed) of different command-line tools available on Windows Server 2008 for both full and server core installation options. What I'm talking about is Arp, Assoc, At, Attrib, BCDEdit Cacls, Certutil, Chdir, chkdsk, Cls, Copy, CScript, Defrag, Dir, and so on. A lot of the commands listed in the "Windows Command-Line Reference A–Z," found on Microsoft TechNet, are available on a Windows server core server—not all, mind you, but a lot of them.

You can also enable Remote Desktop on a Windows server core installation, and this lets you connect to it from another machine using Remote Desktop Connection (RDC) and start a Terminal Services session running on it. Once you've established your session, you can use the command prompt to run various commands on your server, and you can even use the new Remote Programs feature of RDC 6.0 to run a remote command prompt on a Windows server core server from an administrative workstation running Windows Vista. (We'll learn more about that soon.)

There's also a WMI infrastructure on your Windows server core server that includes many of the usual WMI providers. This means you can manage your Windows server core server either by running WMI scripts on the local machine from the command prompt or by scheduling their operation using schtasks.exe. (There's no Task Schedule UI available, however.) Or you can manage your server remotely by running remote WMI scripts against it from another machine. And having WMI on a Windows server core server means that remote UI tools such as MMC snap-ins running on other systems (typically, either a full installation of Windows Server 2008 or an administrator workstation running Windows Vista with Remote Server Administration Tools installed) can connect to and remotely administer your Windows server core server. Plus there's also a WS-Management infrastructure on a Windows server core installation. WS-Management is a new remote-management infrastructure included in Windows Vista and Windows Server 2008, and involves Windows Remote Management (WinRM) on the machine being managed and the Windows Remote Shell (WinRM) for remote command execution from the machine doing the managing. We'll talk about remote management of Windows server core servers later in this chapter.

Then there are various server roles and optional features you can install on a Windows server core server so that the machine can actually do something useful on your network, like be a DHCP server or a domain controller or print server. We'll look later at exactly which roles and features are available for installing on a Windows server core server and which roles/features you can't install.

Then there are a few necessary GUI tools that actually *are* present on a Windows server core server. For example, we already saw that the command prompt (cmd.exe) is available, and so is Task Manager. Another useful tool on a Windows server core server is Regedit.exe, which can be launched either from the command line or from Task Manager. Then there's Notepad.

Notepad?

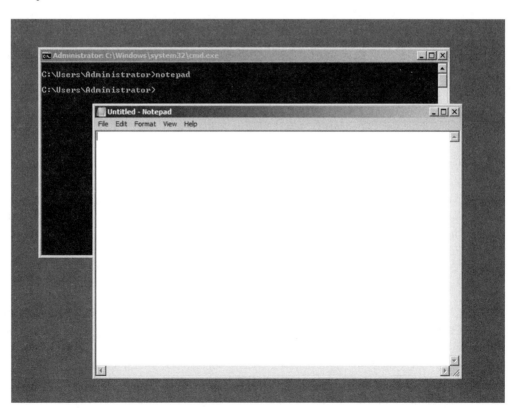

Yes, Notepad. The reason for including Notepad on a Windows server core installation option of Windows Server 2008 is simple: Microsoft listens to its customers. I'm not kidding! (Plus I'm serious about Microsoft listening to customers.) During the early stages of developing and testing Windows Server 2008, one of the most common requests from participants in the Microsoft Technology Adoption Program (TAP) for Windows Server 2008 was this: We need a tool on Windows server core servers that we can use to view logs, edit scripts, and perform other essential administrative tasks. Give us Notepad! We want Notepad!

Who ever expected that the lowly and oft-maligned Notepad would be so important to administrators who work in enterprise environments?

Anyway, before we move on and talk a bit about the rationale behind why Microsoft decided to offer the Windows server core installation option in Windows Server 2008, let's hear from one of our experts about how the Windows server core product team managed to make this thing work. After all, Windows components have a lot of dependencies with one another and especially with the desktop shell and Internet Explorer, so it will be interesting to hear how they took so many components out of this installation option for the product without causing it to break. Plus we'll also learn a bit about how we can try to get applications that we need to have running on a Windows server core server running properly. And finally, we'll learn something about getting Notepad to run properly on a Windows server core server:

From the Experts: Shimming Applications in Windows Server Core

The primary goal of the Windows server core installation option is to minimize the disk and servicing footprint. Thus, a number of Windows components—such as Media Player and Internet Explorer—are not installed as part of a Windows server core installation. This means that because of their dependencies on parts of Internet Explorer, the common dialog boxes are not functional in a Windows server core installation. Thus, the file open and save dialog boxes in Notepad, for example, will not work.

A Windows server core installation leverages the application compatibility shim infrastructure in Windows to develop a clever solution to this problem. A *shim* is a thin layer of code that sits between an application and a Windows API. The shimming infrastructure redirects the API call made by the application to the shim code, which can then make some changes to the parameters, call the original API, or do something else entirely.

A Windows server core installation installs two shims. The first one is called *RegEditImportExportLoadHive* and is a specialized shim that allows *RegEdit* to import and export registry files. The second shim is called *NoExplorerForGetFileName*. It's a general shim for file open and save dialog boxes and is currently used by Notepad. This second shim changes some parameters to the API call that displays the file open or save dialog so that the old-style dialog box from pre-Windows 95 is displayed, instead of the new Explorer-style dialog box.

The shimming engine allows the end user to apply existing shims to other applications. The tool used to do this is the Application Compatibility Toolkit. Copy the sysmain.sdb database located at %SYSTEMROOT%\AppPatch (or %SYSTEMROOT%\AppPatch\ AppPatch64 on x64 machines) on the Windows server core machine to a Windows Server 2008 machine. Use the Application Compatibility Toolkit to edit the database. Copy the new database back to the Windows server core machine, and install it using sdbinst.exe, located at %SYSTEMROOT%\System32.

–Rahul Prasad
   Software Development Engineer, Windows Core Operating System Division

The Rationale for Windows Server Core

The need for something like the Windows server core installation option of Windows Server 2008 is pretty obvious. Windows Server today is frequently deployed to support a single role in an enterprise or to handle a fixed workload. For example, organizations often deploy the DHCP Server role on a dedicated Windows Server 2003 machine to provide dynamic addressing support for client computers on their network. Now think about that for a moment— you've just installed Windows Server 2003 with all its various services and components on a solid piece of hardware, just to use the machine as a DHCP server and nothing more. Or maybe as a file server as part of a DFS file system infrastructure you're setting up for users. Or as a print server to manage a number of printers on your network. The point is, you've got Windows Server 2003 with all its features doing only one thing. Why do you need all those extra binaries on your machine then? And think about when you need to patch your system— you've got to apply all new software updates to the machine, even though the functionality that many of those updates fix will never actually be used on that particular system. Why should you have to patch IIS on your server if the server is not going to be used for hosting Web sites? And might not having IIS binaries on your server make it more vulnerable even though the IIS component is not actually being used on it or is even installed? The more stuff you've got on a box, the more difficult it is to secure (or to be sure that it's secure) and the more complex it is to maintain.

Enter the Windows server core installation option of Windows Server 2008. Now, instead of installing all of Windows Server 2008 on your box while using only a portion of it, you can install a minimal subset of Windows Server 2008 binaries and you need to maintain only those particular binaries. The value proposition for enterprises of the Windows server core installation option is plain to see:

- Fewer binaries mean a reduced attack surface and, hence, a greater degree of protection for your network.
- Less functionality and a role-based paradigm also mean fewer services running on your machine and, therefore, again less attack surface.

- Fewer binaries also mean a reduced servicing surface, which means fewer patches, making your server easier to service and orienting your patch management cycle according to roles instead of boxes. Estimates indicate that using the Windows server core installation option can reduce the number of patches you need to apply to your server by as much as 50 percent compared with full installations of Windows Server 2008.

- Fewer roles and features also mean easier management of your servers and enable different members of your IT staff to specialize better according to the server roles they need to support.

- Finally, fewer binaries also mean less disk space needed for the core operating system components, which is a plus for datacenter environments in particular.

The Windows server core installation option of Windows Server 2008 is all of these and more, and it's included in the Standard, Enterprise, and Datacenter editions of Windows Server 2008. Windows server core is not a separate product or SKU—it's an installation option you can select during manual or unattended install. And it's available on both the x86 and x64 platforms of Windows Server 2008. (It's not available on IA64 and on the Web edition SKU of Windows Server 2008.) The bottom line? The Windows server core installation option of Windows Server 2008 is more secure and more reliable, and it requires less management overhead than using a full installation of Windows Server 2008 for an equivalent purpose in your enterprise.

A Windows server core server provides you with minimal server operating system functionality and a low attack surface for targeted roles. To give you a better idea of the functionality that is (and isn't) available in the Windows server core installation option, Table 6-1 shows included and excluded roles and Table 6-2 shows included and excluded optional features.

Table 6-1   Included/Excluded Roles in the Windows Server Core Installation Option of Windows Server 2008

Roles available	Roles unavailable
Active Directory	Active Directory Certificate Services
Active Directory LDS	Active Directory Federation Services
DHCP Server	Active Directory RMS
DNS Server	Application Server
File Services (includes DFSR and NFS)	Fax Server
Print Services	Network Policy and Access Services
Streaming Media Services	Terminal Services
Windows Server Virtualization	UDDI Services
	Web Server (IIS)
	Windows Deployment Services
	Windows SharePoint Services

Table 6-2   Included/Excluded Features in the Windows Server Core Installation Option of Windows Server 2008

Features available	Features unavailable
BitLocker Drive Encryption	.NET Framework 3.0
Failover Clustering	BITS Server Extensions
Multipath I/O	Connection Manager Administration Kit
Removable Storage Management	Desktop Experience
SNMP Services	Internet Printing Client
Subsystem for UNIX-based Applications	Internet Storage Naming Server
Telnet Client	LPR Port Monitor
Windows Server Backup	Message Queuing
WINS Server	Network Load Balancing
	Peer Name Resolution Protocol
	Remote Assistance
	Remote Server Administration Tools
	RPC over HTTP Proxy
	Simple TCP/IP Services
	SMTP Server
	Storage Manager for SANs
	Telnet Server
	TFTP Client
	Windows Internal Database
	Windows Process Activation Service
	Windows System Resource Manager (WSRM)
	Wireless Networking

Performing Initial Configuration of a Windows Server Core Server

In Chapter 5, "Managing Server Roles," we saw how to perform the initial configuration of a Windows Server 2008 server using the Initial Configuration Tasks screen. Of course, many of these initial configuration tasks can also be performed using an unattend.xml answer file during an unattended installation.

The Windows server core installation option of Windows Server 2008 can also have its initial configuration done in two ways: from the command line after a manual install, or by doing an unattended installation. In this chapter, we're going to look only at the first method (using the command line after a manual install). For more information on unattended installation of Windows Server 2008, see Chapter 13, "Deploying Windows Server 2008."

Performing Initial Configuration from the Command Line

Some of the initial configuration tasks you will want to perform on a Windows server core server include the following:

- Set a password for the Administrator account.

- Set the date, time, and time zone.

- Configure networking, which might mean assigning a static IP address, subnet mask, and default gateway (unless DHCP is being used) and pointing the DNS settings to a domain controller.

- Changing the server's name and joining the domain.

Other initial configuration tasks can include activating your server, enabling Automatic Updates, downloading and installing any available software updates, enabling Windows Error Reporting and the Customer Experience Improvement Program, and so on.

Let's see how to perform some of these tasks.

Changing the Administrator Password

There are two ways you can change the Administrator password on a Windows server core server:

- Press CTRL+ALT+DEL, click Change Password, and enter your old and new password.

- Type **net user administrator** * at the command prompt, and enter your new password twice.

Setting Date, Time, and Time Zone

To set the time zone for your server, type **control timedate.cpl** at the command prompt. This opens the same Date And Time applet that can be opened from Control Panel in the full installation of Windows Server 2008:

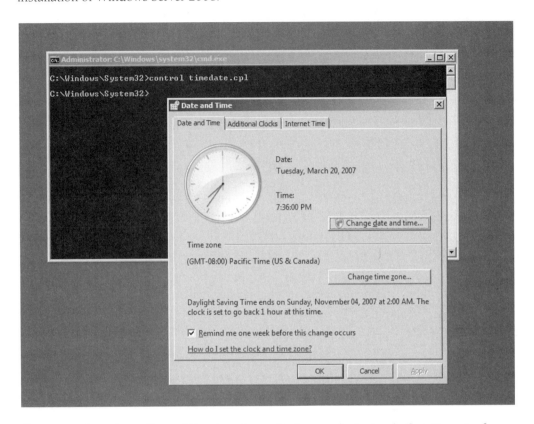

The reason for using a Control Panel applet to do these tasks is simply that it's easier for admins to do it this way than to try and do it from the command line. And because it's a task that is likely to be performed only occasionally (even just once), and because there are no dependencies between the Date And Time applet and other system components that have been removed from the Windows server core installation option, the product team decided to leave this in as one of the few GUI tools still available in the Windows server core installation option of Windows Server 2008. Of course, you can also specify these settings in an unattend.xml answer file if you're performing an unattended installation of your server. And by the way, control.exe by itself doesn't work on a Windows server core installation. Only the two included .cpls work.

Before we go further, let's briefly hear from one of our experts on the Windows Server 2008 product team at Microsoft concerning configuring the Windows server core installation option of Windows Server 2008:

From the Experts: Shell-less vs. GUI-less

If you have been working with a Windows server core installation, you might have noticed that there is some GUI support in a Windows server core installation of Windows Server 2008. To be completely accurate, the GUI of a Windows server core server is shell-less, not entirely GUI-less. There are several low-level GUI DLLs that are included because of current dependencies, such as gdi32.dll and shlwapi.dll. In a future release we hope to be able to remove the dependencies and also remove these files. However, including them does provide some advantages for making a Windows server core server easier to manage using the current tools.

In Beta 1, we didn't include any text editor. Although you could remotely connect to a Windows server core server to view logs, edit scripts, and so on, we heard lots of feedback that there should be an on-the-box text editor. Therefore, we added Notepad. However, because of the reduced environment the Windows server core installation option provides, not all of Notepad is functional—for example, help doesn't work.

In addition, the Windows server core installation option also includes two control panels, which you can access using the following commands:

- Control timedate.cpl
- Control intl.cpl

Timedate.cpl lets you set the time zone for your server, while intl.cpl lets you change your keyboard for different layouts.

–Andrew Mason
Program Manager, Windows Server

Configuring Networking

Now let's configure networking for our server. First let's run **ipconfig /all** and see the server's current networking settings:

```
C:\Windows\System32>ipconfig /all
Windows IP Configuration

    Host Name . . . . . . . . . . . : LH-3TBCQ4I1ONRA
    Primary Dns Suffix  . . . . . . :
    Node Type . . . . . . . . . . . : Hybrid
    IP Routing Enabled. . . . . . . : No
    WINS Proxy Enabled. . . . . . . : No

Ethernet adapter Local Area Connection:

    Connection-specific DNS Suffix  . :
    Description . . . . . . . . . . : Intel 21140-Based PCI Fast Ethernet Adapter
(Emulated)
    Physical Address. . . . . . . . : 00-03-FF-27-88-8C
    DHCP Enabled. . . . . . . . . . : Yes
    Autoconfiguration Enabled . . . . : Yes
    Link-local IPv6 Address . . . . : fe80::c25:d049:5b0c:1585%2(Preferred)
    Autoconfiguration IPv4 Address. . : 169.254.21.133(Preferred)
    Subnet Mask . . . . . . . . . . : 255.255.0.0
    Default Gateway . . . . . . . . :
    DHCPv6 IAID . . . . . . . . . . : 67109887
    DNS Servers . . . . . . . . . . : fec0:0:0:ffff::1%1
                                      fec0:0:0:ffff::2%1
                                      fec0:0:0:ffff::3%1
    NetBIOS over Tcpip. . . . . . . : Enabled

Tunnel adapter Local Area Connection*:

    Connection-specific DNS Suffix  . :
    Description . . . . . . . . . . : isatap.{B4B31F3D-B6C8-4303-BA3C-5A54B05F2FDD}
    Physical Address. . . . . . . . : 00-00-00-00-00-00-00-E0
    DHCP Enabled. . . . . . . . . . : No
    Autoconfiguration Enabled . . . . : Yes
    Link-local IPv6 Address . . . . : fe80::5efe:169.254.21.133%3(Preferred)
    Default Gateway . . . . . . . . :
    DNS Servers . . . . . . . . . . : fec0:0:0:ffff::1%1
                                      fec0:0:0:ffff::2%1
                                      fec0:0:0:ffff::3%1
    NetBIOS over Tcpip. . . . . . . : Disabled
```

Note that **ipconfig /all** displays two network interfaces on the machine: a physical interface (NIC) and an ISATAP tunneling interface. Before we can use netsh.exe to modify network settings, we need to know which interface we need to configure. To determine this, we'll use the **netsh interface ipv4 show interfaces** command as follows:

```
C:\Windows\System32>netsh interface ipv4 show interfaces

Idx  Met   MTU     State         Name
---  ---  -----   -----------    --------------------
  2   20   1500    connected     Local Area Connection
  1   50 4294967295 connected      Loopback Pseudo-Interface 1
```

From this, we can see that our physical interface Local Area Connection has index number 2 (first column). Let's use this information to set the TCP/IP configuration for this interface. Here's what we want the settings to be:

- IP address: 172.16.11.162

- Subnet mask: 255.255.255.0

- Default gateway: 172.16.11.1

- Primary DNS server: 172.16.11.161

- Secondary DNS server: none

To do this, we can use two netsh.exe commands as follows:

```
C:\Windows\System32>netsh interface ipv4 set address name="2" source=static
address=172.16.11.162 mask=255.255.255.0 gateway=172.16.11.1

C:\Windows\System32>netsh interface ipv4 add dnsserver name="2" address=172.16.11.161
index=1
```

Now let's run **ipconfig /all** again and check the result:

```
C:\Windows\System32>ipconfig /all
Windows IP Configuration

    Host Name . . . . . . . . . . . . : LH-3TBCQ4I1ONRA
    Primary Dns Suffix  . . . . . . . :
    Node Type . . . . . . . . . . . . : Hybrid
    IP Routing Enabled. . . . . . . . : No
    WINS Proxy Enabled. . . . . . . . : No

Ethernet adapter Local Area Connection:

    Connection-specific DNS Suffix  . :
    Description . . . . . . . . . . . : Intel 21140-Based PCI Fast Ethernet Adapter
(Emulated)
    Physical Address. . . . . . . . . : 00-03-FF-27-88-8C
    DHCP Enabled. . . . . . . . . . . : No
    Autoconfiguration Enabled . . . . : Yes
    Link-local IPv6 Address . . . . . : fe80::c25:d049:5b0c:1585%2(Preferred)
```

```
           IPv4 Address. . . . . . . . . . : 172.16.11.162(Preferred)
           Subnet Mask . . . . . . . . . . : 255.255.255.0
           Default Gateway . . . . . . . . : 172.16.11.1
           DNS Servers . . . . . . . . . . : 172.16.11.161
           NetBIOS over Tcpip. . . . . . . : Enabled

   Tunnel adapter Local Area Connection*:

           Connection-specific DNS Suffix  . :
           Description . . . . . . . . . . : isatap.{B4B31F3D-B6C8-4303-BA3C-5A54B05F2FDD}
           Physical Address. . . . . . . . : 00-00-00-00-00-00-00-E0
           DHCP Enabled. . . . . . . . . . : No
           Autoconfiguration Enabled . . . . : Yes
           Link-local IPv6 Address . . . . . : fe80::5efe:172.16.11.162%3(Preferred)
           Default Gateway . . . . . . . . :
           DNS Servers . . . . . . . . . . : 172.16.11.161
           NetBIOS over Tcpip. . . . . . . : Disabled
```

So far, so good. Let's move on.

Changing the Server's Name

Next let's change the name of our server. When you install a Windows server core server manually from media, the server is assigned a randomly generated name. We want to change that, and we can use netdom.exe to do this. First let's see what the current name is, and then let's change it to DNSSRV because we're planning on using this particular machine as a DNS server on our network:

```
C:\Windows\System32>hostname
LH-3TBCQ4I1ONRA

C:\Windows\System32>netdom renamecomputer %computername% /NewName:DNSSRV
This operation will rename the computer LH-3TBCQ4I1ONRA
to DNSSRV.

Certain services, such as the Certificate Authority, rely on a fixed machine
name. If any services of this type are running on LH-3TBCQ4I1ONRA,
then a computer name change would have an adverse impact.

Do you want to proceed (Y or N)?
y
The computer needs to be restarted in order to complete the operation.

The command completed successfully.
```

We can restart the server using the **shutdown /r /t 0** command. Once the machine is restarted, typing **hostname** shows that the server's name has been successfully changed:

```
C:\Windows\System32>hostname
DNSSRV
```

Joining a Domain

Now let's join our server to our domain. We'll use netdom.exe again to do this, and we're going to join our server to a domain named contoso.com. Here's how we do this:

```
C:\Windows\System32>netdom join DNSSRV /domain:CONTOSO /userd:Administrator /
passwordd:*
Type the password associated with the domain user:

The computer needs to be restarted in order to complete the operation.

The command completed successfully.
```

Again, we'll use **shutdown /r /t 0** to restart the machine. Once it's restarted, we'll log on as a domain admin this time and use netdom.exe again to verify that our server has established a secure channel to the domain controller.

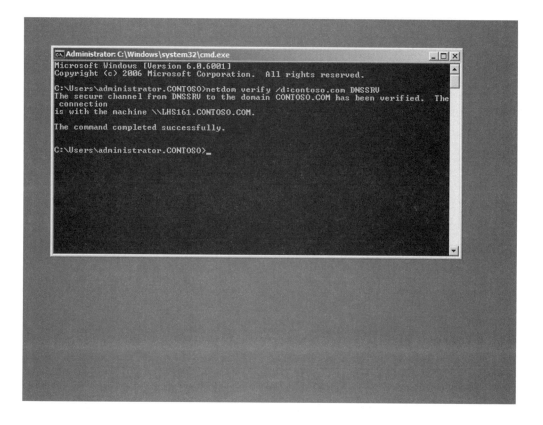

Activating the Server

To activate our server, we can use a built-in script named slmgr.vbs found in the %windir%\System32 directory. (This script is also in Windows Vista and in full installations of Windows Server 2008, and it can be run remotely from those platforms to activate a Windows server core installation.) Typing **cscript slmgr.vbs /?** shows the available syntax for this command:

```
C:\Windows\System32>cscript slmgr.vbs /?
Windows Software Licensing Management Tool
Usage: slmgr.vbs [MachineName [User Password]] [<Option>]
            MachineName: Name of remote machine (default is local machine)
            User:        Account with required privilege on remote machine
            Password:    password for the previous account


Global Options:
-ipk <Product Key>
    Install product key (replaces existing key)
-upk
    Uninstall product key
-ato
    Activate Windows
-dli [Activation ID | All]
    Display license information (default: current license)
-dlv [Activation ID | All]
    Display detailed license information (default: current license)
-xpr
    Expiration date for current license state

Advanced Options:
-cpky
    Clear product key from the registry (prevents disclosure attacks)
-ilc <License file>
    Install license
-rilc
    Re-install system license files
-rearm
    Reset the licensing status of the machine
-dti
    Display Installation ID for offline activation
-atp <Confirmation ID>
    Activate product with user-provided Confirmation ID
```

Let's first use the **−xpr** option to display the expiration date for the current license state:

```
C:\Windows\system32>cscript slmgr.vbs -xpr
Microsoft (R) Windows Script Host Version 5.7
Copyright (C) Microsoft Corporation. All rights reserved.

Initial grace period ends 3/31/2007 1:13:00 AM
```

Now let's use **-dli** to display more info concerning the server's current license state:

```
C:\Windows\system32>cscript slmgr.vbs -dli
Microsoft (R) Windows Script Host Version 5.7
Copyright (C) Microsoft Corporation. All rights reserved.

Name: Windows(TM) Server 2008, ServerEnterpriseCore edition
Description: Windows Operating System - Windows Server 2008, RETAIL channel
Partial Product Key: XHKDR
License Status: Initial grace period
Time remaining: 14533 minute(s) (10 day(s))
```

Now let's activate the server using the **-ato** option:

```
C:\Windows\system32>cscript slmgr.vbs -ato
Microsoft (R) Windows Script Host Version 5.7
Copyright (C) Microsoft Corporation. All rights reserved.

Activating Windows(TM) Server 2008, ServerEnterpriseCore edition
 (f00d81ce-df2c-47cb-a359-36d652296e56) ...
Product activated successfully.
```

Finally, let's try the **-xpr** and **-dli** options again and see the result:

```
C:\Windows\system32>cscript slmgr.vbs -xpr
Microsoft (R) Windows Script Host Version 5.7
Copyright (C) Microsoft Corporation. All rights reserved.

The machine is permanently activated.


C:\Windows\system32>cscript slmgr.vbs -dli
Microsoft (R) Windows Script Host Version 5.7
Copyright (C) Microsoft Corporation. All rights reserved.

Name: Windows(TM) Server code name "Longhorn", ServerEnterpriseCore edition
Description: Windows Operating System - Server code name "Longhorn", RETAIL channel
Partial Product Key: XHKDR
License Status: Licensed
```

Enabling Automatic Updates

To enable Automatic Updates on our server, we'll use another built-in script named scregedit.wsf. This script is unique to the Windows server core installation option of Windows Server 2008, and it's one of the few binaries on a Windows server core server that is not found on a full installation of Windows Server 2008. To view the syntax of this script, type cscript scregedit.wsf /? at the command prompt:

```
C:\Windows\System32>cscript scregedit.wsf /?
Microsoft (R) Windows Script Host Version 5.7
Copyright (C) Microsoft Corporation. All rights reserved.

Automatic Updates - Manage Automatic Windows Updates
These settings can be used to configure how Automatic Updates are applied to the
Windows system. It includes the ability to disable automatic updates and to set the
installation schedule.

/AU [/v][value]

    /v    View the current Automatic Update settings
    value    value you want to set to.


    Options:
    4 - Enable Automatic Updates
    1 - Disable Automatic Updates


Windows Error Reporting Settings
Windows can send descriptions of problems on this server to Microsoft. If you choose
to automatically send generic information about a problem, Microsoft will use the
information to start working on a solution.

This setting might be overridden by the following Group Policy:
    Key : Software\Policies\Microsoft\Windows\Windows Error Reporting\Consent,
        Value : DefaultConsent

/ER [/v][value]
    /v    View the current Windows Error Reporting settings
    value    value you want to set to.

Opt-in Settings:
    2 - Automatically send summary reports (Recommended)
    3 - Automatically send detailed reports
    1 - Disable Windows Error Reporting

For more information on what data information is collected, go to
http://go.microsoft.com/fwlink/?linkid=50163


Terminal Service - Allow Remote Administration Connections
This allows administrators to connect remotely for administration purposes.

/AR [/v][value]

    /v    View the Remote Terminal Service Connection setting
    value    (0 = enabled, 1 = disabled)


Terminal Service - Allow connections from previous versions of Windows
```

This setting configures CredSSP based user authentication for Terminal Service connections

/CS [/v][value]

    /v   View the Terminal Service CredSSP setting
    value   (0 = allow previous versions, 1 = require CredSSP)

IP Security (IPSEC) Monitor - allow remote management
This setting configures the server to allow the IP Security (IPSEC) Monitor to be able to remotely manage IPSEC.

/IM [/v][value]

    /v   View the IPSEC Monitor setting
    value   (0 = do not allow, 1 = allow remote management)

DNS SRV priority - changes the priority for DNS SRV records
This setting configures the priority for DNS SRV records and is only useful on Domain Controllers.
For more information on this setting, search TechNet for LdapSrvPriority

/DP [/v][value]

    /v   View the DNS SRV priority setting
    value   (value from 0 through 65535. The recommended value is 200.)

DNS SRV weight - changes the weight for DNS SRV records
This setting configures the weight for DNS SRV records and is useful only on Domain Controllers.
For more information on this setting, search TechNet for LdapSrvWeight

/DW [/v][value]

    /v   View the DNS SRV weight setting
    value   (value from 0 through 65535. The recommended value is 50.)

Command Line Reference
This setting displays a list of common tasks and how to perform them from the command line.

/CLI

First let's see what the current setting for Automatic Updates is on the machine:

```
C:\Windows\system32>cscript scregedit.wsf /au /v
Microsoft (R) Windows Script Host Version 5.7
Copyright (C) Microsoft Corporation. All rights reserved.

SOFTWARE\Microsoft\Windows\CurrentVersion\WindowsUpdate\Auto Update AUOptions
Value not set.
```

Looks like Automatic Updates is not yet configured, so let's enable it:

```
C:\Windows\system32>cscript scregedit.wsf /au 4
Microsoft (R) Windows Script Host Version 5.7
Copyright (C) Microsoft Corporation. All rights reserved.

Registry has been updated.
```

Now let's verify by using our previous command:

```
C:\Windows\system32>cscript scregedit.wsf /au /v
Microsoft (R) Windows Script Host Version 5.7
Copyright (C) Microsoft Corporation. All rights reserved.

SOFTWARE\Microsoft\Windows\CurrentVersion\WindowsUpdate\Auto Update AUOptions
View registry setting.
4
```

Note that on a Windows server core server you can configure Automatic Updates only to download and install updates automatically. You can't configure it to download updates and prompt you to install them later.

There are other initial configuration tasks we could do, but let's move on. Actually, let's hear first from one of our experts concerning a configuration task that's *not* easy to do from the command line:

From the Experts: Configuring Display Resolution

Although there is no tool on a Windows server core server to allow you to change your display resolution, you can configure this by using an unattend file. However, it is possible to change the display resolution so that you can run at a higher resolution than what you might have ended up with at the end of setup. Doing this requires editing the registry; however, if you pick a resolution your video card or monitor cannot display, you might have to reinstall—although you should still be able to boot and remotely modify the settings in the registry.

To do this, you need to open regedit.exe and navigate to the following location:

HKEY_LOCAL_MACHINE\SYSTEM\CurrentControlSet\Control\Video

Under this will be a list of GUIDs, and you need to determine which one corresponds to your video card/driver. You might have to experiment to determine the right one. Under the GUID, you can set

\0000\DefaultSettings.XResolution

\0000\DefaultSettings.YResolution

to the resolution you would like to use. If these don't exist, you can create them. You must log off and log back on again for the change to take effect. Be careful doing this because if you specify an unsupported display resolution, you might need to reinstall your machine or remotely connect to the registry from another computer to change it, and remotely reboot.

–Andrew Mason
Program Manager, Windows Server

Managing a Windows Server Core Server

Once we've performed initial configuration of our Windows server core server, we can then add roles and optional features so that it can provide needed functionality to our network. In this section, we're going to examine how to perform such common tasks, and we'll also look at different ways of managing a Windows server core server, including using the following:

- Local administration from the command prompt
- Remote administration using Terminal Services
- Remote administration using Remote Server Administration Tools
- Remote administration using Group Policy
- Remote administration using WinRM/WinRS

Local Management from the Command Line

When we log on to the console of a Windows server core server, a command prompt appears. From this command prompt, we can do a lot of things:

- Run common tools such as netsh.exe and netdom.exe to perform various tasks, as we saw previously.
- Use special tools such as oclist.exe and ocsetup.exe to install roles and optional features on our server to give it more functionality.

- Run in-box scripts such as slmgr.vbs and scregedit.wsf, as we saw earlier, to perform certain kinds of tasks.

- Create our own scripts using Notepad, and run them using Cscript.exe and the supported WMI providers.

- Use the WMI command line (WMIC) to do almost anything from the command line that you can do by writing WMI scripts.

As we mentioned before, however, one thing you can't do is run PowerShell commands to administer your server. The reason for this omission is that PowerShell is managed code that requires the .NET Framework in order to work, and the .NET Framework is not included in the Windows server core installation option. Why? Because the .NET Framework has dependencies across the whole spectrum of different Windows components, and leaving it in would have increased the size of the Windows server core installation option until it was very nearly the size of a full installation of Windows Server 2008. For future versions of the Windows server core installation, however, a slimmed-down .NET Framework might be available that can provide PowerShell cmdlet functionality without the need of increasing the footprint significantly. But we'll have to see, as that's something that would happen after RTM. Note that you can however use PowerShell remotely to manage a Windows server core installation if the script strictly uses only WMI commands and not cmdlets.

Let's look how to perform two important tasks from the command line: adding server roles and adding optional features.

Installing Roles

Let's start by seeing what roles are currently installed on our server and what roles are available to install. We'll use the oclist.exe command to do this:

```
C:\Windows\System32\>oclist
Use the listed update names with Ocsetup.exe to install/uninstall a server role or
optional feature.

Adding or removing the Active Directory role with OCSetup.exe is not supported. It can
leave your server in an unstable state. Always use DCPromo to install or uninstall
Active Directory.


============================================================================
Microsoft-Windows-ServerCore-Package
============================================================================
Not Installed:BitLocker
Not Installed:BitLocker-RemoteAdminTool
Not Installed:ClientForNFS-Base
Not Installed:DFSN-Server
Not Installed:DFSR-Infrastructure-ServerEdition
Not Installed:DHCPServerCore
Not Installed:DirectoryServices-ADAM-ServerCore
Not Installed:DirectoryServices-DomainController-ServerFoundation
```

```
Not Installed:DNS-Server-Core-Role
Not Installed:FailoverCluster-Core
Not Installed:FRS-Infrastructure
Not Installed:MediaServer
Not Installed:Microsoft-Windows-MultipathIo
Not Installed:Microsoft-Windows-RemovableStorageManagementCore
Not Installed:NetworkLoadBalancingHeadlessServer
Not Installed:Printing-ServerCore-Role
    |
    |--- Not Installed:Printing-LPDPrintService
    |
Not Installed:ServerForNFS-Base
Not Installed:SIS
Not Installed:SNMP-SC
Not Installed:SUACore
Not Installed:TelnetClient
Not Installed:WindowsServerBackup
Not Installed:WINS-SC
```

Note that the oclist.exe command displays information about both roles and features installed and not installed on the machine. We can see from the command output that the DNS Server role is not presently installed on the machine. We can also verify this by typing **net start** in the command line:

```
C:\Windows\System32>net start
These Windows services are started:

    Application Experience
    Background Intelligent Transfer Service
    Base Filtering Engine
    COM+ Event System
    Computer Browser
    Cryptographic Services
    DCOM Server Process Launcher
    DHCP Client
    Diagnostic Policy Service
    Diagnostic System Host
    Distributed Transaction Coordinator
    DNS Client
    Group Policy Client
    IKE and AuthIP IPsec Keying Modules...
```

In fact, the only DNS binaries presently installed are those for the DNS client:

```
C:\Windows\System32>dir dns*.*
 Volume in drive C has no label.
 Volume Serial Number is FC68-BDF4

 Directory of C:\Windows\system32

02/09/2007  10:00 PM            163,840 dnsapi.dll
02/09/2007  09:59 PM             24,064 dnscacheugc.exe
02/09/2007  10:00 PM             84,480 dnsrslvr.dll
               3 File(s)        272,384 bytes
               0 Dir(s)  27,578,523,648 bytes free
```

Now let's install the DNS Server role using the ocsetup.exe command as follows:

```
C:\Windows\System32>start /w ocsetup DNS-Server-Core-Role
```

After a short while, the command prompt appears again. The reason we used the /**w** switch with **start** is because that way control is not returned to the command prompt until the **ocsetup** command finishes its work. (By the way, note that **ocsetup** is case sensitive.) Now if we type **oclist**, we should see that the DNS Server role has been added to our server:

```
C:\Windows\System32\>oclist
...
Not Installed:DirectoryServices-ADAM-ServerCore
Not Installed:DirectoryServices-DomainController-ServerFoundation
    Installed:DNS-Server-Core-Role
Not Installed:FailoverCluster-Core
Not Installed:FRS-Infrastructure
...
```

We can also see that three additional binaries for DNS are now present on the server:

```
C:\Windows\System32>dir dns*.*
 Volume in drive C has no label.
 Volume Serial Number is FC68-BDF4

 Directory of C:\Windows\system32

03/20/2007  11:59 PM    <DIR>              dns
02/09/2007  11:42 AM            484,864 dns.exe
02/09/2007  10:00 PM            163,840 dnsapi.dll
02/09/2007  09:59 PM             24,064 dnscacheugc.exe
02/09/2007  11:42 AM            162,816 dnscmd.exe
02/09/2007  11:42 AM             13,312 dnsperf.dll
02/09/2007  10:00 PM             84,480 dnsrslvr.dll
               6 File(s)        933,376 bytes
               1 Dir(s)  27,576,926,208 bytes free
```

And if we type **net stop dns**, we can now stop the DNS Server service without getting an error because the service is now present on the machine. Now that our machine is a DNS Server, we can use the dnscmd.exe command to further configure this role if we want from the command line.

Installing other server roles is similar to what we just did and uses the ocsetup.exe command, with the exception being that the process installs the Active Directory role. This is because Dcpromo.exe in Windows Server 2008 now installs the Active Directory binaries during promotion and uninstalls the binaries during demotion, so you should *not* use ocsetup.exe to add or remove the Active Directory role as then the promotion/demotion will not take place and your server may not function correctly.

Anyway, to add or remove the Active Directory role, you therefore have to use the dcpromo.exe tool, but you also have to run it in unattended mode because the GUI form of this tool (the Active Directory Installation Wizard) can't run on a Windows server core server because of the lack of a desktop shell to run it in. The syntax for running dcpromp.exe in unattended mode is **dcpromp /unattend:unattend.txt**, and a sample unattend.txt file you could use (or further customize) for doing this is as follows:

```
[DCInstall]
ReplicaOrNewDomain = Domain
NewDomain=Forest
NewDomainDNSName = contoso.com
AutoConfigDNS=Yes
DNSDelegation=Yes
DNSDelegationUserName=dnsuser
DNSDelegationPassword=p@ssword!
RebootOnSuccess = NoAndNoPromptEither
SafeModeAdminPassword = p@ssword!
```

For more information on using dcpromo in unattended mode, type **dcpromo /?:unattend** at the command prompt.

Installing Optional Features

Installing optional features is very similar to installing roles. Type **oclist** to display a list of installed and uninstalled features and to determine the internal name of each feature. For example, the Failover Cluster feature is named FailoverCluster-Core, and we need to use this internal form of the name when we run ocsetup to install this feature. You can also remove features by adding an **/uninstall** switch to your **ocsetup** command. You can remote roles that way too, but be sure to stop the role's services before you remove the role.

Other Common Management Tasks

There are lots of other common management tasks you might need to perform on a Windows server core server. The following is just a sampling of some of these tasks.

First, you can add new hardware to your server. Windows server core servers include support for Plug and Play. So if your new device is PnP and there's an in-box driver available for your device, you can just plug the device in and the server will recognize it and automatically install a driver for it. But we did mention earlier that the Windows server core server installation option of Windows Server 2008 does not include that many in-box drivers. So what do you do if your device is not supported by an in-box driver because of its date of manufacture? In that case, follow this procedure:

1. Copy the driver files from the driver media for the device to a temporary directory on your server.

2. Change your current directory to this temporary directory, and type **pnputil −i −a <driver>.inf** at the command prompt.

3. Reboot your server if prompted to do so.

Note that if you want to find what drivers are currently installed on your server, you can type **sc query type= driver** at a command prompt.

What if you want to install some application on your server? First of all, beware—any application that has a GUI might not function properly when you install it. Obviously, that means we can't install Microsoft Exchange Server, Microsoft SQL Server, or other Windows Server System products on a Windows server core server, because these products all have GUI management tools (and more importantly, a Windows server core server is missing a lot of components needed by these products such as the .NET Framework for running managed code).

What kinds of applications might you want to install on a Windows server core server? The usual stuff—antivirus agents, network backup agents, system management agents, and so on. Most agents like this are GUI-less and should install fine and work properly on a Windows server core server. And the Windows Installer service is yet another feature that's still present on a Windows server core server—and if you need to install an agent manually, you should try and do so in quiet mode using msiexec.exe with the **/qb** switch to display the basic UI only. For example, you can do this by typing **msiexec /qb <package>** at the command prompt.

If you need to configure Windows Firewall, the NAP client, or your server's IPSec configuration, you can use netsh.exe to do this. I won't go into all the details here, as you can just check TechNet for the proper netsh.exe syntax to use for each task.

What about patch management? We already described how to enable Automatic Updates on the server, and if you have Windows Server Update Service (WSUS) deployed, you can manage patches for your server using that as well. For Windows server core servers that you want to manually perform patch management on, however, you can use the wusa.exe command to install and remove patches from the command prompt. To do this, first download the patch from Windows Update and expand to get the .msu file. Then copy the .msu file to your server, and type **wsua <patch>.msu /quiet** at the command prompt to install the patch. You can also remove installed patches from your server by typing **pkgmgr /up /m:<package>.cab /quiet** at the command prompt.

Let's hear more about patch management on a Windows server core installation of Windows Server 2008 from one of our experts:

From the Experts: Servicing Windows Server Core

When using Windows server core, the new minimal installation option for Windows Server 2008, a common topic of discussion is servicing. First a little background and then some methods to make dealing with patches easier.

With Windows Server 2008, each patch that is released contains a set of applicability rules. When a patch is sent to a server, either by Windows Update or another automated servicing tool, the servicing infrastructure examines the patch to determine if it applies to the system based on the applicability rules. If not, it is ignored and nothing is changed on the server.

If you have already downloaded a set of patches and want to determine if they apply to a Windows server core installation, you can do the following:

1. Run **wusa <patch_name>**.

2. If the dialog box that appears asks if you want to apply the patch, click No. This means that the patch applies, and you should move on to the next step. Otherwise, the dialog box will state that the patch doesn't apply and you can ignore the patch.

3. Run **wusa <patch_name> /quiet** to apply the patch.

After applying patches, you can run either the wmic qfe command or systeminfo.exe to see what patches are installed.

−Andrew Mason
Program Manager, Windows Server

What else can you do in terms of managing your Windows server core installation of Windows Server 2008? Lots! For example, if you need to manage your disks and file system on your server, you can use commands such as diskpart, defrag, fsutil, vssadmin, and so on. And if you need to manage permissions and ownership of files, you can use icacls.

You can also manage your event logs from the command line using the wevtutil.exe command, which is new in Windows Vista and Windows Server 2008. This powerful command can be used to query your event logs for specific events and to export, archive, clear, and configure your event logs as well. For example, to query your System log for the most recent occurrence of a shutdown event having source USER32 and event ID 1074, you can do this:

```
C:\Windows\system32>wevtutil qe System /c:1 /rd:true /f:text /
q:*[System[(EventID=1074)]]
Event[0]:
  Log Name: System
  Source: USER32
  Date: 2007-03-20T22:26:36.000
  Event ID: 1074
  Task: N/A
  Level: Information
  Opcode: N/A
  Keyword: Classic
  User: S-1-5-21-3620207985-2970159875-1752314906-500
  User Name: DNSSRV\Administrator
  Computer: DNSSRV
  Description:
The process C:\Windows\system32\shutdown.exe (DNSSRV) has initiated the restart of
computer DNSSRV on behalf of user DNSSRV\Administrator for the following reason: No
title for this reason could be found
  Reason Code: 0x840000ff
  Shutdown Type: restart
  Comment:
```

To create and manage data collectors for performance monitoring, you can use the logman.exe command. You can also use the relog.exe command to convert a performance log file into a different format or change its sampling rate. And you can use the tracerpt.exe command to create a remote from a log file or a real-time stream of performance-monitoring data.

To manage services, you can use the sc command, which is a very powerful command that provides even more functionality than the Services.msc snap-in.

What else can you do? Lots. Let's move on now to remote management.

Remote Management Using Terminal Services

You can also manage Windows server core servers from another computer using Terminal Services. To do this, you first have to enable Remote Desktop on your server, and because we can't right-click on Computer and select Properties to do this, we'll have to find another way. Here's how—use the scregedit.wsf script we looked at previously. The syntax for performing this task is **cscript scregedit.wsf /ar 0** to enable Remote Desktop and **cscript scregedit.wsf /ar 1** to disable it again. To view your current Remote Desktop settings, type **cscript scregedit.wsf /ar /v** at a command prompt. Note that in order to allow pre-Windows Vista versions of the TS client to connect to a Windows server core installation, you need to disable the enhanced security by running the **cscript scregedit.wsf /cs 0** command.

Once you've enabled Remote Desktop like this, you can connect to your Windows server core server from another machine using Remote Desktop Connection (mstsc.exe) and manage it as if you were logged on interactively at your server's console. In this figure I'm logged on to a full installation of Windows Server 2008 and have a Terminal Services session open to my remote Windows server core server to manage it.

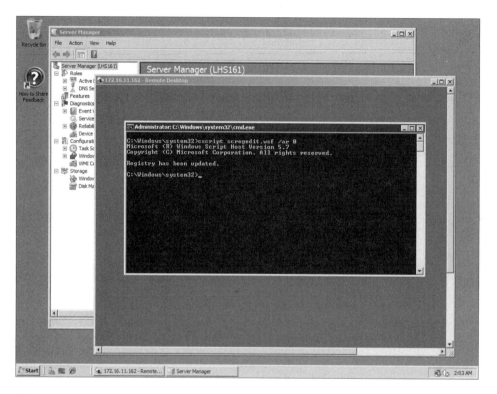

There's more! Later in Chapter 8, "Terminal Services Enhancements," we'll describe a new feature of Terminal Services in Windows Server 2008 that lets you remote individual application windows instead of entire desktops. Let's hear now from one of our experts concerning how this new Terminal Services functionality can be used to make managing Windows server core servers easier.

From the Experts: Enabling Remote Command Line Access on Server Core

There are several ways to administer a Windows server core installation, ranging from using the local console to remote administration from a full Windows Server 2008 server using MMC. A really cool mechanism is to manage the Windows server core installation using Terminal Services RemoteApp to make the command line console available. This allows command-line administration without having to be physically present at the box, and without having a full-blown terminal server session. (After all, a Windows server core installation does not need the full desktop; it just needs the console, and Terminal Services RemoteApp is perfect for this.) A full Windows Server 2008 machine is necessary, along with the Windows server core installation that is to be administered.

On the Windows Server 2008 machine, add the Terminal Server Role using the Server Manager administrative tool. Only the Terminal Server role itself is needed, not the TS Licensing role, TS Session Broker role, TS Gateway role, or TS Web Access role. After the TS role is installed, start MMC and add the TS RemoteApp Manager snap-in, providing the name of the Windows server core machine to the snap-in. Once the snap-in is installed, connect to the Windows server core machine and click Add Remote Apps. Navigate to the %SYSTEMROOT%\System32 folder using the administrative share, select cmd.exe, and complete the wizard. Select the cmd.exe entry in the RemoteApp pane, click Create .rdp File, and follow the wizard to save the RDP file. Ensure that TS is enabled on the Windows server core machine. (Use the scregedit.wsf script.) You can now copy the RDP file to any client machine and connect to the Windows server core installation through it. The console will be integrated into the task bar of the client, like a local application. For more information on Terminal Services and TS RemoteApp, please see Chapter, "Terminal Services Enhancements."

–Rahul Prasad
Software Development Engineer, Windows Core Operating System Division

And here's another expert from the product team at Microsoft sharing some additional tips on managing Windows server core servers using Terminal Services:

From the Experts: Tips for Using Terminal Services with Windows Server Core

When you're using Terminal Services in a Windows server core server without the GUI shell, some common tasks require you to do things a little differently.

Logging off of a Terminal Services Session

On a Windows server core server, there is no Start button and therefore no GUI option to log off. Clicking the X in the corner of the Terminal Services window disconnects your session, but the session will still be using resources on the server. To log off, you need to use the Terminal Services logoff command. While in your Terminal Services session, you simply run logoff. If you disconnect your session, you can either reconnect and use logoff, use the logoff command remotely, or use the Terminal Services MMC to log off the session.

Restarting the Command Prompt

When logged on locally, if you accidentally close the command prompt you can either log off and log on, or press CTRL+ALT+DEL, start Task Manager (or just press CTRL+SHIFT+ESC), click file, and run cmd.exe to restart it. You can also configure the Terminal Services client to have the Windows keys pass to the remote session when not maximized so that you can use CTRL+SHIFT+ESC to start task manager and run cmd.exe.

Working with Terminal Services Sessions

If you ever need to manage Terminal Services sessions from the command line, the query command is the tool to use. Running query sessions (which can also be used remotely) will tell you what Terminal Services sessions are active on the box, as well as who is logged in to them. This is handy if you need to restart the box and want to know if any other administrators are logged on. Query has some other useful options, and there are a variety of other Terminal Services command-line tools.

–Andrew Mason
  Program Manager, Windows Server

Remote Management Using the Remote Server Administration Tools

Although you can manage file systems, event logs, performance logs, device drivers, and other aspects from the command line, there's no law that says you have to. For example, the syntax for wvetutil.exe is quite complex to learn and understand, especially if you want to use this tool to query event logs for specific types of events. It would be nice if you could just use Event Viewer to display, query, and filter your event logs on a Windows server core server. You can! But you have to do it remotely from another computer running either Windows Vista or Windows Server 2008 and with the appropriate Remote Server Administration Tools (RSAT) installed on it.

We talked about RSAT earlier in Chapter 4, "Managing Windows Server 2008," and it's basically the Windows Server 2008 equivalent of the Adminpak.msi server tools on previous versions of Windows Server. So if you want to use MMC snap-in tools to administer a Windows server core server from a Windows Vista computer or a machine running a full installation of Windows Server 2008, you might or might not need to install the RSAT on this machine because both Windows Vista and full installations of Windows Server 2008 already include many MMC snap-in tools that can be accessed from the Start menu using Administrative

Tools. Event Viewer is one such built-in tool, and here it is running on a full installation of Windows Server 2008, showing the previously mentioned shutdown event in the System event log on our remote Windows server core server.

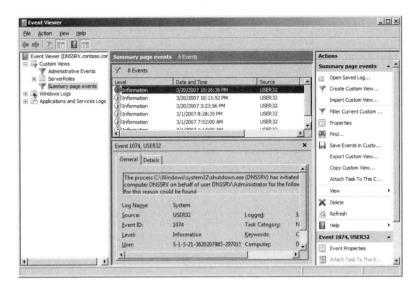

Remote Administration Using Group Policy

Another way of remotely administering Windows server core servers is by using Group Policy. For example, although the **netsh advfirewall** context commands can be used to configure Windows Firewall, doing it this way can be tedious. It's much easier to use the following policy setting:

Computer Configuration\Windows Settings\Security Settings\Windows Firewall With Advanced Security

By creating a GPO that targets your Windows server core servers, either by placing these servers in an OU and linking the GPO to that OU or by using a WMI filter to target the GPO only at Windows server core servers, you can remotely configure Windows Firewall on these machines using Group Policy. For example, you can use the *OperatingSystemSKU* property of the *Win32_OperatingSystem* WMI class to determine whether a given system is running a Windows server core installation of Windows Server 2008 by checking for the following return values:

- 12 – Datacenter Server Core Edition
- 13 – Standard Server Core Edition
- 14 – Enterprise Server Core Edition

You can use this property in creating a WMI filter that causes a GPO to target only Windows server core servers.

Remote Management Using WinRM/WinRS

Finally, you can also manage Windows server core servers remotely using the Windows Remote Shell (WinRS) included in Windows Vista and the full installation of Windows Server 2008. WinRS uses Windows Remote Management (WinRM), which is Microsoft's implementation of the WS-Management protocol developed by the Desktop Management Task Force (DMTF). WinRM was first included in Windows Server 2003 R2 and has been enhanced in Windows Vista and Windows Server 2008.

To use the Windows Remote Shell to manage a Windows server core server, log on to the Windows server core server you want to remotely manage and type **WinRM quickconfig** at the command prompt to create a WinRM listener on the machine:

```
C:\Windows\System32>WinRM quickconfig
WinRM is not set up to allow remote access to this machine for management.
The following changes must be made:

Create a WinRM listener on HTTP://* to accept WS-Man requests to any IP on this
machine.

Make these changes [y/n]? y

WinRM has been updated for remote management.

Created a WinRM listener on HTTP://* to accept WS-Man requests to any IP on this
machine.
```

Now on a different machine running either Windows Vista or the full installation of Windows Server 2008, type **winrs -r:<server_name> <command>**, where <server_name> is your Windows server core server and <command> is the command you want to execute on your remote server. Here's an example of the Windows Remote Shell at work:

```
C:\Users\Administrator>winrs -r:DNSSRV "cscript C:\Windows\System32\slmgr.vbs -dli"
Microsoft (R) Windows Script Host Version 5.7
Copyright (C) Microsoft Corporation. All rights reserved.

Name: Windows(TM) Server Windows Server 2008, ServerEnterpriseCore edition
Description: Windows Operating System - Windows Server 2008, RETAIL channel
Partial Product Key: XHKDR
License Status: Licensed
```

You can also run WinRM quickconfig during unattended installation by configuring the appropriate answer file setting for this service.

Windows Server Core Installation Tips and Tricks

Finally, let's conclude this chapter with a list of 101 things (well, not really 101) you might want to know about or do with a Windows server core installation of Windows Server 2008. Some of these are tips or tricks for configuring or managing a Windows server core server; others are just things you might want to make note of. They're all either interesting, useful, or both. Here goes....

First, if you want quick examples of a whole lot of administrative tasks you can perform from the command line, just type **cscript scregedit.wsf /cli** at the command prompt:

```
C:\Windows\System32\>cscript scregedit.wsf /cli
Microsoft (R) Windows Script Host Version 5.7
Copyright (C) Microsoft Corporation. All rights reserved.

To activate:
    Cscript slmgr.vbs -ato

To use KMS volume licensing for activation:
    Configure KMS volume licensing:
        cscript slmgr.vbs -ipk [volume license key]
    Activate KMS licensing

        cscript slmgr.vbs -ato
    Set KMS DNS SRV record
        cscript slmgr.vbs -skma [KMS FQDN]
Determine the computer name, any of the following:
    Set c

    Ipconfig /all
    Systeminfo

Rename the Server Core computer:
    Domain joined:
        Netdom renamecomputer %computername% /NewName:new-name
  /UserD:domain-username /PasswordD:*

    Not domain joined:
        Netdom renamecomputer %computername% /NewName:new-name

Changing workgroups:
    Wmic computersystem where name="%computername%" call
  joindomainorworkgroup name="[new workgroup name]"

Install a role or optional feature:
    Start /w Ocsetup [packagename]

    Note: For Active Directory, run Dcpromo with an answer file.
View role and optional feature package names and current installation state:
    oclist
Start task manager hot-key:
    ctrl-shift-esc
```

```
Logoff of a Terminal Services session:
    Logoff

To set the pagefile size:
    Disable system pagefile management:
        wmic computersystem where name="%computername%" set
  AutomaticManagedPagefile=False

    Configure the pagefile:
        wmic pagefileset where name="C:\\pagefile.sys" set
  InitialSize=500,MaximumSize=1000
Configure the timezone, date, or time:

    control timedate.cpl
Configure regional and language options:

    control intl.cpl
Manually install a management tool or agent:
    Msiexec.exe /i [msipackage]

List installed msi applications:
    Wmic

    product
Uninstall msi applications:

    Wmic product get name /value
    Wmic product where name="[name]" call uninstall
To list installed drivers:
    Sc query type= driver
Install a driver that is not included:
    Copy the driver files to Server Core
    Pnputil -i -a [path]\[driver].inf
Determine a file's version:
    wmic datafile where name="d:\\windows\\system32\\ntdll.dll" get version
List of installed patches:
    wmic qfe list
Install a patch:
    Wusa.exe [patchame].msu /quiet
Configure a proxy:
    Netsh winhttp proxy set [proxy_name]:[port]
Add, delete, query a Registry value:
    reg.exe add /?
    reg.exe delete /?
    reg.exe query /?
```

Now here are a bunch of random insights into and tips for running a Windows server core installation of Windows Server 2008:

The SMS 2005 and MOM 2005 agents should run fine on Windows server core servers, but for best systems management functionality you probably want to use the upcoming Microsoft System Center family of products instead.

You can deploy the Windows server core installation option using Windows Deployment Services (WDS) just like the full installation option of Windows Server 2008. It's the same product—just a different setup option to choose.

To install the Windows server core installation option on a system, the system needs a minimum of 512 MB RAM. That's not because Windows server core servers need that much RAM, however—in fact, they need just over 100 MB of RAM to run with no roles installed. But the setup program for installing Windows Server 2008 requires 512 MB or more of memory or setup will fail. You *can* install the Windows server core installation option on a box with 512 MB RAM and then after installation pull some of the RAM, but at the time of this writing, this procedure is not supported.

The Windows server core installation option uses much less disk space than a full installation of Windows Server 2008. We're talking roughly 1 MB vs. 5 MB here, and that shows you how much stuff has been pulled out of Windows server core to slim it down.

When patching Windows server core servers, you actually don't need to presort patches into those that apply to the Windows server core installation option and those that don't apply. Instead, you can just go ahead and patch, and only updates that apply to Windows server core servers will actually be applied.

You can manage Windows server core servers remotely using the RSAT, but you can't install the RSAT on Windows server core to manage the server locally.

The Windows server core installation option does support Read Only Domain Controllers (RO DC). This support makes Windows server core servers ideal for branch office scenarios, especially with BitLocker installed as well.

You won't get any User Account Control (UAC) prompts if you log on to a Windows server core server as a nonadministrator and try to perform an administrative task. Why not? UAC needs the desktop shell to function.

One way of seeing how slimmed-down Windows server core is is to compare the number of installed and running services on the two platforms. Table 6-3 shows a rough comparison, assuming no roles have been installed.

Table 6-3 Comparison of default number of services for server core installation vs. full installation

Feature compared	Server core	Server
Number of services installed by default	~40	~75
Number of services running by default	~30	~50

If you're trying to run the Windows Remote Shell from another machine and use it to manage a Windows server core server and it doesn't work, you might not have the right credentials on the Windows server core server to manage it. If this is the case, first try connecting to the

Windows server core server from your machine using the **net use \\<server_name>\ipc$ / u:<domain>\<user_name>** command using a user account that has local admin privileges on the Windows server core server. Then try running your WinRS commands again. Note that this tip also applies to using MMC admin tools to remotely manage a Windows server core installation since the MMC doesn't let you specify different credentials for connecting remotely.

If you're trying to use Computer Management on another machine to manage the disk subsystem on your Windows server core server using Disk Management and you can't, type **net start vds** at the command prompt on your Windows server core server to start the Virtual Disk Service on the server. Then you should be able to manage your server's disks remotely using Disk Management.

If you've enabled Automatic Updates on your Windows server core server and you want to check for new software updates immediately, type **wuauclt /detectnow** at the command prompt.

And yes, the Windows server core installation option does support clustering. A clustered file server running on Windows server core servers would be cool.

Our last tip will be provided by one of our experts:

From the Experts: What Time Is It?

Here is a flash back to the old MS-DOS days. Because Windows server core does not have the system tray, there is no clock. If you are used to having the time available on the screen, you can add it to your prompt in the command prompt window.

Entering the following:

```
prompt [$t]$s$p$g
```

will display:

```
[14:27:06.28] C:\users\default>
```

—Andrew Mason
Program Manager, Windows Server

Conclusion

We're used to Microsoft piling features into products, not stripping features out of them. The Windows server core installation option of Windows Server 2008 is a new direction Microsoft is pursuing in its core product line, but it's a direction being driven by customer demand. When I said that Microsoft listened to their customers, I was serious. And Windows server core is a good example of this.

Additional Resources

You'll find a brief description of the Windows server core installation of Windows Server 2008 at *http://www.microsoft.com/windowsserver/Windows Server 2008/evaluation/overview.mspx*. By the time you read this chapter, this page will probably be expanded or the URL will redirect you to somewhere that has a lot more content on the subject.

If you have access to the Windows Server 2008 beta program on Microsoft Connect (*http://connect.microsoft.com*), you can get some great documentation from there, including these:

- Microsoft Windows Server Code Name 2008 Server Core Step-By-Step Guide
- Live Meeting on Server Core
- Live Chat on Server Core

There's also a TechNet Forum where you can ask questions and help others trying out the Windows server core installation option of Windows Server 2008. See *http://forums.microsoft.com/TechNet/ShowForum.aspx?ForumID=582&SiteID=17* for this forum. (Windows Live registration is required.)

There's a Windows server core blog on TechNet that is definitely something you won't want to miss. See *http://blogs.technet.com/server_core/*.

Finally, be sure to turn to Chapter 14, "Additional Resources," for more sources of information concerning the Windows server core installation option, and also for links to webcasts, whitepapers, blogs, newsgroups, and other sources of information about all aspects of Windows Server 2008.

Chapter 7
Active Directory Enhancements

In this chapter:

Understanding Identity and Access in Windows Server 2008 149

Active Directory Domain Services. 158

Active Directory Lightweight Directory Services 172

Active Directory Certificate Services. 176

Active Directory Federation Services 182

Active Directory Rights Management Services. 186

Conclusion 187

Additional Resources. 187

Active Directory and its related services form the foundation for enterprise networks running Microsoft Windows, and the new features and enhancements to Active Directory and its related services in Windows Server 2008 are numerous. This chapter takes a look at these enhancements and at the direction in which Active Directory and its related services are heading as an integrated identity and access platform for enterprises—that is, as a platform for provisioning and managing network identity.

Understanding Identity and Access in Windows Server 2008

Before we jump in and examine the various enhancements to Active Directory and its related services in Windows Server 2008, however, let's first step back a bit and get the big picture of how Active Directory and its related services have been evolving since they were first introduced in Windows 2000 Server and what these services are becoming in Windows Server 2008 and beyond. It's important to understand this big picture, as otherwise the many improvements to Active Directory and related services in Windows Server 2008 might seem like a miscellaneous grab-bag of changes without much in common. But they have a lot in common as we'll shortly see.

Understanding Identity and Access

So why is identity and access (IDA) important to enterprises? Think for a moment about what goes on when a user on your network needs access to confidential business information stored on a server. Tony is in the Marketing department, and he needs access to a product specification so that he can work on a marketing presentation for a customer. The document containing the specification is stored on a server on the company's network, and Tony tries to open the document so that he can cut and paste information contained in it into his presentation. To safeguard such specifications, you'd like your IDA infrastructure to do the following:

1. Determine who the user is who wants to use the document.

2. Grant the user the appropriate level of access to the document.

3. Protect confidential information contained in the document.

4. Maintain a record of interaction concerning the user's accessing of the document.

For example, you might want to restrict access to product specifications to full-time employees (FTEs) only and provide read-only access to users in the Marketing department so that they can view but not modify specifications. You might also want to prevent Marketing department users from copying and pasting text from specifications into other documents. And you might want an audit trail showing the day and time that the user accessed the specification.

The challenge of implementing an IDA solution that can do all of this becomes even greater once you start extending the boundaries of your enterprise with "anywhere access" devices, Web services, and collaboration tools like e-mail and instant messaging. It becomes even more complicated once you have to start applying the IDA process not just to FTEs but also to contractors, temps, customers, and external partners. The challenge is to build an IDA solution that can handle all these different scenarios, and Microsoft has steadily been working toward this goal since Active Directory was first released with Windows 2000 Server. Let's briefly summarize the evolution of Microsoft's IDA solution, beginning with Windows 2000 Server and working up to the current platform for Windows Server 2003 R2 and then to Windows Server 2008 and beyond.

Identity and Access in Windows 2000 Server

Active Directory directory service is a Windows-based directory service that was first introduced in Windows 2000 Server. Active Directory directory service stores information about various kinds of objects on a network—such as users, groups, computers, printers, and shared folders—and it makes this information available to users who need to access these resources and administrators who need to manage them. Active Directory provides network users with controlled access to permitted resources anywhere on the network using a single logon process. Active Directory directory service also provides administrators with an intuitive, hierarchical view of the network and its resources, and it provides a single point of administration for all network objects.

Windows 2000 Server also included a separate component, called Certificate Services, that can be used to set up a certificate authority (CA) for issuing digital certificates as part of a Public Key Infrastructure (PKI). These certificates can be used to provide authentication for users and computers on your network to secure e-mail, provide Web-based authentication, and support smart-card authentication. Certificate Services also provides customizable services for issuing and managing certificates for your enterprise. What's important to understand here is that in Windows 2000 Server, Active Directory directory service and Certificate Services are two separate components that are not integrated together. In other words, the two services are managed separately and have policy implemented differently.

In addition to these two built-in IDA services, Microsoft also released an out-of-band service for Windows 2000 Server called Microsoft Metadirectory Services (MMS). In its final version, MMS 2.2 was an enterprise metadirectory that enterprises could use to integrate all their various directories together into a single consolidated central repository. MMS 2.2 consisted of one or more metadirectory servers, management agents, and the connected directories, and it provided users with access to this consolidated information via Lightweight Directory Access Protocol (LDAP). The goal of MMS 2.2 was to provide enterprises with a provisioning solution that could be used to effectively provide consistent identity management across many different databases and directories. For example, if you had both an Active Directory directory service infrastructure and a Lotus Notes infrastructure and you wanted Active Directory directory service users to be able to look up e-mail addresses from the Lotus Notes directory, MMS 2.2 could make this possible. MMS 2.2 could also simplify the deployment of Active Directory directory service for enterprises that already had information about employees or customers stored in other directories by enabling real-time synchronization of information from these directories into Active Directory directory service. Finally, MMS 2.2 could also be used to simplify the migration and consolidation of multiple directories into Active Directory directory service.

Identity and Access in Windows Server 2003

Although these Windows 2000 Server offerings did meet the needs of some enterprises, they were still provided as separate services and MMS was even a totally separate product. Customers wanted something more integrated, and they also wanted additional IDA features, such as document rights protection and role-based authorization. In addition to making improvements to how Active Directory directory service and Certificate Services work and how they are managed, Microsoft added a new feature called Authorization Manager to Windows 2003 Server that provided role-based authorization for users of line-of-business applications. Although Active Directory directory service by itself provides object-based access control using ACLs, the role-based access control (RBAC) provided by Authorization Manager enables permissions to be managed in terms of the different job roles users might have. Authorization Manager works by providing a set of COM-based runtime interfaces that enables an application to manage and verify a client's requests to perform operations using the application. Authorization Manager also includes an MMC snap-in that application administrators can use to manage different user roles and permissions.

Another IDA service that Microsoft released for Windows Server 2003 is Windows Rights Management Service (RMS), an information-protection technology that works with RMS-enabled applications to help businesses safeguard valuable digital information from unauthorized use whether online or offline and whether inside the firewall or outside the firewall. Windows RMS was also designed to help organizations comply with a growing number of regulatory requirements that mandated information protection, including the U.S. Sarbanes-Oxley Act, the Gramm-Leach-Bliley Act, the Health Insurance Portability and Accountability Act (HIPAA), and others. To use Windows RMS, enterprises can create central-ized custom usage policy templates, such as "Confidential – Read Only," that can work with any RMS-enabled client and can be directly applied to sensitive business information such as financial reports, product specifications, or e-mail messages. Implementing Windows RMS requires an Active Directory directory service infrastructure, a PKI, and Internet Information Services—all of which are included in Windows Server 2003. In addition, RMS-enabled client applications such as Microsoft Office 2003 and Internet Explorer are needed, plus Microsoft SQL Server to provide the underlying database for the service.

While these additional IDA services and add-ons for Active Directory directory service were being released, Microsoft also released a follow-up to MMS 2.2 called Microsoft Identity Inte-gration Server (MIIS) 2003, which provides a centralized service that stores and integrates identity information for organizations with multiple directories. It also provides a unified view of all known identity information about users, applications, and resources on a network. MIIS 2003 is designed for life-cycle management of identity and access to simplify the provisioning of new user accounts, strong credentials, access policies, rights management policies, and so on. MIIS 2003 is available in two versions. First, there's Microsoft Identity Integration Server 2003 SP1, Enterprise Edition, which includes support for identity integration/directory syn-chronization, account provisioning/deprovisioning, and password synchronization and man-agement. And second, there's Identity Integration Feature Pack 1a for Microsoft Windows Server Active Directory, a free download that provides the same functionality as Microsoft Identity Integration Server 2003 SP1, Enterprise Edition (identity integration/directory syn-chronization, account provisioning/deprovisioning, and password synchronization) but only between Active Directory directory service, Active Directory Application Mode (ADAM), and Microsoft Exchange Server 2000 and later. Enterprises that need to interface with repositories other than Active Directory, ADAM, or Exchange Server, however, must use MIIS 2003, Enterprise Edition, rather than the free Feature Pack version.

Identity and Access in Windows Server 2003 R2

With the R2 release of Windows Server 2003, Microsoft added two more IDA services to the slate of various services already available on Windows Server 2003 either as in-box services, downloadable add-ons, or separate server products built upon Active Directory directory ser-vices. These two new IDA services are Active Directory Application Mode and Active Directory Federation Services.

Active Directory Application Mode (ADAM) is essentially a standalone version of Active Directory directory service that is designed specifically for use with directory-enabled applications. ADAM does not require or depend upon Active Directory forests or domains, so you can use it in a workgroup scenario on standalone servers if desired—you don't have to install it on a domain controller. In addition, ADAM stores and replicates only application-related information and does not store or replicate information about network resources, such as users, groups, or computers. And because ADAM is not an operating system service, you can even run multiple instances of ADAM on a single computer, with each instance of ADAM supporting a different directory-enabled application and having its own directory store, assigned LDAP and SSL ports, and application event log. ADAM is provided as an optional component of Windows Server 2003 R2, but there's also a downloadable version that can be installed on either Windows Server 2003 or Windows XP.

Active Directory Federation Services (ADFS) is another optional component of Windows Server 2003 R2 that provides Web single sign-on (SSO) functionality to authenticate a user to multiple Web applications over the life of a single online session. ADFS works by securely sharing digital identity and entitlement rights across security and enterprise boundaries, and it supports the WS-Federation Passive Requestor Profile (WS-F PRP) Web Services protocol. ADFS is tightly integrated with Active Directory, and it can work with both Active Directory directory services and ADAM. Using ADFS, an enterprise can extend its existing Active Directory infrastructure to the Internet to provide access to resources that are offered by trusted partners across the Internet. These trusted partners can be either external third parties or additional departments or subsidiaries within the enterprise.

Identity and Access in Windows Server 2008

Looking back over this evolution of Active Directory–based IDA services since Windows 2000 Server, we have the following IDA solution for the current platform Windows Server 2003 R2:

- Active Directory directory services and Certificate Services—two core services that can be deployed separately or together.

- Authorization Manager, ADAM, and ADFS—separate optional components that require Active Directory directory services. (Authorization Manager also requires Certificate Services.)

- MIIS 2003, which is available both as a separate product or as a free Feature Pack (depending on whether or not you need to synchronize with non-Microsoft directory services).

- Windows Rights Management Service (RMS), which is available as an optional download from the Microsoft Download Center.

Microsoft's vision with Windows Server 2008 (and beyond) is to consolidate all these various IDA capabilities into a single, integrated IDA solution built upon Active Directory. This consolidation picture as of Beta 3 of Windows Server 2008 is as follows.

As shown in the following diagram, there are four key integrated IDA components present in Windows Server 2008:

- Active Directory Domain Services (AD DS) and Active Directory Lightweight Directory Services (AD LDS), which provide the foundational directory services for domain-based and standalone network environments.

- Active Directory Certificate Services (AD CS), which provides strong credentials using PKI digital certificates.

- Active Directory Rights Management Services (AD RMS), which protects information contained in documents, e-mails, and so on.

- Active Directory Federation Services (AD FS), which eliminates the need for creating and maintaining multiple separate identities.

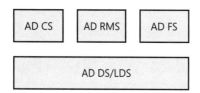

Note the following rebranding of IDA services in Windows Server 2008:

- Active Directory directory services is now known as Active Directory Domain Services (AD DS).

- Active Directory Application Mode is now called Active Directory Lightweight Directory Services (AD LDS).

- Certificate Services is now called Active Directory Certificate Services (AD CS).

- Windows Rights Management Services is now named Active Directory Rights Management Services (AD RMS).

- Finally, Active Directory Federation Services (ADFS) is still called Active Directory Federation Services (AD FS) but now includes an extra space in the abbreviation.

And for identity life-cycle management, Microsoft also plans on releasing a follow-up to MIIS 2003 called Identity Lifecycle Manager (ILM) 2007 in mid-2007. Initially, ILM 2007 will run on Windows Server 2003, Enterprise Edition. ILM 2007 builds on the metadirectory and user-provisioning capabilities in MIIS 2003 by adding new capabilities for managing strong credentials such as smart cards and by providing an integrated approach that pulls together metadirectory, digital certificate and password management, and user provisioning across Microsoft Windows platforms and other enterprise systems. Microsoft is also working on the next version of ILM, which is codenamed Identity Lifecycle Manager "2." This version is planned for release around the same time as Windows Server 2008, but it will install separately. Before we go any further, let's hear from one of our experts at Microsoft concerning plans for ILM "2" as an identity-management solution for Windows Server 2008:

From the Experts: Identity Lifecycle Manager "2"

Identity Lifecycle Manager "2" is the codename for Microsoft's identity management solution for Windows Server 2008. The principles behind Identity Lifecycle Manager "2" are that identity is everywhere and it can be managed how you want it to be.

Identity Is Everywhere

Identity Lifecycle Manager "2" provides a plethora of ready-to-deploy self-service identity and access solutions. Users can manage their own information and that of their staff, and navigate through the organizational hierarchy. They can reset their own passwords, provision their own smart cards, and retrieve their certificates. They can create security groups and distribution lists, request access to one another's groups, and manage approval.

Best of all, they can do all of this right from within their Office applications and Windows desktops. So, with Identity Lifecycle Manager "2," if you want to request to join a group, you can do that right within Outlook. And when you are asked to approve an action by another user, the Approve and Reject buttons are right there in the approval request mail. And if you forget your password and need to reset it, you can do so right where you are most likely to find that you have forgotten it: at the Windows log-in prompt. All the facilities of Identity Lifecycle Manager "2" are also available from a central portal, hosted within Windows SharePoint Services.

Identity Is Managed How You Want It to Be

Identity Lifecycle Manager "2" lets you manage identity your way by allowing you to accurately model your business processes and attach them to identity and access events. Modeling your unique business procedures around identity and access management processes is meant to be something that each staff member can do for themselves, without having to depend on programmers to do it for them. Thus, Identity Lifecycle Manager "2" provides a simple graphical user interface for modeling your business procedures—the Identity Lifecycle Manager "2" Process Designer. Moreover, you don't have to deploy any special software onto your user's desktops for them to be able to use the Process Designer. The Process Designer is fully incorporated within the Identity Lifecycle Manager "2" portal, which is a Windows SharePoint Services 3 application. So all that users of the Process Designer need to access the designer is their browser.

The three fundamental types of processes that you can model in Microsoft Identity Lifecycle Manager "2" are authentication processes, approval processes, and action processes. Indeed, within Identity Lifecycle Manager "2," processing proceeds by first executing your authentication processes, then your approval processes, and finally your action processes.

Authentication processes are for confirming a user's identity. The steps in an authentication process challenge the user for credentials. This process can also include several steps to define a multifactor authentication process required for more sensitive operations. Both the built-in authentication activities and your custom ones can leverage the Windows GINA and Windows Vista Credential Provider technologies to challenge users for their credentials at the Windows log-in prompt. This is a desirable option, because then users are challenged to prove their identity precisely where they expect to be challenged.

A second core type of process in the process model of Microsoft Identity Lifecycle Manager "2" is the approval process. Approval processes are for confirming that a user has permission to perform a requested operation. Typically, an approval process involves sending an e-mail message to the owner of a resource asking them to confirm that a user has permission to perform some requested operation on that resource. Identity Lifecycle Manager "2" allows users to respond to those approval requests right from within Outlook, which is precisely where a user would naturally want to be able to do so. Another type of activity in an approval process is one that requires users to submit a business justification for an operation they want to perform. In Identity Lifecycle Manager "2," approval processes can involve any activities that a user might have to complete before being allowed to proceed with an operation. The enabling power of Identity Lifecycle Manager "2" is that it gives you the freedom to determine how you want to gather approvals for users' actions. Then it surfaces the approvals on the end users' desktops, inside an appropriate application context where they would expect to find them—saving the user from having to go elsewhere to manage permissions.

The third and final core type of process in the process model of Microsoft Identity Lifecycle Manager "2" is the action process. Action processes define what happens as a consequence of an operation. A simple example is just having a notification sent to the owner of a resource to inform the owner of a change. A more interesting and, indeed, more common type of activity to perform as a consequence of an identity management operation is an entitlement activity. Thus, you might define a process that, as a consequence of assigning a user to a particular group, allocates a parking permit in the correct lot and issues the appropriate card key for the user's building. The point is that Identity Lifecycle Manager "2" action processes are truly a blank slate. On that blank slate, you get to define how actions on objects within Identity Lifecycle Manager "2" propagate out to the identity stores and resources of your enterprise.

We've said that the principal idea is that you get to define processes that model the identity management procedures of your enterprise and that you get to attach those processes to identity and access events. Up to this point, we have discussed quite a lot about the processes. Now let us turn to the subject of attaching those processes to events.

Events are the triggers that cause Identity Lifecycle Manager "2" processes to be executed. So, in attaching a process to an event, you are defining the circumstances under which the process will be executed. In the nomenclature of Identity Lifecycle Manager "2," we refer to this as mapping a process to an event. We provide a simple user interface for accomplishing it. You identify the process that you have created using the Process Designer, and then you specify the event to which you want to attach the process.

So what is an *event* in Identity Lifecycle Manager "2?" Well, an event is something that happens to a set of one or more objects. For example, you might update the cost center assigned to a particular team of people, or you might update the office telephone number of a single individual. Both constitute examples of events. Another example is the addition of a person to a team—in that case, there is an event for the person being added, as well as an event for the team that the person is joining.

Because an event is something that happens to a set of one or more objects, when you map a process to an event, you must identify the set of objects to which the event is expected to occur. Identity Lifecycle Manager "2" gives you considerable power to identify the sets of objects. You get to define the rules by which objects are included in sets. Those rules can be as rich and complex or as bare and simple as you want them to be. You can define them so as to include any number of objects in a set, and any variety of types of objects as well. Once you have defined rules to identify a set of objects, you can select the events on those objects that you want to serve as triggers for your processes. There are two types of events in Identity Lifecycle Manager "2" that can trigger your processes: request events and transition events.

Request events are events by which the data of an object or set of objects is retrieved or manipulated. So, included in the category of request events are create, read, update, and delete events. Transition events occur when an object moves in or out of a set of objects. So, in the earlier example of a person joining a team, there is a transition for that person in being included in the group and a transition for the group in having that person join.

All in all, the authentication, approval, and action processes that you compose using approval actions, notification actions, and entitlement actions in the Process Designer can be mapped to any request or transition event on any set of objects that you identify via your rules. We believe that this simple model of designing processes and then mapping those processes to events gives you tremendous power to manage the identity life cycle of your organization. Whatever identity-related occurrences that you can imagine happening in your enterprise can be represented as events within Identity Lifecycle Manager "2," and then you can describe processes to handle those events—processes that confirm the identity of the person initiating the event, that confirm the person's permission to initiate the event, or that define the consequences. Crucially, you get to define those processes as models representing the business policies and procedures that uniquely govern the identity-related assets of your enterprise.

Microsoft Identity Lifecycle Manager "2" is built on the Windows Communication Foundation, Windows Workflow Foundation, and Windows SharePoint Services 3 technologies, and it exposes a thoroughly standards-based API that implements WS-Transfer, WS-ResourceTransfer, WS-Enumeration, and WS-Trust.

–Donovan Follette
  Identity and Access Developer Evangelist, Windows Server Evangelism

After reading all this, you hopefully understand now the big picture of what Microsoft's vision is for identity and access, and how Active Directory in Windows Server 2008 fits into this picture. Now it's time to look at each piece of this picture and learn about the new features and enhancements to Active Directory in Windows Server 2008. We'll begin with core improvements to AD DS/LDS.

Active Directory Domain Services

Let's look at four enhancements to Active Directory in Windows Server 2008:

- AD DS auditing enhancements
- Read-only domain controllers
- Restartable AD DS
- Granular password and account lockout policies

There are other improvements as well, including some changes to the user interface for managing Active Directory and also to the Active Directory Installation Wizard. But we'll focus here on the three enhancements just mentioned, as they're big gains for many enterprises.

AD DS Auditing Enhancements

The first enhancement we'll look at is AD DS auditing. In the current platform, Windows Server 2003 R2 (and in Windows Server 2008 also), you can enable a global audit policy called Audit Directory Service Access to log events in the Security event log whenever certain operations are performed on objects stored in Active Directory. Enabling logging of objects in Active Directory is a two-step process. First, you open the Default Domain Controller Policy in Group Policy Object Editor and enable the Audit Directory Service Access global audit policy found under Computer Configuration\Windows Settings\Security Settings\Local Policies\Audit Policy.

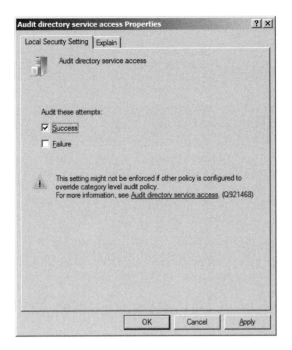

Then you configure the system access control list (SACL) on the object or objects you want to audit. For example, to enable Success auditing for access by Authenticated Users to User objects stored within an organizational unit (OU), you do the following:

1. Open Active Directory Users and Computers, and make sure Advanced Features is selected from the View menu.

2. Right-click on the OU you want to audit, and select Properties.

3. Select the Security tab, and click Advanced to open the Advanced Security Settings for the OU.

4. Select the Audit tab, and click Add to open the Select User, Computer or Group dialog.

5. Type **Authenticated Users**, and click OK. An Auditing Entry dialog opens for the OU.

6. In the Apply Onto list box, select Descendant User Objects.

7. Select the Write All Properties check box in the Select column.

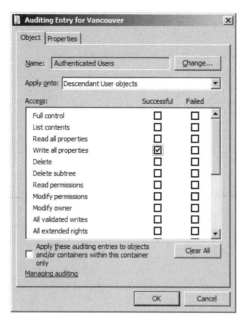

8. Click OK to return to Advanced Security Settings for the OU, which should now show the new SACL you configured.

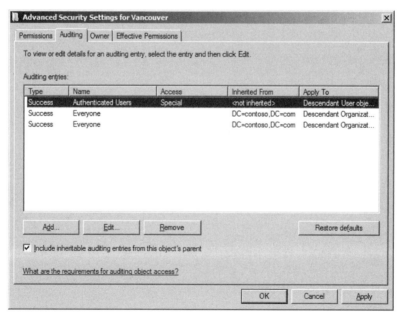

9. Close all dialog boxes by clicking OK as needed.

Now if you go ahead and change a property of one of the user accounts in your OU—for example, by disabling an account—an event should be logged in the Security log with event ID 4662 and source Directory Service Access to indicate that the object was accessed.

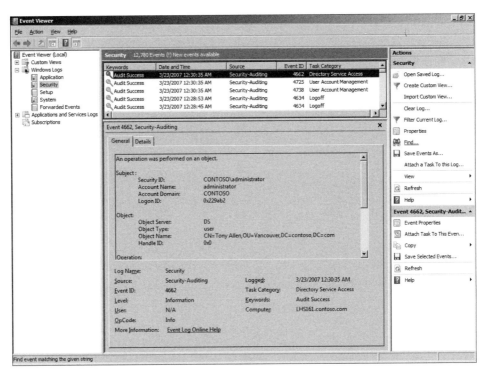

So far, this is the same in Windows Server 2008 as in previous versions of Windows Server. What's new in Windows Server 2008, however, is that while in previous Windows Server platforms there was only one audit policy (Audit Directory Service Access) that controlled whether auditing of directory service events was enabled or disabled, in Windows Server 2008 this policy has been divided into four different subcategories as follows:

- Directory Service Access
- Directory Service Changes
- Directory Service Replication
- Detailed Directory Service Replication

One of these subcategories–Directory Service Changes–has been enhanced to provide the ability to audit the following changes to AD DS objects whose SACLs have been configured to enable the objects to be audited:

- Objects that have had an attribute modified will log the old and new values of this attribute in the Security log.

- Objects that are newly created will have the values of their attributes at the time of creation logged in the Security log.

- Objects that are moved from one container to another within a domain will have their old and new locations logged in the Security log.

- Objects that are undeleted will have the location to which the object has been moved logged in the Security log.

The usefulness of this change should be obvious to administrators concerned about maintaining an audit trail of changes made to Active Directory, and auditing actions like these is an important part of an overall IDA strategy for an organization. For instance, using the Security log and filtering for a particular User object, you can now track in detail all changes to the attributes of that object over the entire lifetime of the object. When you enable Success auditing for the Audit Directory Service Access global audit policy (and this policy has Success auditing enabled for it by default within the Default Domain Controllers Policy), the effect of this is to also enable Success auditing for the first of the four subcategories (Directory Service Access) described earlier, which audits only attempts to access directory objects. If you need to, however, you can selectively enable or disable Success and/or Failure auditing for each of these four auditing subcategories individually by using the Auditpol.exe command-line tool included in Windows Server 2008. For example, if you wanted to enable Success auditing for the second subcategory (Directory Service Changes) so that you can maintain a record of the old and new values of an object's attribute when the value of that attribute is successfully modified, you can do so by typing **auditpol /set /subcategory:"directory service changes" /success:enable** at a command prompt on your domain controller. If we do this in the preceding example and then enable the user account we disabled previously, three new directory service audit events are added to the Security log.

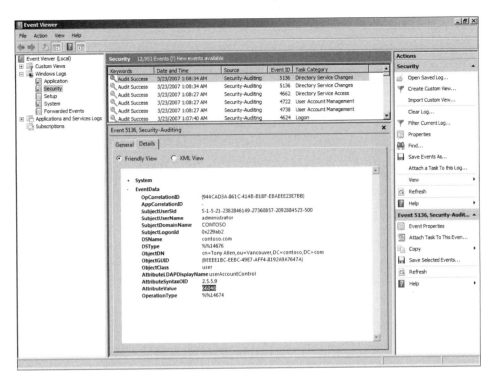

The first (earliest) of these events is 4662, indicating the User object has been accessed, while the second event (5136) records the old value of the attribute modified and the third event (also 5136) records the new value of the attribute. Table 7-1 lists the possible event IDs for Directory Service Changes audit events.

Table 7-1   Event IDs for Directory Service Changes Audit Events

Event ID	Meaning
5136	An attribute of the object has been modified.
5137	The object was created.
5138	The object has been undeleted.
5139	The object has been moved within the domain.

In addition to enabling you to track the history of an object this way, Windows Server 2008 also gives you the option of setting flags in the Active Directory schema to specify which attributes of an object you want to track changes for and which attributes you don't want to track changes for. This can be very useful because tracking changes to objects can lead to a whole lot of audit events and your Security log can fill up awfully fast.

Read-Only Domain Controllers

Another new feature of AD DS in Windows Server 2008 is the Read-Only Domain Controller (RODC), a domain controller that hosts a read-only replica of the AD database. The main rationale for RODCs (apart from nostalgia for the BDCs of good old NT4 days) is to provide a solution for branch offices that have inadequate physical security. For example, a corporate headquarters probably has the resources to adequately protect their domain controllers against theft or other physical dangers—at least, they better have such resources. Small branch offices, however, might not have the facilities, budget, or expertise to ensure a domain controller present there would be physically secure. One solution to this problem might be to not have a domain controller at all at your branch office and just have users there authenticate over a WAN link with a domain controller at headquarters. The problem with this approach is if the WAN link is too slow, unreliable, or saturated with other forms of traffic. The result could be unacceptably slow logons for users or difficulty logging on at all. If your WAN link is unsuitable, the other option is to place a domain controller at your branch office and have users there authenticate locally while the DC itself replicates with DCs at headquarters to ensure its directory database is always up to date. The problem with *this* approach, however, is that domain controllers are the heart and soul of your Windows-based network because they contain all the accounts for all the users and computers on your network. So if the domain controller at your branch office somehow got stolen (perhaps by some clever social engineering like, "Hi, I've come to clean your domain controller, can you show me where it is?"), your whole network should be considered compromised and your only viable solution is to flatten everything and rebuild it all from scratch.

And those are the only two solutions today for branch offices using domain controllers running Windows Server 2003—authenticate over the WAN or risk placing a domain controller at your branch office. RODC, however, solves this dilemma by providing a *secure* way to have a domain controller at your branch office. The only requirement for using RODC is that the domain controller that holds the PDC Emulator FSMO role on your network has to be running Windows Server 2008. Once this is the case and you've deployed an RODC at your branch office, changes made to the directory on your normal (writable) domain controllers replicate to the RODC, but nothing replicates in the opposite direction. That's because the directory database of a RODC is read-only, so you can't write anything to it locally—it has to receive all changes to its database via replication from another (writable) domain controller. (RODCs can't replicate with each other either, so there's no point having more than one RODC at a given site—plus it could cause inconsistent logon experiences for users if you did do this.) So RODC replication is completely unidirectional—and this applies to DFS replication traffic as well.

RODCs also advertise themselves as the Key Distribution Center (KDC) for the branch office where they reside, so they handle all requests for Kerberos tickets from user and computer accounts at the remote site. RODCs don't store user or computer credentials in their directory database, however; so when a user at the branch office tries to log on, the RODC contacts a writable DC at the hub site to request a copy of the user's credentials. How the hub DC responds to the RODC's request depends on how the Password Replication Policy is configured for that RODC. If the policy says that the user's credentials can be replicated to the RODC, the writable DC does this, and the RODC caches the credentials for future use (until the user's credentials change). The result of all this is that RODCs generally have few credentials stored on them. So if an RODC somehow gets stolen (remember the DC cleaning guy), only those credentials are compromised and replacing them is much less work than rebuilding your entire directory from scratch.

Another feature of RODCs is that a domain administrator can delegate the local administrator role for an RODC to an ordinary domain user. This can be very useful for smaller branch offices that have no full-time expert IT person on site. So if you need to load a new driver into your DC at a remote site, you can just give instructions to your "admin" by phone on how to do this. The admin is simply an ordinary user who can follow instructions, and delegating RODC admin rights to him doesn't enable him to perform any domain-wide administrative tasks or log on to a writable DC at headquarters—the damage he can do is limited to wrecking only the RODC.

Let's hear now from a Microsoft MVP and directory services expert concerning some enhancements that have been made to dcpromo.exe in Windows Server 2008 and how these enhancements relate to deploying RODCs:

From the Experts: New Active Directory Setup Wizard (dcpromo.exe)

When you want to install Active Directory, you have to use the Active Directory Setup Wizard (dcpromo.exe). It provides you with some possibilities and assumes that you have a proper design written down and you know what you want to accomplish. However, we have received many support calls and questions on the Internet because Active Directory and DNS were not set up in a way that reflects best practices. Considering the vast amount of installations of Active Directory, it's very clear that it's far easier to find the Active Directory Installation Wizard on the server operating system than it is to find best practices or good consultancy. Common support issues included having the wrong FSMO-Roles together on the same system, not enough Global Catalog servers, or issues in the DNS-Design that were leading to logons over the WAN lines.

In Windows Server 2008, Microsoft has put a huge effort into changing dcpromo.exe. Now it is reflecting best practices. You get a normal mode if you just want to quickly install Active Directory, and you get an advanced mode if you want to do any special configurations. Dcpromo is leveraging best practices, and it provides a lot of additional tasks. It's checking the FSMO roles for you, and it recommends whether to automatically move the Infrastructure Master if necessary. It allows you to enable the Global Catalog on a new domain controller. It is checking the DNS infrastructure, and it allows you to automatically create forwarders and delegations. Also, dcpromo enables you to choose your replication partner for the initial replication so that you can make sure to target a specific DC.

In addition, dcpromo supports the new Read Only Domain Controller (RODC) in multiple ways. You are either able to precreate a RODC-Account in your domain and delegate a site admin to join the RODC to the domain, or you are able to fully install the RODC while selecting whether it should also be a Global Catalog server a DNS-server, or both.

Last but not least, dcpromo finally supports unattended installations from the command line without an answer script. Simply run **dcpromo /?:unattend** to figure out what parameters you have to script the installation of your Windows Server 2008 Active Directory Domain Controller.

–Ulf B. Simon-Weidner
MVP for Windows Server–Directory Services author, consultant, speaker, and trainer

Finally, because domain controllers often host the DNS Server role as well (because DNS is the naming system used by AD), the RODCs need a special read-only form of DNS Server running on them also. To learn more about this feature, however, let's listen to another one of our experts at Microsoft:

From the Experts: Advanced Considerations for DNS on RODCs in Branch Office Sites

When installing a Windows Server 2008 Read Only Domain Controller (RODC) at a branch office site, using the Active Directory Installation Wizard or the DCPromo command-line tool, you are prompted to specify a DNS domain for the Active Directory domain that you are joining the RODC to during promotion. During this process, you are prompted with DNS Server installation options. A DNS Server is required to locate domain controllers and member computers in an Active Directory domain, at both the hub site and the local branch office site. The default option is to install a DNS Server locally on the RODC, which replicates the existing AD-integrated zone for the domain specified and adds the local IP address in the DNS Server list of the domain controller local DNS Client setting.

As a best practice, Microsoft recommends that client computers have Dynamic DNS updates turned on by default and that DHCP Servers be used to configure the DNS Server list. Similarly for branch office sites, clients should be configured to use Dynamic DNS updates, and you should set the Primary DNS Server or use DHCP to set the DNS Server list to direct clients to the DNS Server running on the RODC.

If there is only one DNS Server and RODC running at the branch office site, Microsoft recommends that client computers also point to a DNS Server running on a domain controller at the hub site. This can be done either by configuring clients with an Alternate DNS Server for the hub-site DNS Server or by configuring DHCP Servers to set the DNS Server list to first the local DNS Server and then the remote DNS Server at the hub site. The DNS Server on the RODC should be the first DNS Server in the list to optimize resolution performance for branch office clients.

In larger branch office scenarios, if setting up two or more RODCs at a site, you are provided the default option to install DNS Server locally on all the RODCs. Within the same site, the RODCs do not replicate directly with each other. The RODCs rely mainly on replication with domain controllers at the hub site during scheduled intervals to refresh local data in the directory. Hence, a branch office DNS Server on an RODC receives updated DNS zone data during the normal replication cycle from a hub-site domain controller connected to the local RODC.

In addition to replication from the hub site, DNS Servers on RODCs also attempt to replicate local data after receiving a client update request. The branch office DNS Server redirects the client to a hub-site DNS Server on a domain controller that is writable and can process the update. Shortly thereafter, it attempts to contact a hub-site domain controller to update its local copy of the data with the changed record. Any other branch office DNS Server on RODCs at the site do not attempt to obtain a local copy of the single record update because they did not receive the original client update request. This mechanism has the advantage of allowing an updated client record to be resolved quickly within the branch office, without necessitating frequent and large replication requests for all domain data from the hub site. If network connectivity is lost, or no domain controller at the hub site is able to provide the updated record data to the DNS Server in the branch office, the record will be available locally only after the next scheduled replication from the hub-site domain controllers, and it will be available to all RODCs at the branch office site.

As a consequence of a DNS Server's attempt to replicate individual records between replication cycles, if DNS zone data is stored across multiple RODCs, the local branch office records might accumulate some incongruities. To ensure a high level of consistency for DNS data, the recommendation is to configure all client computers at the branch office site with the same DNS Server list—for example, by using DHCP.

If, however, in the more rare case that timely resolution of local branch office client records is absolutely critical, to avoid any inconsistencies for resolution, you can install DNS Servers on all RODCs at the site, but point clients only to a single DNS Server.

−Moon Majumdar
  Program Manager, DNS (Server and Client) and DC Locator, Directory and Service Team

Restartable AD DS

Another new feature of AD DS in Windows Server 2008 is the ability to restart the Active Directory directory services without having to restart your domain controller in Directory Services Restore Mode. In previous versions of Windows Server, when you wanted to do some maintenance task on a domain controller—such as performing offline defragmentation of the directory database or performing an authoritative restore of the Active Directory directory service database—you had to restart your domain controller in Directory Services Restore Mode by pressing F8 during startup and selecting this from the list of startup options. You then logged on to your domain controller by using the local Administrator account specified previously when you ran the Active Directory Installation Wizard (dcpromo.exe) on your machine to promote it from a member server to a domain controller. Once logged on in Directory Services Restore Mode, you could perform maintenance on your domain controller and clients couldn't authenticate with it during your maintenance window.

Having to reboot a domain controller like this to perform maintenance operations resulted in longer downtime for clients who needed to be authenticated by your domain controller. To reduce this downtime window, AD DS has been re-architected in Windows Server 2008. Instead of rebooting your machine and logging on in Directory Services Restore Mode, you simply stop the Domain Controller service by using the Services snap-in (shown in Figure 7-1) or typing **net stop ntds** at a command line, perform your maintenance tasks while still logged on as a domain admin, and when you're finished start this service again using the snap-in or the **net start ntds** command. Stopping and starting the Domain Controller service like this also has no effect on other services such as the DHCP Server service that might be running on your domain controller.

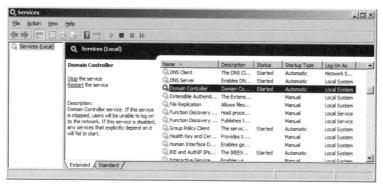

Figure 7-1   You can now stop and start the Domain Controller (NTDS) service without rebooting your domain controller and logging on in Directory Services Restore Mode

While domain controllers running previous versions of Windows Server had two Active Directory directory service modes (normal mode and Directory Services Restore Mode), domain controllers running Windows Server 2008 now have three possible modes or *states* they can be running in:

- **AD DS Started**   This is the normal state when the NTDS service is running and clients can be authenticated by the domain controller. This state is similar to how AD directory services worked in Windows 2000 Server and Windows Server 2003.

- **Directory Services Restore Mode**   This state is still available on domain controllers running Windows Server 2008 through the F8 startup options, and it's unchanged from how it worked in Windows 2000 Server and Windows Server 2003.

- **AD DS Stopped**   This is the new state for domain controllers running Windows Server 2008. A domain controller running in this state shares characteristics of both a domain controller running in Directory Services Restore Mode and a member server that is joined to a domain. For example, as in Directory Services Restore Mode, a domain controller running in the AD DS Stopped state has its directory database (Ntds.dit) offline. And similar to a domain-joined member server, a domain controller running in this state is still domain-joined, and users can log on interactively or over the network by using another domain controller. But it's a good idea not to let your domain controller remain in the AD DS Stopped state for an extended period of time because not only will it be unable to service user logon requests, it also will be unable to replicate with other domain controllers on the network.

Granular Password and Account Lockout Policies

New in Beta 3 of Windows Server 2008 is the ability to have multiple password policies and account lockout policies in a domain. To learn about this particular feature, let's hear from a Microsoft MVP and directory services expert:

From the Experts: Granular Password Policies in Windows Server 2008

If you want to deploy multiple password policies in your forest, the domain has always been the boundary for this. This was confusing for many customers because you are able to change passwords in every Group Policy Object (GPO). However, remember that password settings (and account lockout settings) are configured in the Computer Settings part of the GPO. They apply only to computer objects, and therefore, to local accounts on those computer objects. An exception to this rule is policies that are linked to the domain head (the top node of the domain). GPOs linked here that hold password settings are the administrative interface for the password and account lockout settings for domain objects. Actually, they are written back to attributes on the domain head object and take effect from there. Domain controllers that receive a password change request compare the settings on the domain head with the password, and they either allow the password change or deny it. So it's important to understand that password and account lockout settings are maintained on the domain head in Active Directory. You also need to keep in mind that Group Policies are only the administrative interface and that password settings configured in any GPO linked to any other OU or site are applied only to the local user accounts of the computer object to which the policy applies.

So, in the past, password and account lockout settings were limited to the domain and we were able to apply only one setting per domain. If we wanted to have different password policies, we were required to deploy multiple domains.

This has been changed in Windows Server 2008. Active Directory is extended, and the password settings validation on the domain controllers have been extended so that we are able to configure multiple password and account lockout settings for each domain now. How are they administered? Not via GPO—as mentioned before, GPO has been only an administrative interface. So the new fine-grained password policies are configured as new objects in the domain and are linked to either groups or users in the domain.

If you want to experiment with this, simply use ADSIEdit.msc. Expand the Password Settings Container underneath the System Container in the domain, right-click, and select New. You are prompted to fill in the following mandatory attributes, which define password and account lockout policies:

- *msDS-PasswordSettingsPrecendence* This attribute is just a virtual number you can make up. (Be sure you leave some space in the numbering for future use.) It defines which password settings take effect if multiple settings apply to the same object (user or group, but settings on the user always take precedence over settings on the group).

  This will usually reflect on the "level" of the settings object. For example, if you have stronger settings, they have a lower value, and if you have higher settings, you're probably assigning a higher precedence to them.

- *msDS-PasswordReversibleEncryptionEnabled* This attribute is Boolean and defines whether you want to store the passwords of the accounts (that is, specify to whom the password settings object applies) in reversible encryption or not. The default and best practice is to set this value to FALSE.

- *msDS-PasswordHistoryLength* This setting defines how many old passwords the user cannot reuse again (to prevent the user from changing the password back and forward to the same one or changing it multiple times until he's able to reuse his old password).

  The domain default is to not allow the last 24 passwords of that user.

- *msDS-PasswordComplexityEnabled*   This attribute is also a Boolean and defines whether the password needs to be complex (that is, it has at least three of the following character sets applied: lower letters, capital letters, numbers, symbols, or unicode characters).

  The domain default and best practice is to turn it on (TRUE).

- *msDS-MinimumPasswordLength*   This attribute defines the minimum length of a password in characters. The domain default is seven characters long.

- *msDS-MinimumPasswordAge*   The msDS-MinimumPasswordAge attribute does just what its name suggests—it defines the minimum age for passwords. The minimum age is necessary to prevent a user from changing her password x amount of times on the same day until she exceeds the Password History limit and can change the password back to the same value as before.

  This is a negative number that you can compile or decompile, using the scripts at *http://msdn2.microsoft.com/en-us/library/ms974598.aspx* as a guideline. (The domain default is 1 day, which equals -864000000000.)

- *msDS-MaximumPasswordAge*   This attribute is just the opposite of the previous one. It defines when you have to change your password. It is also a negative number just like the previous one. (The domain default is 42 days, which equals -36288000000000.)

- *msDS-LockoutThreshold*   Defines how many failed attempts at entering a password a user can have before the user object will be locked. (The domain default is 0, which equals "Don't lock out accounts after invalid passwords.")

- *msDS-LockoutObservationWindow*   This attribute determines at which time the bad password counter should be reset. (The domain default is 6 minutes, which equals -18000000000.)

- *msDS-LockoutDuration*   This attribute determines how long a password should be locked. (The domain default is 6 minutes, which equals -18000000000.)

After you create your own password settings object (PSO), you have to link it to a user or group. I recommend, for administrative purposes, always linking it to groups instead of to users. (Otherwise, it will get messy and hard to administer.) To link the PSO to a group or user, you simply change its *msDS-PSOAppliesTo* attribute to the distinguished name of the group or user (for example, *cn=Administrators,cn=Users,dc=example,dc=com*). This is a multivalued attribute, so you are able to link the same PSO to multiple groups or users.

For administrative purposes, there are also two attributes that help you determine which password policies are applied to which users or groups. On the group or user, you will find the *msDS-PSOApplied* attribute, which is actually the back link of the *msDS-PSOAppliesTo* attribute and lists all PSOs that are directly linked to this object.

To help you figure out which PSO is the effective one, there's the constructed attribute *msDS-ResultantPSO*, which shows you which PSO is effective for the object in question.

At the beta stage that is current at the writing of this book, this is a new feature that lacks adequate administrative support in the graphical user interface. However, you are able to administer it easily using ADSIEdit.msc. And Joe Richards, a Directory Services MVP who wrote Active Directory command line tools such as ADFind and ADMod, has created a new command-line utility named PSOMgr.exe, which helps you create and link PSOs. You'll find it at *www.joeware.net*.

–Ulf B. Simon-Weidner
  MVP for Windows Server–Directory Services author, consultant, speaker, and trainer

Active Directory Lightweight Directory Services

Another feature of Active Directory in Windows Server 2008 is the new built-in Active Directory Lightweight Directory Services (AD LDS) server role. Well, actually it's not new because this is essentially the same Active Directory Application Mode (ADAM) feature that was available as an out-of-band download for Windows Server 2003 and Windows XP. What's new is mainly that this directory service is now available as an in-box role that can be added to your Windows Server 2008 server using the Role Manager tool described in Chapter 4, "Managing Windows Server 2008," instead of it needing to be downloaded from the Microsoft Download Center as in previous versions of Windows.

So AD LDS is basically just ADAM, but what's ADAM? ADAM (we'll call it by its new name now, AD LDS) is basically a stripped-down version of AD DS that supports a lot of the features of AD DS (multimaster replication, application directory partitions, LDAP over SSL access, the ADSI API) but doesn't store Windows security principals (such as domain user and computer accounts), domains, global catalogs, or Group Policy. In other words, AD LDS gives you all the benefits of having a directory but none of the features for managing resources on a network. Instead, AD LDS is designed to support applications that need a directory for storing their configuration and data instead of storing these in a database, flat file, or other form of repository. Examples of directory-enabled LOB apps that could use AD LDS include CRM and HR applications or global address book apps. Because such apps often require schema changes in order to work with AD DS, a big advantage of AD LDS is that you can avoid having to make such changes to your AD DS schema, as making mistakes when you modify your AD DS schema can be costly—think flatten and rebuild everything from scratch! And it's particularly useful also if your directory-enabled LOB apps will be made available to customers or partners over an extranet or VPN connection because using AD LDS instead of AD DS in this scenario means you don't have to risk exposing your domain directory to nondomain users and computers.

Once you've added the AD LDS role in Server Manager, to use this feature you create an AD LDS instance. An AD LDS instance is an application directory that is independent of your domain-based AD DS and can run on either a member server or a domain controller if desired. (There's no conflict when running AD DS and AD LDS on the same machine as long as the two directories use a different LDAP path and different LDAP/SSL ports for accessing them. And you can even run multiple AD LDS instances on a single machine—for example, one instance for each LOB app on the machine—without conflict as long as their paths and ports are unique.)

Let's quickly walk through creating a new AD LDS instance and show how you can manage it:

1.   After installing the AD LDS role on your server, select the Active Directory Lightweight Directory Services Setup Wizard from Administrative Tools on your Start menu. This launches a wizard for creating a new instance of AD LDS on the machine:

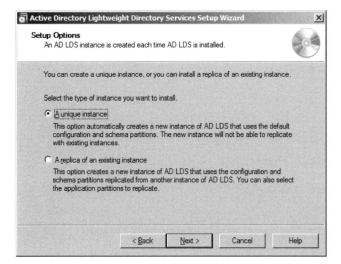

2.   Select the A Unique Instance option, and click Next. Then specify a name for the new instance (using only alphanumeric characters and the dash in your name):

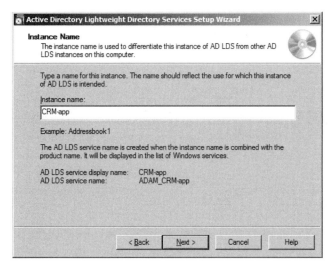

3. Click Next, and specify LDAP and SSL ports for accessing your instance:

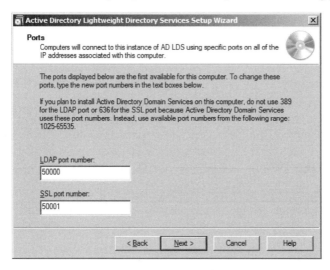

4. Click Next, and either allow the application to create its own directory partition when you install the application or type a unique distinguished name (DN) for the new application partition you are going to create:

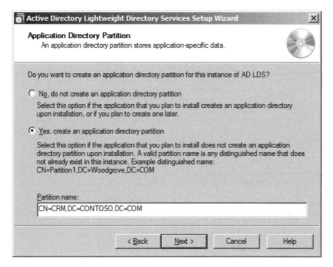

5. Click Next, and in the following wizard pages specify the location where data and recovery files for the partition will be stored, the service account under whose context the AD LDS instance will be running, and the user or group who will have administrative privileges for managing your instance. After completing these steps, you'll be asked to select from a list of default LDIF files you can import to add specific functionality to your instance:

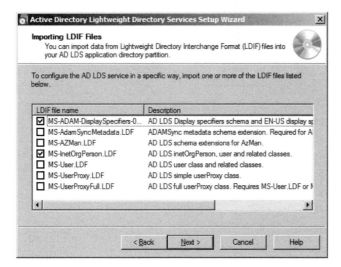

6.   Click Next to confirm your selections, and then click Finish to run the wizard and create the instance.

Once you've created your new AD LDS instance, you can manage it using ADSI Edit, an MMC snap-in available from Active Directory Lightweight Directory Services under Administrative Tools. To do this, open ADSI Edit, right-click on the root node, and select Connect To. When the Connection Settings dialog opens, specify the DN for the connection point to your instance (which was CN=CRM,DC=CONTOSO,DC=COM in our example) and click the Advanced button to specify the LDAP port (50000 in our example) for connecting to the instance:

Clicking OK then opens your AD LDS instance in ADSI EDIT. Then you can navigate the directory tree and view and create or modify objects and their attributes in your application directory partition as needed to support the functionality of your directory-enabled LOB app.

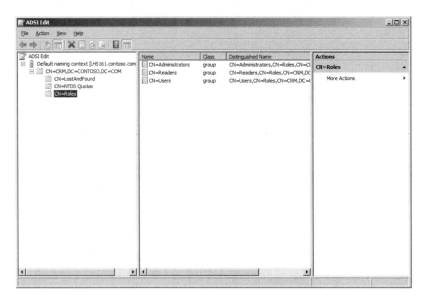

Active Directory Certificate Services

Let's move on and briefly describe improvements to Active Directory Certificate Services (AD CS) in Windows Server 2008. We'll focus on the following key improvements:

- Improvements to certificate Web enrollment support

- Support for Network Device Enrollment Service to allow network devices such as routers to enroll for X.509 certificates

- Support for the Online Certificate Status Protocol to easily manage and distribute certificate revocation status info

- The inclusion of PKIView for monitoring the health of Certification Authorities (CAs)

There are other improvements as well for AD CS—such as new Group Policy settings—but we'll pass over these for now because they'll be well documented once Windows Server 2008 RTMs. But we will also hear from the AD CS product group concerning some other enhancements to AC CS in Windows Server 2008.

Certificate Web Enrollment Improvements

Enrollment is the process of issuing and renewing X.509 certificates to users and computers when a PKI has been deployed in your enterprise. Users and computers belonging to an Active Directory domain can take advantage of a mechanism called *autoenrollment*, which allows them to automatically enroll domain-joined computers when they boot and domain users when they log on. Windows Server 2003 also includes a Certificate Request Wizard to enable domain users to request a new certificate manually when they need to.

Users and computers that are not domain joined or that run a non-Microsoft operating system can use Web enrollment instead. Web enrollment is built on top of Internet Information Services and allows a user to use a Web page to request a new certificate or renew an existing one over an Internet or extranet connection.

What's changed with this feature in Windows Server 2008 is that the old XEnroll.dll ActiveX control for the Web enrollment Web application has now been retired for both security and manageability reasons. In its place, a new COM control named CertEnroll.dll is now used, which is more secure than the old control but whose use can pose some compatibility issues in a mixed environment. For reasons of time, we can't get into these compatibility issues here, but see the "Additional Resources" section at the end of this chapter for more information on this topic.

Network Device Enrollment Service Support

Another enhancement in AD CS in Windows Server 2008 is the inclusion of built-in support for the Network Device Enrollment Service (NDES). Let's listen to one of our experts at Microsoft briefly describe this new feature (and see the "Additional Resources" section at the end of the chapter for links to more information on the subject):

From the Experts: Network Device Enrollment Service

Network Device Enrollment Service is one of the optional components of the Active Directory Certificate Services (AD CS) role. This service implements the Simple Certificate Enrollment Protocol (SCEP). SCEP defines the communication between network devices and a Registration Authority (RA) for certificate enrollment.

SCEP enables network devices that cannot authenticate to enroll for x.509 certificates from a Certification Authority (CA). At the end of the transactions defined in this protocol, the network device will have a private key and associated certificate that are issued by a CA. Applications on the device can use the key and its associated certificate to interact with other entities on the network. The most common usage of this certificate on a network device is to authenticate the device in an IPSec session.

–Oded Shekel
Program Manager, Windows Security

Online Certificate Status Protocol Support

Another new feature of AD CS in Windows Server 2008 is support for the Online Certificate Status Protocol (OCSP). In a traditional PKI, such as one implemented using Certificate

Services in Windows Server 2003, certificate revocation is handled by using certificate revocation lists (CRLs). There has to be a way of revoking certificates that expire or are compromised; otherwise, a PKI system won't be secure. CRLs provide a way of doing this by enabling clients to download a list of revoked certificates from a CA to ensure the certificate they're trying to verify (for example, a certificate belonging to a server the client is trying to connect to) is valid. Unfortunately, once a lot of certificates have been revoked in an enterprise, the CRL can become quite large and have an impact on performance when authenticating over slow WAN links or during peak traffic times, like the beginning of the workday when everyone is trying to log on to the network at the same time.

To improve performance in checking for revoked certificates and increase the scalability of a PKI system, Windows Server 2008 includes an optional Online Certificate Status Protocol role service you can install on a server by adding the Active Directory Certificate Services role using Server Manager. OCSP provides an Online Responder that can receive a request to check for revocation of a certificate without the client having to download the entire CRL. This speeds up certificate revocation checking and reduces the network bandwidth used for this process, which can be especially helpful when such checking is done over slow WAN links. AD CS in Windows Server 2008 even supports *Responder* arrays, in which multiple OCSP Online Responders are linked together to provide fault tolerance, increased scalability, or functionality needed for geographically dispersed PKI deployments.

OCSP support is described in more detail in one of the links in the "Additional Resources" section at the end of this chapter. Meanwhile, let's hear from one of our experts at Microsoft concerning this new feature:

From the Experts: Online Responder

The Online Responder server rule implements the server component of the Online Certificate Status Protocol (OCSP).

OCSP uses Hypertext Transfer Protocol (HTTP) and allows a relying party to submit a certificate status request to an OCSP responder. This returns a definitive, digitally signed response indicating the certificate status. The Microsoft Online Responder was built with scalability, performance, security, and manageability in mind. It includes the following two components:

- **Online Responder Web Proxy Cache**   First and foremost, this component is the service interface for the Online Responder. It is implemented as an Internet Server API (ISAPI) Extension hosted by Microsoft Windows Internet Information Services (IIS).

- **Online Responder Service**   This component is a Microsoft Windows NT service (ocspsvc.exe) that is running with NETWORK SERVICE privileges.

−Oded Shekel
Program Manager, Windows Security

Enterprise PKI and CAPI2 Diagnostics

Monitoring the health of CAs in an enterprise PKI deployment is important to prevent problems from arising and to troubleshoot issues when they arise. The Windows Server 2003 Resource Kit included a tool called PKI Health that could be used to display the status of each CA in a chain of CAs; in Windows Server 2008, this tool has been renamed Enterprise PKI (PKIView) and has been re-implemented as an MMC snap-in. Using PKIView, enterprise PKI admins can check the validity or accessibility status of authority information access (AIA) locations and certificate revocation list (CRL) distribution points (CDPs) for multiple CAs within an enterprise that has a Windows Server–based PKI deployed:

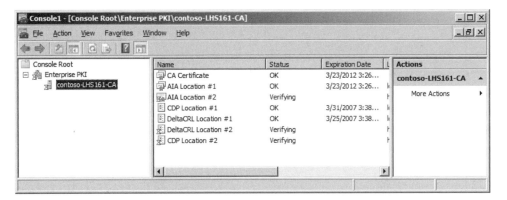

PKIView isn't the only way of troubleshooting problems with a Windows Server 2008–based PKI, however. Another useful tool is CAPI2 Diagnostics, which is described in the next sidebar contributed by one of our experts:

From the Experts: Troubleshooting PKI Problems on Windows Vista and Windows Server 2008

Microsoft Windows Vista and Microsoft Windows Server 2008 have a new feature—CAPI2 Diagnostics—that can help you with PKI troubleshooting. This feature enables administrators to troubleshoot PKI problems by collecting detailed information about certificate chain validation, certificate store operations, and signature verification. In case of errors in PKI-enabled applications, detailed information—such as the low-level API results and errors, objects retrieved, and status flags raised at different steps—is available in the logs. This functionality can help reduce the time required to diagnose problems. For troubleshooting purposes, enable CAPI2 logging, reproduce the problem, and use the data in the logs to identify the root cause. To enable logging, follow these steps:

1. Open the Event Viewer, and go to Application And Services Logs\Microsoft\ Windows\CAPI2 to get the CAPI2 channel.

2. Right-click Operational, and select Enable Log to enable CAPI2 Diagnostics logging.

3. To save the log to a file, right-click Operational and select the Save Events As option. You can save the log file in the .evtx format (which can be opened through the Event Viewer) or in XML format.

4. If there is data present in the logs before you reproduce the problem, it is recommended that you clear the logs before the repro. This allows only the data relevant to the problem to be collected from the saved logs. To clear the logs, right-click Operational and select the Clear Log option.

5. The default size for the event log is 1 MB. For CAPI2 Diagnostics, the logs tend to grow in size quickly, and it is recommended that you increase the log size to at least 4 MB to capture relevant events. To increase the log size, right-click Operational and select the Properties option. In the log properties, increase the maximum log size.

To learn more about CAPI2 Diagnostics, check out the whitepaper titled "Troubleshooting PKI Problems on Windows Vista" at *http://www.microsoft.com/downloads/details.aspx?FamilyID=FE8EB7EA-68DA-4331-9D38-BDBF9FA2C266&displaylang=en.*

−Yogesh Mehta
Program Manager, Windows Security

Other AD CS Enhancements

Finally, let's briefly hear from one of our experts on the product team at Microsoft concerning two more enhancements to AD CS in Windows Server 2008. Our first sidebar outlines some important changes to V3 certificate templates and the cryptographic algorithms they support in Windows Server 2008 (and in Windows Vista):

From the Experts: V3 Certificate Templates

One important change in Windows Server 2008 and Windows Vista is the support for CNG (Suite-B). With Suite-B algorithms, it is possible to use alternate and customized cryptographic algorithms for encryption and signing certificates.

To support these algorithms, a new certificate template version was added—V3. A V3 certificate template is enhanced in the following ways:

■ Support for asymmetric algorithms implemented by a Key Service Provider (KSP) for CNG. By default, Windows implements the following algorithms: DSA, ECDH_P256, ECDH_P384, ECDH_P521, ECDSA_P256, ECDSA_P384, ECDSA_P521, and RSA.

- Support for hash algorithms implemented by a KSP. By default, Windows implements the following algorithms: MD2, MD4, MD5, SHA1, SHA256, SHA384, and SHA512.

- A discrete signature (PKCS#1 V2.1) can be required for certificate requests. Activating this option forces a client that uses the certificate autoenrollment functionality or enrolls a certificate through the Certificates MMC snap-in to generate a certificate request that carries a discrete signature. Selecting this option does not mean that a certificate that is issued from this template also carries a discrete signature. The setting applies to the certificate request only. Also, the setting is not relevant for certificate requests that are created with the certreq.exe command-line tool.

- The Advanced Encryption Standard (AES) algorithm can be specified to encrypt private keys while they are transferred to the CA.

- For machine templates, read permissions on the private key can be added to the Network Service so that services such as IIS have permission to use certificates and keys that are available in the computer's certificate store. In previous versions of Windows, manually adjusting permissions on the computer's certificate store is required.

- The list of asymmetric algorithms is filtered based on the template purpose in the Request Handling tab.

–Oded Shekel
Program Manager, Windows Security

And our second sidebar describes the new restricted enrollment agent functionality in Windows Server 2008's implementation of Enterprise CA:

From the Experts: Restricted Enrollment Agent

Enrollment agents are one or more authorized individuals within an organization. The enrollment agent needs to be issued an Enrollment Agent certificate, which enables the agent to enroll for certificates on behalf of users. Enrollment agents are typically members of the corporate security, IT security, or help desk teams because these individuals have already been trusted with safeguarding valuable resources. In some organizations, such as banks that have many branches, help desk and security workers might not be conveniently located to perform this task. In this case, designating a branch manager or other trusted employee to act as an enrollment agent is required.

The Windows Server 2003 Enterprise CA does not provide any configurable means to control enrollment agents except from enrollment agents' certificates enforcement. The enrollment agent certificate is a certificate containing the Certificate Request Agent application policy extension (OID=1.3.6.1.4.1.311.20.2.1).

The restricted enrollment agent is a new functionality that allows limiting the permissions that enrollment agents have for enrolling on behalf of other users. On a Windows Server 2008 Enterprise CA, an enrollment agent can be permitted for one or many certificate templates. For each certificate template, you can configure which users or security groups the enrollment agent can enroll on behalf of. You cannot constrain an enrollment agent based on a certain Active Directory organizational unit (OU) or container. As mentioned previously, you must use security groups. Note that the restricted Enterprise enrollment agent is not available on a Standard CA.

–*Oded Shekel*
Program Manager, Windows Security

Active Directory Federation Services

Active Directory Federation Services (AD FS) is another important part of the overall IDA solution provided by Windows Server 2008. AD FS is designed to address a situation that is common in business nowadays—a partner or client that resides on a different network has to access a Web application exposed by your own organization's extranet. In a typical scenario, the client has to enter secondary credentials to this when she tries to access a Web page on your extranet. That's because the client's credentials on her own network might not be compatible or might not even be known by the directory service running on your own network.

AD FS is designed to eliminate the need for entering such secondary credentials by providing a mechanism for supporting single sign-on (SSO) between different directories running on different networks. AD FS does this by providing the ability to create trust relationships between the two directories that can be used to project a client's identity and access rights from her own network to networks belonging to trusted business partners. By deploying one or more federation servers in multiple organizations, federated business-to-business (B2B) partnerships can also be established to facilitate B2B transactions between trusted partners.

To deploy AD FS, at least one of the networks involved must be running either AD DS or AD LDS. AD FS has been around since Windows Server 2003 R2, but it has been enhanced in several ways in Windows Server 2008. For example, AD FS is now easier to install and configure in Windows Server 2008 because it can be added as a server role using Server Manager. AD FS is also easier to administer in Windows Server 2008, and the process of setting up a federated trust between two organizations by exporting and importing policy files is now simpler and more robust. Finally, AD FS now includes improved application support and is more tightly integrated with Microsoft Office SharePoint Services 2007 and also the Active Directory Rights Management Services (AD RMS) component of Windows Server 2008.

Let's learn some more about the improved import/export functionality in AD FS in Windows Server 2008 from some of our product group experts:

From the Experts: Using Import/Export Functionality to More Efficiently Create Federation Trusts

There's no doubt about it. Setting up a federation trust between two organizations can be a daunting task because of the many sequential steps involved in manually setting up both partners for successful AD FS communications. In this scenario, both administrators are equally responsible for entering in values and addresses (that is, URIs, URLs, and claims) within the AD FS snap-in that are unique to their company's federation environment.

Once this initial setup phase has been completed, each administrator must then provide these values to the administrator in the other organization so that a federation trust can be properly established. Even when these values are sent to the intended partner administrator, there is the distinct possibility that an administrator can accidentally type in a value incorrectly and inadvertently cause himself or herself many hours of headaches trying to locate the source of the problem with the new trust.

In Windows Server 2008, improvements have been made that allow partner administrators to export their generic trust policy and partner trust policy into a small xml file format that can easily be forwarded via e-mail to a partner administrator in another organization. The generic trust policy contains the Federation Server Display Name, URI, Federation Server Proxy URL, and any verification certificate information; whereas the partner trust policy file also includes information about each of the claims. With this in mind, the second-half of the federation trust can then be quickly established by importing the partner's trust policy and mapping the claims.

This "export and e-mail" process adds the following benefits for the partner administrator who receives the xml file:

- Expedites the process of establishing a federation trust because the administrator can choose to import the contents of the xml file in the Add Partner Wizard and simply click through the wizard pages to verify that the imported settings are suitable

- Eliminates the additional step of importing the account verification certificate because the import process does this automatically

- Provides for easy claim mapping

- Eliminates the possibility of manual typing errors

You can test-drive this new functionality by walking through the Windows Server 2008 version of the AD FS Step-by-Step Guide.

−Nick Pierson
  Technical Writer of CSD (Connected System Division) UA team

−Lu Zhao
  Program Manager, Active Directory Federation Service

−Aurash Behbahani
  Software Design Engineer, Active Directory Federation Service

Another new feature of AD FS in Windows Server 2008 is the ability to use Group Policy to prevent setting up unauthorized federation servers in your domain. Here's how some of our experts at Microsoft describe this enhancement:

From the Experts: Limiting Federation Service Deployment Using Group Policy

In Windows Server 2003 R2, AD FS did not provide control mechanisms that prevented users from installing or configuring their own federation service. In Windows Server 2008, AD FS administrators can now turn on Group Policy settings that prevent unauthorized federation servers in their domain. This new setting helps to satisfy the needs of an IT department when they want to enforce compliance or legal process requirements.

Once the Group Policy setting has been enabled, the value *DisallowFederationService* is inserted into the registry key on each federation server in that domain. Before an AD DS domain-joined computer running the Windows Server 2008 operating system can install the Federation Service server role, the server first checks to make sure that the Don't Allow Non-authorized Federation Servers In This Domain Group Policy setting is enabled. If this setting is enabled, the installation of the Federation Service will fail. If it is not enabled, which is the default setting, installation of a Federation Service will be allowed and the installed Federation Service will function normally.

The registry key value is checked only when the trust policy file is loaded, so there might be a delay between when the update appears that brings down the policy and when the Federation Service observes the policy. By default, the policy is read when a file change notification is received and also once every hour.

Note that this feature applies only to Windows Server 2008 federation servers and does not affect new or existing installations of a Federation Service in Windows Server 2003 R2.

–*Lu Zhao*
 Program Manager, Active Directory Federation Service

–*Nick Pierson*
 Technical Writer of CSD (Connected System Division) UA team

Finally, AD FS can be integrated with AD CS, but when problems occur with this scenario you need to know how to troubleshoot them. Here are some more of our experts explaining how to do this:

From the Experts: Troubleshooting Certificate Revocation Issues

Certificate issues are among the top five AD FS troubleshooting hot spots for the product support team here at Microsoft. One particular AD FS-related certificate issue centers on a known routine process that checks for the validity of a certificate by comparing it to a CA-issued list of revoked certificates. This process, in the world of PKI, is known as certificate revocation list (CRL) checking.

The revocation verification setting configured for an account partner on a federation server is used by the federation server to determine how revocation verification will be performed for tokens sent by that account partner. The revocation verification setting of the federation server itself, configured on the Trust Policy node of the AD FS snap-in, is used by the federation server and by any AD FS Web agent bound to the federation server to determine how the revocation verification process will be performed for the federation server's own token signing certificate. The verification process will make use of CRLs imported on the local machine or that are available through the CRL Distribution Point.

When troubleshooting certificate issues, it is important to be able to quickly disable revocation checking to help you locate the source of the problem. For example, this can be helpful in deployment scenarios where there are no CRLs available for the token-signing certificates.

To help troubleshoot CRL-checking issues, the AD FS product team has provided a method within the AD FS snap-in in Windows Server 2008 where you can adjust or disable how revocation checking behaves within the scope of a federation service. For example, you can set revocation checking to check for the validity of all the certificates in a certificate chain or only the end certificate in the certificate chain.

–Nick Pierson
 Technical Writer of CSD (Connected System Division) UA team

–Lu Zhao
 Program Manager, Active Directory Federation Service

–Aurash Behbahani
 Software Design Engineer, Active Directory Federation Service

–Marcelo Mas
 Software Design Engineer in Testing, Active Directory Federation Service

Active Directory Rights Management Services

The last (but certainly not least) IDA component in Windows Server 2008 that we'll look at is Active Directory Rights Management Service (AD RMS). As we mentioned at the beginning of this chapter, AD RMS is the follow-up to Windows RMS. Windows RMS is an optional component for the Windows Server 2003 platform that can be used to protect sensitive information stored in documents, in e-mail messages, and on Web sites from unauthorized viewing, modification, or use. AD RMS is designed to work together with RMS-enabled applications such as the Microsoft Office 2007 System and Internet Explorer 7.0, and it also includes a set of core APIs that developers can use to code their own RMS-enabled apps or add RMS functionality to existing apps.

AD RMS works as a client/server system in which an AD RMS server issues rights account certificates that identify trusted entities such as users and services that are permitted to publish rights-protected content. Once a user has been issued such a certificate, the user can assign usage rights and conditions to any content that needs to be protected. For example, the user could assign a condition to an e-mail message that prevents users who read the message from forwarding it to other users. The way this works is that a publishing license is created for the protected content and this license binds the specified usage rights to the piece of content. When the content is distributed, the usage rights are distributed together with it, and users both inside and outside the organization are constrained by the usage rights defined for the content.

Users who receive rights-protected content also require a rights account certificate to access this content. When the recipient of rights-protected content attempts to view or work with this content, the user's RMS-enabled application sends a request to the AD RMS server to request permission to consume this content. The AD RMS licensing service then issues a unique use license that reads, interprets, and applies the usage rights and conditions specified in the publishing licenses. These usage rights and conditions then persist and are automatically applied wherever the content goes. AD RMS relies upon AD DS to verify that a user attempting to consume rights-protected content has the authorization to do so.

AD RMS has been enhanced in several ways in Windows Server 2008 compared with its implementation in Windows Server 2003. These enhancements include an improved installation experience whereby AD RMS can be added as a role using Server Manager; an MMC snap-in for managing AD RMS servers rather than the Web-based interface used in the previous platform; self-enrollment of the AD RMS cluster without the need of Internet connectivity; integration with AD FS to facilitate leveraging existing federated relationships between partners; and the ability to use different AD RMS roles to more effectively delegate the administration of AD RMS servers, policies and settings, rights policy templates, and log files and reports.

Conclusion

Identity and access is key to how businesses communicate in today's connected world. Active Directory in Windows Server 2008 is a significant advance in the evolution of a single, unified, and integrated IDA solution for businesses running Windows-based networks that need to connect to other businesses that are running either Windows or non-Windows networks. Keeping the big picture for IDA in mind helps us to see how all these various improvements to Active Directory work together to provide a powerful platform that can unleash the power of identity for your enterprise.

I know, the Marketing Police are knocking at my door after that last sentence and they want to get me for that one. But whether it sounds like marketing gobbledygook or not, it's true!

Additional Resources

The starting point for finding information about all things IDA on Microsoft platforms is *http://www.microsoft.com/ida/*. Although this link currently redirects you to *http://www.microsoft.com/windowsserver2003/technologies/idm/default.mspx*, I have a feeling this will change as Windows Server 2008 approaches RTM.

The Windows Server 2008 main site on Microsoft.com also has a general overview called "Identity and Access in Windows Server Longhorn" that you can read at *http://www.microsoft.com/windowsserver/longhorn/ida-mw.mspx*. By the time you read it, there probably will be more details on the site than there are at the time of writing this.

You can also find a developer-side overview of the directory, identity, and access services included in Windows platforms (including Windows Server 2008) on MSDN at *http://msdn2.microsoft.com/en-us/library/aa139675.aspx*.

If you have access to the Windows Server 2008 beta program on Microsoft Connect (*http://connect.microsoft.com*), you can get a lot of detailed information about AD DS, AD CS, AD FS, and so on. First, you'll find the following Step-By-Step guides (and probably others will be there by the time you read this):

- Installing, Configuring, and Troubleshooting OCSP
- Auditing Active Directory Domain Services Changes
- Active Directory Domain Services Backup and Recovery
- Planning, Deploying, and Using a Read-Only Domain Controller
- Restartable Active Directory

- Certificate Settings

- Active Directory Rights Management Services

- Identity Federation with Active Directory Rights Management Services

- Active Directory Domain Services Installation and Removal

- Active Directory Federation Services

Be sure also to turn to Chapter 14, "Additional Resources," for more sources of information concerning the Windows server core installation option, and also for links to webcasts, whitepapers, blogs, newsgroups, and other sources of information about all aspects of Windows Server 2008.

Chapter 8
Terminal Services Enhancements

In this chapter:

Core Enhancements to Terminal Services 190

Terminal Services RemoteApp. 216

Terminal Services Web Access 226

Terminal Services Gateway. 232

Terminal Services Licensing 238

Other Terminal Services Enhancements. 243

Conclusion 249

Additional Resources. 250

Terminal Services has been available on the Microsoft Windows platform since the days of Windows NT 4.0. So most readers of this book (all seasoned IT pros, I'll bet) have some familiarity with it as a group of technologies that provides access to the full Windows desktop from almost any computing device, including other Windows computers, Mobile PC devices, thin clients, and so on. When you access a terminal server from one of these devices, the server is doing all the hard work of running your applications, while a protocol named Remote Desktop Protocol (RDP) sends keyboard and mouse input from client to server and displays information in return. In addition to enabling administrators to run programs remotely like this, Terminal Services also lets administrators remotely control Windows computers that have Remote Desktop (a Terminal Services feature) enabled on them.

Anyway, if you work in a medium-sized organization, you likely have at least one Windows terminal server running either Windows 2000 Server or Windows Server 2003. And larger enterprises likely have a whole farm of them load-balanced together. Either way, you need to take a good hard look at what improvements are coming to Terminal Services in Windows Server 2008, and that's what this chapter is about.

Because this book is brief and covers so many different new features and enhancements found in Windows Server 2008, I'm going to assume you're already familiar with basic Terminal Services concepts and terminology, including Remote Desktop Protocol (RDP), the two Terminal Services clients (Remote Desktop Connection and the Remote Desktop Web Connection ActiveX control), the two Terminal Service modes (Remote Desktop for Administration and the Terminal Server role), and Terminal Services Session Broker—plus various other things, such as console session, client resource redirection, and the different tools (MMC snap-ins, Group Policy, WMI scripts) you can use to configure and manage Terminal servers and their clients. If you're not up to speed on any of these topics, you can find a good overview a whitepaper titled "Technical Overview of Windows Server 2003 Terminal Services," which is available from *http://go.microsoft.com/?linkid=2606110*. Another good general source of information concerning Terminal Services is the Windows Server 2003 Terminal Services Technology Center found at *http://www.microsoft.com/windowsserver2003/ technologies/terminalservices/default.mspx*. Or you can just buy a mainframe if you find your server room too quiet for your liking. (See Chapter 3, "Windows Server Virtualization," for why we need to bring back the mainframe–remember those days? You can probably get one at a bargain on eBay.)

Because there have been so many enhancements to Terminal Services in Windows Server 2008, we'll need a roadmap to navigate this chapter. So here's a quick list of the new and enhanced features we're going to cover:

- Core Enhancements to Terminal Services
- Terminal Services RemoteApp
- Terminal Services Web Access
- Terminal Services Gateway
- Terminal Services Easy Print
- Terminal Services Session Broker
- Terminal Services Licensing
- Terminal Services WMI Provider
- Deploying Terminal Services
- Other Terminal Services Enhancements

Before we start looking at these enhancements, however, be warned–I'm not just going describe their features. I'll also provide you with tons of valuable insights, recommendations, and troubleshooting tips from the people who are bringing you Terminal Services in Windows Server 2008. In other words, you'll hear from members of the Terminal Services product team themselves! Well, that's not a warning, is it? Do you warn your kids at the end of June by saying, "Warning, summer vacation ahead?"

Core Enhancements to Terminal Services

Windows Server 2008 has a number of core improvements in how Terminal Service works. Most of the improvements we'll look at were first introduced in Windows Vista, but for some of these enhancements to work in Windows Vista you need Windows Server 2008 running on the back end as your terminal server. Many of these improvements center around changes to the Remote Desktop Connection client that comes with Windows Vista and Windows Server 2008, so let's begin there. After that, we'll look at some core changes on the server side that change some of the ways Terminal Services operates and that terminal server admins need to know about. Finally, we'll briefly look at how to install Terminal Services, and then move on to other new features such as TS Gateway, TS Web Access, and TS RemoteApp.

Remote Desktop Connection 6.0

On previous versions of Windows, there were effectively two Terminal Services clients:

- Remote Desktop Connection, a Win32 client application that is the "full" Terminal Services client and is included in Windows XP and Windows Server 2003. You could also download a version of this client (msrdpcli.exe) that could be installed on earlier Windows versions to provide similar functionality.

- Remote Desktop Web Connection, an ActiveX control you could download from a Web page running on IIS and then use to connect over the Internet to a terminal server. Remote Desktop Web Connection has slightly less functionality than the full Terminal Services client but is easy to deploy—just download it using a Web browser and you can open a Terminal Services session within your Web browser.

Starting with Windows Vista, however (and in Windows Server 2008 too), this ActiveX control has been integrated into the Remote Desktop Connection client, so there is only one client now and users don't have to download anything to access terminal servers over the Internet. This is good because some organizations might have security policies in place that prevent users from downloading ActiveX controls onto their client machines.

This new version 6.0 client (which is also available for Windows XP Service Pack 2—see article 925876 in the Microsoft Knowledge Base for more info) provides a number of significant improvements in the areas of user experience and security. Let's look at security first.

Network Level Authentication and Server Authentication

Remote Desktop Connection 6.0 (let's shorten this to RDC 6.0) supports Network Level Authentication (NLA), a new authentication method that authenticates the user, the client machine, and server credentials against each other. This means client authentication is now performed before a Terminal Services session is even spun up and the user is presented with a logon screen. With previous RDC clients, the Terminal Services session is started as soon as the user clicks Connect, and this can create a window of opportunity for malicious users to perform denial of services attacks or steal credentials via man-in-the-middle attacks.

To configure NLA, open the System item from Control Panel, click Remote Settings, and select the third option as shown here:

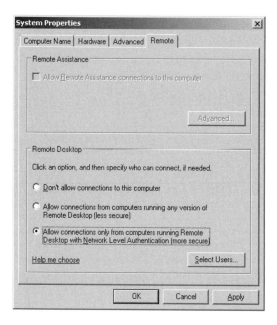

The other security enhancement in RDP 6.0 is Server Authentication, which uses Transport Layer Security (TLS) and enables clients to be sure that they are connecting to the legitimate terminal server and not some rogue server masquerading as the legitimate one. To ensure Server Authentication is used on the client side, open RDC and on the Advanced tab select the Don't Connect If Authentication Fails (Most Secure) setting from the drop-down list box (the default setting is Warn Me If Authentication Fails).

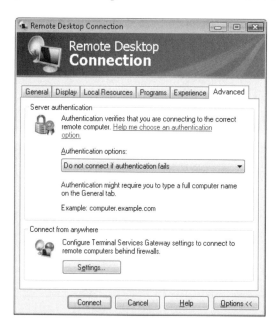

You can also configure Server Authentication using the Terminal Services Configuration snap-in. Using Network Level Authentication together with Server Authentication can help reduce the threat of denial of service attacks and man-in-the-middle attacks.

Display Improvements

RDC 6.0 also provides users with a considerably enhanced user experience in the area of display improvements. For one thing, Terminal Services sessions now support a maximum display resolution of 4096 × 2048. (Boy, I wish I had a monitor that supported that!) And although before only 4:3 display resolution ratios were supported, now you can define custom resolutions like 16:9 or 16:10 to get the more cinematic experience supported by today's wide-screen monitors. Setting a custom resolution can be done from the RDC UI or by editing a saved .rdp file using Notepad or by starting RDC from a command line using switches—that is, typing **mstsc /w:*width* /h:*height*** at a command prompt.

Another display improvement is support for spanned monitors—that is, spreading the display across multiple monitors. Note that to do this you have to make sure that all your monitors have the same resolution configured and their total resolution doesn't exceed 4096 × 2048. Additionally, you can span monitors only horizontally, not vertically (better for the neck, actually) using the /span switch.

A third display improvement is that RDC now supports full 32-bit color depth, which means that users can now experience maximum color quality when running applications in Terminal Services sessions. Personally, I can't tell the difference between True Color (24-bit) and Highest Quality (32-bit), but I suppose someone who works with Photoshop can quickly notice the difference. To get 32-bit color, you need to configure it both on the client (on the Display tab of the RDC properties) and on the terminal server, which must be running Windows Server 2008. Or you can configure 32-bit color from the server by opening the Terminal Services Configuration snap-in and double-clicking on the RDP connection you want to configure (like the default RDP-Tcp connection). Then switch to the Client Settings tab of the connection's properties dialog box and change the color depth to 32 bits per pixel. In fact, 32-bit color is now the default; this is because for typical higher-color applications, such as IE and PowerPoint, the new compression engine in RDP6 typically sends less data over the network in 32-bit color mode rather than in 24-bit color mode. If you need high color you should consider 15-bit, 16-bit, and 32-bit color before you consider 24-bit.

Yet another display enhancement is support for ClearType in Terminal Services sessions. This feature of RDC 6.0 is known as *font smoothing* because it makes the fonts of displayed text a lot easier to read. You can enable this on RDC by selecting the Font Smoothing check box on the Experience tab.

To ensure font smoothing is enabled on the server side of your Windows Server 2008 terminal server, open Appearance And Personalization from Control Panel, click Personalization, click Windows Color And Appearance, click Effects, and make sure ClearType is selected.

Let's now hear from one of our experts at Microsoft concerning the new font-smoothing feature of Terminal Services in Windows Server 2008.

From the Experts: Pros and Cons of Font Smoothing

ClearType is a Microsoft font smoothing technique that improves the readability of text on LCD screens. With the proliferation of LCD screens and the release of Windows Vista and Microsoft Office 12, ClearType has become very important. Most of the fonts available in Vista and Office 12 are tuned for ClearType and look ugly when it is turned off. For these reasons, the Terminal Services team decided to give the end user the option to turn on ClearType. You can get ClearType in RDP 6.0 by going to the Experience tab and selecting Enable Font Smoothing.

But the high fidelity of ClearType comes at a cost. Normally (with font smoothing disabled), fonts are remoted (sent across the wire) as glyphs. Remote Desktop Protocol remotes glyphs efficiently and caches them to reduce bandwidth consumption. With ClearType enabled, fonts are remoted as bitmaps and not as glyphs. Remote Desktop Protocol does not remote these bitmaps efficiently, resulting in increased bandwidth consumption. From our initial internal testing, we found that the impact of enabling ClearType for text editing/scrolling scenarios could range from 4 to 10 times the bandwidth consumed when the scenario was run with ClearType disabled.

−Somesh Goel
* Software Development Engineer in Test, Terminal Services*

Display Data Prioritization

I'm separating out this feature from the other display-related improvements because it's related both to display experience and to network utilization. In previous versions of RDC, you could be doing stuff on your remoted desktop when you decided to print a long document or transfer a large file, and then suddenly your keyboard/mouse responded sluggishly and your display became jerky and slow to update. What was happening? The file or print operation was consuming most of the available bandwidth between your client machine and the terminal server, and as a result, the RDP stuff (keyboard, mouse, display info) was having trouble getting through.

RDC 6.0 solves this problem by using a new feature called *display data prioritization*, which automatically controls virtual channel traffic so that your keyboard, mouse, and display data is given a higher priority than other virtual channel traffic (such as the file and print data). The result of this prioritization is that your mouse and keyboard won't become sluggish and your display won't be adversely affected when you perform bandwidth-intensive actions like this.

The default setting for display data prioritization in Windows Vista and Windows Server 2008 is 70% allocated for display/input data and 30% for everything else. This ratio can be adjusted by modifying certain DWORD registry values located under the HKLM\SYSTEM\CurrentControlSet\Services\TermDD registry key on your terminal server. The values you can tweak are these:

- Setting *FlowControlDisable* to 1 disables display data prioritization, and all requests are then handled on a first-in-first-out (FIFO) basis.

- *FlowControlDisplayBandwidth* specifies the relative priority for display/input data; its default value is 70, and its maximum value is 255.

- *FlowControlChannelBandwidth* specifies the relative priority for all other data; its default value is 30, and its maximum value is 255.

- Setting *FlowControlChargePostCompression* to 0 means that flow control calculates bandwidth allocation based on precompression bytes, although setting it to 1 uses postcompression bytes. (The default is 0.)

The key values you probably want to tweak are *FlowControlDisplayBandwidth* and *FlowControlChannelBandwidth*, as it's the ratio between these two values (not their absolute values) that defines the display data prioritization ratio for your server.

Desktop Experience

RDC 6.0 also enhances the user's desktop experience by offering the option to provide users with desktop themes, photo management, Windows Media Player, and other desktop experiences provided by Windows PCs. Previous versions of Terminal Services didn't provide this. Instead, users who use RDP to connect to terminal servers were presented with a Windows Server 2008 desktop look and feel that couldn't be customized using themes, while popular applications such as Windows Media Player were also unavailable for them to use.

To get the full desktop experience in a Terminal Services session, however, you need both RDC 6.0 on the client plus Windows Server 2008 as your terminal server. To enable desktop experience on the server, log on to your terminal server as administrator, start Server Manager, right-click the Features node, and select Add Feature from the context menu. When the Add Feature Wizard appears, select the check box beside Desktop Experience and continue through the wizard. After that, you need to start the Themes service on your server and con-figure the theme you want users to have in their sessions. Note that you don't have to do any-thing on the client side, as support for the full desktop experience is built into the RDC 6.0 client.

Desktop Composition

This enables the full Windows Aero desktop experience with its translucent windows, thumb-nail-sized taskbar button window previews, and Flip 3D to be remoted. Desktop composition requires that client computers be running Windows Vista and that they have hardware that can support the full Aero experience. Remote desktop composition is supported only in two instances:

- Remote Desktop to a Windows Server running terminal services in single user mode
- Remote Desktop to a Windows Vista host machine

To enable desktop composition, first configure desktop experience on the terminal server, and then configure the server to use the Windows Vista theme. Then on the client, open the RDP properties, switch to the Experience tab, and select the Desktop Composition check box.

Plug and Play Device Redirection Framework

RDC 6.0 also supports redirection of specific Plug and Play (PnP) devices in Terminal Services sessions, and it includes inbox support for redirection of Windows Portable Devices—that is, media players based on the Media Transfer Protocol (MTP) and digital cameras based on the Picture Transfer Protocol (PTP). PnP device redirection is designed to allow applications to access PnP devices seamlessly, regardless of whether they run locally or remotely, and it works with both full Terminal Services remote desktop sessions and with TS Remote App.

When you launch your Terminal Services session, the redirected PnP device is automatically installed in the remote session, and PnP notifications and AutoPlay popups will appear in the remote session. The redirected device is scoped to that particular remote session only and is not accessible from any other session, either remote or console, on the remote computer. To enable PnP device redirection on the client, open the RDP properties, select the Local Resources tab, click More, and select the appropriate check boxes.

Selecting the Devices That I Plug In Later check box lets you see PnP devices get installed on the remote machine when you plug the PnP device into your local machine while the Terminal Services session to is active. Or you can enable PnP device redirection from the server by opening the Terminal Services Configuration snap-in, double-clicking on the RDP connection you want to configure, switching to the Client Settings tab, and selecting the Supported Plug And Play Devices check box.

Once the redirected PnP device is installed on the remote machine, the device is available for use within your Terminal Services session and can be accessed directly from applications running on the server, such as RemoteApp programs you have launched from your client machine. Note that PnP device redirection doesn't work over cascaded terminal server connections.

How does PnP device redirection work under the hood? Let's gain some insight by listening to another one of our Microsoft experts who works on the Terminal Services team:

From the Experts: Inside the PnP Device Redirection Framework

One new feature in Microsoft Windows Vista was support for redirecting certain Plug and Play devices over a Remote Desktop Connection. Windows Server 2008 now adds this functionality to server scenarios. Although Windows Server 2008 includes only in-box support for Windows Portable Devices and Point of Service for .NET 1.11 devices, the PnP Device Redirection Framework is generic enough to support a variety of devices. PnP device redirection works by redirecting I/O request packets (IRPs). This approach provides several advantages. The server needs only a generic redirected device driver, rather than requiring a function driver for each device a client could possibly redirect.

This also protects the server from possible instability caused by problematic third-party device drivers. On the client, IRP redirection allows local applications to continue to use a device while it is being redirected, and the same device can also be redirected to several simultaneous remote sessions.

When a new connection is established with device redirection enabled, terminal server creates a proxy device node on the server for each device being redirected. Windows then starts WUDFhost.exe, which then loads usbdr.dll to act as the driver for each redirected device. One instance of WUDFhost.exe can support multiple devices, which improves terminal server's scalability. When a server-side application calls *NtCreateFile* on a redirected device, usbdr.dll forwards this call over the RDP connection. On the client, Remote Desktop Connection then calls *NtCreateFile* on the real device and returns the result to the server. Additional I/O operations are handled in a similar manner.

A generic redirected device driver is included, but special handling is needed for certain types of devices. For example, a digital camera needs to be identified as such so that the Windows Shell can provide the appropriate user interface. Likewise, additional information is needed about portable media players so that Windows Media Player will recognize that it can synchronize with the device. If the redirected device is a Point of Service for .NET device, additional steps are taken to enable it with Microsoft Point of Service for .NET 1.11.

Third parties can add support for redirecting their devices as well, provided several requirements are met. It is recommended that redirected device drivers be based on the User-Mode Device Framework, although this is not strictly required. The driver's INF file needs several additional sections to support the redirected version of the device. Windows Server 2008 includes the file ts_generic.inf, which can be included in driver INF files to easily add specific support for redirection. Including ts_generic.inf instructs Windows Server 2008 to use usbdr.dll as the device driver during a Terminal Services session, and usbdr.dll will automatically forward all operations to the client-side device driver. The relevant sections can be referenced using *Include=* and *Needs=* directives in the driver's new sections describing the device in redirected scenarios. These added sections might also provide additional hints to optimize the driver under redirection, as was done for Windows Portable Devices and Point of Service for .NET devices.

–*Eric Holk*
  Software Design Engineer, Terminal Services

Microsoft POS for .NET Device Redirection

RDC 6.0 also supports redirection of Microsoft Point of Service (POS) for .NET 1.1 devices. Microsoft POS for .NET 1.1 is a class library that provides an interface for .NET applications to allow them to communicate with and run POS peripheral devices—for example, bar-code scanners, biometrics devices, and magnetic card readers. Note that Microsoft POS for .NET 1.1 device redirection is supported only for x86-based terminal servers running Windows Server 2008.

Terminal Services Easy Print

Another enhanced device redirection feature of Windows Server 2008 is Terminal Services (TS) Easy Print. This enhancement greatly improves printer redirection by eliminating the need for administrators to install any printer drivers on the terminal server while guaranteeing client printer redirection and the availability of printer properties for use in remote sessions. TS Easy Print leverages the new XPS print path used in Windows Vista and Windows Server 2008, and here's another of our product team experts to tell us more about it:

From the Experts: Inside TS Easy Print

In the past, to successfully redirect a given printer, the proper driver needed to be installed on both the TS client machine and TS server machine. As many customers have experienced, the requirement of having the TS server host a matching printer driver caused configuration problems on the server. Simply put, this requirement had to go. As a result, TS Easy Print presents a printing redirection solution that is "driverless." The only driver required is the TS Easy Print system that comes installed by default.

The implementation of this solution comes in two pieces.

The first piece is presenting the user with printing preferences through the UI so that he can configure the print job on any arbitrary printer. Instead of creating some server-side UI that shows the bare minimum of preferences users need (such as number of copies, landscape vs. portrait, and so on) and applying this UI to all printers, the TS Easy Print driver acts as a proxy and redirects all calls for the UI to the actual driver on the client side. When the user goes to edit preferences for a print job on a redirected printer, the TS client launches this UI from the local machine on top of the remote session. As a result, the user sees the same detailed printer-specific UI (ensuring that all printer options are available to the user) he would see if he were printing something locally. This is what creates the more "consistent printing experience." The user's selected preferences are then redirected to the server for use when printing.

The second piece is the ability to send a print job from the server to the client and reliably print the job. To do so, we take advantage of Microsoft's new document format, XPS. When redirecting print jobs, on the server, we create an XPS file using the preferences the user has selected, send the XPS file to the client, and, with the help of other printing components, print the job on the appropriate printer. The biggest advantage to using the XPS format is that it provides a high-quality print rendering system that is agnostic to the printer the job will actually be printed on.

–Zardosht Kasheff
  Software Design Engineer, Terminal Services

Single Sign-On for Domain-joined Clients

A key enhancement of Terminal Services in Windows Server 2008 is the ability to allow users with domain accounts to log on once and gain access to the terminal server without being asked to enter their credentials again. This new feature is called single sign-on (SSO), and it can work with both password-based logons and smart card logons. It's designed to make it easier for enterprises to run business applications using terminal servers–users can use SSO when running either the full Remote Desktop or individual RemoteApp programs. I don't know about you, but I hate having to enter my password twice–I hate passwords, too, because I have so many of them to remember. Smart cards are great because all you need to remember is your PIN, but I have several smart cards, which means several PINs, which means I hate PINs too. What a world we live in!

Anyway, to implement Terminal Services SSO, you need both Windows Vista on the client side and Windows Server 2008 running on the back end for your terminal server. Plus you need an Active Directory domain environment. Enabling SSO is a two-step process that requires configuring authentication on the Terminal Server and then configuring the client to allow default credentials to be used for logging on to your terminal servers.

To enable SSO on the terminal server, open the Terminal Services Configuration snap-in, double-click on the RDP connection you want to configure, switch to the General tab, and make sure either Negotiate or SSL (TLS 1.0) is selected for Security Layer. (The default is Negotiate.) Configuring SSO on the client can be done using Group Policy by enabling the Computer Configuration\Administrative Templates\System\Credentials Delegation\Allow Delegating Default Credentials policy setting and adding your terminal servers to the list of servers for this policy.

To configure clients for SSO to a TS Gateway server, you need to enable the User Configuration\Administrative Templates\Windows Components\Terminal Services\TS Gateway\Set TS Gateway Server Authentication Method policy setting and set it to Use Locally Logged-On Credentials. And, if you do this, you should also select the Allow Users To Change This Setting check box as shown here:

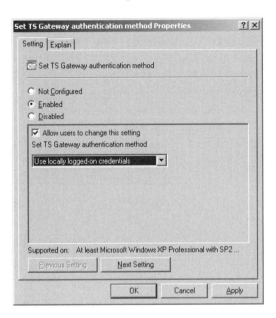

The reason behind this check box is that TS Gateway supports Group Policy settings slightly differently than other Windows components. Normally, Group Policy settings are enforced so that end users can't change them. But when Group Policy is enabled for TS Gateway and this check box is selected, end users can change the way they authenticate with the TS Gateway server, for example, by using another user account to authenticate with the TS Gateway server. So enabling this setting as described above while also selecting this check box means that the TS Gateway admin is only suggesting the setting instead of enforcing it.

Other Core Enhancements

There are other core enhancements to how Terminal Services works in Windows Server 2008, and to hear an explanation of these changes let's listen to another of our experts from the Terminal Server team at Microsoft. First, here's a description of an under-the-hood change in how the core Terminal Services engine works in Windows Server 2008.

From the Experts: Terminal Services Core Engine Improvements

In Windows Vista and Windows Server 2008, we did a bunch of improvements to the core TS engine. The core engine (termsrv.dll) was split into two components: lsm.exe (the core session manager component), and the termsrv.dll (which takes care of remote connectivity).

LSM stands for Local Session Manager. It's one of the core system processes started during boot, and it does session management. LSM also interacts with other key system components—such as smss.exe, winlogon.exe, logonui.exe, csrss.exe, and win32k.sys—to make sure that the rest of the OS is in sync with session management operations, loading the appropriate graphics driver, unloading the driver during session disconnect, and so on. The LSM manages all connections and provides Vista with features such as Fast User Switching (FUS) even if Remote Desktop isn't enabled.

The Termsrv service (termsrv.dll running inside svchost.exe) hosts the listener, which talks to a kernel-mode TDI driver to listen for incoming connection requests. It also does a bunch of session arbitration, interacts with License Server, supports Media Center extender sessions, talks to RDP layers in the protocol stack, and also communicates with LSM.

Because of this, when someone needs to turn off remote connections, it can be done without turning off Fast User Switching (FUS), which enables multiple users to use the machine locally without a user ever having to log off! This is because LSM takes care of all the session management functionality needed by FUS.

The other significant benefit here is security—only LSM runs with system privilege, and all the termsrv.dll code runs with network service privilege, which is at a much lesser privilege level. Only one-third of the old Termsrv code runs in LSM; hence, this is significant attack surface reduction when compared to Windows XP and Windows Server 2003.

–Sriram Sampath
Development Lead, Terminal Services

The next sidebar deals with the impact that session 0 isolation has for those developing Terminal Services applications. *Session 0 isolation* is a new feature of Windows Vista and Windows Server 2008 that is designed to enhance the security of the platform. In previous versions of Windows, all services run in Session 0 together with user applications, and this poses a security risk because services run with elevated privileges and are therefore targets for malware trying to elevate privilege level. In Windows Vista and Windows Server 2008, however, services are now isolated in session 0 while user applications run in other sessions, which means that services are protected from attacks caused by exploiting faulty application code. This design change affects how applications should be developed to run on terminal servers. Let's listen to our expert explain this issue:

From the Experts: Session 0 Isolation and App Development Tips

In Windows Vista and Windows Server 2008, session 0 is reserved for running System services—no interactive user logon is permitted in session 0 (called the *console session* in Windows Server 2003—that is, the session at the physical keyboard and mouse). One of the primary reasons for sandboxing services in their own session is for security—services, such as LocalSystem, usually run under very high privilege, and user apps run with far lesser privilege. However, if both of these run in the same interactive session, the lower-privilege apps can easily attack the higher-privilege services. The most common way to do this is by using something called *shatter attacks*, which exploit the UI thrown by some services—for example, an error message UI or a status message UI.

Because services run in their own session, service writers and app developers should follow these guidelines:

- Don't assume in your code that apps will run in session 0, and don't assume that apps and services will run in the same session. For example, if your service created an event (which was not prefixed with the Global\ flag), don't assume that your app will be able to see the event (or wait on it) automatically. Explicitly create named objects with the Global\ flag if you plan to use this model.

- To determine whether the app is running in a physical console session, some apps these days check whether they are running in session ID 0. This is plain wrong to do, even in Windows XP and Windows Server 2003, but the fact of the matter is that some apps still do this. The correct way to do this check is to find the current session ID of the application using the *ProcessIdToSessionId* API. Then use the *WTSGetActiveConsoleSessionId* API to find the session ID of the physical console session; then check whether both of them are the same.

- If the services want to display a UI (say, a status message), the best way to do it is to use the *CreateProcessAsUser* API and create a process in the target user's session. This process should run with the same privileges of the logged-on user.

- If the services need to interact with the app, the best way to design it is through a regular client-server mechanism—for example, the service and the app in a different session could communicate through a protocol such as RPC or COM, and the app could do the work in the user session on behalf of the service.

–Sriram Sampath
Development Lead, Terminal Services

Actually, this whole concept of Terminal Services sessions is worth digging into further, as there are some additional significant changes in how Terminal Services works in Windows Server 2008 compared with Windows Server 2003. What is a Terminal Services session, anyway? What possible states can a session have? What happens when a session disconnects and you try to reconnect to your terminal server? How does licensing work with Terminal Services sessions? (We'll also look at Terminal Services licensing in more detail later in this chapter.) What's the difference between a user session and an administrative session? What happens when contention occurs—that is, when your session limit is exceeded and you try to connect to another session? And how has the effect of the /**console** switch changed in Windows Server 2008 for Terminal Services sessions given the session 0 isolation feature described in the previous sidebar? These are all fascinating questions that have been bugging me for a while—and here comes another expert from the Terminal Services team to explain! Let's listen and learn:

From the Experts: Understanding the Console Session

This sidebar describes in detail the changes to the console session in Windows Server 2008.

Sessions and Their States

Whenever a user logs on to a machine (locally or remotely), he gets an interactive session. A session is a defined space which contains a collection of running processes representing the system or the user and his desktop and applications.

Each session is identified by an ID. In Windows Server 2008, the first interactive user session is session 1, whether the user is logged on to the local terminal or connected remotely. The session IDs then increment as more users log on to the server. The session IDs are reused as users log off and previous sessions are terminated.

The session, during its lifetime, transits through various states. The most interesting states are active and disconnected. If a user is actively working in the session, the session is in an *active* state. And if the user is not connected to the session while his application is still running, the session is in a *disconnected* state.

Terminals—Local and Remote

Whenever a session is in an active state, the session is attached to a set of input and output devices (keyboard, mouse, monitor, and so on). This set of devices will be referred to as the *terminal* for the purposes of this discussion.

The terminal can be a local terminal—that is, the keyboard, mouse, and monitor, are physically connected to the server.

The terminal can be a remote terminal—that is, the session on the server is bound to a keyboard, mouse, and monitor on the client machine. The remote terminal is also associated with a connection. The connection is an object that contains information about the remote connection—the protocol, stack drivers, listener, session extension drivers, and so on.

When the session is disconnected, it is not attached to any terminal. When the remote session (or rather, connection) is disconnected, the remote terminal and connection objects are destroyed. The local terminal, on the other hand, is never destroyed permanently. When the session at the local terminal gets disconnected, a new "console session" is created and a new local terminal is attached to that session. In this case, although the session is not in active state, it is attached to a terminal. Such a session is said to be in a *connected* state. For example, if you list the sessions that occur while no one is logged on to a local terminal, you will notice the session state of "console" session is reported as connected (this is displaying the CTRL+ALT+DEL screen).

Session Reconnection

The disconnected sessions might get reattached to different terminals, local or remote, when reconnect happens. The following example illustrates the sequence of events that takes place during a disconnect and reconnect scenario that involves logon at a local terminal:

1. When a user logs on to the local terminal, a session (session 1) is attached to the local terminal and is in the active state. The session local terminal is displayed on the local terminal; the name of the session is "console."

2. When the user disconnects (or locks) the session, the session gets disconnected. At this point, session 1 is not attached to any terminal. When the local terminal is terminated, it creates a new session (session 2) that represents the local terminal (displaying the CTRL+ALT+DEL screen). A new local terminal is created and is attached to session 2. Session 2 is now in connected state. The session 1 remains in disconnected state. The name "console" is now assigned to session 2.

3. When the same user connects remotely to the server, a new remote terminal is created. By default, each user is restricted to single session. Because this user already had a disconnected session, his new remote terminal gets attached to the already existing session (session 1). Session 1 state changes to the active state with a remote terminal attached to it.

4. When the user disconnects the session, the remote terminal is destroyed and session 1 remains in the disconnected state.

5. Session 1 terminates only when the user initiates logoff or the administrator forcefully logs off that session using admin tools.

Meaning and Purpose of /console and /admin

In Windows Server 2003, the "console" is a special session with ID 0. This session is always bound to the local terminal. When a user logs on to the local terminal, he or she gets logged on to session 0. This session is never terminated unless the machine is shut down. There are certain things that could be done only in session 0. For example, several applications ran well only in console session. Several services ran only in session 0 and popped up UI, which could be viewed only by logging on to the local terminal (or session 0).

The purpose of the /console switch in Windows Server 2003 is to connect remotely to the local terminal, specifically session 0. This is needed by administrators to install and execute those applications or view pop-ups given by services or simply to get back to the session on the local terminal. Also, it is the only way to administer the server remotely without consuming a TS CAL when Terminal Server is installed.

In Windows Server 2008, session 0 is not an interactive session anymore; it hosts only services. The "console" session is the one that is bound to the local terminal. However, there is no single session that acts as "console" at all times. The session bound to a local terminal may be logged off or disconnected and a new session will be created and associated with the local terminal. At any point, whatever session is associated with the local terminal is named as "console" session.

In Windows Server 2008, there is no need to connect remotely to this session called "console" because all sessions with remote terminals have the same capabilities as the session that is on the local terminal. For the applications that used to run only in session 0 before, fixes will be provided through shims by the OS App Compat component. The UI popped up in the services session (session 0) by legacy services will be available for viewing by a separate feature called "session 0 viewer."

In addition, the /console switch has been repurposed in Windows Server 2008 to administer the server without consuming a TS CAL, and because there is no longer a need to connect to the "console" session, this switch has been changed in Windows Server 2008 to /admin.

In Windows Server 2003, when the /console switch is used to connect to the server, the user is connected to session 0. This behavior is applicable to both Remote Administration mode and Terminal Server mode. In Windows Server 2008, when the TS role is installed, the /admin switch either results in the creation of a new session or it reconnects to any existing session. In Remote Administration mode, /admin has no effect.

In Windows Server 2003, when /console is not used, the user gets a new session even if he or she already has a session on the local terminal—no matter what the "Restrict user to single session" policy says. In Windows Server 2008, whether or not /admin is specified, the user will be reconnected to the existing session if the "Restrict user to single session" policy is set (this is the default).

Remote Administration Sessions Using /admin

When the TS role is installed, remote connections initiated using mstsc.exe consume a TS CAL. To administer the machine remotely without consuming a TS CAL, you can use the /admin switch (for example, mstsc /admin). By using /admin, you can have a maximum of two administrative sessions—just as the remote administration mode works—including the one on the local terminal. The /admin switch has no effect in remote administration mode.

There is a difference in the permissions needed to obtain an administrative session at the local terminal vs. at the remote terminal using /admin. To obtain administrative sessions remotely using /admin, the user must be part of the Remote Desktop Users group and should be listed in SD_CONSOLE. By default, only administrators are part of this ACL as well as the Remote Desktop Users group. The SD_CONSOLE ACL can be modified by administrators using WMI to provide more users with privileges to have administrative sessions using /admin. There is no UI to do this because, normally, there should be no need to change this.

To obtain the administrative session at the local terminal the user needs to have the interactive user logon right (which is the highlighted policy below in secpol.msc):

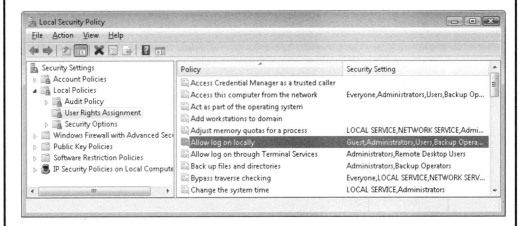

Differences between Administrative Sessions and User Sessions

There are a few behavioral differences between administrative sessions and user sessions:

- For administrative sessions, the time zone is not redirected, even if it is enabled, whereas for the user sessions it is. This essentially means time-zone redirection is not available in Remote Administration mode because there are no CAL sessions.

- The administrative sessions are exempted from the "Deny User Permissions To Log On To Terminal Server" policy in the Terminal Services profile of the user.

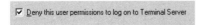

For example, if this check box is selected for any user, he cannot connect remotely by using mstsc without /admin. However, if the same user is listed in the SD_CONSOLE or is part of the administrators group, he can connect remotely using /admin.

- The administrative sessions are exempted from the drain mode. If the server is in drain mode, you will not be able to connect remotely without /admin, unless you have an existing session on the server. However, you can connect by using /admin regardless of whether you have the required permissions.

- The administrative sessions are exempted from the maximum session limit configured on the server (note that there still can be only two active /admin sessions at one time).

- When the limit on number of administrative sessions is exceeded, the contention is handled by allowing the new user to negotiate with existing users (described below). There is no contention handling for CAL sessions. You can connect remotely as long as you have a valid CAL.

Changing an Administrative Session to a User Session (or Vice Versa)

When a user connects to a server remotely using /admin, a remote terminal is created that consumes no TS CAL. When the user disconnects the session, the terminal is destroyed; however, the session is still an administrative session consuming no TS CAL.

Now, when the same user connects to the server remotely again without using /admin, a new remote terminal is created. This remote terminal is connected to the existing session and consumes a TS CAL. This means, for example, that the session will no longer be listed in session contention UI when the maximum number of active administrative type sessions is exceeded.

Contention Handling

In Windows Server 2003, in Remote Administration mode, you can have a total of three sessions, regardless of their state. This can be one session at the local terminal and two remote sessions, or two remote sessions without /console and one with /console.

In Windows Server 2003, in Remote Administration mode, when the number of sessions exceeds three, the fourth session gets an error message saying "Maximum number of sessions exceeded."

In Windows Server 2003, in Terminal Server mode, you can have a maximum of one remote connection for administration purposes that does not consume a CAL. If anyone is already logged on to the console, that user must be logged off.

In Windows Server 2008, you can have a maximum of two active sessions (local or remote) for administration purposes. When a third user attempts to logon to an administrative session (for example, when a user initiates a remote connection using /admin or logs on to the local terminal) while two administrators are active, the user gets a dialog in which she can request that existing users disconnect. The dialog looks like this (in this example, Admin1 and Admin2 are the active users using administrative sessions):

The check box for forcibly disconnecting an existing user does not exist if the new user is not a member of the administrators group.

When you select a user in this dialog, the selected user gets a disconnect request similar to the one in Windows XP or Windows Vista clients; if the user does not respond, they will be disconnected after 30 seconds (the session is not logged off).

The list of users contained in this contention UI does not include users who are using normal user sessions. Only those sessions that are created at the local terminal or at the remote terminal using /admin are listed in this UI.

Note that while there can be maximum of 2 active sessions (local or remote), there can be multiple disconnected sessions coexisting on the server.

–Mahesh Lotlikar
Software Development Engineer, Terminal Services

Installing and Managing Terminal Services

Before we end our discussion of core Terminal Services enhancements in Windows Server 2008 and move on to talk about other new Terminal Services features in this platform, let's talk briefly about installing and managing the Terminal Services role. For small and mid-sized organizations, your friend here is Server Manager, which we introduced previously in Chapter 4, "Managing Windows Server 2008." When you use the Add Roles Wizard to add the Terminal Services role, you're presented with the following five role services:

- **Terminal Server**   Installs core Terminal Server functionality, and lets you share either the full desktop as in previous versions of Terminal Server or individual applications using the new TS RemoteApp feature. See the upcoming "Terminal Services RemoteApp" section for more information.

- **TS Licensing**   Lets you install a Terminal Services Licensing Server for managing Terminal Server CALs. See the upcoming "Terminal Services Licensing" section for more information.

- **TS Session Broker**   The new name in Windows Server 2008 for the Terminal Services Session Directory feature of Windows Server 2003. See the upcoming "Other Terminal Services Enhancements" section for more information.

- **TS Gateway**   Lets clients use HTTPS to securely access terminal servers on internal networks from outside clients over the Internet. See the upcoming "Terminal Services Gateway" section for more information.

- **TS Web Access**   Lets clients access terminal servers via the Web and start applications using a Web browser. See the upcoming "Terminal Services Web Access" section for more information.

You can choose one or more of these role services to install on your machine. Note that choosing TS Gateway or TS Web Access prompts you to install the Web Server (IIS) role and some additional features if these have not already been installed. Note also that choosing TS Gateway prompts you to install the Network Policy And Access Services role if this has not already been installed. For additional information on how to install roles and features, see Chapter 5, "Managing Server Roles."

Unattended Setup of Terminal Services

Larger organizations, however, will want to perform an unattended setup of Windows Server 2008 terminal servers. You can find more information about deploying Windows Server 2008 in Chapter 13, "Deploying Windows Server 2008." For now, let's hear from another of our experts from the Terminal Services product team concerning performing an unattended setup of the Terminal Services role. Isn't it great how the product team took time out of their busy schedule to contribute these "From the Experts" sidebars to provide us with insights and share their expertise with us? Here's our next sidebar:

From the Experts: Unattend.xml Settings for the Terminal Services Role

This sidebar describes the Terminal Services settings that can be specified in your Unattend.xml answer file and applied during unattended installation. Thanks to Kevin London and Ajay Kumar for providing some of the descriptions of the settings covered here.

Don't forget that the recommended way to author answer files is to create them in Windows System Image Manager (Windows SIM). If you use one at all, you use a manually authored answer file and validate the answer file in Windows SIM to verify that it works. Because available settings and default values can change from time to time, you must revalidate your answer file when you reuse it. For information on Windows SIM,

---

please refer to *http://technet2.microsoft.com/WindowsVista/en/library/d9f7c27e-f4d0-40ef-be73-344f7c7626ff1033.mspx.*

Enabling Remote Connections (*fDenyTSConnections*)

This setting is specified in the answer file to enable Remote Desktop using unattended installation:

```
Component name: "Microsoft-Windows-TerminalServices-LocalSessionManager"
Setting: fDenyTSConnections
Possible values: false or true
Default: true
```

If the value is true, Remote Desktop is enabled. If it's false or the setting is not specified, Remote Desktop is disabled by default.

If you want to enable Remote Desktop and if you use Windows Firewall, along with this setting, you need to enable a firewall exception for Remote Desktop. For the details on adding a firewall exception, refer to *http://technet2.microsoft.com/WindowsVista/en/library/aadfdd06-7e68-4c56-928e-f943d3cc4a421033.mspx.*

User Authentication Setting (*UserAuthentication*)

This setting specifies how users are authenticated before the Remote Desktop Connection is established. If you do not specify this setting, by default you won't be able to remotely connect to the machine from computers that do not run Remote Desktop with Network Level Authentication.

```
Component name: "Microsoft-Windows-TerminalServices-RDP-WinStationExtensions"
Setting: UserAuthentication
Possible values: 0 or 1
Default: 1
```

The value 0 specifies that user authentication using Network Level Authentication is not required before the Remote Desktop Connection is established. This value corresponds to the following option in the system properties Remote tab:

If this setting is not specified or if the specified value is 1, user authentication using Network Level Authentication is not required. This corresponds to the following option in the system properties Remote tab:

Security Layer Setting (*SecurityLayer*)

This setting specifies how servers and clients authenticate each other before a Remote Desktop Connection is established.

```
Component name: "Microsoft-Windows-TerminalServices-RDP-WinStationExtensions"
Setting: UserAuthentication
Possible Values: 0 or 1 or 2
Default: 1
```

This setting corresponds to the following options in the General tab of rdp-tcp properties in tsconfig:

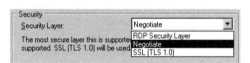

The value 0 results in the RDP Security Layer option being selected during unattended installation. It means that the Remote Desktop Protocol (RDP) is used by the server and client for authentication before a Remote Desktop Connection is established.

The value 1 results in the Negotiate option being selected. This is also the default option if this setting is not specified in the answer file. It means that the server and client negotiate the method for authentication before a Remote Desktop Connection is established.

The value 2 results in the SSL (TLS 1.0) option being selected during unattended installation. It means that the Transport Layer Security (TLS) protocol is used by the server and client for authentication before a Remote Desktop Connection is established.

Licensing Mode Setting (*LicensingMode*)

This setting is applicable only when the Terminal Server role is installed. It specifies the licensing mode.

```
Component name: "Microsoft-Windows-TerminalServices-RemoteConnectionManager"
Setting: LicensingMode
Possible Values: 2 or 4 or 5
Default: 5
```

This setting corresponds to the following UI option in the server configuration:

Specify the terminal server licensing mode

- ⊙ Not yet configured
- ○ Per device
- ○ Per user

The value 2 means the licensing mode is "Per Device"; the value 4 means "Per User"; and the value 5 means "Not yet configured."

Disable Allow List Setting (*fDisabledAllowList*)

This setting allows you to specify whether or not the unlisted applications are allowed to be used in single app mode.

```
Component name: "Microsoft-Windows-TerminalServices-Publishing-WMIProvider"
Setting: fDisabledAllowList
Possible values: false or true
Default: false
```

The value true means all the unlisted applications are allowed to be launched as an initial program. The value false means only unlisted applications are allowed to be launched as an initial program.

Scope of License Server Automatic Discovery (*Role*)

This configuration setting decides the scope of the License Server automatic discovery.

```
Component name: "Microsoft-Windows-TerminalServices-LicenseServer"
Setting: Role
Possible values: 0 or 1
Default: 0
```

When this value is set to 1 and the License Server is installed on a domain machine, the License Server discovery scope is set to Forest. If it's set to zero and the License Server is installed on a domain machine, the discovery scope is set to Domain. If it's set to zero and the License Server is installed on a workgroup machine, the discovery scope of the License Server is set to Workgroup. You cannot set this setting to 1 on a workgroup. All other values are invalid, and a default value of zero will be used if an invalid value is provided.

Also, if you have set the role setting to 1 on a domain machine—that is, the discovery scope is set to Forest—the admin needs to publish the License server in Active Directory after an unattended setup is complete. While applying unattended settings, we can modify only License Server registry settings and we cannot actually publish the License Server in Active Directory because Enterprise admin credentials are required to publish the License Server there. We have introduced two new ways in Beta 3 to publish the License Server after installation:

- The first way is to use the new License Server configuration dialog in TS Licensing Manager (the admin console for TS License Server). Following are the steps to publish a License Server through TS Licensing Manager:

    1. Connect to License Server.

    2. Right-click on Server, and choose Review Configuration in the menu.

    3. If the License Server is configured to be in the Forest discovery scope and it is not published, the configuration dialog will show the appropriate message. There will be a Publish button as well on this dialog if the condition in the previous sentence holds true. Just click the button and License Server will be published.

    4. The TS Licensing Manager needs to be launched with Enterprise admin credentials for publishing to succeed.

- The other process involves using the WMI method *Win32_TSLicenseServer:: Publish()*. You need to run this API under Enterprise admin credentials.

TS Licensing Database Folder (*DBPath*)

This setting allows you to specify the folder in which the TS licensing data files will be stored.

```
Component name: "Microsoft-Windows-TerminalServices-LicenseServer"
Setting: DBPath
Default: %SystemRoot%\System32\LServer
```

TS Web Access Web Site

This setting allows you to set the TS Web Access to a nondefault Web site.

```
Component name: "TSPortalWebPart"
Setting: WebSite
Default: Empty
```

TS Web Client Web Site

This setting allows you to set the TS Web client to a nondefault Web site.

```
Component name: "Microsoft-Windows-TerminalServices-WebControlExtension"
Setting: WebSite
Default: Empty
```

—Mahesh Lotlikar
Software Development Engineer, Terminal Services

Managing Terminal Services

Managing Terminal Services is a snap using the new Server Manager console we examined earlier in Chapter 4. Figure 8-1 shows the Terminal Services role management tools available in Server Manager after adding the Terminal Services role with the Terminal Server role service, as described earlier in this section. Additional snap-ins for managing features such as TS Gateway and TS Web Access will be displayed if these role services are also installed on the machine.

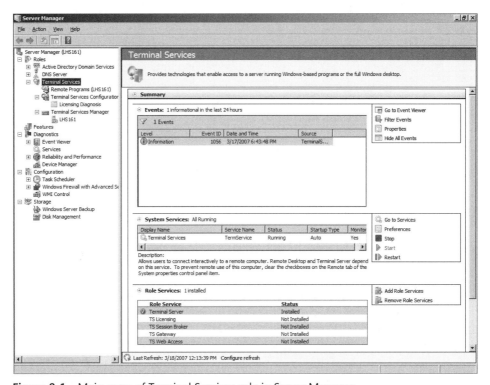

Figure 8-1   Main page of Terminal Services role in Server Manager

From the main page of the Terminal Services role in Server Manager, you can add or remove role services for this role, start and stop services, and view event log information involving Terminal Services. From there, you can select any of the sub-nodes beneath the Terminal Services role node and view information or configure settings relating to that role service. For example, Figure 8-2 shows the Terminal Services Configuration node selected, which displays key configuration settings for your terminal server. From this page, you can create a new connection using the Terminal Services Connection Wizard, double-click on an existing connection such as the default RDP-Tcp connection and configure its properties, or edit key Terminal Services settings displayed in the lower part of the details pane in the middle of the console.

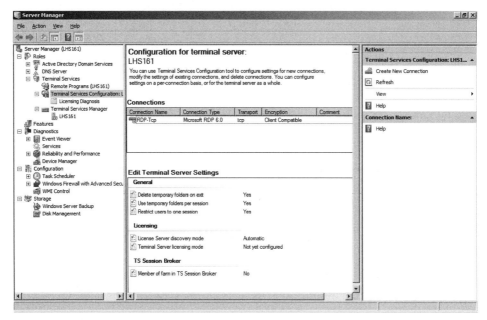

Figure 8-2   Main page of Terminal Services Configuration snap-in

Terminal Services RemoteApp

Let's move on now and discuss some other new features and enhancements of Terminal Services in Windows Server 2008. One of the biggest improvements in the area of experience features is Terminal Services RemoteApp, which enables users to access standard Windows-based programs from anywhere by running them on a terminal server instead of directly on their client computers. In previous versions of Terminal Services, you could remote only the entire desktop to users' computers. So when a user wanted to run a program remotely on the terminal server, she typically double-clicked on a saved .rdp file that the administrator previously distributed to her. This connected her to the terminal server, and after logging in (or being automatically logged in using saved credentials), a remote desktop would appear on her computer with a pin at the top pinning the remote desktop to her local (physical) desktop. The user could then run applications remotely on the terminal server from within her remote desktop, or she could minimize the remote desktop if she wanted to run applications on her local computer using her physical desktop.

In other words, the user had two desktops. Needless to say, some users found this confusing, and I can hear the tired help desk person responding to the user's call by asking, "Which desktop are you looking at now?" and the user responding "Huh?"

TS RemoteApp solves this problem (and makes the lives of harried help desk staff easier) by allowing users to run Terminal Services applications directly on their physical desktop. So instead of having to switch between two desktops, the user sees the RemoteApp program (the program that is running remotely on the terminal server instead of on her local computer) sitting right there on her desktop, looking just like any other locally running program. Figure 8-3 shows an example of two programs running on a user's desktop: one of them a RemoteApp program, and the other one running locally on the user's computer.

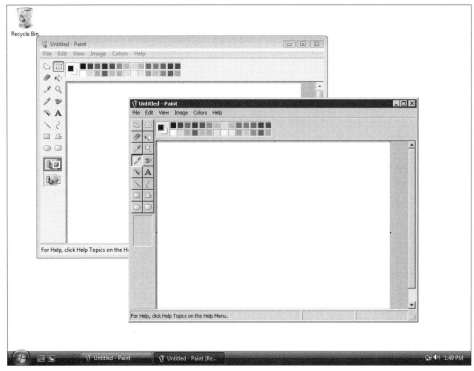

Figure 8-3   Local and RemoteApp programs running simultaneously on a user's desktop

Can you tell which program is the remote one running on the terminal server and which is running locally? I'll give you a clue—the Desktop Experience feature that we mentioned earlier in this chapter hasn't been installed on the terminal server.

Figured it out yet? That's right, the client computer is running Windows Vista. The left copy of Microsoft Paint is running locally on the computer, while the right copy of Paint is running on the terminal server as a RemoteApp program. Both copies of Paint (the local program and the RemoteApp program) are running on the same desktop, which is the user's normal (that is, local or physical) desktop—the new TS RemoteApp feature of Windows Server 2008 Terminal Services at work! Let's see how we can make this work.

Using TS RemoteApp

First, we'll open Server Manager and select the TS RemoteApp Manager node under Terminal Services. (We could also open TS RemoteApp Manager from Administrative Tools.)

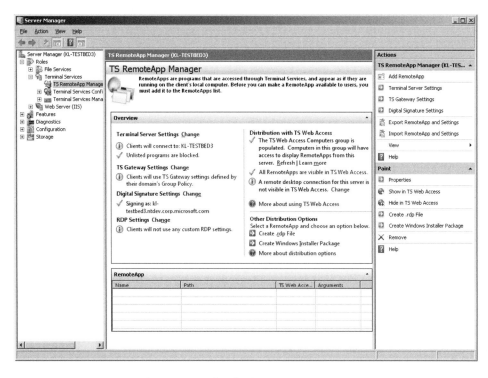

TS RemoteApp Manager lets us specify which programs our Terminal Services users will be able to run remotely on their normal desktops. Right now, we have no programs on the Allow list, so let's click Add RemoteApp in the Action pane at the right. This launches the RemoteApp Wizard. Clicking Next presents us with a page that allows us to choose which installed programs we want to add to the RemoteApp programs list. We'll choose Paint.

Clicking Next and then Finish causes Paint to be added to the RemoteApp programs list with default settings. (We'll examine these defaults in a moment.)

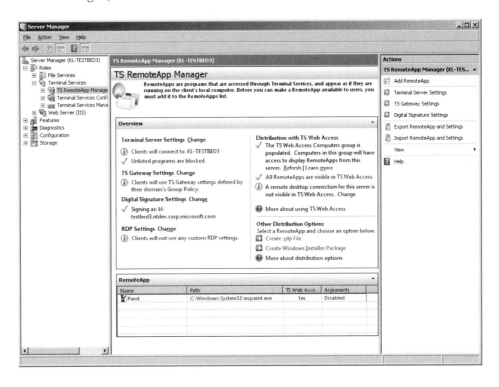

If we select Paint in the center (Details) pane and click Properties in the Action pane, we see the default settings for running this RemoteApp program:

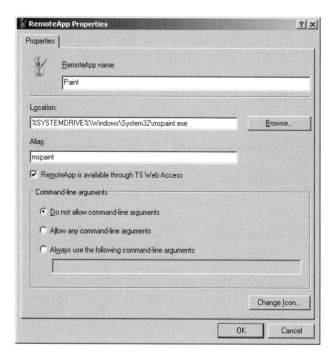

What these default settings indicate are that users will not be allowed to add their own command-line arguments when running Paint. (This is usually a good idea, though as far as I know, Paint doesn't have any command-line switches.) The settings also indicate that the RemoteApp program will automatically be made available to users through Terminal Services Web Access (though we actually haven't added that role service yet to our terminal server). In addition, we could change the name of the RemoteApp program to something other than "Paint" if we want users to know that they're running the RemoteApp version of the program and not the version installed on their local computer—let's not do this though as it's more fun to confuse the user. (I'm talking like a jaded administrator here.)

Anyway, once we've added Paint to the RemoteApp programs list, how do we actually enable the user to run the RemoteApp program? To do this, we need to deploy a package containing the RemoteApp information for Paint to our users. We can package our RemoteApp program in two ways: as a Windows Installer file or as a Remote Desktop Protocol file. Let's use the Windows Installer file approach because as administrators we're used to deploying Windows Installer packages to client computers using Group Policy.

Start by selecting Paint in our RemoteApp programs list, and then click Create Windows Installer Package in the Action pane. This starts the RemoteApp Wizard again, but after you click Next the wizard displays the following page instead of the previous one:

By default, we see that our Windows Installer package (which will actually be created with the extension .rap.msi, with *RAP* presumably standing for RemoteApp Package) will be saved at C:\Program Files\Packaged Programs. We could elect to save it there, or we could save it on a network share instead, which is likely the better choice. This page of the wizard also lets us customize the terminal server settings (server name, port, and authentication settings), specify that the package is digitally signed to prevent tampering, or specify Terminal Services Gateway settings if we're using this feature. (We'll talk about this later.)

Accepting the default and clicking Next brings us to this wizard page:

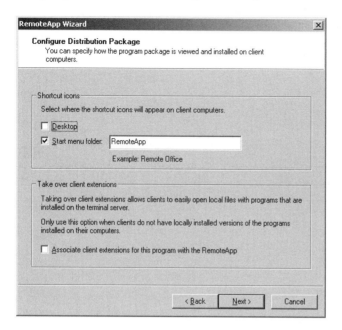

Note that by default the RemoteApp program is going to be added to the user's Start menu in a folder named RemoteApps. (We'll see that in a moment.) By selecting the check box at the bottom of this page, we can also cause the RemoteApp program to launch whenever the user double-clicks on a file extension like .bmp that is associated with the program. Click through now to finish the wizard.

Now we just need to deploy the .rap.msi package by using Group Policy. I won't show the details because we're all pretty familiar with this procedure, so let's just say we've deployed our package to our client computers and the package has been installed on these computers. Now when the user clicks Start and then Programs, the RemoteApp program can be seen on the Start menu:

Now we select Paint under RemoteApp, and the following appears:

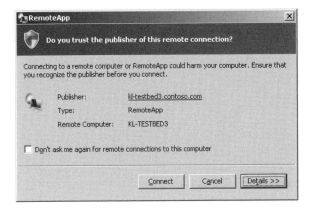

We're also prompted for our user credentials because it's the first time we're running this RemoteApp program from our terminal server. After having our credentials authenticated, the following appears:

Once the RemoteApp is running, if we also start a copy of Paint locally from Accessories, then we've come full circle to our earlier screen shot, where we had two copies of Paint running, one showing the Vista theme (local mspaint.exe) and the other Classic Windows (remote mspaint.exe). We're done!

One more thing—what if we *did* have the Desktop Experience feature installed on our terminal server? In that case, both copies of Paint on our desktop would look identical. How could we tell then whether or not we're using TS RemoteApp to run one of these copies? Try Task Manager—opening Task Manager displays the two copies of Paint that are running:

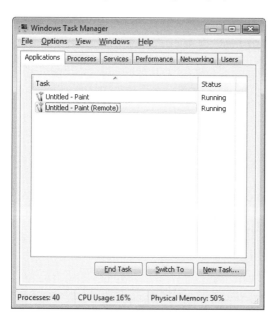

Notice that the remote version of Paint is clearly marked this way. Now right-click on the remote Paint application and select Go To Process. The Process tab now opens, and we see that mstsc.exe (in other words, RDC 6.0) is the actual process hosting our remote copy of Paint:

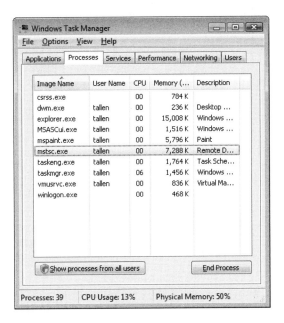

What do you think would happen if we start another remote copy of Paint? We'd have three Paint windows on our desktop, one local and two remote—but how many mstsc.exe processes would we see running on the Processes tab? Take a guess and then try it yourself to see whether you guessed right. See Chapter 13 for more information on trying out Windows Server 2008 for yourself.

Benefits of TS RemoteApp

Now that we've examined the new RemoteApp feature of Terminal Services in Windows Server 2008, what do you think the benefits are? Several come to my mind:

- No more user confusion over why they need to have two desktops instead of one. And that's not to forget the gratitude your help desk staff will have for you.

- A great new method for easily deploying new applications to users—that is, using small (generally less than 100-KB) .rap.msi files deployed using Group Policy software distribution.

- Less work for you as administrator because you no longer have to configure entire remote desktops for users but only RemoteApp programs, and this you can easily do using a wizard.

■ No more getting caught up in the argument of whether Terminal Services is for rich clients or thin clients—RDP 6.0 together with RemoteApp makes every client rich.

What are some best practices for using TS RemoteApp? Well first, if you have some programs that are intended to work together—that is, they share data by embedding or linking using DDE—it's a good idea to run these RemoteApp programs from the same terminal server instead of dividing the programs up onto different terminal servers. That way, the experience for users will be enhanced, and they will see better integration between different programs when they run them. And second, you should put different programs on different terminal servers if you have application compatibility issues between several programs or if you have a single heavy-use application that could result in users filling the capacity of one of your terminal servers. (Use the x64 architecture instead of x86, however, if you want much greater capacity for your terminal servers.)

Terminal Services Web Access

Terminal Services Web Access (or simply TS Web Access) is another Terminal Services feature that has been enhanced in Windows Server 2008. The previous version of Terminal Services in Windows Server 2003 includes a feature called Remote Desktop Web Connection, which is an ActiveX control that provides essentially the same functionality as the full Terminal Services client but is designed to deliver it using a Web-based launcher. By embedding this ActiveX control in a Web page hosted on Internet Information Services (IIS), you enable a user to access the Web page using a Web browser such as Internet Explorer, download and install the ActiveX control, and initiate a session with a remote terminal server. The user's computer does not require RDC—instead, the TS session runs within the user's Web browser using ActiveX functionality.

Remote Desktop Web Connection was limited, however, to running entire remote desktop sessions, not individual applications. In addition, the user had to be able to download and install the ActiveX control to connect to and start a session with the terminal server. And if the security policy on the user's computer prevented him from downloading and/or installing ActiveX controls, he was out of luck and couldn't use Remote Desktop Web Connection.

Windows Vista, together with Windows Server 2008, enhances Remote Desktop Web Connection functionality in two basic ways. First, the RDC 6.0 client has this ActiveX control built into it, so users no longer need to download and install an ActiveX control to start a Terminal Services session within a Web browser—at least, they don't have to do this if their client computer is running Windows Vista (which includes RDC 6.0) or if they are running Windows XP SP2 and have the RDC 6.0 update for Windows XP installed. (The RDC 6.0 update for Windows XP is described in KB 925876 and is available from the Microsoft Download Center or via Windows Update.)

And second, TS Web Access integrates with the TS RemoteApp feature, allowing users to go to a Web page, view a list of available RemoteApp programs they can run, click an icon link for a particular RemoteApp program, and run that program on their computer. In fact, TS Web

Access includes a default Web page that you can use for deploying RemoteApp programs from a Web page. This default page consists of a frame together with a customizable Web Part that displays the list of RemoteApp programs within the user's Web browser. And if you don't want to use this default Web page, you can add the Web Part into a Microsoft Windows SharePoint Services site.

Once a RemoteApp program has been started from the default Web page, the application appears as if it is running on the local computer's desktop just like with the TS RemoteApp feature described previously. In addition, if the user starts more than one RemoteApp program from the Web page and these programs are all running on the same terminal server, all the RemoteApp programs will run within the same Terminal Services session.

Using TS Web Access

Let's take a quick look at how to make TS Web Access work. First you need to add the TS Web Access role service to a server running Windows Server 2008, and when you do this you're also required to add the Web Server (IIS) role to your server, plus a feature called Windows Process Activation Service (WPAS). Once you've installed TS Web Access, you next need to specify a data source to use to populate the list of RemoteApp programs that will be displayed within the Web Part.

Note that IIS can populate the list of RemoteApp programs displayed within the Web Part from either a local or an external data source, plus this list is dynamically updated so that if you add another application to the RemoteApp programs list in TS RemoteApp Manager, it will be displayed to the user the next time she opens the default Web page for TS Web Access. In other words, the Windows Server 2008 machine on which you add the TS Web Access role service (and hence, also IIS 7.0) doesn't need to have the core Terminal Server role service installed on it as well. Thus, you could have one or more terminal servers for remotely running applications, and a single IIS 7.0 server that has TS Web Access installed on it to provide a way for users to access your terminal servers from a Web page and run RemoteApp programs on your terminal servers.

The data source for populating the Web Part can be a specific terminal server, which causes all applications on the RemoteApp programs list on the terminal server to be made available for all users. In other words, using this approach means that all users will see the same list of RemoteApp programs when they view the page that has the Web Part embedded in it.

Before we look at how to configure the data source, let's jump ahead and actually try TS Web Access. Remember from our previous discussion of TS RemoteApp earlier in this chapter that, by default, when you add an application to the RemoteApp programs list using the TS RemoteApp Manager snap-in, the application is also made available for users to access via TS Web Access (even if TS Web Access has not been installed at that point). So you've already made Paint available using TS RemoteApp, which means the application should also be available to users via TS Web Access.

Let's check: from a Windows Vista client computer to which we've logged on using a domain user (non-admin) account, let's open Internet Explorer and go to the URL http://<*server_name*>/ts where <*server_name*> is the name (hostname or FQDN) or IP address of our terminal server. When we open this URL and enter our credentials (and optionally save them in CredMan for future reuse), we see the following Web page:

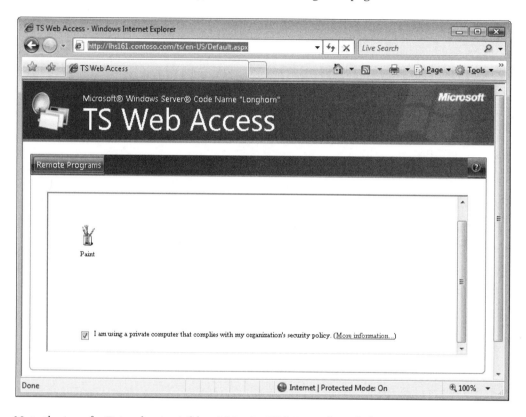

Note the icon for Paint that is visible within the Web Part. If we click on this icon and respond to a couple of security dialogs (some of these security hurdles will likely go away between now and RTM to make the user's experience even smoother), we see the same Connecting Remote-App window followed by a "Do you trust the computer you are connecting to?" dialog (unless we previously selected the check box to not display that dialog any more). Then, once we've been authenticated and RDC have successfully connected to the terminal server, a remote copy of Paint appears running on our desktop—just as before with the TS RemoteApp feature. Note that Paint runs right on our desktop, not within our Web browser.

What if you are an administrator and you want to configure the data source for TS Web Access? You might have noticed that when you installed the TS Web Access role service to your Windows Server 2008 machine that it didn't add any TS Web Access sub-node under

Terminal Services in Server Manager. That's because TS Web Access is really just an IIS application, which means you configure it using the Internet Information Services (IIS) Manager console. (See Chapter 11, "Internet Information Services 7.0," for more information concerning IIS.) But you actually don't need to do this here–instead, you can configure your data source using your Web browser! Just follow the same steps as shown earlier, but this time instead of specifying domain user credentials from a Windows Vista client computer, open Internet Explorer on your TS Web Access server and use your local Administrator credentials. (Alternatively, you can open IE either locally or remotely and specify credentials that belong to the TS Web Access Administrators local group on the TS Web Access server.) Once you do this, the Web page we just saw is displayed again, but with one significant difference:

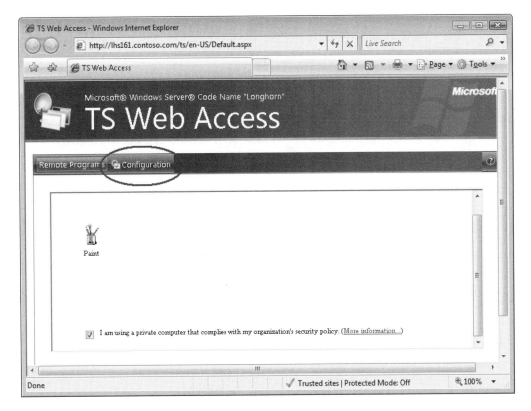

Note the Configuration button that was not displayed when we accessed this page as an ordinary user.

Of course, the UI might change to some degree by RTM, and this chapter is currently being written using a near-Beta 3 build of Windows Server 2008, but the basic idea of how TS Web Access is deployed, configured, and used should stay pretty much the same. And if you want users to be able to securely access this TS Web Access Web page over the Internet, you can deploy the new TS Gateway feature of Windows Server 2008 to help ensure that users' remote connections over the Internet to your terminal servers are secure. We'll learn more about TS Gateway later in this chapter.

Finally, if your client computer is running an older version of Windows, or if it is running Windows XP SP2 but doesn't have the RDC 6.0 update installed on it, you can still access an entire remote desktop on the terminal server from within your Web browser by opening the URL http://<server_name>/tsweb instead of http://<server_name>/ts. By doing this, you can use Remote Desktop Web Connection on your client computer, download and install the ActiveX control needed, and run a separate remote desktop on top of your physical desktop.

Now let's learn some more about administering this feature from one of our experts on the Terminal Services team at Microsoft.

 First, let's look at how we can increase the number of remote desktops available to any terminal server on our network. We'll hear again from our expert on the team concerning this and see that the procedure involves editing the registry so that all the usual warnings apply concerning this:

From the Experts: Setting Up Multiple Remote Desktops for TS Web Access to Discover

The RemoteApp manager has only a setting to show the desktop connection for the Terminal Server that the RemoteApp manager is connected to. But you can easily have an arbitrary number of desktops connected to any server in your network. First, for desktops to be available you have to make sure the TS Web Access (TSWA) site is set up in the Terminal Server mode. That is, it should be pointed at a single Terminal Server. There are then two tasks you need to accomplish to make a new desktop available for TSWA: create a registry entry for the new desktop, and create an RDP file that represents the connection settings for the desktop. You can use the WMI interface or manually create the entries, but I will discuss how to manually create the entries. Also, remember you must be an administrator on the Terminal Server box while making these changes.

First, create the registry key for the new desktop. All desktop registry keys are located in HKEY_LOCAL_MACHINE\SOFTWARE\Microsoft\Windows NT\CurrentVersion\ Terminal Server\TSAppAllowList\RemoteDesktops.

Create a new key with the name of the desktop—for example, server1.mycorp.net. Inside this new registry key, you need to create the following values:

1. Create *IconPath* as a REG_SZ. This should be the fully qualified path to either the executable or dll that contains the icon you want to use or the path to the icon file itself. If it is an icon file, it must end in *.ico*. If you leave this empty, the mstsc client icon will be used instead.

2. Create *IconIndex* as a REG_DWORD. This should be the index of the icon in the file specified by *IconPath*. If you use an icon ID instead of an index, it needs to be negative. For example: −2 specifies the icon with an ID of 2, while 2 specifies the third icon in the file. (The index starts at 0.)

3. Create *Name* as a REG_SZ. This will be the name shown to the users that visit the TSWA site.

4. Create *ShowInTSWA* as a REG_DWORD. Set this to 1 or the desktop will not be shown in the TSWA site.

Next, the RDP file needs to be created for the desktop. The easiest way to do this is to open up the mstsc client. Apply the settings that you want to use, and save this from the client as the name of the registry key that you created under the *RemoteDesktops* registry key. In this example, you want to save it as server1.mycorp.net.rdp. This file needs to be moved to %WINDIR%\RemotePackages\RemoteDesktops, and all users need to be able to read the RDP file. Once this is done, the desktop will show up in the TSWA site (though there might be some lag time until the cache expires or is reset by an administrator of the TSWA site).

−Kevin London
Software Design Engineer, Terminal Services

Next, here's how you can move the Web site for TS Web Access in IIS from the Default Web Site to some other Web site running on your IIS server should you need to do this:

From the Experts: Changing TS Web Access from the Default Web Site

You might want to have TSWA on a non-default Web site because you might want to use a nonstandard port to connect to TSWA. Or you might have other reasons to move TSWA to a non-default Web site. Several steps need to be done before installing TSWA to accomplish this task, but they are easy and straightforward:

1. Install IIS.

2. Start the management console for IIS.

3. Right-click on the top-level node and click Add Website.

4. Give it a name, and note that you need to use a nonstandard port or a different NIC.

> **5.** Create the registry key HKLM\SOFTWARE\Microsoft\Terminal Server Web Access Website (which is a REG_SZ), and set this to the name specified in step 4.
>
> **6.** Install the TS WebAccess role.
>
> After you complete this procedure, TS Web Access will be created on a non-default Web site.
>
> *–Kevin London*
> *Software Design Engineer, Terminal Services*

Benefits of TS Web Access

What are some possible benefits of using TS Web Access? How about really simple application deployment? ("Hey user, go to this Web page and click this icon and Excel will open.") We're talking about a technology that is ideal for low-complexity scenarios. Plus it can be customized to use with SharePoint, which is enormously popular in the enterprise environment nowadays.

How should you best implement this feature? Use it mainly if you have a single terminal server, as it's really not intended for multiserver scenarios. That's about it.

Terminal Services Gateway

Another new feature of Windows Server 2008 is Terminal Services Gateway (or TS Gateway), which is designed to provide authorized users with secure, encrypted access over the Internet to terminal servers on your internal corpnet. In other words, a salesperson arriving at a hotel in Hong Kong could open his Windows Vista laptop to bring it out of sleep mode, connect to the Internet using a hot spot in the lobby, and launch a RemoteApp program on his machine that actually runs far away on a Terminal Server hidden behind your company's perimeter firewall at headquarters in New York. Or, depending on how your administrator has defined its resource authorization policies, the user might be able to access the remote desktop of his own desktop computer in New York, provided Remote Desktop has been enabled on it. And if the remote user is an administrator, he could access the remote desktop of any servers within his internal corpnet (provided Remote Desktop is enabled on them) and securely manage those servers and do whatever tasks he needs to perform on them. All I can say concerning this TS Gateway feature is what Edward Norton said in one of my favorite movies, *Rounders*: "Wow. Wow. A lot of action. A *lot* of action."

And you can do all this without having to use a virtual private network (VPN) connection. Plus this will work regardless of the type of perimeter firewall your company has set up, or even if your business is using Network Address Translation (NAT). As Figure 8-4 illustrates, all it takes to make all this work is that your perimeter firewall has to allow TCP port 443 so that HTTP SSL traffic can pass through from the outside.

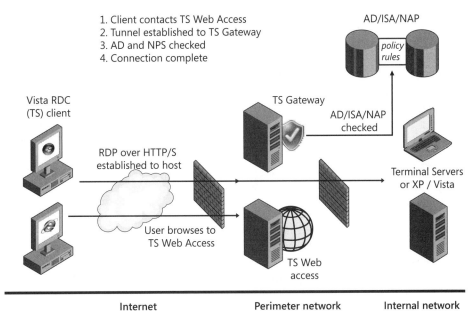

1. Client contacts TS Web Access
2. Tunnel established to TS Gateway
3. AD and NPS checked
4. Connection complete

AD/ISA/NAP

policy rules

Vista RDC (TS) client

TS Gateway

AD/ISA/NAP checked

RDP over HTTP/S established to host

Terminal Servers or XP / Vista

User browses to TS Web Access

TS Web access

Internet   **Perimeter network**   **Internal network**

Figure 8-4   How TS Gateway works

As this figure illustrates, TS Gateway works by enabling tunneling of RDP traffic over HTTPS (HTTP with SSL encryption). The client computer at the left is attempting to connect to the terminal servers at the right that are hidden behind a pair of firewalls with a perimeter network subnet in between them. The TS Gateway is sitting between the firewalls on the screened subnet, and when the incoming RDP over HTTP traffic reaches the external firewall, the firewall strips off the HTTP part and passes the RDP packets to the TS Gateway. The TS Gateway can then use the Network Policy Server to verify whether the user is allowed to connect to the terminal server, and will use Active Directory to authenticate the remote user. Once the user is authenticated, she can access the internal terminal servers and run RemoteApp programs on them as described previously in this chapter.

TS Gateway will support NAP so that when a remote client computer tries to connect to a terminal server on your internal corpnet, the remote client first has to undergo the required health check to make sure it has the latest security updates installed, has an up-to-date antivirus signature, has its host firewall enabled, and so on. After all, you don't want unhealthy (read: infected with worms and other malware) remote computers to be able to connect to your internal terminal servers and infect your whole network! One thing to note, however, is that NAP will not be able to perform remediation for unhealthy clients connecting through TS Gateway—it simply blocks them from accessing your internal terminal servers. In addition, device redirection is blocked for remote clients connecting via TS Gateway (though best practice is actually to block such redirection on your terminal servers and not on your TS Gateway).

An alternative to placing your TS Gateway on the perimeter network is to put it on your corp-net—that is, behind your internal firewall. Then place an SSL terminator in your perimeter network to forward incoming RDP traffic securely to your TS Gateway. Either way you implement this, however, one advantage of this new feature is that you don't need to worry about using an SSL VPN any longer and all the headaches associated with getting this working properly.

This integration with Network Access Protection (NAP) is an important aspect of TS Gateway because many mid- and large-sized organizations that will deploy Windows Server 2008 will probably do so because of NAP (and also, of course, because of the many enhancements in Terminal Services on the new platform). (We'll be covering NAP in Chapter 10, "Implementing Network Access Protection.")

Before we go any further, let's hear from one more of our experts:

From the Experts: Better Together: TS Gateway, ISA Server, and NAP

Terminal Services–based remote access has long been used as a simpler, lower-risk alternative to classical layer 2 VPN technologies. Whereas the layer 2 VPN has often provided "all ports, all protocols" access to an organization's internal network, the Terminal Services approach restricts connectivity to a single well-defined port and protocol. However, as more and more capability has ascended the stack into RDP (such as copy/paste and drive redirection), the potential attack vectors have risen as well. For example, a remote drive made available over RDP can present the same kinds of security risks as one mapped over native CIFS/SMB transports.

With the advent of TS Gateway, allowing workers to be productive from anywhere has never been easier. TS Gateway also includes several powerful security capabilities to make this access secure. In addition to its default encryption and authentication capabilities, TS Gateway can be combined with ISA Server and Network Access Protection to provide a secure, manageable access method all the way from the client, through the perimeter network, to the endpoint terminal server. Combining these technologies allows an organization to reap the benefits of rich RDP-based remote access, while mitigating the potential exposure this access can bring.

ISA Server adds two primary security capabilities to the TS Gateway solution. First, because it can act as an SSL terminator, it allows for more secure placement of TS Gateway servers. Because ISA can be the Internet-facing endpoint for SSL traffic, the TS Gateway itself does not need to be placed within the perimeter network. Instead, the TS Gateway can be kept on the internal network and the ISA Server can forward traffic to it. However, if ISA were simply performing traffic forwarding, it would be of little real security benefit. Thus, the second main security value ISA brings to the solution is pre-authentication capabilities. Rather than simply terminating SSL traffic and forwarding frames on to the TS Gateway, ISA authenticates users before they ever contact the TS Gateway, ensuring that only valid users are able to communicate with it. Using ISA as the SSL endpoint and traffic inspection device allows for better placement of TS Gateway resources and ensures that they receive only inspected, clean traffic from the Internet.

Although ISA Server provides important network protection abilities to a TS Gateway solution, it does not address client-side threats. For example, users connecting to a TS Gateway session might have malicious software running on their machines or be non-compliant with the organization's security policy. To mitigate against these threats, TS Gateway can be integrated with Network Access Protection to provide enforcement of security and healthy policies on these remote machines.

NAP is included in Windows Server 2008 and can be run on the same machine as TS Gateway, or TS Gateway can be configured to use an existing NAP infrastructure running elsewhere. When combined with TS Gateway, NAP provides the same policy-based approach to client health and enforcement as it does on normal (not RDP-based) network connections. Specifically, NAP can control access to a TS Gateway based on a client's security update, antivirus, and firewall status. For example, if you choose to enable redirected drives on your terminal servers, you might require that clients have antivirus software running and up to date. NAP allows organizations to ensure that computers connecting to a TS Gateway are healthy and compliant with its security policies.

–John Morello
Senior Program Manager, Windows Server Division

One other thing about ISA is that it does inspect the underlying HTTP stream when being accessed over port 80, and although this is not RDP/HTTP inspection, it does afford additional protection from anything that might try to piggyback on the HTTP connection itself.

Implementing TS Gateway

Implementing TS Gateway on a server running Windows Server 2008 requires that you add the TS Gateway role service for the Terminal Services role. When you do this using Server Manager, you are prompted to add the following roles and features as well (if they are not already installed):

- Network Policy and Access Server role (specifically, the Network Policy Server role services)

- Web Server (IIS) role (plus various role services and components)

- RPC Over HTTP Proxy feature

Note that for smaller environments, it's all right to install TS Gateway and the Network Policy Server (NPS) on the same Windows Server 2008 machine. Larger enterprises, however, will probably want to separate these two different role services for greater isolation and manageability.

Adding the TS Gateway role service also requires that you specify a server certificate for your server so that it can use SSL to encrypt network traffic with Terminal Services clients. A valid digital certificate is required for TS Gateway to work, and you have the choice during installation of this role to import a certificate (for example, a certificate from VeriSign if you want clients to be able to access terminal servers running on your corpnet from anywhere in the world via the Internet), create a self-signed certificate (good for testing purposes), or delay installing a certificate until later:

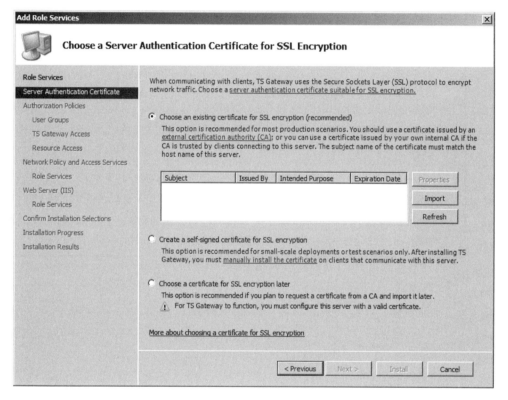

After importing a certificate for your server, you're given the option of creating authorization policies now or doing so later using the TS Gateway Management console. There are two kinds of authorization policies you need to create:

- **Connection authorization policies**   These are policies that enable remote users to access your network based on conditions you have specified.

- **Resource authorization policies**   These are policies that grant access to your terminal servers only to users whom you have specified.

Finally, the Add Role Services Wizard indicates which additional roles and role services will be installed for the Network Policy and Access Server and Web Server (IIS) roles (if these roles and role services are not installed already). And finally you're done.

Once your TS Gateway is set up, you can configure it by creating additional connections and resource authorization policies. For example, you could create a resource authorization policy (RAP) to specify a group of terminal servers on your internal corpnet that you want the TS Gateway to allow access to by authorized remote clients:

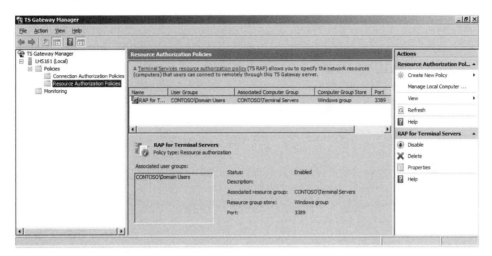

When you create and configure connection authorization policies, you specify which security groups of users they apply to and, optionally, which groups of computers as well. You also specify whether authorization will use smart cards, passwords, or both. When you create and configure resource groups, you define a collection of resources (for example, terminal servers) that remote users will be allowed to access. You can specify these resources either by selecting a security group that contains the computer accounts of these computers, by specifying individual computers using their names (hostname or FQDN) or IP addresses, or by allowing remote users to access any computer (client or server) on your internal network that has Remote Desktop enabled on it. You need to create both connection and resource authorization policies for TS Gateway to do its job.

Finally, the Monitoring node in the TS Gateway Management console lets you monitor connections happening through your TS Gateway and disconnect them if needed.

Benefits of TS Gateway

Why is TS Gateway a great feature? It gives your users remote access to fully firewalled terminal servers on your corpnet, and it does so without any of the headache of having to configure a VPN connection to those servers. That's not to say that VPNs aren't still useful, but if users don't need a local copy of data, network bandwidth is limited, or the amount of application data that needs to be transferred is large, you'll likely get better performance out of using TS Gateway than trying to let your users VPN into your corpnet to access your terminal servers.

Best practices for deploying this feature? Use a dedicated TS Gateway (it can coexist with Outlook RPC/HTTP), and consider placing it behind Microsoft Internet and Acceleration Server (ISA) rather than using a simple port-based firewall.

Terminal Services Licensing

Let's move on and talk briefly about Terminal Services Licensing (or TS Licensing) and also hear from more of our experts on the Terminal Services team at Microsoft. The job of TS Licensing is to simplify the task of managing Terminal Services Client Access Licenses (TS CALs). In other words, TS Licensing helps you ensure your TS clients are properly licensed and that you aren't purchasing too many (or too few) licenses. TS Licensing manages clients that are unlicensed, temporarily licensed, and client-access (that is, permanent) licensed clients, and it manages licenses for both devices and users that are connecting to your terminal servers. The TS Licensing role service in Windows Server 2008 supports terminal servers that run both Windows Server 2008 and Windows Server 2003.

Device-based TS Licensing basically works like this: When a client tries to connect to a terminal server, the terminal server first determines whether the client requires a license (a TS CAL). If the client requires a license, the terminal server contacts your TS Licensing server (usually a separate machine, but for small environments this could also be the terminal server) and requests a license token, which it then forwards to the client. Meanwhile, the TS Licensing server keeps track of all the license tokens you've installed on it to ensure your environment complies with licensing requirements. Note that if a client requires a permanent license token, your TS Licensing server must be activated. (Nonactivated TS Licensing servers can issue only temporary tokens.)

A new feature of TS Licensing in Windows Server 2008 is its ability to track issuance of TS Per-User CALs. If your terminal server is configured to use Per-User licensing mode, any user attempting to connect to it must have a TS Per-User CAL. If the user doesn't, the terminal server will contact the license server to obtain a CAL for her, and administrators can track the issuance of these CALs by using the TS Licensing management tool. Note that TS Per-User CAL tracking and reporting requires an Active Directory infrastructure.

To learn more about managing licensing servers, let's hear now from our experts. First let's learn how to configure TS Licensing after this role service has been installed:

> ## From the Experts: Configuring Terminal Server License Server After Installation
>
> TS Licensing Manager, the admin console for Terminal Server License Server, can now find configuration-related issues with a Terminal Server License Server. It displays the License Server configuration status under a new column, Configuration, in the list view. If there are some issues with the License Server configuration, the configuration status will be set to Review.

TS Licensing Manager also allows the admin to view the current License Server configuration settings in detail. The admin can choose Review Configuration from the right-click menu for a License Server, which opens the configuration dialog. The License Server configuration dialog displays the following information:

- TS License Server Database Path

- Current scope for the license server

- Membership of the Terminal Server License Server group at the Active Directory Domain Controller. During installation of the TS Licensing role on a domain machine, the setup tries to add the License Server in the Terminal Server License Server group at the Active Directory Domain controller, for which it requires domain administrator privileges. Membership to this group enables the License Server to track Per-User license usage.

- Status of the global policy License Server Security Group (TSLS). If this policy is enabled and the Terminal Server Computers group is not created, a warning message will be displayed. If the policy is disabled, no message/status will be displayed.

Admins can take corrective actions if some License Server configuration issues are found. The License Server configuration dialog allows an administrator to take the following actions:

- Change the License Server scope.

- If the License Server scope is set to Forest and the License Server is not published in Active Directory, the License Server configuration dialog shows a warning message to the administrator and allows the administrator to publish the License Server in Active Directory.

- Add to the TSLS group in AD.

- If the License Server Security Group Group Policy is enabled and the Terminal Server Computers local group is not created, the License Server configuration dialog displays the warning message and allows the administrator to create the Terminal Server Computers local group on the License Server.

–Ajay Kumar
Software Design Engineer, Terminal Services

Next, let's learn how revocation of TS CALs works in Windows Server 2008. CAL revocation can be done only with Per-Device CALs, not Per-User ones, and there are some things you need to know about how this works before you begin doing it. Here's what our next expert has to say concerning this:

From the Experts: CAL Revocation on Terminal Services License Server

CAL Revocation is supported only for Windows Server 2008 TS Per-Device CALs. Terminal Services License Server's *automatic CAL reclamation* mentioned later in this sidebar applies only to Per Device CALs.

Per-Device CALs are issued to clients for a certain *validity period*, after which the CAL expires. If the client accesses the terminal server often, the validity of the CAL is renewed accordingly before its expiration. If the client does not access the terminal server for a long time, the CAL eventually expires. The Terminal Services License Server reclaims all the expired CALs periodically with its automatic CAL reclamation mechanism.

Occasionally, an administrator might need to transfer a Per-Device CAL from the client back into the free license pool on the License Server (a process referred to as *reclaiming* or *revoking*) when the original client has been permanently removed from the environment and one needs to reallocate the CAL to a different client. Historically, there was no way to do it. An administrator would have had to wait until the CAL expired or lost its validity and was automatically reclaimed by its mechanism. So it was desired to have the License Server support a mechanism to reclaim or revoke CALs.

Using the new Revoke CAL option in TS Licensing Manager, administrators can now reclaim issued CALs and place them back into a free license pool on the License Server. An administrator has to also select the specific client whose CAL needs to be revoked.

But there are certain restrictions on the number of CALs that can be revoked at a given time. This is a restriction imposed by the License Server to prevent misuse. The restriction can be stated as follows: At any given point in time, the number of LH PD CALs in a revoked state cannot exceed 20 percent of the total number of LH PD CALs installed on the License Server. A CAL goes into a revoked state right after revocation, and its state is cleared when it goes past its original expiration date. One can see the list of CALs in the revoked state in the TS Licensing Manager tool by observing the Status column in the client list view. When the administrator has exceeded this limit, he is given a date when further revocation is possible.

Note that TS CALs should not be revoked to affect concurrent licensing. TS CALs can only be revoked when it is reasonable to assume that the machine they were issued to will no longer participate in the environment, for example, when the machine failed. Client machines, no matter how infrequently they may connect, are required to have a TS CAL at all times. This also applies for per user licensing.

–Harish Kumar Poongan Shanmugam
  Software Design Engineer in Test, Terminal Services

Finally, let's dig into some troubleshooting stuff and learn how we can diagnose licensing problems for terminal servers. Our expert will look at four different troubleshooting scenarios in this next sidebar:

From the Experts: Running Licensing Diagnosis on a Terminal Server

The Licensing Diagnosis tool is now integrated into the Terminal Services Configuration MMC snap-in (TSConfig.msc). This tool on the terminal server, in conjunction with the TS Licensing Manager's Review Configuration option on the License Server, can be useful in finding problems arising because of a misconfigured TS Licensing setup. The Diagnostic tool does not report all possible problems in all possible scenarios during diagnosis. However, it collates the entire TS Licensing information of Terminal Services and the License Servers at a single place and identifies common licensing configuration errors.

Upon launch of the Licensing Diagnosis tool, it first makes up a list of License Servers that the terminal server can discover via auto-discovery and also those that can be discovered via manual specification by using either the Use The Specified License Servers option in TSConfig.msc (registry-by-pass) or the Use The Specified Terminal Services License Servers Group Policy. It then contacts each License Server in turn to gather its configuration details, such as the activation state, License Key Pack information, relevant Group Policies, and so on. For this to work properly, we need to make sure that the Licensing Diagnosis tool has been launched with credentials that have administrator privileges on the License Servers. If needed, use the Provide Credentials option to specify appropriate credentials for each License Server individually at run time. Then the terminal server's licensing settings—such as the licensing mode, Group Policies, and so on—are analyzed and compared, together with the License Servers information, to summarize common TS Licensing problems. A summary of diagnostic messages, with the possible resolution steps, is provided by this tool at the end of diagnosis.

We can understand how the tool can be used by considering some sample scenarios.

Case 1: Basic Diagnosis

The terminal server has just been set up, and the licensing mode of the server has remained in Not Yet Configured mode. No other Licensing settings have been done on the TS, and a License Server has not been set up. Within the grace period of 120 days, TS has allowed connection to clients.

Past the grace period, the administrator observes that the clients are no longer able to connect. The administrator launches the diagnostic tool and finds that two diagnostic messages are reported. One message is that the TS mode needs to be configured to either Per-User or Per-Device mode, and the other is that no License Servers have been discovered on the terminal server. The administrator now sets the TS licensing mode to Per-Device mode using TSConfig.msc. (If the TS licensing mode is set up using the Set The Terminal Services Licensing Mode Group Policy, the Licensing tab in TSConfig.msc is disabled.) A License Server is also set up by the administrator in the domain. When rerunning the tool, it now reports that the License Server needs to be activated and License Key Packs of the required TS mode need to be installed on the License Server. And so on.

Case 2: Advanced Diagnosis Cases

The Terminal Services License Server Security Group Policy has been enforced on the domain. The administrator has not added the TS computer name into the Terminal Server Computers local group on the License Server. When the Licensing Diagnosis tool is launched, it displays a diagnostic message indicating that licenses cannot be issued to the given terminal server because of the Group Policy setting. This can be corrected by using the Review Configuration option in TS Licensing Manager to create the TSC group, and TS can be added to the group using the Local Users And Groups MMC snap-in.

If the License Server computer name is not a member of the Terminal Server License Servers local group in the Active Directory Domain Controller of the TS's domain, per-user licensing and per-user license reporting will not work. In such case, when the Licensing Diagnosis tool is opened on TS, the Per-User Reporting And Tracking field in the License Server Configuration Details panel indicates that per-user tracking is not available. This can be corrected by using the Review Configuration option in TS Licensing Manager to add the License Server computer name into the Terminal Server License Servers group.

Case 3: License Server Discovery Diagnosis on the Terminal Server

During License Server setup, the administrator selected to install the License Server in the Forest Discovery Scope. But as the administrator ran the installation without the required Active Directory privileges, the License Server did not get published in the Active Directory licensing object. When the Licensing Diagnosis tool is launched on the TS, it is unable to discover the License Server. For diagnosing discovery problems, the administrator can initially specify the License Server by manually configuring it in the

Use The Specified License Servers option in TSConfig.msc so that the License Server shows up in the diagnostic tool. When rerunning the Licensing Diagnosis tool, the administrator notices that the License Server's discovery scope is visible in the License Server Configuration Details section. The discovery scope shows up as Domain Scope, instead of Forest Scope. This can be corrected by using the Review Configuration option in TS Licensing Manager and exercising the Change Scope option to set the License Server discovery scope to Forest Scope.

Case 4: Licensing Mode Mismatch Diagnosis

The terminal server is configured in Per-Device licensing mode, but the administrator has installed Per-User licenses on the License Server. On launching the Licensing Diagnosis tool, a diagnostic message shows that the appropriate type of licenses are not installed on the License Server, indicating a potential mode mismatch problem.

–Harish Kumar Poongan Shanmugam
   Software Design Engineer in Test, Terminal Services

For a look at how one can use WMI to manage licensing for terminal servers, see the "Terminal Services WMI Provider" section upcoming.

Other Terminal Services Enhancements

Finally, let's briefly talk about three other features of Terminal Services in Windows Server 2008:

- WMI Provider for scripted management of Terminal Services features
- Integrating Windows System Resource Manager with Terminal Services
- Terminal Services Session Broker

Terminal Services WMI Provider

Windows Server 2008 and Windows Vista have many enhancements to WMI compared with previous versions of Microsoft Windows, and we've already covered these enhancements earlier in Chapter 4. Let's hear from our experts on the Terminal Services team concerning these WMI enhancements, including some tips on how to use WMI for managing Terminal Services:

From the Experts: Using the TS WMI Provider

The TS WMI (tscfgwmi) provider offers a rich set of class templates that allows a TS server to be configured remotely or locally. For it to work properly, however, several things need to happen:

1. By default, only user accounts that are part of the administrators group are allowed to read and write WMI properties and methods.

2. There is a User Account Control (UAC) consideration if you use the TS WMI provider locally. Run the script or application that uses TS WMI as an elevated process. If you receive a message that says, "Access Denied (0x80041003), Unspecified Error (0x80004005)," most likely you're using the TS WMI provider with a protected administrator and the process or application is not being elevated.

   If you are using the TS WMI provider remotely, the user account needs to be a domain user that is part of the local administrators group on the remote machine.

3. If you are using the TS WMI provider remotely, make sure the following firewall exceptions are selected:

   ❑ If the remote machine is in TS Remote Administration mode: File And Printer Sharing, Windows Management Instrumentation (WMI)

   ❑ If the remote machine is in TS Application mode: Terminal Services

   If firewall exceptions are not properly configured, the return error code HRESULT can be WBEM_E_ACCESS_DENIED (0x80041003), RPC Server Is Unavailable (Win32 0x800706ba).

4. 4. Note that in Win2k3/XP, the TS WMI provider is grouped in the *root/cimv2* namespace. In Windows Vista/Windows Server 2008, it is grouped in the *root/cimv2/TerminalServices* namespace. WMI security impersonation level *wbemImpersonationLevelImpersonate* and security authentication level *wbemAuthenticationLevelPktPrivacy* settings are also required for Windows Vista/Windows Server 2008. If an incorrect namespace is specified, the return error code HRESULT is WBEM_E_INVALID_NAMESPACE (0x8004100E).

TS WMI is also the abstraction layer of the Terminal Services Configuration UI tool (TSConfig.msc). Essentially, TSConfig is a UI tool that uses TS WMI to do the actual work. This also means that TS WMI can be used to troubleshoot errors when using TSConfig. For example, if you get an "Unspecified error" message when using TSConfig, you need to set the Remote Control Setting by writing a small script with TS WMI that uses the *Win32_TSRemoteControlSetting* class template. If you get the same error with the script, most likely it is a UAC issue.

Other Tips

Wbemtest.exe (which comes with Windows Vista/Windows Server 2008 at %windir%\System32\Wbem) is a great tool to use if you want to find out more information about a particular WMI class template and which WMI class templates are available. It can be used to query all class templates within a namespace. It is also able to show a brief description of what a particular property or method does. For example, to list all available class templates for the namespace *TerminalServices*, follow these steps:

1. Open a cmd shell running as administrator.

2. Type **wbemtest**.

3. Click the Connect button, connect to the namespace *root\cimv2\TerminalServices*, select Packet Privacy under Authenticationlevel, and click the Connect button.

4. Under Method Invocation Options, select the Use Amended Qualifiers check box.

5. Click the Enum Classes button, leave the Enter Superclass Name edit box empty, select the Recursive option, and then click the OK button. A Query Result dialog will show up with all the class templates under the *TerminalServices* namespace.

Now if you want to know more about remote control settings, all you need to do is double-click on the *Win32_TSRemotecontrolSetting* within the Query Result list, and a new Object Editor dialog will show up. Clicking on the Show MOF button will give you a brief description concerning each of the *Win32_TSRemotecontrolSetting* properties and methods.

For more info on Wbemtest, see *http://technet2.microsoft.com/WindowsServer/en/library/28209472-b3ed-4b96-a6dd-c43ffdd913691033.mspx?mfr=true*. And please visit *http://blogs.msdn.com/ts/archive/2006/10/03/Terminal-Services-_2800_TS_2900_-Remote-Configuration-Primer-Part-1.aspx* for a quick primer on the TS WMI provider.

–Soo Kuan Teo
Software Development Engineer in Test, Terminal Services

And here's a sidebar from another expert concerning another new feature of Windows Server 2008—the ability to use WMI to track Terminal Services licensing:

From the Experts: Monitoring TS Licensing Using WMI

Up until Windows Server 2003, TS Licensing did not have a way to dynamically monitor the usage of licenses. With the WMI providers introduced in Windows Server 2008, you can write scripts that track the number of licenses issued to devices or users. No more worrying about being caught unaware—write a script, put it in as a scheduled task for whatever interval you want the monitoring to happen, and track license usage.

Here are the WMI providers that you can use for tracking Per-Device and Per-User CAL usage:

- For tracking Per-Device license usage, you need to query all the instances of key packs installed on the License Server. To do this, query all instances of *Win32_TSLicenseKeyPack*. Within each instance, you can get the count of issued vs. available licenses using the properties *TotalLicenses* and *AvailableLicenses*.

- For tracking Per-User license count, you can query the most recent report generated or create one if it does not exist. To generate a report, call the static method *GenerateReport* on the class *Win32_TSLicenseReport*. This method returns a file name that you can use to go through the details. You can also enumerate existing reports by enumerating instances of the *Win32_TSLicenseReport* class. The report names are generated based on the date and time. Choose the latest from the set, and then look at the properties *InstalledLicenses* and *LicenseUsageCount* to get a number for how many licenses were used up for Per-User licensing.

–Aruna Somendra
Program Manager, Terminal Services

Windows System Resource Manager

Windows System Resource Manager (WSRM) is an optional feature of Windows Server 2008 that can be used to control how CPU and memory resources are allocated to applications, services, and processes running on a computer. WSRM is not a feature of Terminal Services, but if you install it on a terminal server you can control allocation of such resources for Terminal Services users and sessions.

WSRM works by using resource allocation policies to manage how computer resources (memory and CPU) are allocated to processes running on the machine. When you install the WSRM feature on a terminal server, you have a choice of two policies you can use:

- **Equal_Per_User**   This means that CPU allocation is divided on an equal-shares basis among all users, and any processes created by the user are able to use as much of the user's total CPU allocation as might be necessary.

- **Equal_Per_Session**   This policy is new to Windows Server 2008 and means that each user session with its associated processes gets an equal share of the CPU resources of the system.

The usefulness of the new Equal_Per_User resource allocation policy in a Terminal Services environment where WSRM is being used is when you have multiple sessions running for the same user. For example, say you have two sessions running for the same user, and another session running for a second user. In this case, the first two sessions will get same amount of CPU resources allocated as the third session. By contrast, if the Equal_Per_Session policy is being used, the first user will get twice the CPU resources as the second user. Note, however, that the default setting in Windows Server 2008 is for Terminal Services users to be restricted to running only a single session. (You can configure this restriction from the main page of the Terminal Services Configuration snap-in in Server Manager.)

Terminal Services Session Broker

Terminal Services Session Broker (TS Session Broker) is the new Windows Server 2008 name for what used to be called Terminal Services Session Directory, a feature that allows users to automatically reconnect to a disconnected session in a load-balanced Windows Server 2003 terminal server farm. The session directory maintains a list of sessions indexed by user name and terminal server name. It enables the user, after disconnecting a session, to reconnect to the same terminal server where the disconnected session resides so that she can resume working in that session. Furthermore, this reconnection process will work even if the user connects from a different client computer than the one used to initiate the session.

In Windows Server 2003, load balancing for terminal servers can be provided by using either the built-in Network Load Balancing (NLB) component or a third-party load balancing solution. As terminal servers become more and more mission-critical for hosting business applications, doing this becomes more and more important. By combining NLB with Terminal Services Session Directory, Windows Server 2003 terminal server farms can thus provide scale-out capability and also help ensure business continuity.

In Windows Server 2008, Terminal Services Session Directory is now called TS Session Broker and includes out-of-the-box load-balancing capability designed to replace Microsoft NLB; however, Session Broker will continue to work with both NLB and third-party solutions. In addition, while Session Directory required the Enterprise or higher SKU of Windows Server 2003, TS Session Broker is available even in the Standard Edition of Windows Server 2008.

Enabling TS Session Broker is done using the Terminal Services Configuration snap-in. Double-click the Member Of Farm In TS Session Broker link at the bottom of the center Details pane to open a Properties sheet. Then, on the TS Session Broker tab, select the check box labeled Join A Farm In TS Session Broker and fill in the remaining details (you need to do this on all terminal servers in your farm).

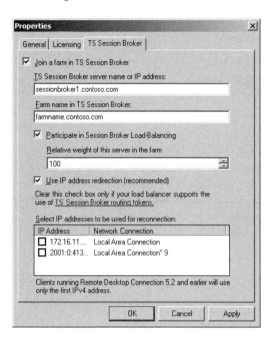

With Windows Server 2008, there are two key deployment scenarios for Session Broker:

- **Session Broker Load Balancing** Session Broker provides a simple-to-deploy load balancing solution for small scale deployments. Create a DNS record for the farm that contains the IP address of the terminal servers in the farm. DNS (or DNS round robin) will direct the initial connection to a server in the farm; however, Session Broker will perform the actual load balancing and direct the user to the least loaded terminal server in the farm (based on number of Windows sessions). The TS Client provides basic failover support for the initial connection, and in the case of a server failure, will automatically try the next entry in the DNS record after a 20 second time-out. Session Broker is capable of detecting server failures and not direct users to a server that is down. Alternatively, NLB or another connection routing mechanism can be used in place of DNS.

- **Third-party Load Balancing (or MS NLB)** Session Broker can be deployed in the same configuration as Windows Server 2003 Session Directory, using any third-party hardware load balancers.

Finally, with the regular stream of patches and application updates admins are faced with these days, it can be difficult to find a time when a terminal server can be brought offline without interrupting user experience. Starting with Beta 3 of Windows Server 2008, the new Server Draining feature enables planned maintenance for TS Session Broker load balancing farms without interruption of user experience. The following sidebar explains more.

From the Experts: Terminal Server Draining

Administrators typically would like to drain their servers to apply security update patches and keep the machine up to date. In this scenario, they would try to prevent new users from logging on to the server; at the same time, they would want to get current users actively using the machine to save their work and log off in a phased manner.

In Windows Server 2003, a very primitive form of server draining is supported by using a command-line tool called chglogon.exe. The chglogon.exe /disable switch prevents any new logons from occurring in the machine. However, it also prevents users who already have disconnected sessions from reconnecting to their disconnected sessions enabling them to log off gracefully and save their work.

In Windows Server 2008, server draining is introduced. This can be enabled by using a command-line tool (new flags to chglogon.exe), using the Terminal Services Configuration tool, and also via WMI. When a server is put in drain mode, new logons are not allowed, but users who already have a disconnected session are allowed to reconnect. In addition, for remote administration purposes, administrators who connect with the /admin switch are allowed to log on, even if drain mode is set. This mode is supported only when the TS role is installed.

We expect that this enhanced drain support will enable IT administrators to patch their servers in a way that causes minimal trouble to all the remote users. Before taking the server down for patching and installing updates, administrators can enable drain mode and then send a message that prompts users to save their work and log off in a day or two!

Also, we have relevant events logged in the Windows event log when somebody is not allowed to log on because the server is in drain mode. We recommend that administrators check the event log for relevant events to determine whether drain mode was indeed the cause for someone to be denied logon from a remote site.

−Sriram Sampath
Development Lead, Terminal Services

Conclusion

As we've seen in this chapter, Terminal Services has been greatly enhanced in Windows Server 2008 with new features such as TS RemoteApp, TS Web Access, and TS Gateway—plus lots of security, manageability, and user experience improvements too numerous to list here and many of which we've described. In my mind, Windows Server 2008 has changed the whole meaning of Terminal Services from a platform for providing remote access to different types of clients (thin/fat, Windows/non) to a powerful and secure application-deployment platform that enterprises can use to provide remote users with access anywhere and anytime. The evolution of this platform is remarkable—I can't wait to see what there will be in future versions!

Additional Resources

You'll find a brief overview of Terminal Services features in Windows Server 2008 at *http://www.microsoft.com/windowsserver/2008/evaluation/overview.mspx*. By the time you read this chapter, this site will probably redirect you to something with a lot more content.

If you have access to the Windows Server 2008 beta program on Microsoft Connect (*http://connect.microsoft.com*), you can get some great Terminal Services documents from there, including:

- Windows Server 2008 Terminal Services RemoteApp Step-by-Step Guide
- Windows Server 2008 Terminal Services TS Gateway Server Step-by-Step Setup Guide
- Windows Server 2008 Terminal Services TS Licensing Step-by-Step Setup Guide

Plus you'll also find chats there, saved Live Meeting presentations, and lots of other useful stuff, with more being added all the time.

There's also a TechNet Forum where you can ask questions and help others trying out the Terminal Services features; see *http://forums.microsoft.com/TechNet/ShowForum.aspx?ForumID=580&SiteID=17* for this forum. (Windows Live registration is required.)

The Terminal Services Team Blog is definitely something you won't want to miss. See *http://blogs.msdn.com/ts/*.

Finally, be sure to turn to Chapter 14, "Additional Resources," for more sources of information concerning new Terminal Services features, and also for links to webcasts, whitepapers, blogs, newsgroups, and other sources of information about all aspects of Windows Server 2008.

Chapter 9
Clustering Enhancements

In this chapter:

Failover Clustering Enhancements 252

Network Load Balancing Enhancements 278

Conclusion 283

Additional Resources. 283

Don't tell my local bookstore, but I don't shop there anymore—even though I'm frequently seen browsing the shelves. Instead, I browse the latest titles while sitting in one of the comfortable chairs the bookstore generously provides its customers (big mistake on their part) and when I find a book that interests me, I make a note of the title, author, and ISBN.

Then, when I get home, I order the book from an online bookstore. Shhh—don't tell my local bookstore I do this, otherwise they might bar me from using their comfy chairs next time I visit them.

Online bookstores and similar sites have changed the way I do much of my shopping. But what if an online bookstore ran their entire Web site on a single server and that server died? Chaos! Frustration!! Lost business!!! I might even go back to my local bookstore and buy from there!

What keeps sites like these always available is clustering. A single server is a single point of failure for your business, and when that server goes down so does your revenue. The same goes for a single source of storage, a single network link, or even having all your computing resources located at a single geographical site. Fault-tolerant technologies such as RAID can mitigate the risk of storage failures, while redundant network links can reduce the impact of a network failure. And data backup and archival solutions are essential if you want to ensure continuity of your business after a catastrophe. But it's also important to implement clustering technologies if you want to fully protect your business against downtime and ensure high availability to customers.

A cluster is simply a collection of nodes (servers) that work together in some fashion to ensure high availability for your applications. Clusters also provide scalability for applications because they enable you to bring additional nodes into your cluster when needed to support increased demand. And since the days of Microsoft Windows NT 4.0, there have been two types of clustering technologies supported by Microsoft Windows: server clusters and Network Load Balancing (NLB).

First, let's look at server clusters. Originally code-named "Wolfpack" when the technology was first developed, server clusters provide failover support for long-running applications and other network services, such as file, print, database, or messaging services. Server clusters ensure high availability for these services because when one node in your cluster dies, other nodes take over and assume the workload of the failed node and continue servicing client requests to keep your applications running. In Windows NT 4.0, server clusters were known as the Microsoft Cluster Services (MSCS); in Windows 2000 Server, this feature was renamed Server Clusters. Now in Windows Server 2008, we call this technology Windows Server Failover Clustering (WSFC) or simply Failover Clustering, which communicates clearly the purpose of this form of clustering and how it works.

Then there's Network Load Balancing, which was originally called Windows Load Balancing Service (WLBS) in Windows NT 4.0. This form of clustering technology was renamed Network Load Balancing (NLB) in Windows Server 2003, which is still the name for this technology in Windows Server 2008. NLB provides a highly available and scalable environment for TCP/IP services and applications by distributing client connections across multiple servers. Another way of saying this is that NLB is a network driver that balances the load for networked client/server applications by distributing client connections across a set of servers. NLB is especially great for scaling out stateless applications running on Web servers when the number of clients is growing, but you can also use it to ensure the availability of terminal servers, media servers, and even VPN servers.

Let's look at the improvements the Windows Server team has made to these two clustering technologies in Windows Server 2008. As with everything in this book, the new features and enhancements I'm going to describe here are subject to change before RTM. And who knows? Maybe after you read this you'll want to go out, buy Windows Server 2008, and start your own online bookstore! Well, maybe not—the competition is already pretty stiff in that market.

Failover Clustering Enhancements

Let's start with improvements to Failover Clustering, as the most significant changes have occurred with this technology. Here's a quick list of enhancements, which we'll unpack further in a moment:

- A new quorum model that lets clusters survive the loss of the quorum disk.

- Enhanced support for storage area networks and other storage technologies.

- Networking and security enhancements that make clusters more secure and easier to maintain.

- An improved tool for validating your hardware configuration *before* you try to deploy your cluster on it.

- A new server paradigm that sees clustering as a feature rather than as a role.

- A new management console that makes setting up and managing clusters a snap.

- Improvements to other management tools, including the cluster.exe command and WMI provider.

- Simplified troubleshooting using the Event logs instead of the old cluster.log.

But before we look at these enhancements in detail, let me give you some insight into *why* Microsoft has implemented them in Windows Server 2008.

Goals of Clustering Improvements

Why is Microsoft making all these clustering improvements in Windows Server 2008?

For their customers.

I know, you're IT pros and you want to read the technical stuff. And you probably wish the Marketing Police would step in and put me in jail for making a statement like that. But think about it for a moment—it's *you* who are the customer! At least, you are if you are an admin for some company. So what have been *your* complaints with regard to Microsoft's current (Windows Server 2003 R2 Enterprise and Datacenter Edition) version of server clustering technology?

Well, perhaps you've said (or thought) things similar to the following:

"Why do I have to assign one of my 26 available drive letters to the quorum resource just for cluster use? This limits how many instances of SQL I can put on my cluster! And why does the quorum in the Shared Disk model have to be a single point of failure? I thought the whole purpose of server clusters was to *eliminate* a single point of failure for my applications."

"Why do we as customers have to be locked in to a single vendor of clustering hardware whose products are certified on the Hardware Compatibility List (HCL) or Windows Server Catalog? I found out I couldn't upgrade the firmware driver on my HBA because it's not listed on the HCL so it's unsupported, argh. So I called my vendor and he says I'll have to wait months for the testing to be completed and their Web site to be updated. Maintaining clusters shouldn't be this hard!"

"Why is it so darned hard to set up a cluster in the first place? I was on the phone with Microsoft Premier Support for hours until the support engineer finally helped me discover I had a cable connected wrong—plus I forgot to select the third check box on the second property sheet of the first node's configuration settings on the left side of the right pane of the cluster admin console."

"We had to hire a high-priced clustering specialist to implement and configure a cluster solution for our IT department because our existing IT pros just couldn't figure this clustering stuff out. They kept asking me questions like, "What's the difference between *IsAlive* and *LooksAlive*?", and I kept telling them, "I don't understand it either!" Why can't they make it so simple that an ordinary IT pro like me can figure it out?"

"I want to create a cluster that has one node in London and another in New York. Is that possible? Why do you say, 'Maybe'?"

And here's my favorite:

"All I want to do is set up a cluster that will make my file share highly available. I'm an experienced admin who's got 100 file servers and I've set up thousands of file shares in the past, so why are clusters completely different? Why do I have to read a 50-page whitepaper just to figure out how to make this work?"

OK, I think I've probably got your attention by now, so let's look at the enhancements. I'm assuming that as an experienced IT pro you already have some familiarity with how server clustering works in Windows Server 2003, but if not you can find an overview of this topic on the Microsoft Windows Server TechCenter. See the "Server Clusters Technical Reference" found at *http://technet2.microsoft.com/WindowsServer/en/library/8ad36286-df8d-4c53-9aee-7a9a073c95ee1033.mspx?mfr=true.*

Understanding the New Quorum Model

For Windows Server 2003 clusters, the entire cluster depends on the quorum disk being alive. Despite the best efforts of SAN vendors to provide highly available RAID storage, sometimes even they fail. On Windows Server 2003, you can implement two different quorum models: the shared disk quorum model (also sometimes called the standard quorum model or the shared quorum device model), where you have a set of nodes sharing a storage array that includes the quorum resource; and the majority node set model, where each node has its own local storage device with a replicated copy of the quorum resource. The shared disk model is far more common mainly because a very high percentage of clusters are 2-node clusters.

In Windows Server 2008, however, these two models have been merged into a single hybrid or mixed-mode quorum model called the majority quorum model, which combines the best of both these earlier approaches. The quorum disk (which now is referred to as a *witness disk*) is now no longer a single point of failure for your cluster as it was in the shared disk quorum model of previous versions of Windows server clustering. Instead, you can now assign a *vote* to each node in your cluster and also to a shared storage device itself, and the cluster can now survive any event that involves the loss of a single vote. In other words—drum roll, please—a two-node cluster with shared storage can now survive the loss of the quorum. Or the loss of either node. This is because each node counts as one vote and the shared storage device also gets a vote, so losing a node or losing the quorum amounts to the same thing—the loss of one vote. (Actually, technically the voting thing works like this: Each node gets one vote for the internal disk where the cluster registry hive resides and the "witness disk" gets one vote because a copy of the cluster registry is also kept there. So not every disk a node brings online equates to a vote. Finally, the file share witness gets one vote even though a copy of the cluster registry hive is *not* kept there.)

Or you can configure your cluster a different way by assigning a vote only to your witness disk (the shared quorum storage device) and no votes for your nodes. In this type of clustering configuration, your cluster will still be operational even if only one node is still online and talking to the witness. In other words, this type of cluster configuration works the same way as the shared disk quorum model worked in Windows Server 2003.

Or if you aren't using shared storage but are using local (replicated) storage for each node instead, you can assign one vote to each node so that as long as a majority of nodes are still online, the cluster is still up and any applications or services running on it continue to be available. In other words, this type of configuration achieves the same behavior as the majority node set model worked on the previous platform and it requires at least three nodes in your cluster.

In summary, the voting model for Failover Clustering in Windows Server 2008 puts you in control by letting you design your cluster to work the same as either of the two cluster models on previous platforms or as a hybrid of them. By assigning or not assigning votes to your nodes and shared storage, you create the cluster that meets your needs. In other words, in Windows Server 2008 there is only one quorum model and it's configurable by assigning votes the way you choose.

There's more. If you want to use shared storage for your witness, it doesn't have to be a separate disk. (The file share witness can't be a DFS share, however.) It can now simply be a file share on any file server on your network (as shown in Figure 9-1) and one file server can even function as a witness for multiple clusters. (Each cluster requires its own share, but you can have a single file server with a number of different shares, one for each cluster.) This approach is a good choice if you're implementing GeoClusters (geographically dispersed clusters), something we'll talk about in a few moments.

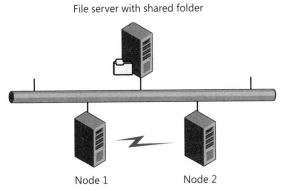

Figure 9-1   Majority quorum model using a file share witness

A few quick technical points need to be made:

- If you create a cluster of at least two nodes that includes a shared disk witness, a \Cluster folder that contains the cluster registry hive will be created on the witness.

- There are no longer any checkpoint files or quorum logs, so you don't need to run **clussvc −resetquorumlog** on startup any longer. (In fact, this switch doesn't even exist anymore in Windows Server 2008.)

- You can use the Configure Quorum Settings wizard to change the quorum model after your cluster has been created, but you generally shouldn't. Plan your clusters before you create them so that you won't need to change the quorum model afterwards.

Understanding Storage Enhancements

Now let's look at the storage technology enhancements in Windows Server 2008, many of which result from the fact that Microsoft has completely rewritten the cluster disk driver (clusdisk.sys) and Physical Disk resource for the new platform. First, clustering in Windows Server 2008 can now be called "SAN friendly." This is because Failover Clustering no longer uses SCSI bus resets, which can be very disruptive to storage area network operations. A SCSI reset is a SCSI command that breaks the reservation on the target device, and a bus reset affects the entire bus, causing all devices on the bus to become disconnected. Clustering in Windows 2000 Server used bus resets as a matter of course; Windows Server 2003 improved on that by using them only as a last resort. Windows Server 2008, however, doesn't use them at all–good riddance. Another improvement this provides is that Failover Clustering never leaves your cluster disks (disks that are visible to all nodes in your cluster) in an unprotected state that can affect the integrity of your data.

Second, Windows Server 2008 now supports only storage technologies that support persistent reservations. This basically means that Fibre Channel, iSCSI, and Serial Attached SCSI (SAS) shared bus types are allowed. Parallel-SCSI is now deprecated.

Third–and this might seem like a minor point–the quorum disk no longer needs a drive letter because Failover Clustering now supports direct disk access for your quorum resource. This is actually a good thing because drive letters are a valuable commodity for large clusters. You can, however, still assign the quorum a drive letter if you need to do so for some reason.

Fourth, Windows Server 2008 supports GUID Partition Table (GPT) disks. These disks support partitions larger than 2 terabytes (TB) and provide improved redundancy and recoverability, so they're ideal for enterprise-level clusters. GPT disks are supported by Failover Clustering on all Windows Server 2008 hardware platforms (x86, x64, and IA64) for both Enterprise and Datacenter Editions.

Fifth, new self-healing logic helps identify disks based on multiple attributes and self-heals the disk if found by any attribute. There's a sidebar coming up in a moment where an expert from the product team will describe this feature in more detail. And in addition, new validation logic helps preserve mount point relationships and prevent them from breaking.

Sixth, there is now a built-in mechanism that helps re-establish relationships between physical disk resources and logical unit numbers (LUNs). The operation of this mechanism is similar to that of the Server Cluster Recovery Utility tool (ClusterRecovery.exe) found in the Windows Server 2003 Resource Kit.

Seventh (and probably not finally) there are revamped chkdsk.exe options and an enhanced DiskPart.exe command.

Did I mention the improved Maintenance Mode that lets you give temporary exclusive access to online clustered disks to other applications? Or the Volume Shadow Copy Services (VSS) support for hardware snapshot restores of clustered disks? Or the fact that the cluster disk driver no longer provides direct disk fencing functionality (disk fencing is the process of allowing/disallowing access to a disk), and that this change reduces the chances of disk corruption occurring?

Oh yes, and concerning dynamic disks, I know there has been customer demand that Microsoft include built-in support for dynamic disks for cluster storage. However, this is not included in Windows Server 2008. Why? I would guess for two reasons: first, there are already third-party products available, such as Symantec Storage Foundation for Windows, that can provide this type of functionality; and second, there's really no need for this functionality in Failover Clusters. Why? Because GPT disks can give you partitions large enough that you'll probably never need to worry about resizing them—plus if you do need to resize a partition on a basic disk, you can do so in Windows Server 2008 using the enhanced DiskPart.exe tool included with the platform, which now allows you to shrink volumes in addition to being able to extend them.

The bottom line for IT pros? You might need to upgrade your storage gear if you plan on migrating your existing Windows server clusters to Windows Server 2008. That's because some hardware will simply not be upgradable and you can't assume that what worked with Windows Server 2003 will work with Windows Server 2008. In other words, there won't be any grandfathering of storage hardware support for qualified Windows server clustering solutions that are currently listed in the Windows Server Catalog. But I'll get to the topic of qualifying your clustering hardware in a few moments.

Now here's the sidebar I mentioned earlier.

From the Experts: Self-Healing Cluster Storage

The storage stack and how shared disks are managed as well as identified has been completely redesigned in Windows Server 2008 Failover Clustering. In Windows Server 2008, the Cluster Service still uses the Disk Signature located in the Master Boot Record of the disk to identify disks, but in addition it also now leverages SCSI Inquiry data to identify disks as well. The Disk Signature is located in sector 0 of the disk and is actually data on the disk, but data on the disk can change for a variety of reasons. SCSI Inquiry data is an attribute of the LUN provided by the storage array. The new mechanism in 2008 is that if for any reason the Cluster Service is unable to identify the disk based on the Disk Signature, it then searches for the disk based on the SCSI Inquiry data. If the disk is found, the Cluster Service then self-heals and updates its entry for the disk signature. In the same respect, if the disk is found by the Disk Signature and the previously known SCSI Inquiry data has changed, the Cluster Service self-heals, updates its known value, and brings the disk online. The big win in the end is that disks are now identified based on multiple attributes, the service is flexible enough to deal with a variety of failures of modifications, and such failures will not result in downtime. This is a big win and will resolve one of the top supportability issues in previous releases.

There might be extreme situations where both the Disk Signature and the SCSI Inquiry data for a LUN change—for example, in the case of a complete disaster recovery. To handle this situation, a new recovery tool has been built into the product in 2008. If a disk is in a Failed or Offline state because it cannot identify the disks (which is a condition that is identified by Event ID 1034 in the System event log), perform the following steps. Open the Failover Cluster Management snap-in (CluAdmin.msc), right-click the Physical Disk resource, and select Properties. At the bottom of the General tab, find and click the Repair button. A list is displayed of all the disks that are shared but not clustered yet. The Repair action allows you to specify which disk this disk resource should control, and it allows you to rebuild the relationship between logical disks and the cluster physical disk resources. Once you select the newly restored disk, the properties are updated and you can bring the disk online so that it can be used again by highly available services or applications.

–Elden Christensen
Program Manager, Windows Enterprise Server Products

Understanding Networking and Security Enhancements

If you've picked up a copy of the *Microsoft Windows Vista Resource Kit* (Microsoft Press, 2007), you'll have already read a lot about the new TCP/IP networking stack in Windows Vista. (If you haven't picked up a copy of this title yet, why haven't you? How am I supposed to retire if the books I've been involved with don't earn royalties?) Windows Server 2008 is built on the same TCP/IP stack as Windows Vista, so all the features of this stack are present here as well. The Cable Guy has a good overview of these features in one of his columns, found at *http://www.microsoft.com/technet/community/columns/cableguy/cg0905.mspx*.

One implication of this is that Failover Clustering in Windows Server 2008 now fully supports IPv6. This includes both internode network communications and client communications with the cluster. If you're thinking of migrating your IPv4 network to IPv6 (or if you have to do so because of government mandates or for industry compliance), there's a good overview chapter on IPv6 deployment in the *Windows Vista Resource Kit*. (Did I mention royalties?)

Another really nice networking enhancement in Failover Clustering is DHCP support. This means that cluster IP addresses can now be obtained from a DHCP server instead of having to be assigned manually using static addressing. Specifically, if you've configured the servers that will become nodes in your cluster so that they receive their addresses dynamically, all cluster addresses will also be obtained dynamically. But if you've configured your servers with static addresses, you'll need to manually configure your cluster addresses as well. At the time of this writing, this works only for IPv4 addresses, however, and I don't know if there are any plans for IPv6 addresses to be assigned dynamically to clusters before RTM–though DHCPv6 servers are supported in Windows Server 2008. (See Chapter 12, "Other Features and Enhancements," for more information on DHCP enhancements in Windows Server 2008.)

Another improvement in networking for Failover Clusters is the removal of all remaining legacy dependencies on the NetBIOS protocol and the standardizing of all name resolution on DNS. This change eliminates unwanted NetBIOS name resolution broadcast traffic and also simplifies the transport of SMB traffic within your cluster.

Another change involves moving from the use of RPC over UDP for cluster heartbeats to more reliable TCP session-oriented protocols. And IPSec improvements now mean that when you use IPSec to safeguard communication within a cluster, failover is almost instantaneous from the client's perspective. And now Network Name resources can stay up if only one IP address resource is online–in previous clustering implementations, all IP address resources had to be online for the Network Name to be available to the client.

Finally–and this can be a biggie for large enterprises–you can now have your cluster nodes reside in different subnets. And that means different nodes can be in different sites–really different sites that are geographically far apart! This kind of thing is called Geographically Dispersed Clusters (or GeoClusters for short) and although a form of GeoClusters was supported on earlier Windows server platforms, you had to use technologies such as Virtual LANs (VLANs) to ensure that all the nodes in your cluster appeared on the same IP subnet, which could be a pain sometimes. In addition, support for configurable heartbeat time-outs in Windows Server 2008 effectively means that there are no practical distance limitations on how far apart Failover Cluster nodes can be. Well, maybe you couldn't have one node at Cape Canaveral, Florida, and another on Olympus Mons on Mars, but it should work if one node is in New York while another is in Kalamazoo, Michigan. In addition, the cluster heartbeat, which still uses UDP port 3343, now relies on UDP unicast packets (similar to the Request/ Reply process used by "ping") instead of less reliable UDP broadcasts. This also makes Geo-Clusters easier to implement and more reliable than before. (By default, Failover Clustering waits five seconds before considering a cluster node as unreachable, and you can view this and other settings by typing **cluster . /prop** at a command prompt.)

Let's hear an expert from Microsoft add a few more insights concerning GeoClusters.

From the Experts: Dispersing Failover Cluster Nodes

One of the restrictions placed on previous versions of Failover Clusters (in Windows NT 4.0, Windows 2000 Server, and Windows Server 2003) was that all members of the cluster had to be located on the same logical IP subnet—for example, communications among all the cluster nodes could not be routed across different networks. Although this was not much of a restriction for clusters that were centrally located, it proved to be quite different for IT professionals who wanted to implement geographically dispersed clusters that were stretched across multiple sites as part of a disaster recovery scenario.

As described later in this chapter in the "From the Experts: Validating a Failover Cluster Configuration" sidebar, cluster solutions were required to be listed in the Windows Server Catalog. A subset of that listing is the Geographically Dispersed category. Geographically dispersed cluster solutions are typically implemented by third-party hardware vendors. With the exception of Microsoft Exchange Server 2007 deployed as a 2-Node Cluster Continuous Replication (CCR) cluster, there is no "out-of-the-box" data replication implementation available from Microsoft for geographic clusters.

In addition to the storage replication requirement, there were networking requirements as well. Because of the restriction previously stated regarding the nodes having to reside on the same logical subnet, organizations implementing geographic clusters had to configure VLANs that stretched between geographic sites. These VLANs also had to be configured to guarantee a maximum round-trip latency of no more than 500 milliseconds. Allowing Windows Server 2008 Failover Cluster nodes to reside on different subnets now does away with this restriction.

Accommodating this new functionality required a complete rewrite of the cluster network driver and a change in the way cluster Network Name resources were configured. In previous versions of Failover Clusters, a Network Name resource required a dependency on at least one IP Address resource. If the IP address resource failed to come online or failed to stay online, the Network Name resource also failed. Even if a Network Name resource depended on two different IP Address resources, if one of those IP Address resources failed, the Network Name resource also failed. In the Windows Server 2008 Failover Cluster feature, this has changed. The logic that is now used is no longer an AND dependency logic but an OR dependency logic. (This is the default, but it can be changed.) Now a Network Name resource that depends on IP Address resources that are supported by network interfaces configured for different networks can come online if at least one of those IP Address resources comes online.

Being able to locate cluster nodes on different networks has been one of the most highly requested features by those using Microsoft high-availability technologies. Now we can accommodate that request in Windows Server 2008.

–Chuck Timon, Jr.
Support Engineer, Microsoft Enterprise Support, Windows Server Core Team

Other Security Improvements

Failover Clustering also includes security improvements over previous versions of Failover Clusters. The biggest change in this area is that the Cluster Service now runs within the security context of the built-in LocalSystem account instead of a custom Cluster Service Account (CSA), a domain account you needed to specify in order to start the service on previous versions of Windows Server. This change means you no longer have to prestage user accounts for your cluster, and also that you'll have no more headaches from managing passwords for these accounts. It also means that your cluster is more protected against accidental account changes—for example, when you've implemented or modified a Group Policy and the CSA gets deleted or has some of its privileges removed by accident.

Another security enhancement is that Failover Clustering relies exclusively on Kerberos for authentication purposes—that is, NTLM is no longer internally leveraged. This is because the cluster nodes now authenticate using a machine account instead of a user account. There are other security enhancements, but let's move on.

Validating a Clustering Solution

A significant change in Microsoft's approach to qualified hardware solutions for clustering is that it is moving away from the old paradigm of certifying whole cluster solutions in the HCL or the Windows Server Catalog. Microsoft is now providing customers with tools that enable them to self test and verify their solutions. Not that you should try to mix and match hardware from different vendors to build your own home-grown Failover Cluster solutions—Microsoft is just trying to make the model more flexible, not to encourage you to start duct-taping your clusters together. Anyway, what this means is that Failover Clustering solutions are now defined by "best practices" and self testing, not by static listings on some Web site. Of course, you still have to buy hardware that has been certified by the Windows Logo Program, but you no longer need to buy a complete solution from a single vendor (although it's still probably a good idea to do this in most cases). So what you would generally now do when implementing a Failover Clustering solution would be the following:

1. Buy your servers, storage devices, and network hardware, and then connect everything together the way you want to for your specific clustering scenario. (Note that all components must have a Designed For Windows logo.)

2. Enable the Failover Clustering feature on each server that will function as a node within your cluster. (See Chapter 5, "Managing Server Roles," for information on how to enable features in Windows Server 2008. Note that Failover Clustering is a feature, not a role— this is because Failover Clustering is designed to *support* roles such as File Server, Print Server, DHCP Server, and so on.)

3. Run the new Validate tool (shown in Figure 9-2) to verify whether your hardware (and the way it's set up) is end-to-end compatible with Failover Clustering in Windows Server 2008. Note that depending on the type of clustering solution you've set up, it can sometimes take a while (maybe 30 minutes) for all the built-in validation tests to run.

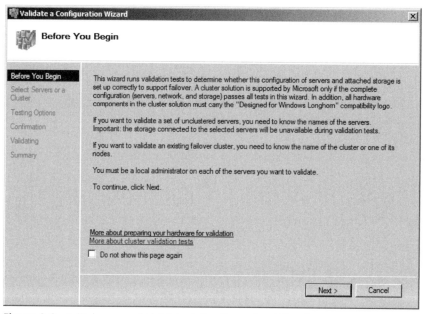

Figure 9-2   Initial screen of Validate A Configuration Wizard

Here's a sidebar, written by an expert at Microsoft, that provides detailed information about this new Validate tool. Actually it's not so new—it's essentially the same ClusPrep.exe tool (actually called the Microsoft Cluster Configuration Validation Wizard) that's available from the Microsoft Download Center, and it can be run against server clusters running on Windows 2000 Server SP4 or later to validate their configuration. However, the tool is now integrated into the Failover Clustering feature in Windows Server 2008.

From the Experts: Validating a Failover Cluster Configuration

Microsoft high-availability (HA) solutions are designed to provide applications, services, or both to end users with minimal downtime. To achieve this, Microsoft requires the hardware running high-availability solutions be qualified that they have been tested and proven to work correctly. Hardware vendors are required to download a test kit from the Microsoft Windows HCL and upload test results for their solutions before they are listed as Cluster Solutions in the Windows Server Catalog. Users depend on the vendors to test and submit their solutions for inclusion in the Windows Server Catalog. A user can request that a vendor test and submit a specific solution for inclusion in the catalog, but there are no guarantees this will be done. This sometimes leaves users with little choice for clustering solutions on current Windows platforms.

Beginning with Windows Server 2008 Failover Clustering, however, the qualification process for clusters will change. Microsoft will still require that the hardware or software meet the requirements set forth in the Windows Logo Program for Windows Server 2008, but users will have more control over the choices they can make.

Once the hardware is properly configured in accordance with the vendor's specifications, all the user has to do is install the correct version of the server software (Windows Server 2008 Enterprise or Datacenter Edition), join the servers to an Active Directory–based domain, and add the Windows Server 2008 Failover Clustering feature. With the feature installed on all nodes that will be part of the cluster, connectivity to the storage verified, and the disks properly configured, the first step is to open the Failover Cluster Management snap-in (located in Administrative Tools) and select Validate A Configuration located in the Management section in the center pane of the MMC 3.0 snap-in.

The Validate A Configuration process is wizard-based, as are most of the configuration processes in Windows Server 2008 Failover Clustering. (See the "From the Experts: Simplifying the User Experience" sidebar later in this chapter.) After entering the names for all the servers in the Select Servers Or A Cluster screen and accepting all the defaults in the remaining screens, the validate process runs and a Summary report is presented once the process completes. This report can be viewed in the last screen of the Validate A Configuration Wizard, or it can be viewed inside Internet Explorer as an MHTML file by selecting View Report. Each time Validate is run, a copy of this report is placed in the *%systemroot%*\cluster\reports directory on all nodes that were tested. (All cluster configuration reports are stored in this location on every node of the cluster.)

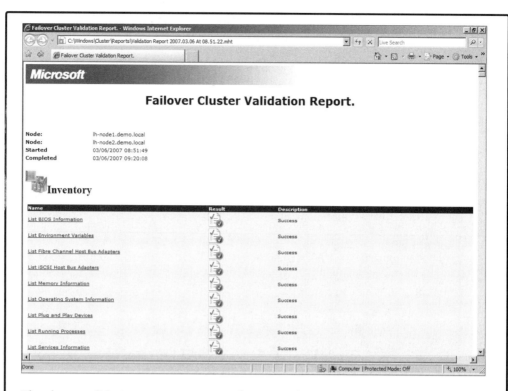

The cluster validation process consists of a series of tests that verify the hardware configuration, as well as some aspects of the OS configuration on each node. These tests fall into four basic categories: Inventory, Network, Storage, and System Configuration.

- **Inventory** These tests literally take a basic inventory of all nodes being configured. The inventory tests collect information about the system BIOS, environment variables, host bus adapters (HBAs), memory, operating system, PnP devices, running processes and services, software updates, and signed and unsigned drivers.

- **Network** The network tests collect information about the network interface card (NIC) configuration (for example, whether there is more than one NIC in each node), IP configuration (for example, static or DHCP assigned addresses), communication connectivity among the nodes, and whether the firewall configuration allows for proper communication among all nodes.

- **Storage** The storage area is probably where most failures will be observed because of the more stringent requirements placed on hardware vendors and on the restrictions on what will and will not be supported in Windows Server 2008 Failover Clustering. (For example, parallel SCSI interfaces will no longer be supported in a cluster.) The storage tests first collect data from the nodes in the cluster and determine what storage is common to all. The common storage is what will be considered *potential cluster disks*. Once these devices have been enumerated, tests are run to verify disk latency, proper arbitration for the shared disks, proper failover of the disks among all the nodes in the cluster, the existence of multiple-arbitrations scenarios, file system, the use of the MS-MPIO standard (if multipath software is being used), that proper SCSI-3 SPC3 commands are being adhered to (specifically Persistent Reservations, or PR, and Unique Disk IDs), and simultaneous failover scenarios.

■ **System Configuration**   This final category of tests verifies the nodes are members of the same Active Directory domain, the drivers being used are signed, the OS versions and service pack levels are the same, the services that the cluster needs are running (for example, the Remote Registry service), the processor architectures are the same (note that you cannot mix X86 and X64 nodes in a cluster), and that the processor architectures all have the same software updates installed.

The configuration tests report a status of Success, Warning, or Failed. The ideal scenario is to have all tests report Success. This status indicates the configuration should be able to run as a Windows Server 2008 Failover Cluster. Any tests that report a status of Failed have to be addressed and the validation process needs to be run again; otherwise, the configuration will not properly support Windows Server 2008 Failover Clustering (even if the cluster creation process completes). Tests that report a status of Warning indicate that something in the configuration is not in accordance with cluster best practices and the cluster should be evaluated and potentially fixed before actually deploying the cluster in a production environment. An example is if one or more nodes tested had only one NIC installed. From a clustering perspective, that arrangement equates to a single point of failure and should be corrected.

An added benefit of having a validation process incorporated into the product is that it can be used to assist in the troubleshooting process should a problem arise. The cluster validation process can be run against an already configured cluster. Either all the tests can be run or a select group of tests can be run. The only restriction is that for the storage tests to be run, all physical disk resources in the cluster must be placed in an Offline state. This will necessitate an interruption in services to the clients.

Incorporating cluster validation functionality into the product empowers the end user not only by allowing them to verify their own configuration locally, but by also providing them a set of built-in troubleshooting tools.

−*Chuck Timon, Jr.*
Support Engineer, Microsoft Enterprise Support, Windows Server Core Team

Tips for Validating Clustering Solutions

Here are a few tips on getting a successful validation from running this tool:

- If you're going to use domain controllers as nodes, use domain controllers. If you're going to use member servers instead, use member servers. You can't do both for the same cluster or validation will fail. (Note that Microsoft generally discourages customers from running clustering on domain controllers.)

- All the servers that will be nodes in your cluster need to have their computer accounts in the same domain and the same organizational unit.

- All the servers in your cluster need to be either 32-bit systems or 64-bit systems; you can't have a mix of these architectures in the same cluster (and you can't combine x64 and IA64 either in the same cluster).

- All the servers in your cluster need to be running Windows Server 2008—you can't have some nodes running earlier versions of Windows.

- Each server needs at least two network adapters, with each adapter having a different IP address that belongs to a separate subnet on which all the servers reside.

- If your Fibre Channel or iSCSI SAN supports Multipath I/O (MPIO), a validation test will check to see whether your configuration is supported. (See Chapter 12 for more information about MPIO.)

- Your cluster storage needs to use the Persistent Reserve commands from the newer SCSI-3 standard and not the older SCSI-2 standard.

And here are a couple of best practices to follow as well. If you ignore these, you might get warnings when you run the validation tool:

- Make sure all the servers in your cluster have the same software updates (including service packs, hotfixes, and security updates) applied to them or you could experience unpredictable results.

- Make sure all drivers on your servers are signed properly.

Setting Up and Managing a Cluster

Once you've added the Failover Cluster feature on the Windows Server 2008 servers that you're going to use as your cluster nodes and you have validated your clustering hardware and network and storage infrastructure, you're ready to create your cluster. Creating a cluster is much easier in Windows Server 2008 than in previous versions of Windows Server. For example, in Windows Server 2003 you had to create your cluster first using one node and then adding the other nodes one at a time. Now you can add all your nodes at once when you create your cluster.

To create your new cluster, you open the Failover Clustering Management console from Administrative Tools, right-click on the root node, and select Create A Cluster. Then you simply follow the steps presented in the Create A Cluster Wizard by specifying your server names, typing a name for your cluster (following standard naming conventions) to define the Client Access Point (CAP) for your cluster, specifying static IP address information (which is needed only if DHCP is not being used by your nodes), and then clicking Finish. An XML report is generated after you've finished, and you can view it later from the %windir%\cluster\reports directory if you need to. (The report is saved on every node in the cluster.) Note that when you're specifying the names of servers for your cluster, the number of nodes you can specify depends on your processor architecture. Specifically, clusters on x64 hardware support up to 16 nodes, while only 8 nodes are supported on both x86 and IA64 architectures. This is true whether you're using the Enterprise or Datacenter edition of Windows Server 2008. (Failover Clustering is not supported on the Standard or Web Edition.)

Once you've created your cluster, you're ready to manage it. Figure 9-3 shows the Failover Cluster Management console for a cluster of two nodes. You can use this tool to change the quorum model, make applications and\or services highly available, configure cluster permissions (including a new feature that lets you audit access to your cluster if auditing has been enabled on your servers), and perform other common cluster management tasks. In fact, you can now use this new MMC console to manage multiple clusters at once—something you couldn't do with the previous version of the tool, which looked like an MMC console but really wasn't. (But you can't manage server clusters running on earlier versions of Windows using the new Failover Cluster Management console.) In addition, you can use the cluster.exe command to manage your cluster from the command line (but again you can't use the new cluster.exe command to manage clusters running on previous Windows platforms). And finally, you can use the clustering WMI provider to automate clustering management tasks using scripts.

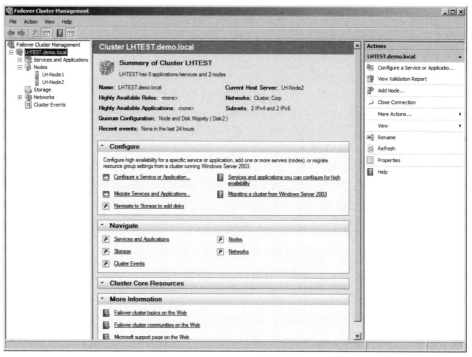

Figure 9-3   Managing a cluster using the Failover Cluster Management snap-in

Of course, the real purpose of setting up a cluster is to be able to use it to provide high availability for your network applications and services. But before we look at that, let's hear what an expert at Microsoft has to say about the new MMC snap-in for managing clusters.

From the Experts: Simplifying the User Experience

Failover Clusters in previous versions of the Windows operating system were difficult for many users to configure and maintain. A primary design goal for Windows Server 2008 Failover Clustering was to make it easier for the IT generalist to implement high availability. To achieve this goal required that changes be made to both the user interface (UI) and to the process for configuring the cluster and the associated highly available applications and services.

The Cluster Administration tool in previous versions of the operating system was a pseudo-MMC snap-in. You could not open a blank MMC console and add it as a valid snap-in. Once the Cluster Administration console was open, it was not very intuitive. It was not easy to understand the default resource group configuration (with the possible exception of the default Cluster Group), and it took a little bit of trial and error to figure out how to configure high availability. This level of complexity has changed in Windows Server 2008. The Failover Cluster Management interface is a true MMC 3.0 snap-in. When the feature is installed, the snap-in is placed in the Administrative Tools group. It can also be added into a blank MMC snap-in along with other tools. The Windows Server 2008 Failover Cluster manager cannot be used to manage clusters in previous versions of Windows and vice versa.

The Failover Cluster Management snap-in consists of three distinct panes. The left pane provides a listing of all the managed clusters in an organization if they have been added in by the user. (All Windows Server 2008 clusters can be managed inside one snap-in). The center pane displays information based on what is selected in the left pane, and the right pane lists actions that can be executed based on what is selected in the center pane. If the Failover Cluster Management snap-in has been added to a noncluster node (must be added as a feature called "Remote Server Administration Tools"), the user needs to manually add each cluster that will be managed. If the Failover Cluster Management snap-in is opened on a cluster node, a connection is made to the cluster service if it is running on the local node. The cluster that is hosted on the node is listed in the left pane.

The cluster configuration processes have also changed significantly in Windows Server 2008. One of those processes, cluster validation, has already been discussed. (See the "From the Experts: Validating a Failover Cluster Configuration" sidebar.) Once a cluster configuration has passed validation, the next step is to create a cluster. Like the cluster validation process, the process for creating a cluster is also wizard-based. All major configuration changes in a Windows Server 2008 Failover Cluster are made using a wizard-based process. Users are stepped through a process in an orderly fashion. Information is requested and information is provided until all the required information has been gathered, and then the requested task is executed and completed in the background. Administrators can now accomplish in simple three-step wizards what used to be very long, complex, and error-prone tasks in previous versions. For each wizard-based process, a report is generated when the process completes. As with other reports, a copy is placed in the %systemroot%\cluster\reports subdirectory of each node in the cluster.

Incorporating the innovative features listed here should make deploying and managing Windows Server 2008 Failover Clusters much easier for IT shops of any size.

–Chuck Timon, Jr.
Support Engineer, Microsoft Enterprise Support, Windows Server Core Team

Creating a Highly Available File Server

A common use for clustering is to provide high availability for file servers on your network, and you can now achieve this goal in a straightforward manner using Failover Clustering in Windows Server 2008. Let me quickly walk you through the steps, and if you're testing Windows Server 2008 Beta 3 you can try this on your own. (See Chapter 13, "Deploying Windows Server 2008," for more information on setting up a test environment for Windows Server 2008.)

Here's all you need to do to configure a two-node file server cluster instance on your network:

First, add the Failover Clustering feature to both of your servers, which must of course be running Windows Server 2008. See Chapter 5 for information about how to add features and roles to servers.

Now run the Validation tool to make sure your cluster solution satisfies the requirements for Failover Clustering in Windows Server 2008. Make sure you have a witness disk (or file share witness) accessible by both of your servers.

Now open the Failover Cluster Management console, and click Configure A Service Or Application in the Actions pane on the right. This starts the High Availability Wizard. Click Next, and select File Server on the Select Service Or Application screen of the wizard.

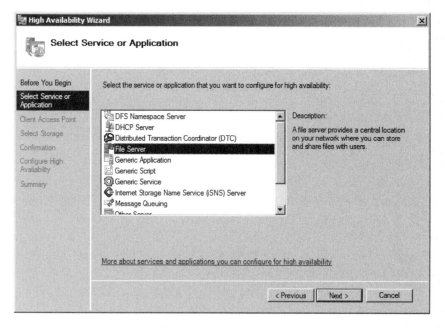

Click Next, and specify a Client Access Point (CAP) name for your cluster (again following standard naming conventions). Then specify static IP address information if DHCP is not being used by your servers. If your servers are connected to several networks and you're using static addressing, you need to specify an address for each subnet because the wizard assumes you want to ensure that your file server instance will be highly available for users on each connected subnet.

Click Next again, and select the shared disks on which your file share data will be stored. Then click through to finish the wizard. Now return to the Failover Cluster Management console, where you can bring your new file server application group online.

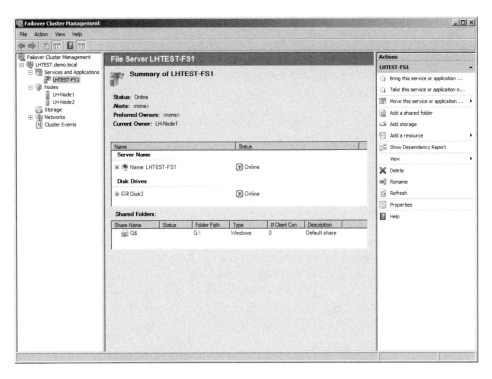

The middle pane displays the CAP name of the file server instance (which is different from the CAP name of the Failover Cluster itself that you defined earlier when you created your cluster) and the shared storage being used by this instance. The Action pane on the right gives you additional options, such as adding a shared folder, adding storage, and so on. If you click Add A Shared Folder, the Create A Shared Folder Wizard starts. In this wizard, you can browse to select a folder on your shared disk and then share this folder so that users can access data stored on your file server. And in Windows Server 2008, you can also easily create new file shares on a Failover Cluster by using Explorer—something you couldn't do in previous versions of Windows server clustering.

And that's basically it! You now have a highly available two-node file server cluster that your users can use for centrally storing their files. Who needs a dedicated clustering expert on staff when you've deployed Windows Server 2008?

Here are a few additional tips on managing your clustered file share instance. First, you can also manage your cluster using the cluster.exe command-line tool. For example, typing **cluster . res** displays all the resources on your cluster together with the status of each resource. This functionality includes displaying your shared folders in UNC format—for example, \\<file_server_instance>\<share_name>. In addition, typing **cluster .res < file_server_instance > /priv** displays the Private properties of your file server instance (for example, your Network Name resource), while **cluster .res < file_server_instance > /prop** displays its Public properties.

Another new feature of clustered file servers in Windows Server 2008 is *scoping* of file shares. This feature is enabled by default, as can be seen by viewing the *ScopedName* setting when you display the Private properties of your Network Name resource. Scoping restricts what can be seen on the server via a NetBIOS connection—for example, when you type **net view** **\\<CAP_name>** at the command prompt, where *CAP_name* is the Network Name resource of your Failover Cluster, not one of your file server instances. On earlier Windows clustering platforms, running this command displayed all the shares being hosted on your cluster. However, in Windows Server 2008 you don't see anything when you run this command because shared folders are scoped to your individual file server instances and not to the Failover Cluster itself. Instead, you can see the shares that have been scoped against a specific file server instance by typing **net view \\<file_server_instance>** at your command prompt.

Finally, you can also enable Access Based Enumeration (ABE) on the shared folders in your file server cluster. ABE was first introduced in Windows Server 2003 Service Pack 1, and it was designed to prevent domain users from being able to see files and folders within network shares unless they specifically had access permissions for those files and folders. (If you're interested, ABE works by setting the SHARE_INFO_1055 flag on the shared folder using the NetShareSetInfo API, which is described on MSDN.) To enable ABE for a shared folder on a Windows Server 2008 file server cluster, just open the Advanced Settings dialog box from the share's Properties page and select the Enable Access Based Enumeration check box.

One final note concerning creating a highly available file server: One of the really cool things that was added in Beta 3 is Shell Integration. This means you can now just open up Explorer and create file shares as you normally would, and Failover Clustering is smart enough that it will detect if the share is being created on a clustered disk. And if so, it will then do all the right things for you by creating a file share resource on your cluster. So admins who are not cluster savvy don't need to worry—just manage file shares on clusters as you would for any other file server!

Performing Other Cluster Management Tasks

You might need or want to perform lots of other management tasks using the management tools (snap-ins, the cluster.exe command, and WMI classes) for Failover Clustering. The following paragraphs provide a quick list of a few of these tasks, and I'm sure you can think of more.

First, you'll probably need to replace a physical disk resource when the disk fails. This task can be done as follows: Initialize the new disk using the Disk Management snap-in found under the Storage node in Server Manager. (See Chapter 4, "Managing Windows Server 2008," for more information on Server Manager.) Then partition it and assign it a drive letter. Now open the Failover Cluster Management console, right-click on the failed disk resource, select Properties, click Repair, and specify the replacement disk. Then bring the disk online and change the drive letter back to the original one. Now you can bring your cluster back online. And this process works even if the disk being replaced is your shared quorum disk!

Second, if you're already running server clusters on Windows Server 2003 and you're thinking of migrating them to Windows Server 2008, a new Cluster Migration Tool will be included in Failover Clustering that can help you to migrate a cluster configuration from one cluster (either Windows Server 2008 or an earlier platform) to another (running Windows Server 2008). This tool copies both resources and cluster configurations and is fairly easy to use, but you can't perform a rolling upgrade—for example, you can't migrate one node at a time from the old cluster to the new one. And you can't have a Failover Cluster that contains a mix of nodes running Windows Server 2008 and nodes running earlier Windows platforms.

Finally, you'll also want to know how to monitor and troubleshoot cluster issues. On earlier clustering platforms, you had to use a combination of the standard Windows event logs (Application, System, and so on) together with the cluster.log file found in the *%systemroot%*\cluster folder. Plus there were some additional configuration logs under *%systemroot%*\system32\LogFiles\Cluster that you could use to try and diagnose cluster problems. In Windows Server 2008, however, cluster logging has changed significantly. Let's listen now to one of our experts at Microsoft as he explains these changes:

From the Experts: Failover Cluster Logging in Windows Server 2008

In Windows Server 2008, cluster logging has been changed. The cluster log implemented in previous versions of server clustering, which was located in the %windir%\cluster directory, is no longer there. As a result of the new Windows Eventing model implemented in Windows Server 2008, the cluster logging process has evolved. Critical cluster events will still be registered in the standard Windows System event log; however, a separate Operational Log has also been created. This log will contain informational events that pertain to the cluster, an example of which is shown here:

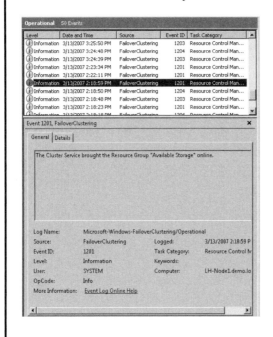

The Operational Log is a standard Windows event log (.evtx file format) and can be viewed in the Windows Event Viewer. In the Event Viewer, the log can be found under Applications and Services Logs\Microsoft\Windows\FailoverClustering:

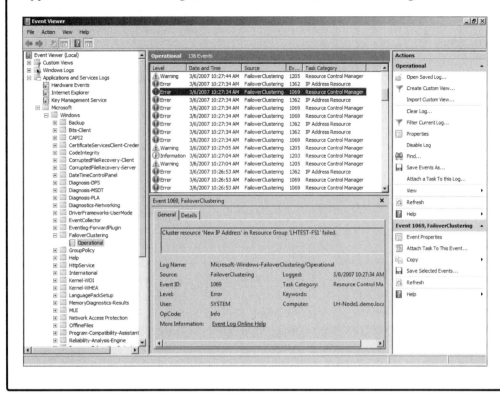

The "live" cluster log, on the other hand, cannot be viewed inside the Windows Event Viewer. As a result of the new Eventing model implemented in Windows Server 2008, and the requirement for the cluster log to be a "running" record of events that occur in the cluster, the cluster log has now been implemented as a "tracing" session. Information about this tracing session can be viewed using the "Reliability and Performance Monitor" snap-in as shown in these two screen shots:

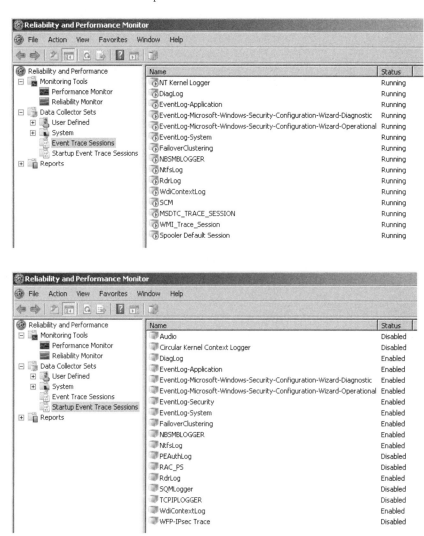

The log is in Event Trace Log (.etl) format and can be parsed using the tracerpt command-line utility that comes in the operating system. The ClusterLog.etl.xxx file(s) are located in the same directory as the Operational Log i.e. %windir%\system32\winevt\logs. There can be multiple ClusterLog.etl files in this location. Each log, by default, can grow to 40 MB in size (configurable) before a new one is created. Additionally, a new log will be created every time the server reboots. As mentioned, the tracerpt command-line utility can be used to parse these log files as shown here:

```
Z:\Tools\xml>tracerpt -lr %SystemRoot%\System32\Winevt\Logs\ClusterLog.* -o clusterlog.xml -of xml
Input
File(s):
        C:\Windows\System32\Winevt\Logs\ClusterLog.etl
        C:\Windows\System32\Winevt\Logs\ClusterLog.etl.001
        C:\Windows\System32\Winevt\Logs\ClusterLog.etl.002
        C:\Windows\System32\Winevt\Logs\ClusterLog.etl.003
100.00%
Output
DumpFile:          clusterlog.xml
The command completed successfully.
Z:\Tools\xml>
```

Additionally, the cluster.exe CLI has been modified so the cluster log can be generated for all nodes in the cluster or a specific node in the cluster. Here is an example:

```
C:\>cluster . log /?
The syntax of this command is:

CLUSTER [[/CLUSTER:]cluster-name] LOG <options>
<options> =
   /G[ENERATE]] [/COPY[:directory]] [/NODE:"node-name"]
   /SIZE:logsize-MB [/NODE:"node-name"]

Note:
   The /SIZE option will flush and restart the log.


CLUSTER LOG /?
CLUSTER LOG /HELP

C:\>cluster . log /gen /copy:"c:\temp"
Generating cluster log on node 'LH-Node1'...
Generating cluster log on node 'LH-Node2'...
The cluster log(s) have been copied to 'c:\temp'...


C:\>cd temp

C:\temp>dir
 Volume in drive C has no label.
 Volume Serial Number is 307C-400A

 Directory of C:\temp

03/14/2007  12:36 PM    <DIR>          .
03/14/2007  12:36 PM    <DIR>          ..
03/14/2007  12:36 PM        21,357,938 LH-Node1.log
03/14/2007  12:36 PM        15,836,463 LH-Node2.log
               2 File(s)     37,194,401 bytes
               2 Dir(s)  13,828,612,096 bytes free

C:\temp>
```

These logs can be read using Notepad:

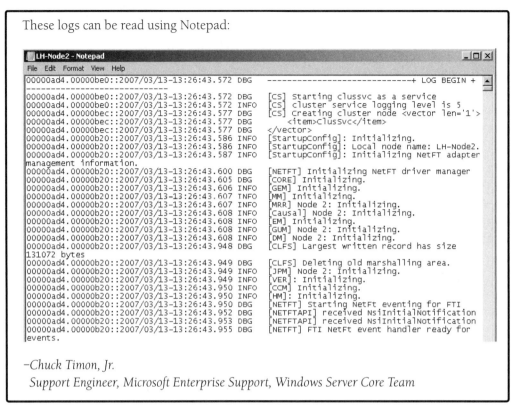

–Chuck Timon, Jr.
Support Engineer, Microsoft Enterprise Support, Windows Server Core Team

Network Load Balancing Enhancements

Let's conclude this chapter with a brief look at enhancements to Network Load Balancing (NLB) in Windows Server 2008. This particular list of new features and enhancements is shorter than others in this chapter.

First, although the overall architecture and functionality of NLB remains the same as far as deploying and managing this feature are concerned, the picture under the hood is quite different: the NLB driver has essentially been rewritten to conform with the new NDIS 6.0 filter driver model used in Windows Server 2008. As shown in Figure 9-4, the NLB driver is a kernel-mode driver that runs on each server in an NLB cluster, and this is essentially the same as in previous versions of Windows Server.

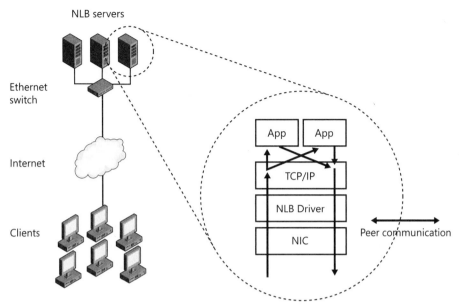

Figure 9-4   How NLB works

The biggest reason for rewriting the NLB driver from scratch is that now the NLB driver is an NDIS 6.0 lightweight filter module. This means that it's a cleaner, lighter, and faster driver when compared with the NDIS 5.1 intermediate driver that NLB had in Windows Server 2003.

One of the most valued improvements done in Windows Server 2008 was to provide full IPv6 support for NLB servers. In other words, IPv6 nodes can now join an NLB cluster and IPv6 traffic can be load-balanced between nodes. There is also support now for multiple dedicated IP addresses (DIPs). This also means that NLB clusters can now have multiple IPv6 DIPs in addition to the support for multiple virtual IP addresses (VIPs) that existed in previous versions.

Another helpful improvement has to do with consolidated management using Network Load Balancing Manager—you no longer need to work with the network configuration user interface on every single node of the cluster. This welcome change will ultimately minimize NLB configuration problems. NLB Manager is also more reliable because of WMI enhancements that enable auto recovery of the repository when it becomes corrupted or accidentally deleted.

Other NLB enhancements include the following:

- Improved DoS attack protection for interested apps. Using a public callback interface, NLB can notify applications of SYN attacks so that steps can be taken to remediate the problem.

- Support for a rolling upgrade of NLB clusters from Windows Server 2003 to Windows Server 2008.

- Support for unattended installation of NLB.

- Support for NLB in Server Core.

Let's end this chapter with a couple of insights from experts at Microsoft regarding new features and enhancements to NLB in Windows Server 2008. First let's learn how you can use the public WMI provider to add health monitoring and dynamic load balancing to applications running on your NLB cluster:

From the Experts: Add Health Monitoring to Your NLB App!

The Network Load Balancing (NLB) service does not monitor the health of your application. Instead, it allows the application developer to determine how healthy a load-balanced application is. Since each application has its own notion of load and health, measuring and monitoring these quantities is best achieved by the application itself. By using collected measurements from your application and NLB's public WMI provider, it is a relatively simple task to add load and health monitoring to your load-balanced application.

If your application has a service that runs on each node of the NLB cluster, or a service that runs on a single (master) node that can communicate with the other nodes in the cluster, this service can double as a monitoring service that periodically queries each node for performance data and application-specific load and health information. Queries for performance data can be made locally or remotely using WMI. For example, you can query a particular node for its CPU load or the number of active TCP connections (the latter can also be determined by running the nlb params command locally and parsing the output). Queries for application-specific data can be made locally or remotely using the application's protocol. For example, you can send a request to a particular node targeted at the port the application is listening on and measure the amount of time it takes to get a response. Even if your load-balanced application does not have its own service to issue these queries from–this is generally true of Web sites that run on Microsoft Internet Information Services (IIS) or some other web server–you can still gather load and health data by writing a script that periodically issues queries to each node. A VBScript script running in a loop on one node, for example, can issue WMI or application-specific queries to every other node in the cluster. The ultimate goal is to gather enough data to determine how healthy and loaded each instance of the application is.

Once you have gathered all the appropriate load and health metrics from each node, you need to act on this information. If you find that a given node has become unresponsive–either because the application instance is experiencing problems or the machine itself has died–you may want to remove this node from the NLB cluster. You can do this by executing the DrainStop or Stop method on the instance of the MicrosoftNLB_Node class running on that node (refer to MSDN documentation of the MicrosoftNLB_Node class). Keep in mind that these operations will affect all traffic being handled by the node and will eventually remove it from the cluster. If the problem is confined to a particular port or virtual IP address-port combination, you can use the Drain/DrainEx or Disable/DisableEx methods to drain or disable the affected port rule instead. Once the problem goes away or the machine has been recovered, you can use the Enable/EnableEx methods to resume traffic handling on a per-port rule basis, or the Start method to restart cluster operations on a previously stopped node. Congratulations–you have added a simple but effective health monitoring scheme to your load-balanced application!

It may not always be the case that you want to drain or disable all traffic associated with a port rule. For example, you may find that a given application instance is responsive but severely overloaded, in which case the best course of action might be to temporarily reduce the amount of load it is configured to handle, and restore this amount only after things have subsided. You can achieve this by adjusting the LoadWeight property of the MicrosoftNLB_PortRuleEx class running on that node (refer to MSDN documentation of the MicrosoftNLB_PortRuleEx class). By changing this quantity, you can decrease/increase the amount of future traffic handled by the node on that port rule. Congratulations–you have added a simple but effective dynamic load balancing scheme to your load-balanced application!

By monitoring the health of your application across the cluster, and making appropriate adjustments to the load handled by each node, you will increase the overall responsiveness, reliability, and performance of your load-balanced application – all in a way that makes sense to your app.

–Siddhartha Sen
Software Design Engineer, Clustering & High Availability Group, Windows Server

And last but not least, here are some helpful troubleshooting tips when you have Network Load Balancing deployed in your environment:

From the Experts: Tips on Troubleshooting NLB Issues

If you see that some of your clients are not getting serviced by NLB hosts, you can take the following steps to isolate the issue:

1. The first thing to check is whether the application running on top of all hosts in a cluster is behaving as expected. When a application running on top of a host dies, NLB doesn't automatically move the traffic to a different host in the cluster. The trick to narrow down the problem is to first see if you see the issue with one node

NLB cluster (stop all other hosts and then the one being tested). If you can isolate the host, try to reproduce the problem without NLB bound.

2. Next start Network Load Balancing Manager from a client/host that has access to all the hosts in the cluster. If Network Load Balancing Manager gives you any errors, try to fix them. The errors shown by Network Load Balancing Manager can be fixed most of the time by reapplying the last known configuration on the host one connects. This can be done by right-clicking on the cluster name in Network Load Balancing Manager, selecting cluster properties, and clicking OK.

3. Make sure next that all the port rules you want are correct by re-verifying your port rules. To do this, right-click the cluster, select cluster properties, and take a look at the Port Rules tab. Many times rules are incorrectly defined, so make sure you read the description about how various port rules behave and be sure you understand the difference between single affinity, no affinity, diabled rules, rules with different weight, default host rules, and so on.

4. The next step in troubleshooting would be to check whether the information shown by Network Load Balancing Manager is consistent with the output of command-line utilities like the nlb params and nlb display commands.

5. The next step in triaging would be to make sure each host in the cluster is seeing all the incoming traffic. This can be done by sending ICMP ping commands to the cluster from a few clients. If ping works then also make sure you can connect to other services (RPC, WMI, and so on) on each host. This can be done by starting Network Monitor on each host. Network Monitor can be downloaded from *http://www.microsoft.com/downloads/details.aspx?FamilyID=AA8BE06D-4A6A-4B69-B861-2043B665CB53&displaylang=en*. You should see client traffic received on each host. In your network capture you should also see NLB heartbeats (an Ethernet broadcast packet with the bytes 0x886f after the source address in the Ethernet frame) being exchanged among the hosts. If traffic is being handled by only one host, make sure that your switch has not learned the MAC address of the cluster.

−Amit Date
Software Design Engineer in Test, Clustering & High Availability Group, Windows Server

Conclusion

Clustering improvements are manifold in Windows Server 2008, making the platform ideal for running applications and services that need to be highly available to support your business. I found it fun learning about these new features, and I hope you're as excited about them as I am. Now let's move on to another hot feature of Windows Server 2008–namely, (Cough! Cough!) Network Access Protection. I should have taken my zinc tablets while I was finishing this chapter around 4 a.m., and I think I'm coming down with a sore throat. We IT pros just work way too hard, don't we?

Additional Resources

There's a brief overview of the new features and enhancements in Failover Clustering in Windows Server 2008 on the Microsoft Web site at *http://www.microsoft.com/windowsserver/ longhorn/failover-clusters.mspx.* I think by the time you have this book in your hands, this page will likely be fleshed out some more, so keep it bookmarked.

If you've signed up for the Longhorn beta on Microsoft Connect, you'll find several useful resources there, including a Live Meeting on Clustering, a Step By Step guide titled "Configuring a Two-Node File Server Failover Cluster," another Step By Step guide called "Configuring Network Load Balancing with Terminal Services," a live chat on clustering, and probably more.

Finally, be sure to turn to Chapter 14, ""Additional Resources," for more information on Failover Clustering and NLB, and also references to webcasts, whitepapers, blogs, newsgroups, and other sources of information about all aspects of Windows Server 2008.

Chapter 10
Network Access Protection

In this chapter:

The Need for Network Access Protection 286

Understanding Network Access Protection. 287

Understanding the NAP Architecture. 297

A Walkthrough of How NAP Works 299

Implementing NAP 301

Troubleshooting NAP 319

Conclusion 339

Additional Resources. 340

Before we dig into this feature, let me tell you a brief background story concerning this book. Why write a book about a beta version of a product? Won't a book like this become obsolete once the final release version of the product appears? Probably, yes. After all, at the time of writing this particular chapter, Microsoft Windows Server 2008 has not quite reached Beta 3, so features are bound to change between now and RTM.

Doesn't that mean that this is basically a "throwaway" book? I suppose that's true of many books like this. But why would Microsoft throw away money to have this published? The answer's simple—to help get customers ready for what's coming. Whenever Microsoft is in the process of developing a major new platform—a new Microsoft Windows client or server operating system, a new release of Microsoft Visual Studio, the .NET Framework, and so on—they like to produce a book like this describing a prerelease version of the product. And usually these books are throwaways—that is, IT pros read them and learn about the capabilities of the product, and when the final release of the product appears, Microsoft publishes other books on the product such as an Administrator's Companion, a Pocket Consultant, a Resource Kit, and so on. Usually, after the IT pros buy these additional titles, they toss away the "beta book" because they figure it's no longer useful.

Well, as you've probably noticed by now, this book is different. Why? Because it's more than just an overview—it's got real meat in it. That is, it has insights and recommendations from the experts at Microsoft who are actually developing Windows Server 2008 and its different features. For instance, in this chapter alone you'll find sidebars contributed by eight different members of the Network Access Protection (NAP) team at Microsoft, including program managers, software design engineers, and software development engineers. And these sidebars are deep, they're technical, and they're full of meat you can chew on. I mean, how many IT pros are vegans, really?

Dropping the silly metaphors, what I really mean is that even after Windows Server 2008 RTMs and other great books about it are published by Microsoft Press, you'll still want to keep this particular book on your shelf and refer back to it whenever you need to draw on the insights that the product team has contributed to this and other chapters. Am I tooting my own horn too much? Not really—I'm tooting a "long horn" actually! But even if I am shamelessly promoting myself and my book, what's wrong with that? How do you think The Donald earned his first billion, anyway? Certainly not by making puns on product names, I guess. Let's move on to NAP.

The Need for Network Access Protection

Protecting the network is the number one challenge of most organizations today. What makes this difficult for many organizations is that many different kinds of users need to access their networks, including full-time employees who work on desktop computers, mobile sales professionals who need to VPN into corpnet using their laptops, teleworkers who use their desktop computers to work from home, consultants and other "guests" who come on site and need to connect their laptops to either LAN drops or wireless access points, business partners who need access via the extranet, and so on. Many of these computers need to be domain-joined, but others are not and therefore don't have Group Policy applied when users log on. And not all of these computers are running the latest version of Microsoft Windows—in fact, some of them might not be running Windows at all!

Some of these computers will have a personal firewall enabled and configured, which might be either the Windows Firewall or some third-party product. Others might have no firewall at all on them. Most will have antivirus software installed on them, but some of these might not have downloaded the latest AV signature files from their vendor. Client computers that are permanently connected to corpnet will likely have the latest service packs, hotfixes, and security patches installed, but guest computers and machines that are not domain-joined might be lacking some patches.

The overall effect of all this is that today's enterprise network is a dangerous place to live. If you are a network administrator and a machine wants to connect to your network, either via a LAN drop or access point or RAS or VPN connection, how do you know it's safe to let it do so? What if you allow an "unhealthy" machine—one missing the latest security updates or with its firewall turned off or with an outdated AV signature file—to connect to your network? You might be jeopardizing your network's integrity. How can you prevent this from happening? How can you make sure only machines that are "healthy" are allowed to access your network? And what happens when an unhealthy machine does try to connect? Should you bump him off immediately, or is it possible to "quarantine" the machine and help it become healthy enough so that it can be allowed in?

Understanding Network Access Protection

There are already solutions around that can do some of these things. Some of them are homegrown. For example, one organization I'm familiar with uses a DHCP registration system that links MAC addresses to user accounts stored in Active Directory to control which machines have access to the network. But homegrown solutions like this tend to be hard to manage and difficult to maintain, and they can sometimes be circumvented—for example, by using a static IP address configuration that allows access to a subnet scoped by DHCP.

Vendors also have their own solutions to this problem, and Microsoft has one for Windows Server 2003 called Network Access Quarantine Control, but although this solution can enhance the security of your network if implemented properly, it has its limitations. For example, although Network Access Quarantine Control can perform client inspection on machines trying to connect to the network, it's only intended to do so for remote access connections. Basically, what Network Access Quarantine Control does is delay normal remote access to a private network until the configuration of the remote computer has been checked and validated by a quarantine script. And it's the customers themselves who must write these scripts that perform the compliance checks because the exact nature of these scripts depends upon the customer's own networking environment. This can make Network Access Quarantine Control challenging to implement.

Other vendors, such as Cisco Systems, have developed their own solutions to the problem, and Cisco's solution is called Network Access Control (NAC). NAC is designed to enforce security policy compliance on any devices that are trying to access network resources. Using NAC, you can allow network access to devices that are compliant and trusted, and you can restrict access for devices that are noncompliant. NAC is both a framework that includes infrastructure to support compliance checks based on industry-common AV and security management products, and a product called NAC Appliance that you can drop in and use to build your compliance checking, remediation, and enforcement infrastructure.

Network Access Protection (NAP) in Windows Server 2008 is another solution, and it's one that is rapidly gaining recognition in the enterprise IT community. NAP consists of a set of components for both servers (Windows Server 2008 only) and clients (Windows Vista now, Windows XP soon), together with a set of APIs that will be made public once Windows Server 2008 is released. NAP is not a product but a platform that is widely supported by over 100 different ISVs and IHVs, including AV vendors like McAfee and Symantec, patch management companies like Altiris and PatchLink, security software vendors like RSA Security, makers of security appliances including Citrix, network device manufacturers including Enterasys and F5, and system integrators such as EDS and VeriSign. Those are all big names in the industry, and the number of vendors supporting NAP is increasing daily. And that's not marketing hype, it's fact—and it's important to IT pros like us because we want a platform like NAP to support our existing enterprise networks, which typically already have products and solutions from many of the vendors I just listed.

What NAP Does

If you want a short definition of NAP, it's this: NAP is a platform that can enforce compliance by computing devices with predetermined health requirements before these devices are allowed to access or communicate on a network. By itself, NAP is not designed to protect your network and is not intended to replace firewalls, AV products, patch management systems, and other protection elements. Instead, it's designed to work together with these different elements to ensure devices on your network comply with policy that you have defined. And by *devices* I mean client computers (Windows Vista and soon Windows XP as well), servers running Windows Server 2008, PDAs running Windows Mobile (soon), and eventually also computers running other operating systems such as Linux and the Apple Macintosh operating system (using NAP components developed by third-party vendors).

Let's unpack this a bit further. NAP supplies an infrastructure (components and APIs) that provides support for the following four processes:

- **Health policy validation**   NAP can determine whether a given computer is compliant or not with a set of health policy requirements that you, the administrator, can define for your network. For example, one of your health requirements might be that all computers on your network must have a host-based firewall installed on them and enabled. Another requirement might be that all computers on your network must have the latest software updates installed on them.

- **Network access limitation**   NAP can limit access to network resources for computers that are noncompliant with your health policy requirements. This limiting of access can range from preventing the noncompliant computer from connecting to any other computers on your network to quarantining it on a subnet and restricting its access to a limited set of machines. Or you can choose to not limit access at all for noncompliant computers and merely log their presence on the network for reporting purposes; it's you're choice—NAP puts you, the administrator, in control of how you limit network access based on compliance.

- **Automatic remediation**   NAP can automatically remediate noncompliant computers that are attempting to access the network. For example, say you have a laptop that doesn't have the latest security updates installed on it. You try to connect to corpnet, and NAP identifies your machine as noncompliant with corpnet health requirements, and it quarantines your machine on a restricted subnet where it can interact only with Windows Server Update Services (WSUS) servers. NAP then points your machine to the WSUS servers and tells it to go and get updates from them. Your machine downloads the updates, NAP then verifies that your machine is now healthy, and you're let in the door and can access corpnet. Automatic remediation like this allows NAP to not just prevent unhealthy machines from connecting to your network, but also help those machines become healthy so that they can have access to needed network resources without bringing worms and other malware into your network. Of course, NAP puts you, the administrator, in the driver's seat, so you can turn off auto-remediation if you want to and instead have NAP simply point the noncompliant machine to an internal Web site that gives the user instructions on what to do to make the machine compliant (or simply states why the noncompliant machine is not being allowed access to the network). Again, it's your choice how you want NAP to operate with regard to how remediation is performed.

■ **Ongoing compliance**   Finally, NAP doesn't just check for compliance when your computer joins the network. It continues to verify compliance on an ongoing basis to ensure that your machine remains healthy for the entire duration of the time it's connected to your network.

As an example, let's say your NAP health policy is configured to enforce compliance with the requirement that Windows Firewall be turned on for all Windows Vista and Windows XP clients connected to the network. You're on the road and you VPN into corpnet, and NAP—after verifying that Windows Firewall is enabled on your machine—lets you in. Once you're in, however, you decide for some reason to turn Windows Firewall off. (You're an administrator on your machine, so you can do that—making users local administrators is not best practice, but some companies do that.) So you turn off Windows Firewall, which means the status of your machine has now changed and it's out of compliance. What does NAP do? If you've configured it properly, it simply turns Windows Firewall back on! How does this work? The client computer has a NAP agent running on it and this agent detects this change in health status and tries to immediately remediate the situation. It can be a bit more complicated than that (for example, agent detects noncompliance, health certificate gets deleted, client goes into quarantine, NAP server remediates, agent confirms compliance, client becomes healthy again and regains access to the network) but that's the basic idea—we'll talk more about the NAP architecture in a moment.

NAP Enforcement Methods

So NAP can enforce compliance with network health policies you define for your network. But how does it enforce compliance? What are the enforcement mechanisms available? NAP actually has five different enforcement mechanisms you can use: DHCP, VPN, 802.1X, IPSec, and TS-Gateway. Let's briefly look at each of these mechanisms and how NAP uses them to verify health and enforce compliance with health policies you've defined.

DHCP Enforcement

DHCP is the network administrator's friend. It makes managing IP addresses across an enterprise easy. You don't want to have to go back to managing addresses manually, do you? But DHCP is a notoriously unsecure protocol that basically just gives an address to any machine that wants one. You want an IP address? Here, you can have this one—don't bother me for a while. Once your machine has an IP address (and subnet mask, default gateway, and DNS server addresses), you're on the network and you can communicate with other machines. If you have the right permissions, you can access shared resources on the network. If you don't have any permissions, you can't access any resources, but you can still wreak havoc on the network if your machine is infected with Blaster, Slammer, or some other worm.

So how does NAP help prevent such infected machines from damaging your network? It's easy if your DHCP server is running Windows Server 2008 and either has the Network Policy Server (NPS) role service installed as a RADIUS server (with policies) or has NPS installed as a RADIUS proxy that redirects RADIUS requests to a different NPS server running as a RADIUS server somewhere else on your network. Basically, what happens in this enforcement scenario is this (for simplicity we'll assume the first option above is true, that is NPS and DHCP servers are installed on the same Windows Server 2008 machine):

1. Client configured to obtain IP address configuration using DHCP tries to connect to DHCP server on network to obtain address and access the network.

2. DHCP (NAP) server checks the health of the client. If the client is healthy, it leases a full, valid IP address configuration (address, mask, gateway, and DNS) to the client and the client enters the network. If the client is unhealthy (not in compliance with NAP health policy requirements), the DHCP server leases a limited IP address configuration to the client that includes only the following:

    ❑ IP address

    ❑ Subnet mask

    ❑ Set of host routes to remediation servers on the restricted network

3. Once configured, the client has no default gateway and can access only the specified servers on the local subnet. These servers (called *remediation servers*) can apply patches, provide updated AV sigs, and perform other actions to help bring the client into compliance.

4. Finally, once the client has been brought into compliance (made healthy), the DHCP server leases a full IP address configuration to it and it can now connect to the intranet.

VPN Enforcement

VPN is the most popular way today's enterprises provide remote access to clients. Remember the old days when large businesses had to buy modem banks and lease dozens of phone lines to handle remote clients that needed to dial in and connect to corpnet? Those days are long gone now that secure VPN technologies have arrived that encrypt all communication between VPN clients and servers. Windows Vista has a built-in VPN client that enables a client computer to tunnel over the Internet and connect to a VPN server running Windows Server 2008. To use VPN as an enforcement mechanism for NAP, your VPN server needs to be running Windows Server 2008 and have the Routing And Remote Access Services role service installed on it. (This role service is part of the Network Policy And Access Services role. (See Chapter 5 for more information about roles and role services.)

Basically, VPN enforcement works like this:

1. The remote VPN client attempts to connect to the VPN server on your perimeter network.

2. The VPN server checks the health of the client by contacting the NAP server (which again is either a separate NPS or RADIUS server running Windows Server 2008 or a RADIUS proxy redirecting RADIUS requests to a different NPS on your network). If the client is healthy, it establishes the VPN connection and the remote client is on the network. If the client is unhealthy, the VPN server applies a set of packet filters that quarantines the client by letting it connect only to your restricted network where your remediation servers are located.

3. Once your client gets remediated (for example, by downloading the latest AV sig file) the VPN server removes the packet filters from the client and the client can then connect freely to corpnet.

802.1X Enforcement

802.1X is an IEEE standard that defines a mechanism for port-based network access control. It's used to provide authenticated network access to Ethernet networks and was originally designed for wired networks but also works with 802.11 wireless networks. By *port-based network access control* I mean that 802.1X uses the physical characteristics of a switched LAN infrastructure to authenticate a device that is attached to a port on a switch. If the device is authenticated, the switch allows it to send and receive frames on the network. If authentication is denied, the switch doesn't allow the device to do this. The authentication mechanism used by 802.1X is EAP (Extensible Authentication Protocol), which is based on PPP (Point-to-Point Protocol), and for Windows Vista and Windows Server 2008 the exact supported authentication protocols are EAP-TLS, PEAP-TLS, and PEAP-MS-CHAP v2. We're talking acronym city here—we won't go into that.

802.1X enforcement basically works like this:

1. An EAP-capable client device (for example, a computer running Windows Vista, which has an EAPHost NAP enforcement client) tries to connect an 802.1X-capable switch on your network. Most modern managed Ethernet switches support 802.1X, and in order to support NAP the switch must support 802.1x authentication and V-LAN switching based on the authentication results from the auth submitted to the RADIUS server (in this case the RADIUS server is NPS, which will also do NAP).

2. The switch forwards the health status of the client to the NPS, which determines whether it complies with policy. If the client is healthy, the NPS tells the switch to open the port and the client is let into the network. If the compliance test fails, either the switch can close the port and deny the client entry, or it can VLAN the client to place it on an isolated network where it can talk only to remediation servers. Then once the client is remediated, the switch lets it onto corpnet.

IPSec Enforcement

IPSec enforcement for NAP works a little differently than the other enforcement methods just described. Specifically, IPSec enforcement doesn't quarantine a noncompliant client by isolating it on a restricted network or VLAN. Instead, a noncompliant client simply doesn't receive a health certificate as these are only given to machines that connect to a Health Registration Authority (HRA), submit a Statement of Health (SoH), pass the health check and then receive that certificate back. Then, other machines that have IPSec policy that mandates that they only receive incoming connections from machines that have a health certificate will ignore incoming connections from noncompliant machines since they don't have a health certificate. So in other words, in IPSec NAP enforcement, a noncompliant machine is allowed onto the network in a physical sense (in the sense that it can send and receive frames), but compliant computers on the network simply ignore traffic from the noncompliant machine.

To configure IPSec enforcement, you configure IPSec policy for your client machines to require a health certificate. This is easy to do in Windows Vista because this functionality is built into the new Windows Firewall With Advanced Security. (See the *Windows Vista Resource Kit* from Microsoft Press for more information.) Then you set up a HRA on your network, and the HRA works together with the Network Policy Server (NPS) to issue X.509 health certificates to clients that are determined to comply with NAP health policy for the network. These certificates are then used to authenticate the clients when they attempt to initiate IPSec-protected connections with other machines (called *peers*) on your network.

The HRA is a key component of using IPSec for NAP enforcements, and it has to be a machine running Windows Server 2008 and having the IIS7 component (Web Server role) installed. The HRA obtains health certificates for compliant NAP clients from a certification authority (CA), and the CA can be installed either on the Windows Server 2008 machine or on a different system. The HRA obtains health certificates. Let's learn more about HRA from an expert at Microsoft:

From the Experts: HRA Auto Discovery for Network Access Protection IPSec Enforcement

Large enterprises often have complex deployments involving many domains, multiple forests, and a large number of sites within this hierarchy. NAP clients require the configuration of Health Registration Authorities (HRAs), which clients need to contact to acquire a health certificate. This can be configured on the client either locally or pushed out via Group Policy, which requires the administrators to create site-specific GPOs to specify which HRAs a client should hit to acquire a health certificate and which HRAs are perceived to be too costly. This can be complex.

An alternative solution is to use the HRA Auto Discovery feature built into the NAP client, which enables clients to dynamically discover the appropriate HRA based on DNS SRV records.

How HRA Auto Discovery Works

A client will dynamically discover HRAs only when there is no NAP Group Policy or NAP Local configuration on the client. Also, clients need to be explicitly set to discover HRA. Here's how it works.

The client first checks to see whether there are SRV records for HRAs in the "site" the host is in:

- If yes, add the HRA as the discovered one.
- Or else, try to see if there are SRV records for the AD domain the host is in and derive the HRA list from there.
- If not, the client discovers the HRA from the SRV records for the DNS domain the host is in.

Domain-joined clients discover HRA from the "DNS site SRV" records of the DNS server, while site-less domain clients discover HRA from the "Domain SRV records." Workgroup clients look up the "DNS domain name" from the DHCP server and then discover HRA from the "Domain SRV records" of that DNS server.

With HRA Discovery, the client discovers HRA dynamically when it roams from one network to another. Also, to ensure that posture information is sent only to trusted HRAs, the NAP client always attempts an HTTPS connection with Server certificate validation. The NAP client communicates only with an HRA that has a certificate issued by the enterprise CA.

HRA Discovery Setup

Setting up HRA Discovery requires actions to be performed on the DNS server, the DHCP server, and the client.

On the DNS Server: Add site SRV records (one for each HRA) as follows:

- DNS\<machine_name>\Forward Lookup Zones\<domain_name>_sites\Default-First-Site-Name_tcp
- SRV record name: "_hra"
- SRV record data: <HRA_machine_name>

  Also add Domain SRV records (one for each HRA) as follows:

- DNS\<machine_name>\Forward Lookup Zones\<domain_name>_tcp
- SRV record name: "_hra"
- SRV record data: <HRA_machine_name>

On the DHCP Sever: Add the DNS domain name and DNS Server in the Scope options of the DHCP server.

On the Client: Enable HRA Discovery on the client using the following registry key:

- HKEY_LOCAL_MACHINE\SYSTEM\CurrentControlSet\Services\napagent\LocalConfig\Enroll\HcsGroups

- EnableDiscovery REG_DWORD = 1

Some Troubleshooting Steps

- The client will discover HRAs only if it is configured to do so, so verify that the client does not have any NAP configuration pushed down through Group Policy or configured locally.

- The client will send requests to the discovered HRA only if IPSec QEC is enabled.

- If the client fails to discover HRA, make sure that the client is able to contact the DNS server and look up the DNS records. Nnslookup can help in troubleshooting.

- In case of workgroup clients, make sure that the client has acquired an IP address from the correct DHCP server and that the client is able to look up the DNS records.

- On the server side, make sure that the DNS and DHCP records are configured properly.

- If the client discovers HRA correctly but fails to acquire a health certificate, investigate the following:

  - Verify that there are no network issues that are preventing the client from being able to reach the discovered HRA.

  - Verify that the discovered server is a trusted enterprise server.

  - Verify that the discovered server is configured to accept SSL requests, as by default the client sends HTTPS requests to the discovered HRA.

For further troubleshooting procedures, see the additional sidebars later in this chapter.

–Harini Muralidharan
Software Development Engineer in Test, Network Access Protection

TS Gateway Enforcement

TS Gateway is yet another NAP enforcement method—see Chapter 8, "Terminal Services Enhancements," for more information about what TS Gateway is and how it works. TS Gateway NAP enforcement, however, supports only quarantine enforcement and does not support auto-remediation of the client when the client fails to meet health checks. To understand how TS Gateway NAP enforcement works, let's examine a "clean machine" scenario where a TS Gateway client is used for the first time from a non-domain-joined client computer:

1. The user clicks on a Remote Desktop Connection icon, and the TS Gateway Client (TSGC) on his computer attempts to connect through TCP and HTTP transports simultaneously (the client tries TCP first and then HTTP). As soon as Terminal Services (TS) name resolution or TCP fails, the TSGC will attempt to connect to a TS Gateway server (TSGS) and authenticate the user at IIS and RPC layers.

2. During the user authentication process and after SSL handshake but before the GAP/RAP authorization sequence begins, the TSGS challenges the client for a "SoH request" blob and in its challenge/response it includes its certificate in PKCS#7 formats plus a random generated nonce value.

3. Since the request for a SoH was made on behalf of an untrusted TSGS name, the TSG-QEC will block the request. First the TS user must add to the TSG URL in the trusted gateway server list in the registry, and this requires admin privilege on the machine. Network administrators can also use SMS or logon scripts to populate this regkey setting.

4. The TSG_QEC will then talk to the QA to get the SoHs from SHAs. The TSG_QEC will then create a "SoH request blob" by combing SoHs from QAs, the nonce from the TSGS, a randomly generated symmetric key, and the client's machine name. The TSG QEC will encrypt this "SoH request" blob using the TSGS's public key and give it to the TSGC.

5. The TSGC then passes this encrypted blob to the TSG server, which decrypts the blob and extracts the SoH, the TSGS nonce, and the TSG_QEC symmetric key. The TSGS then verifies that the nonce it received from the TSG_QEC is the same as the one it sent out previously, and if it is the same, the TSGS sends the decrypted SoH blob to the NPS (RADIUS) server for validation.

6. The NPS server then calls SHVs and sends the "SoH request" blob for validation. The NPS server calls SHVs to validate the SoHs and replay with a response back to the NPS server, and based on SHVs' pass/fail response the NPS server will create a "SoH response" and send it to the TSGS.

7. The TSGS passes this information to the TSGS RADIUS proxy for GAP (Gateway Authorization Policy) authorization, and if this succeeds, the TSGS RADIUS proxy returns success with its gateway level of access info. Based on this result, the TSGS then allows the TS client to connect to the TS server.

Let's hear from another expert at Microsoft to learn more about TS Gateway and NAP:

From the Expert: Better Together—TS Gateway, ISA Server, and NAP

Terminal Services–based remote access has long been used as a simpler, lower-risk alternative to classical layer 2 VPN technologies. Whereas the layer 2 VPN has often provided "all ports, all protocols" access to an organization's internal network, the Terminal Services approach restricts connectivity to a single well-defined port and protocol. However, as more and more capability has ascended the stack into RDP (such as copy/paste and drive redirection), the potential attack vectors have risen as well. For example, a remote drive made available over RDP can present the same kinds of security risks as one mapped over native CIFS/SMB transports.

With the advent of TS Gateway, allowing workers to be productive from anywhere has never been easier. TS Gateway also includes several powerful security capabilities to make this access secure. In addition to its default encryption and authentication capabilities, TS Gateway can be combined with ISA Server and Network Access Protection to provide a secure, manageable access method all the way from the client, through the perimeter network, to the endpoint Terminal Server. Combining these technologies allows an organization to reap the benefits of rich RDP-based remote access, while mitigating the potential exposure this access can bring.

ISA Server adds two primary security capabilities to the TS Gateway solution. First, because it can act as an SSL terminator, it allows for more secure placement of TS Gateway servers. Because ISA can be the Internet-facing endpoint for SSL traffic, the TS Gateway itself does not need to be placed within the perimeter network. Instead, the TS Gateway can be kept on the internal network and the ISA Server can forward traffic to it. However, if ISA were simply performing traffic forwarding, it would be of little real security benefit. Thus, the second main security benefit ISA brings to the solution is application-layer inspection capabilities. Rather than simply terminating SSL traffic and forwarding frames on to the TS Gateway, ISA can perform advanced application layer inspection of the traffic to ensure that only desired IP frames are forwarded on to the TS Gateway. Using ISA as the SSL endpoint and traffic inspection device allows for better placement of TS Gateway resources and ensures that they receive only inspected, clean traffic from the Internet.

Although ISA Server provides important network protection abilities to a TS Gateway solution, it does not address client-side threats. For example, users connecting to a TS Gateway session might have malicious software running on their machines or be noncompliant with the organization's security policy. To mitigate against these threats,

TS Gateway can be integrated with Network Access Protection to provide enforcement of security and healthy policies on these remote machines.

NAP is included in Windows Server 2008 and can be run on the same machine as TS Gateway, or TS Gateway can be configured to utilize an existing NAP infrastructure running elsewhere. When combined with TS Gateway, NAP provides the same policy-based approach to client health and enforcement as it does on normal (not RDP-based) network connections. Specifically, NAP can control access to a TS Gateway based on a client's security update, antivirus, and firewall status. For example, if you choose to enable redirected drives on your Terminal Servers, you can require that clients have antivirus software running and up to date. NAP allows organizations to ensure that computers connecting to a TS Gateway are healthy and compliant with its security policies.

–John Morello
   Senior Program Manager, Windows Server Division

Understanding the NAP Architecture

Let's dig into the NAP architecture a bit so that we can understand these enforcement mechanisms better. So it's time for a couple of diagrams and some explanation. Let's start with the big picture (shown in Figure 10-1).

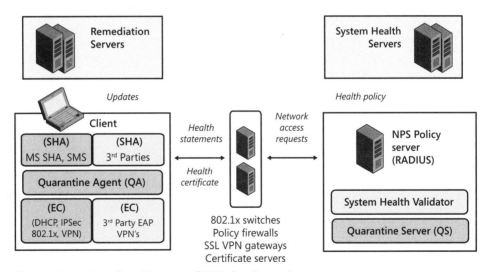

Figure 10-1   Overall architecture of NAP showing various components

On the left of this figure are the clients trying to get onto your network and the remediation servers that can provide updates to them to move the health status of these clients from unhealthy (noncompliant) to healthy (compliant). These remediation servers can be Microsoft products such as System Center Configuration Manager 2007 (currently in beta) or Windows Server Update Services (WSUS), or they can be third-party server products from AV vendors, patch management solution providers, and so on.

Now for a client machine to participate in a NAP infrastructure, the machine must include a NAP client. This NAP client comes built into Windows Vista and Windows Server 2008, and Microsoft is currently working on a NAP client for Windows XP that is planned for release around the time Windows Server 2008 RTM's.

This NAP client has several layers as follows:

- **System Health Agents (SHAs)**   These are components that verify whether the client machine satisfies given health requirements. For instance, one SHA might determine whether the client has AV software installed and whether the sig file is up to date. Another SHA might determine whether the client has the latest software updates installed for some enterprise LOB application. By default, Windows Vista includes its own Microsoft SHA (MS SHA) that can do things like check whether Windows Firewall is turned on, verify whether Automatic Updates is enabled, and determine whether the system has AV or spyware protection software installed and enabled on it. This built-in SHA basically interacts with Security Center on the machine to verify this information. Other SHAs are typically provided by third-party ISVs to support their AV, patch management, firewall and other security products.

- **Quarantine Agent (QA)**   Also called the *NAP Agent*, this is basically a broker layer that takes health status information collected by SHAs and packages them into a list that is then handed to the Enforcement Clients to handle accordingly.

- **Enforcement Clients (ECs)**   These are the client-side components that are involved in helping enforce whether the client is granted full (or partial, or no) network access based upon compliance with your predefined health policy. In Windows Vista and Windows Server 2008, there are built-in ECs for each of the different NAP enforcement mechanisms described previously in this chapter. And because the platform is extensible, third-party ISVs and IHVs are also being encouraged to develop ECs for their own network access and security products.

In the middle of Figure 10-1 are your network access devices that control access to the network. These devices need to be able to interoperate with the NAP infrastructure to pass the statements of health (SOHs) to the NPS servers for health evaluation. In some cases, this will require that the server be enabled for NAP, which is why you need to use Windows Server 2008 DHCP and VPN servers if you are going to use those NAP enforcement methods. However, some existing network access devices (such as 802.1X authenticating switches) are already able to integrate with NAP using their built-in RADIUS capabilities. These network access devices, if running Windows Server 2008 (for example, DHCP or VPN servers) must include a component called an Enforcement Server (ES) that corresponds to an EC on the clients. For example, Windows Server 2008 has a DHCP NAP ES that corresponds to the DHCP NAP EC in the NAP client for Windows Vista, and an ES on the server works together with its corresponding EC on the client to make the enforcement mechanism work. We'll walk through how that happens in a moment.

Finally, on the right of the figure is your Network Policy Server (NPS) and your system health servers. The health servers (also called *policy servers*) provide NAP health policy information to the NPS upon request. The heart and soul of the NAP platform, however, is the NPS server, which is a RADIUS server that is basically the replacement for the Internet Authentication Service (IAS) found in previous versions of the Windows Server operating system. The NPS server is a key component of Windows Server 2008 and is installed by adding the Network Policy Server role service from the Network Policy And Access Services role using the Add Roles Wizard. (See Chapter 5.)

The NPS also has a layered architecture as follows:

- **System Health Validators (SHVs)**   These are the server-side components on the NPS that correspond to the SHAs on the client. Again, this includes both a Microsoft SHV (MS SHV) that ensures the different security components managed by Security Center are enabled on the client, and third-party SHVs developed by ISVs that are enhancing their security products to support the NAP platform. We'll see how the SHAs and SHVs communicate in a moment.

- **Quarantine Server (QS)**   This is basically a broker between the SHVs running on the NPS and the ESs running on the NAP servers. Note that in a large enterprise deployment of NAP, the NPS servers and NAP servers are typically running on different boxes. It's possible, however, to implement NPS and NAP server functionality on a single machine—for example, by installing the DHCP Server role on an NPS server. However, this actually makes managing NAP more complicated instead of simplifying things because if you do this, each NAP server must be separately configured with its own network access and health policy. In most scenarios, however, the NPS and NAP servers will be running on different machines and the QS on the NPS server will use the RADIUS protocol to send and receive messages with the NAP servers.

A Walkthrough of How NAP Works

Now that we understand a bit about NAP enforcement mechanisms and the architecture of the NAP platform, let's walk through an example of NAP at work. Figure 10-2 shows a VPN NAP scenario that we're going to analyze. (Other NAP scenarios such as DHCP and IPSec work a bit differently.) We'll leave out a few elements, like Active Directory for performing authentication, so that we don't complicate things too much, and some of the interactions between the different components are simplified. If you want a more detailed explanation of how NAP works, you can always look at some of the references listed under "Additional Resources" at the end of this chapter.

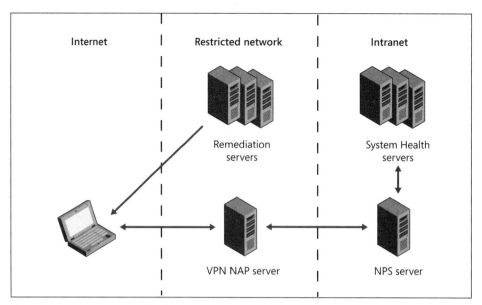

Figure 10-2   A VPN scenario showing NAP at work

Here's a simplified description of what happens when a noncompliant laptop running Windows Vista tries to VPN into corpnet by connecting to a VPN server running Windows Server 2008 when a NAP infrastructure has been deployed:

1. The VPN client uses PEAP to try and establish an authenticated connection with the VPN server. Keep in mind that the VPN client is a NAP client and the VPN server is a NAP server in this scenario.

2. The VPN server, which is also a NAP server, relays the health status information provided by the client to the NPS. What's happening under the hood is that each SHA running on the client performs a system health policy check to determine whether the client is healthy (with respect to the function being performed by the SHA—firewall on, AV enabled, and so on). The result of each check is a data blob, called a Statement of Health (SoH), that indicates compliance or noncompliance with policy. The QA caches these SoHs and consolidates them into a list. The QA then waits for an EC to request this health status information.

3. When the VPN client tries to connect to the VPN server, the server notifies the client that it needs information concerning the client's health status before it will let the client into the corporate intranet. The way it works is that the ES component on the NAP server (the VPN server) communicates using PEAP with the EC component on the NAP client and requests the SoH information from the client.

4. Once the client has sent this SoH information to the NAP server, the NAP server then uses the RADIUS protocol to communicate with the NPS. Specifically, what's happening here is that the SoH information (along with the other non-NAP user authentication

stuff) is being sent from the SHAs on the client (where it was collected) to the corresponding SHVs on the NPS (where it is analyzed against the policy information obtained from the System Health Servers).

5. One of the SHVs on the NPS now determines that the client is noncompliant (for example, Windows Firewall is turned off on the machine). Each SHV produces a Statement of Health Response (SoHR) in response to its compliance analysis of the SoH information it received from the corresponding SHA. The QS uses these SoHRs to construct a System Statement of Health Response (SSoHR), which indicates that the noncompliant client should be denied network access until remediated. The QS then uses RADIUS to send this information from the NPS back to the NAP server.

6. The VPN (NAP) server now applies a set of packet filters to the client to quarantine the client. The client has now been authenticated but can access only the resources on the restricted network, which basically means the VPN server and the remediation servers. The NAP server passes the SoHRs to the NAP client, and the SHAs on the client perform their designated remediation actions (assuming auto-remediation is enabled). The result might then be that the client's firewall is turned on, the client downloads the latest AV sig, or some other remediation action or actions are performed.

7. Once the SHAs on the client have determined that the client is now compliant, an updated list of SoHs is sent by the client to the NAP server and forwarded to the NPS to verify compliance. The procedure repeats as described here, only this time the VPN server recognizes that the client is now healthy, so it removes the restrictive filters from the client and allows it free access to the intranet.

Implementing NAP

Let's move on now and talk about how to implement NAP in an enterprise environment. Obviously, this is a big topic and we can't do it justice in a brief book like this—plus Windows Server 2008 is only at Beta 3 at the time of writing this book, so some aspects of implementing NAP might still change. Still, the NAP platform is pretty far evolved at this point, and we can at least cover some of the important points for deploying it. So let's look at three aspects in particular:

-   Choosing the NAP enforcement methods you want to use

-   Deploying your NAP solution using a phased implementation method

-   Configuring the NPS and other aspects of the NAP platform

Note that you'll also find references to other available documentation on deploying NAP in the "Additional Resources" section at the end of this chapter.

Choosing Enforcement Methods

One choice you need to make when planning your NAP deployment is which enforcement method (or methods) to use. DHCP enforcement is probably the easiest solution to deploy, as it relies on modifying the IP routing table of NAP clients and makes no other changes to these clients. But being the easiest NAP solution to implement means DHCP is probably also the weakest NAP enforcement method. So if you're going to use DHCP enforcement, you probably also want to couple this with another enforcement method, typically 802.1X or IPSec, in order to provide defense-in-depth protection for your network.

802.1X port-based enforcement is a good way of enhancing network protection for both wired and wireless networks within your enterprise, but it requires supporting hardware (802.1X-capable switches) and client computers that have 802.1X supplicant software. This supplicant software has been built into Microsoft Windows since Windows 2000, but it has gone through several updates and is best supported in Windows Vista. This method of NAP enforcement can provide strong network access control, as clients with valid authentication credentials will receive different VLAN identifiers based on their compliance with your network health requirements.

IPSec policies were difficult and sometimes confusing to configure and manage on previous versions of Windows, but in Windows Vista and Windows Server 2008, IPSec connection rules are easy to configure using the Windows Firewall With Advanced Security snap-in. Using IPSec as a NAP enforcement method requires that you set up a PKI infrastructure with an HRA for issuing health certificates to clients in quarantine, which means more planning and deployment overhead when implementing NAP. But because IPSec can be used to restrict communication with compliant clients on a per-IP address or per-port basis, IPSec is the strongest network access control method you can implement using NAP and can be considered a host protection scenario for deploying NAP. However, if you plan on implementing IPSec NAP enforcement, you need to implement IPSec across your entire corpnet because IPSec NAP doesn't quarantine noncompliant clients on a restricted network. Instead, when a noncompliant client obtains physical access to corpnet, IPSec-enabled hosts on corpnet simply drop any traffic received from the client. So if you still have hosts on corpnet that are not IPSec-enabled, these hosts might be susceptible to malware infection from the noncompliant client. So basically, IPSec NAP is an all-or-nothing solution, so if you implement this as your enforcement solution you need to do it everywhere . Other NAP enforcement methods might require adding network infrastructure (such as a restricted network for quarantining noncompliant clients), but they don't require making changes to hosts already on your corpnet.

Finally, VPN enforcement is obviously something you should consider deploying if your enterprise has mobile clients that need to remotely connect into corpnet. VPN enforcement provides strong limited network access for any computer trying to access your network using a VPN connection, and is therefore a good choice for implementing perimeter protection using NAP.

Phased Implementation

The best way to deploy the NAP platform in an enterprise is to do this in stages. Begin with a test implementation using an isolated test network so that you can learn how NAP works and test whether your hosts and network infrastructure can support it. Then try a pilot rollout, maybe by deploying NAP for users in your IT department. (They're used to having headaches, so they won't be too upset when they can't RAS into corpnet Monday morning–well, maybe they will be upset, but they're paid to solve such problems anyway.) Then, depending on the size of your enterprise, you can start rolling out NAP for different business units or in different locations.

Even when you're deploying NAP, however, you have different options you can implement in terms of the level of enforcement you use. So rather than starting by configuring NAP to refuse network access to noncompliant clients, it's better to follow a more measured approach like this:

- **Phase 1: Reporting only**   Implement NAP so that client access is logged in the Event logs on the NPS but no remediation or quarantining is performed. If you follow this approach at first, you can monitor how NAP is doing without users becoming frustrated over network access problems and without having to tie your remediation infrastructure together with NAP.

- **Phase 2: Reporting and remediation**   Once you've monitored NAP in reporting mode for a while and you've gained some understanding of the possible health states of NAP clients, you can now enable remediation in addition to reporting. During phase 2, clients that are noncompliant get automatically remediated (if they can be) but nonremediated clients are not prevented from accessing your network.

- **Phase 3: Delayed enforcement**   After you're sure that autoremediation is working properly, bump NAP enforcement up a notch and implement delayed enforcement. What this does is allow unhealthy clients to still have access to the network but only for a predetermined period of time. For example, a client that is missing the latest security update would be allowed to connect to corpnet, but if after one week has elapsed the client still hasn't downloaded and installed the update, the client is moved into quarantine and denied corpnet access until the client can be remediated.

■ **Phase 4: Immediate enforcement**   Finally, once you're ready (and your users are ready), you can remove the grace period and configure NAP to quarantine noncompliant clients immediately if NAP determines them to be unhealthy. Clients are remediated automatically whenever possible, and when for some reason this is not possible, the client remains in quarantine until it can be manually remediated. Phase 4 is the most secure NAP deployment you can do, but not every organization will need to go this far—you need to balance your security requirements against usability/manageability to determine whether Phase 4 is necessary or Phase 3 (or some earlier phase) might be enough to meet the needs of your business. In general, however, the more managed the environment, the more likely you'll be to implement Phase 4 (or perhaps Phase 3 with a very short grace period).

Let's find out more about implementing NAP by listening to another of our experts at Microsoft talk about it deploying it:

From the Experts: Planning the Deployment of Network Access Protection

Deploying solutions that enforce policy compliance by restricting network access is a powerful tool for protecting the network. However, the time during which the deployment is taking place can also be intimidating because of the concern of unintentionally blocking network access. Appropriate deployment planning and execution can significantly reduce the risk of unintended network restrictions and greatly smooth the process of getting NAP deployed. A recommended process for planning and deploying NAP is the following one:

1. Plan an enforcement type.
2. Plan the health policy.
3. Deploy the NAP components.
4. Enable NAP in reporting mode.
5. Enable NAP in deferred enforcement mode.
6. Enable NAP in full enforcement mode.

A significant decision that needs to be made early in the NAP deployment planning is what type of access enforcement will be used. There are four enforcement types supported natively with NAP: Server and Domain Isolation using IPSec policies, 802.1x authentication, VPN remote access, and DHCP. Other options might be provided by NAP partners. The decision of which enforcement type to use depends on many factors, including what is currently in use in the network, the desired robustness of the enforcement, and cost of deployment and maintenance.

NAP depends on the administrator to define the health policy for the network. This commonly includes standards regarding antivirus measures, firewalls, patch management, and other items that are viewed as critical for protecting or managing the network. By defining the health requirements of the network, the administrator can then plan the software required to check for and enforce compliance with those standards using the NAP infrastructure. Once health policies are defined, administrators can ensure that the appropriate software and tools are deployed in advance of enabling NAP.

After the initial planning, the NAP components and servers need to be deployed. This deployment process includes installing and configuring the required Network Policy Servers, System Health Validators, and System Health Agents. This should be done while NAP policies are operating in reporting mode. When operating in this mode, the NAP health policies are in place and all clients connecting to the network are requested to participate in health checks. However, in reporting mode, regardless of compliance to the health policy, no access restriction is applied. The results of the health check are logged, but all clients are given full network access. This mode allows administrators to validate the operation of the NAP infrastructure, see the level of compliance with the health policies, and take steps to get the compliance rates to the desired levels, without causing any disruption to the end user. One of those steps is to enable automatic remediation of noncompliant clients to elevate compliance rates.

After compliance levels are at an acceptable level, the administrator can enable NAP deferred enforcement. In this operating mode, computer health is checked and noncompliant clients receive a notification that they are out of compliance. This allows for additional elevation of the compliance rates, introducing the operation of NAP to the end users, while giving noncompliant users time to address any lingering problems before network restrictions are applied. As with reporting mode, the results of the client health checks are logged and can be analyzed by the network administrator to verify client compliance rates and the operation of the NAP infrastructure.

The final step is to enable NAP in enforcement mode. This mode applies the defined access restrictions to clients that fail the health compliance check, protecting the network from clients that are unhealthy. As with the other modes, the results of the health check are logged for monitoring the NAP infrastructure operation. Automatic remediation can be applied to noncompliant machines to return them to a compliant state and restore full network access with as minimal impact to the user as possible.

–Kevin Rhodes
  Lead Program Manager – Network Access Protection

One thing to consider when you're deploying NAP is how to handle exceptions. A good example is when a contractor comes on site and has to connect to corpnet using her laptop to perform some task. Now in situations like this, you often can't just let NAP take control of her computer and try and remediate it if the machine is not compliant. Why not? Well, first there's the ownership issue—the contractor's computer belongs to her, not the enterprise. Second, how can NAP remediate her machine if it's running different AV software than you use in your enterprise? Or a different host-based firewall? Or a different operating system, like Linux?

What should you do in these types of situations? Let's hear some insights concerning this issue from another of our experts:

From the Experts: Managing NAP Policy Exceptions

It's inevitable: as soon as you get NAP deployed in your organization someone way more important than you will demand an exception to the policy. Or perhaps you have some non–NAP capable machines on your network and you want a simple method for exempting them from the policy. Or maybe you have a vendor coming on site who needs network access for the afternoon. In any case, managing exceptions to your policy is a key part of a successful NAP deployment. Because NAP is built around RADIUS, you can build exception policies based around many types of attributes. The following are three common scenarios that occur frequently.

The first and most common scenario of all involves non–NAP capable computers. NAP policies can include a conditional statement about whether or not a machine is NAP capable. This provides a convenient method for allowing access to machines that are not NAP capable, while still enforcing health on those that are. For example, your policy set can be expressed as follows:

1. Healthy Full Access: Grant access when "Computer Health matches 'Healthy' AND Computer is NAP-capable."

2. Not Healthy Restricted Access: Quarantine when "Computer Health matches 'Not Healthy' AND Computer is NAP-capable."

3. Not NAP Capable Full Access: Grant access when "Computer is not NAP-capable."

Because the Network Policy Server processes rules sequentially, any machines that are NAP capable will be judged against one of the first two rules, while any machines that are not NAP capable will fall back to the third rule. This exception method is a useful way to preserve interoperability with existing machines as you go through your NAP deployment.

The second scenario involves a machine that is NAP capable but that you want to exempt from policy. Using the NAP-capable Computers attribute would not help in this case because the machine would match one of the first two policies from the previous example. Instead of exempting based upon NAP capability, you can design a policy that exempts based upon group membership. These groups can include user and machine accounts, and complex rules can be built combining the two (for example, allow when user is in DOMAIN\Finance Users and machine is in DOMAIN\Finance Workstations). In the preceding example, you would want to list group-based policies first because these rules must be matched for the exemptions to be granted. If the group-based rules are not listed first, the match will occur within the original two Healthy / Not Healthy rules and the exemptions will never be triggered.

In the final example, what about the vendor who comes on site briefly and needs network access? In this case, the computer and user will not have group memberships to build rules around. If you've completed your NAP deployment or taken a more aggressive enforcement stance, you might not have the "Not NAP Capable" rule to fall back on either. In this case, a simple way to exempt a user on a short-term basis is by MAC address. A new rule could be created that utilizes the Calling Station ID RADIUS Client Property. This rule could be expressed as "Exempt by MAC Address: Grant access when Calling Station ID matches '0015B7A6F653'." Once your rules are ordered properly, the visitor's connection attempt will match this rule first and will gain network access based purely on its MAC address.

–*John Morello*
  Senior Program Manager, Windows Server Division

Configuring the Network Policy Server

Let's now look at configuring the NPS, which you'll remember is the "heart and soul" of NAP. The discussion that follows is not meant to be a tutorial on how to do this. (You'll find references to "Step by Step" guides for NAP under "Additional Resources" at the end of this chapter.) Instead, we're just going to take a bird's-eye view of the Network Policy Server MMC snap-in and see what's there and how certain configuration tasks are performed. These screen shots were taken using a near-Beta 3 build, so they should be nearly accurate for Beta 3 and probably beyond also. They were also taken on a test NAP deployment that uses 802.1X for the NAP enforcement method.

Let's start by opening Network Policy Server from Administrative Tools.

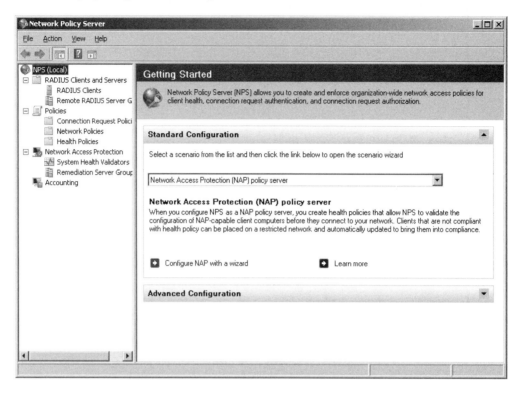

From the root node of the NAP console, you can configure NAP various ways. For example, by selecting Network Access Protection (NAP) policy server from the drop-down list, you can define health policies your NPS can use to check the health of clients when they try to access your network. Other options available include configuring a RADIUS server for dial-up or VPN connections, and configuring a RADIUS server for 802.1X wireless or wired connections.

Selecting the RADIUS Clients And Server node lets you configure RADIUS clients and remote RADIUS server groups. Your RADIUS clients will be your network access servers that perform NAP enforcement. Because we're using 802.1X as the enforcement method for our test network, typical RADIUS clients might be 802.1X-compliant Ethernet switches or wireless access points.

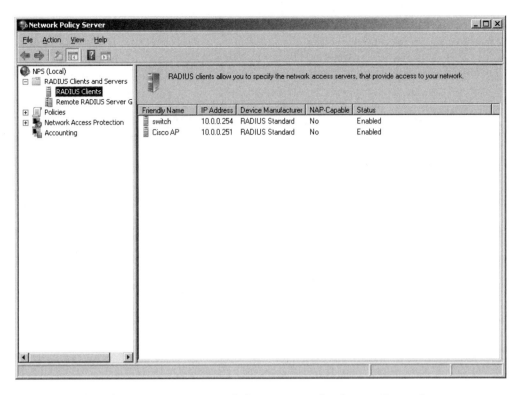

The Remote RADIUS Server Groups node lets you specify where to forward connection requests when the local NPS server is configured as a RADIUS proxy.

Selecting the Policies node lets you configure connection request policies, network policies, and health policies for your NAP deployment. Connection request policies (the first node) let you designate whether connection requests are handled locally or are forwarded to a remote RADIUS server for processing. Because we're using 802.1X NAP enforcement, we also need to configure PEAP authentication as part of our connection request policy. Health policies (the third node) let you define the configuration required for NAP-capable clients to access the network. You deploy a health policy by configuring System Health Validators (SHVs), creating a health policy, and adding the policy to the Health Policies condition in network policy.

The Network Policies node (second node in the preceding figure) is where some key NAP configuration settings reside. Here is where you specify who will be authorized to connect to your network and also the conditions under which they can (or can't) connect. In our test setup, we have three network policies defined: one for 802.1X clients that are compliant, another for clients that aren't compliant, and a third for clients that are not NAP-capable.

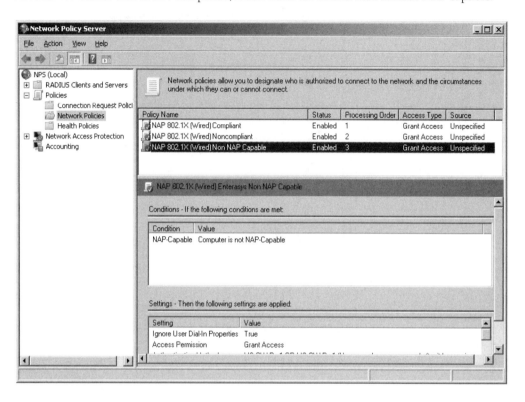

Let's examine the properties of the first policy mentioned (the one for compliant clients) and see what settings can be configured here. Let's double-click on this policy to open its properties.

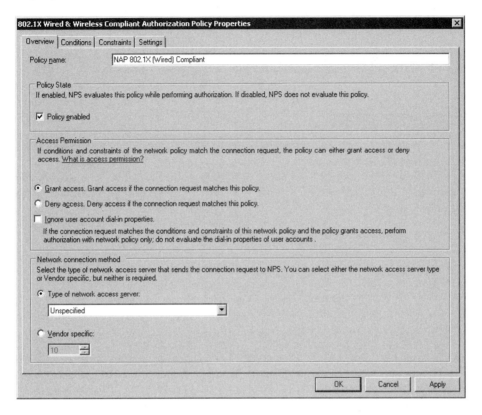

Notice that it's here on the Overview tab that you can enable or disable your network access policy and specify whether clients that match this policy should be granted or denied access to your network. Note that this particular policy setting can be confusing. For example, when you think of "noncompliant" policy you might expect this to be "Deny Access" because you don't want noncompliant computers accessing your network. But this is actually not the right place to do that—this should be "Grant Access" for all policies that are going to be allowing clients to be checked for health.

Now let's switch to the Settings tab and select NAP Enforcement on the left.

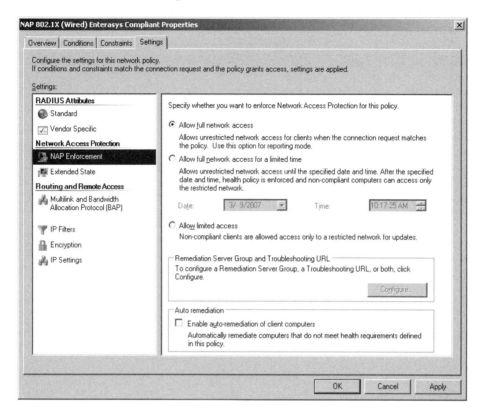

Note that here is where we can configure the level of enforcement (full access, full access with grace period, or limited access to the restricted network only) and also whether auto-remediation is attempted or not. For example, the settings you configure here for a network policy for compliant clients might look like this:

■ Allow full network access

■ Auto-remediation turned off

By contrast, the settings you configure for a policy for noncompliant clients might be these:

■ Allow limited access

■ Auto-remediation turned on

Looking back under the root node in the NPS console, the Network Access Protection node is where you can configure SHVs and also remediation server groups, which are groups that let you specify the remediation servers that will store and provide software updates for NAP clients that need them. By default, the NPS includes one predefined SHV called the Windows Security Health Validator.

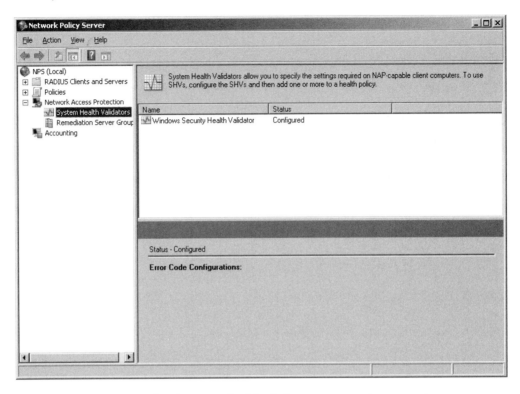

To configure the settings for this SHV, double-click on it to open its properties.

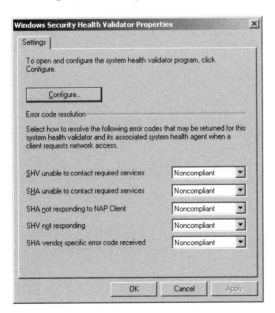

If we click the Configure button, we can see the different kinds of health checks that are performed by this default SHV.

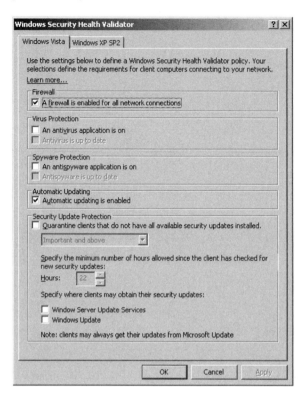

As we described earlier in this chapter, the Windows SHV performs the following kinds of health checks on NAP clients:

- Check whether the Windows Firewall (or any other NAP-compliant host-based firewall) is enabled.

- Check whether AV software is running (and optionally whether its sig file is up to date).

- Check whether Windows Defender or some other antispyware program is running (and up to date).

- Check whether Automatic Updates is turned on for the machine.

- Check whether all available security updates above a specified level of criticality are installed, the minimum time since the client last checked for security updates, and where the client obtains its updates from.

How does the NPS know how to handle a NAP client whose health satisfies (or fails to satisfy) the requirements you've specified in this Windows SHV? Look back under the Policies node again, where you'll find a subnode called Health Policies. If you select this node in our test network, you'll see two kinds of health policies that have been defined.

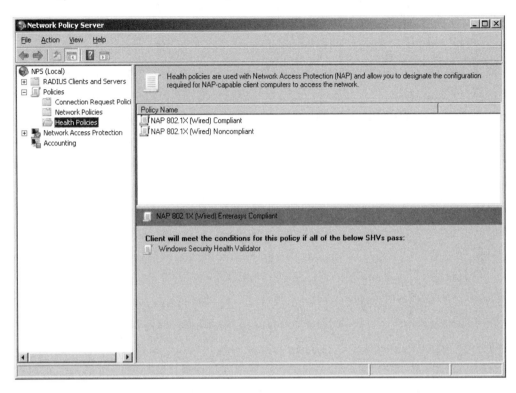

If you double-click on the "compliant" health policy, you'll see that the Windows SHV is being used to check for compliance.

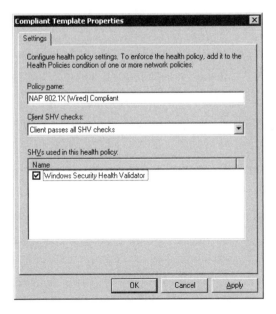

Looking back under the root node, the fourth and final subnode, called Accounting, can be used to configure logging for the NPS. This logging can be in the form of local logging (for display in Event Viewer) or remote logging to a SQL server.

That's a brief whirlwind tour of the Network Policy Server snap-in, which is used for configuring your NPS. There's another way of configuring NPS, however, and that's by doing it programmatically. Let's hear from an expert at Microsoft concerning how this can be done:

From the Experts: Programmatic Method for Configuring NPS Using Netsh

Pre-Windows Server 2008, the Server Data Objects (SDO) API made it possible to programmatically configure and administer Microsoft's RADIUS server (IAS). The SDO API was designed for programmers who use C/C++ and Visual Basic.

With NPS however, programmatic configuration is now possible using scripts and batch files. The new netsh nps context has made this possible. Following is a sample VBScript called AddClient.vbs that can programmatically add a list of RADIUS clients provided in a text file using one of the new netsh nps commands:

```
If WScript.Arguments.Count = 1 Then
 Set objShell = CreateObject("WScript.Shell")
 Set objFSO = CreateObject("Scripting.FileSystemObject")
 Set objTextFile = objFSO.OpenTextFile(WScript.Arguments.Item(0), 1)
 Do While objTextFile.AtEndOfStream <> True
  arrclientinfo = split(objTextFile.Readline, ",")
  netshcmd = "netsh nps add client name = """ & arrclientinfo(0) &_
  """ address = """ & arrclientinfo(1) &_
  """ state = ""enable"" sharedsecret = """ & arrclientinfo(2) &_
  """ requireauthattrib = ""no"" napcompatible = ""no"" vendor = ""RADIUS Standard"""
  objShell.Run "cmd /c"& netshcmd
  wscript.sleep 15000
 Loop
 objTextFile.Close
Else
 Wscript.Echo "Usage: addclients.vbs filename"
 Wscript.Quit
End If
```

The AddClient.vbs vbscript just shown makes use of the netsh nps add client command and a text file named clients.txt containing per-line comma-delimited RADIUS client friendly names, the hostnames, and the RADIUS client shared secrets:

```
radiusclient1,host1,secret1
radiusclient2,host2,secret2
radiusclient3,host3,secret3
radiusclient4,host4,secret4
```

Running this script adds these RADIUS clients to the NPS configuration, and the NPS snap-in displays the four new RADIUS clients.

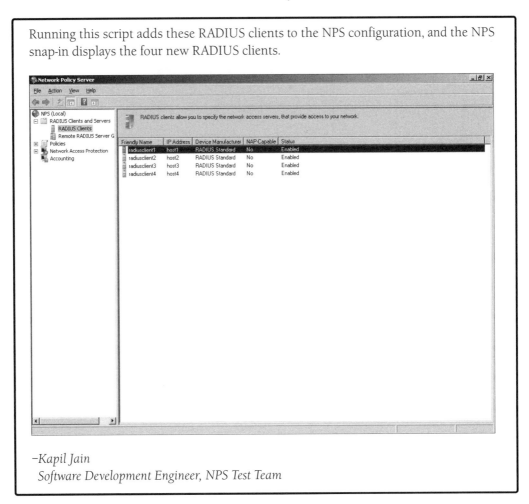

−Kapil Jain
Software Development Engineer, NPS Test Team

Configuring NAP Clients

Now that we've examined how to configure NAP on the server end (that is, the NPS), what sort of configuration do NAP clients need and how is this done? Windows Vista and Windows Server 2008 include an MMC snap-in called NAP Client Configuration that you can use to manually configure client-side NAP settings.

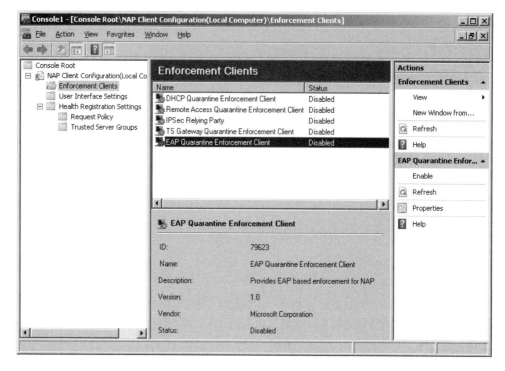

For example, to configure the NAP client to respond to 802.1X enforcement policy on the NPS, you simply select the Enforcement Clients node as shown in the preceding figure, right-click on EAP Quarantine Enforcement Client, and select Enable.

Obviously, you'll get tired of configuring NAP clients manually like this if your enterprise has thousands of client computers. The solution? Use Group Policy to configure your NAP clients. In Windows Server 2008 and Windows Vista, the Group Policy settings for NAP are found under this policy location:

Computer Configuration\Windows Settings\Security Settings\Network Access Protection

Here's a screen shot showing NAP client settings in Group Policy for configuring supported enforcement methods. Compare what you see here with the previous screen shot and you'll see that the same user interface for locally configuring NAP clients is used by the Group Policy Object Editor, which is pretty cool indeed.

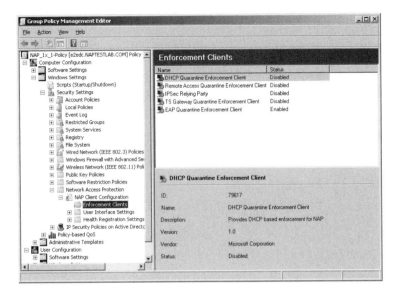

Troubleshooting NAP

Let's end this chapter with some more meat from the Windows Server 2008 product team. If you plan on deploying NAP soon in your enterprise, the following pages alone might be worth the price of the book. And if you don't want to keep the whole book, you can always tear these pages out and throw away the rest!

First let's look at some general tips on how to diagnose various kinds of NAP enforcement issues:

From the Experts: Network Access Protection Diagnostics

The following is designed to be a support aid to diagnose Network Access Protection issues in various enforcements, including IPSec, 802.1x, and DHCP. It is meant to provide additional information to the administrator to identify the root cause of the problem and refers to Microsoft troubleshooting procedures and related information. These Network Access Protection diagnostics involve the Vista/XP client (we will use the term *NAP Client* to refer to them), the network access devices (DHCP Server, HRA Server, 802.1x switch), and the Network Policy Server.

The goal is to collect information to help classify the problem. The first step in diagnosing the NAP system is collecting the following information for diagnosis:

1. Client operating system and the corresponding version (example: Is it Windows Vista or Windows XP?)

2. Network connection information (ipconfig /all details)

3. NAP Client configuration

4. Event logs for the NAP and corresponding enforcement components

The key to identifying the problem quickly is getting to know the scope of the issue. "Who is affected by the problem?" If the problem is shared by many users, it is better to start the investigation by verifying the connectivity and the health of NAP servers—for example:

■ Are the servers running as expected?

■ Are there any errors in the server event logs pointing to various issues?

■ Are the clients receiving the configuration from group policy?

In the following section, we will focus on the NAP client-specific problems—that is, NAP Client Diagnostics.

Information Gathering

Open a command prompt with administrator credentials, and issue the following commands:

```
ipconfig /all netsh nap client show state sc query
```

Troubleshooting Flowchart

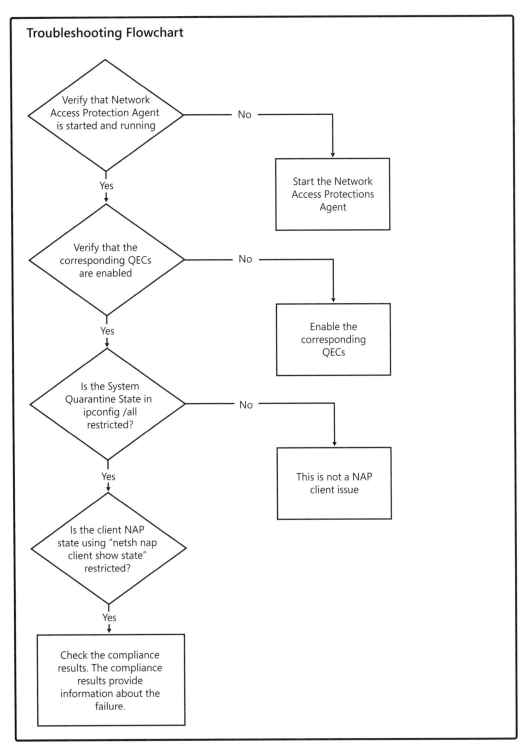

Detailed Investigation

The following steps help identify failures and misconfigurations in the NAP system. The NAP system can have various points of failure. The following diagram illustrates the failure points and the process for debugging them.

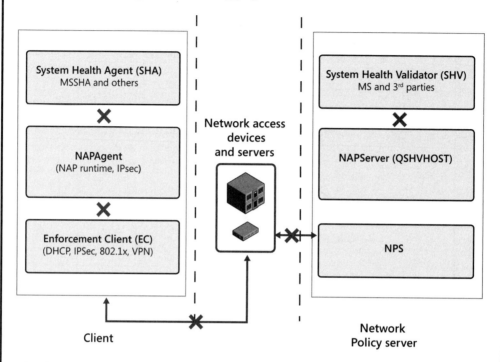

The diagnosis of a NAP client failure starts with the verification of NAP client configuration:

1. Is NAP turned on? (Is NAPAgent service running?)

2. Is the corresponding NAP Enforcement client enabled?

3. Are there any NAP client events in the event logs?

There are a number of events on the client that provide information about the failures. The following diagram shows the informational events logged on the client when the NAP transaction crosses the component boundaries.

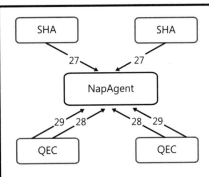

The following is a description of various NAP events that can help the diagnosis:

Event ID	Event Details
27	Indicates that a Statement of Health (SoH) was received from the System Health Agent (SHA)
28	Indicates that the Statement of Health (SoH) was received by the Quarantine Enforcement client indicated in the event
29	Indicates the Statement of Health Response from the server, and it also contains the client health state
18	Indicates a NAP Health state change

All the events have a unique correlation ID that identifies a NAP transaction.

–Chandra Nukala
Program Manager, Network Access Protection

–Ram Vadali
Software Design Engineer, Network Access Protection

Next let's examine how to troubleshoot NAP IPSec enforcement. We'll start by troubleshooting on the client side because this is generally the best way to begin your troubleshooting when an issue arises.

From the Experts: NAP IPSec Enforcement: Client-Side Trouble-shooting

Here are the client-side troubleshooting steps to identify the root cause of the problem when the client fails to acquire a health certificate in the NAP IPSec environment. These are common to both Windows Vista and Windows XP clients (we will use the term *NAP IPSec Client* to refer to them and the term *NAP Server* to refer to the Windows Server 2008 system, with HRA/NPS/IIS).

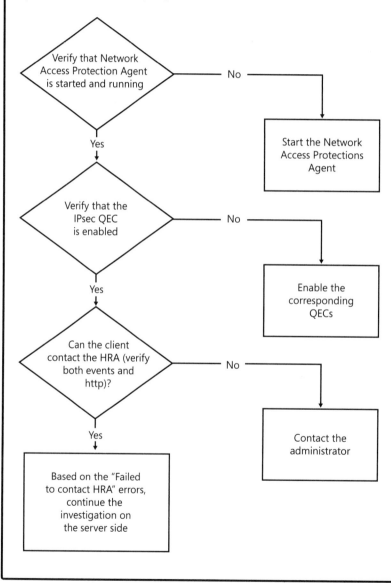

Verify Client Configuration

1. Check for the NAP health certificate in the client's machine store.

   Mmc.exe Certificates Snap-in Computer Account Local Computer Personal Certificates Store

   Proceed to the following troubleshooting steps if the health certificate is not found. A client would not have acquired a certificate if any of the following aren't true.

2. Verify NAP Agent service is running–sc query napagent.

3. Verify Security Center service is running–sc query wscsvc.

4. Confirm the client is in "nonrestricted" state–netsh nap client show state. If the client is restricted, follow the remediation steps to get the client out of restriction state.

5. Validate IPSec Relying Party (QEC) is "Enabled".

   Make sure the client is configured with the correct URL needed to contact HRA Server.

   ❑ If NAP settings are configured locally–netsh nap client show config

   ❑ If NAP settings are configured through Group Policy–netsh nap client show grouppolicy

Verify Client's Connectivity

1. Try to ping HRA. If it fails, there might be a network issue. (Recheck your firewall settings, IPSec Policies, and potential DNS/DHCP issues.)

2. Validate that the client can access the HRA's URL by typing the address into a browser (IE). Following is a list of HTTP errors and the possible causes of these errors:

HTTP Errors	Failures Indicated by the Error Codes
401	Access Denied.
403	Forbidden. This error indicates that the client is sending HTTP requests to HTTPS URL or vice-versa.
404	Page not found. This error indicates that this could be a server-side issue, and investigation has to continue on the server. (Is the HRA installed and set up?)
500	Server error. This error indicates that the client request reached the HRA and because this could be a server-side issue, investigation has to continue on the server.

Client-Side Event Errors

Once the administrator verifies that the client is configured accurately, he can use the following steps to help identify failures and misconfigurations in the IPSec scenario. The administrator can start the investigation by looking at the various "Network Access Protection" events, particularly looking for events 21 and/or 22 in the event log. All NAP-related events are logged in the "Event Viewer/Windows Logs/Applications and Services logs\Microsoft\Windows\Network Access Protection" channel. All NAP events use the event source name "Network Access Protection."

Event 22 indicates that the NAP Agent successfully acquired a health certificate from the HRA Server.

Event 21 indicates that the NAP Agent failed to acquire a certificate from the HRA. The event also provides an error code associated with the failure. The following table shows various error codes and the corresponding failures:

Error Codes	Failures indicated by the Error codes
2147954407	Indicates a name resolution problem. This could indicate a DNS problem. Use ping <destination name> and nslookup to further investigate the issue.
2147954430	Indicates a connection error.
2147954429	Indicates a connection error.
2147954575	Indicates secure failure. There is a problem setting up an SSL channel with the server. (This could indicate a SSL Certificate configuration problem.)

−Wai-O Hui
  Software Development Engineer in Test, Network Access Protection

−Harini Muralidharan
  Software Development Engineer in Test, Network Access Protection

Having seen how to perform client-side troubleshooting of NAP IPSec enforcement, now let's examine how to approach troubleshooting on the server end of things. Event Viewer is going to be especially useful here.

From the Experts: NAP IPSec Enforcement: Server-Side Troubleshooting

Here are the server-side troubleshooting steps to identify the root cause of the problem when the client fails to acquire a health certificate in the NAP IPSec environment. It is assumed that you have already gone through the client-side troubleshooting steps in the previous sidebar.

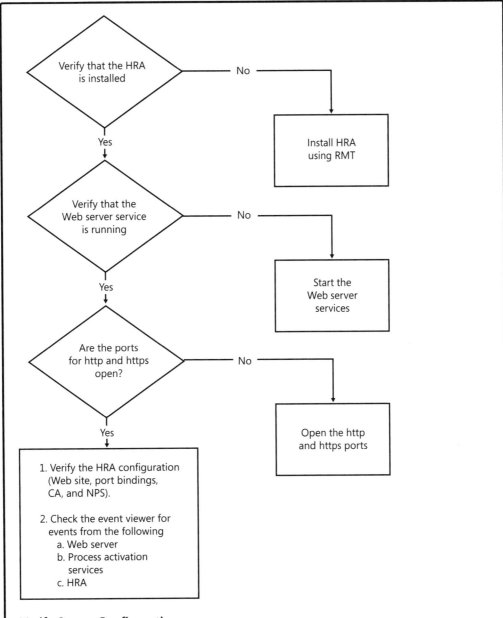

Verify Server Configuration

Use the following steps to verify the server configuration:

1. Verify that HRA and IIS services are installed on the NAP IPSec server.

2. Make sure HRA is configured to point to the correct Certificate Authority.

3. Validate IIS has configured port bindings to support HTTP and HTTPS (SSL) requests.

4. Confirm that the server's firewall settings have exemption for both HTTP and HTTPS traffic.

5. Make sure that HRA is configured to accept anonymous requests (requests from workgroup clients). This is configured during HRA installation. To verify, in the IIS snap-in check whether a non-domain hra root is configured.

6. When configuring the NAP health certificate validity period, make sure it is greater than 15 minutes or else the client will fail to obtain a certificate.

Verify Certificate Authority Configuration

Use the following steps to verify the Certificate Authority configuration:

1. Confirm that the CA is set to auto-issue certificates. The option is located in CA Properties Policy Module Properties Choose "Follow the settings in cert template, if applicable, otherwise automatically issue the cert".

2. Verify that the HRA server is configured with permissions to request and delete certificates from the Certification Authority on behalf of the client. Both the Issue And Manage Certificates option and the Manage CA option need to be verified in the security configuration of the CA properties.

3. After making any changes to the Certification Authority, make sure to restart the certificate services to allow the settings to take effect.

Verify Server Connectivity

Make sure that the HRA server could reach the configured CA. If not, there might be a network issue. (Recheck your firewall settings, IPSec Policies, and potential DNS/DHCP issues.)

Server-Side Event Errors

All HRA-related events are logged in the "Event Viewer/Windows Logs/System" channel. All HRA events use the event source name "HRA".

The following table indicates the HRA error events and the possible failures causing the errors:

Event Number	Event Type	Event Text	Resolution Steps
7	Error	The Health Registration Authority denied the request with the correlation-id %1 at %2 (principal: %3) because the request could not be authorized (%4) by the provided DNS. Discarding the request.	A client domain configuration problem. Make sure the client is joined to the correct domain.

Event Number	Event Type	Event Text	Resolution Steps
8	Error	The Health Registration Authority is misconfigured or cannot read its configuration, stopping Health Registration Authority. Verify the Health Registration Authority configuration or contact an administrator for more information.	Certification Authority Configuration error. Verify that Certification Authorities are configured in HRA by doing the following: In a command window run: `netsh nap hra show configuration` and verify that the HRA configuration is correct. If no Certification Authorities are configured, set any available Certification Authorities using the MMC Health Registration Authority snap-in or by using the following netsh command: `netsh nap hra set caserver name = "\\server1\CA" processingorder = "1"`
9	Error	The Health Registration Authority was unable to acquire a certificate for request with the correlation-id %1 at %2 (principal: %3). Discarding the request. The Certification Authority %4 denied the request with the following error: %5 (%6). Contact the Certification Authority administrator for more information.	Health Registration Authority (HRA) does not have the proper permissions to request a certificate from the Certification Authority (CA). Contact the CA administrator, and configure to grant the HRA permission to request certificates.
10	Error	The Health Registration Authority was unable to acquire a certificate for request with the correlation-id %1 at %2 (principal: %3). The Certification Authority %4 denied the request with the following error: %6 (%7). This failure was possibly due to a network related issue. The request will be discarded if no other Certification Authorities are available. This server will not be tried again for %5 minutes. Contact the Certification Authority administrator for more information.	Unable to connect to a Certification Authority because of a network failure. Perform the following resolution steps: Verify the server's network connection. Verify the CA's network address, computer name, and connectivity. Inform the CA administrator of connectivity problems.

Event Number	Event Type	Event Text	Resolution Steps
11	Error	The Health Registration Authority could not contact NPS: %1	Contact the Network Policy Server (NPS) administrator to verify that the NPS service is running and is not disabled. Ensure that Network Policy Server is installed correctly.
20	Error	The Health Registration Authority failed to validate the certificate request against the HRA configuration. The Health Registration Authority denied the request with the correlation-id %1 at %2 (principal: %3) because it did not satisfy the cryptographic policy (%4). Discarding the request.	A configuration problem between the client and the Health Registration Authority (HRA). Verify the client's cryptographic policy. If the problem persists or shows up with multiple clients, verify the applied group policy's cryptographic settings against the HRA configuration regarding Hash and Asymmetric Key algorithm.
24	Error	The Health Registration Authority was unable to validate the request with the Correlation ID %1 at IP address %2 (Principal: %3). The Network Policy Server had no policy matching the request (%4). Contact the Network Policy Server administrator for more information.	The client did not match any of the policies on the Network Policy Server (NPS). Review the client health state. If the problem appears across multiple clients, consider creating additional NPS policies.
25	Error	The Health Registration Authority was unable to validate the request with the Correlation ID %1 at IP address %2 (Principal: %3). The Network Policy Server denied the request because the request was not authorized (%4). Contact the Network Policy Server administrator for more information.	Network Policy Server (NPS) configuration problem. Verify that the NPS proxy is authorized to forward requests to the correct NPS.
28	Error	The Health Registration Authority was unable to validate the request with the Correlation ID %1 at IP address %2 (Principal: %3). The Network Policy Server (NPS) was unable to contact the Active Directory Global Catalog necessary to validate the request (%4). Contact the Network Policy Server administrator for more information.	NPS cannot connect to the Global Catalog. Verify the Global Catalog status, its network connectivity, and the NPS permissions in the forest.

Event Number	Event Type	Event Text	Resolution Steps
29	Error	The Health Registration Authority denied the certificate request with the correlation-id %1 at %2 for (principal: %3). Either no Certification Authorities are configured or none are available. Verify the Health Registration Authority configuration or contact its administrator for more information.	Certification Authority Configuration error. Verify that Certification Authorities are configured in HRA by doing the following: In a command window run `netsh nap hra show configuration` If Certification Authorities are configured, all of them might be blacked out. Contact the CA administrator, and examine whether the current configuration meets the traffic requirements for the network.
30	Error	The Health Registration Authority was unable to connect to the Certification Authority to remove expired records. The Certification Authority [ca-name] denied the request with the following error: [ca-error-number]. Contact the Certification Authority administrator to check the permissions and for more information.	Health Registration Authority (HRA) does not have the proper permissions to delete expired certificates on the Certification Authority (CA). Contact the CA administrator, and configure to grant the HRA permission to delete expired certificates.

–*Wai-O Hui*
  Software Development Engineer in Test, Network Access Protection

–*Harini Muralidharan*
  Software Development Engineer in Test, Network Access Protection

Now let's look at troubleshooting NAP 802.1X enforcement. Once again, we'll begin on the client side, as problems most often begin there—especially if only some clients and not all of them have difficulties.

From the Experts: Debugging NAP 802.1x Enforcement Using Client-Side Troubleshooting

These instructions are designed to be a support aid to diagnose Network Access Protection issues in 802.1x enforcement. They are meant to provide additional information to the administrator to identify the root cause of the problem and refer to Microsoft troubleshooting procedures and related information. Network Access

Protection diagnostics involve the Vista/XP client (we will use the term *NAP Client* to refer to them), the 802.1x switch, and the Network Policy Server.

Is NAP the Problem?

The goal of this section is to collect the information to help classify the problem. The first step in diagnosing the NAP system is collecting the following information for diagnosis:

1. Client Operating system and the corresponding version (Example: Is it Windows Vista or Windows XP?)

2. Network connection information (ipconfig /all details)

3. NAP Client configuration

4. Event logs for the NAP and corresponding enforcement components

802.1x Enforcement

802.1x provides client authentication to the network devices. When diagnosing 802.1x issues, information can be gathered from the NAP Client, the network device, and the Network Policy Server (NPS).

NAP utilizes the PEAP authentication to pass health data, enabling the use of 802.1x as a NAP enforcement. 802.1x NAP health policy is enforced on the network access device through the use of VLANs, which are assigned through RADIUS attributes from NPS to the switch.

Information Gathering

Use the following steps to gather the necessary information:

1. Open the "services.msc," and verify that the following services are running (this can also be verified using the command line by using the command 3c – sc query):

   ❑ NAP Agent

   ❑ EAP Host

   ❑ Wired AutoConfig (for wired scenarios)

   ❑ WLAN AutoConfig (for wireless scenarios)

2. Open a command prompt with administrator credentials, and issue the following commands:

   ```
   netsh nap client show config > C:\napconfig.txt netsh nap client show state >
   C:\state.txt sc.exe query > C:\services.txt
   ```

Troubleshooting Flowchart

The following is the troubleshooting flowchart that administrators can use to debug the 802.1x NAP system.

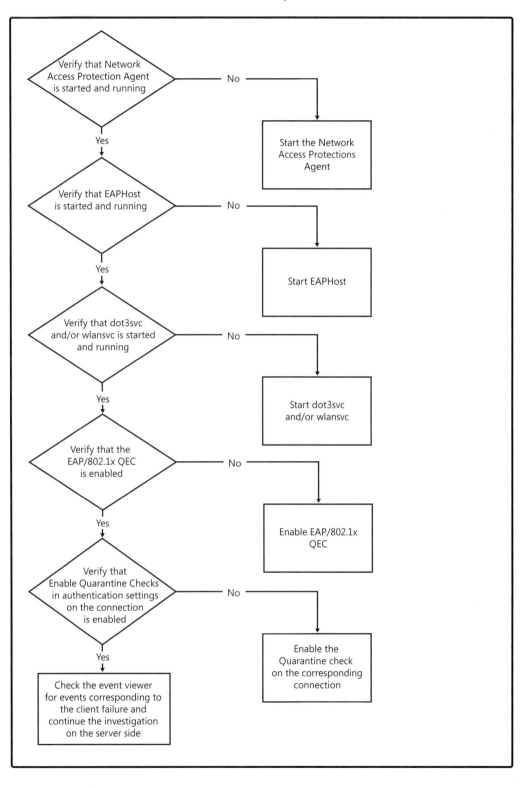

Detailed Investigation

The administrator has to first verify the configuration of the client:

1. The following services are enabled:

    ❑ Network Access Protection Agent ("napagent")

    ❑ Extensible Authentication Protocol ("eaphost")

    ❑ Wired AutoConfig ("dot3svc"). This service is used if the administrator is setting up a wired 802.1x environment.

    AND/OR

    ❑ WLAN AutoConfig ("wlansvc"). This service is used if the administrator is setting up a wireless 802.1x environment.

2. The EAP/802.1x QEC is enabled.

3. The Enable Quarantine Checks option in the Authentication settings for the corresponding connection is configured. (Enable Quarantine Checks is a setting in the connection profile; this setting is new and enables NAP.)

4. Verify the PEAP configuration on the wired connection profile. (Verify the EAP method configuration, and also verify that the certificate is chained back to the same root for validation of the server certificate.)

Once the administrator verifies that the client is configured accurately, he can use the following steps to help identify failures and misconfigurations in the 802.1x/EAP scenario. The administrator can start the investigation by looking at the various Wired AutoConfig (for wired 802.1x scenarios) and Wireless AutoConfig (for wireless 802.1x scenarios) events, particularly looking for events 15505 and/or 15514 (for wired 802.1x scenarios) and events 12013 and/or 12011 (for wireless 802.1x scenarios) in the event log.

Events 15505 and 12011 indicate "Authentication success."

Events 15514 and 12013 indicate "Authentication failures." For authentication failures, look for the reason code and reason text to help with further debugging. (The investigation needs to continue on the NPS server.)

−*Tom Kelnar*
Lead Software Design Engineer, Network Access Protection

−*Chris Edson*
Software Development Engineer in Test, Network Access Protection

Finally, here's the server side of NAP 802.1X troubleshooting. Once again, Event Viewer will be of invaluable use in determining the nature of the problem.

From the Experts: Troubleshooting the Network Policy Server for 802.1x PEAP-Based NAP

Use these instructions if you have already configured 802.1x PEAP-based NAP and have attempted authentication, but you do not see the expected behavior on the client. It is expected that the client-side troubleshooting procedure outlined in the previous sidebar has already been used.

Information Gathering

Use the following steps to gather the necessary information:

1. Dump all NPS events into an Event viewer file for later analysis: `wevtutil.exe epl System NPS.evtx /q:"*[System[Provider[@Name='NPS'] and TimeCreated[timediff(@SystemTime) <= 86400000]]]"`

   Or create a custom (or filtered) view folder in the Event Viewer that displays only the NPS events.

2. Open the Network Policy Server snap-in for examining policy configuration.

Troubleshooting Flowchart

Most 802.1x PEAP-based NAP troubleshooting is done by analyzing the Events posted by NPS into the System event log store. Take a look at the events, and proceed along the flowchart, referring back to the events as needed.

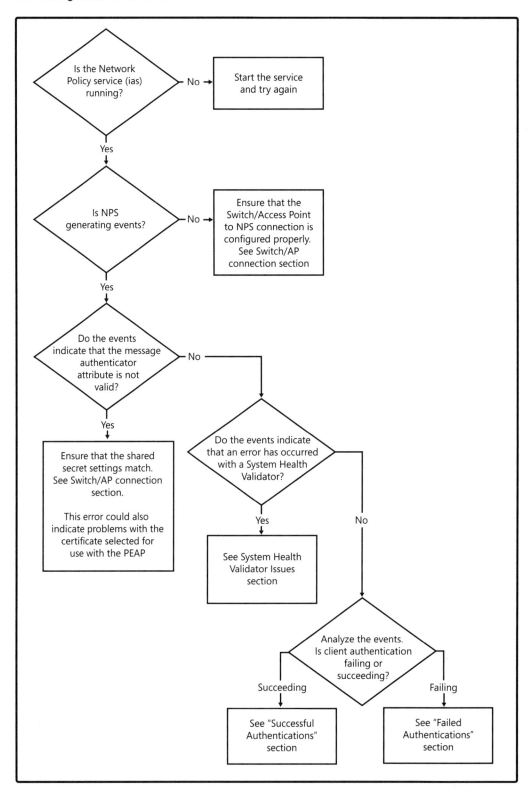

Switch/Access Point Connection

Several issues can prevent the switch or access point from properly communicating with the Network Policy Server:

1. The Network Policy Server machine must have the correct ports open in the firewall to allow the RADIUS requests through to the NPS service:

   ❑ UDP:1812 for authentication

   ❑ UDP:1813 for accounting

2. The switch or access point must be configured to forward 802.1x authentication requests to the Network Policy Server; this includes setting the correct IP address for the NPS machine, as well as the proper ports (for some switches).

3. The Network Policy Server must also be configured to recognize the switch or access point; this is done by configuring a RADIUS client table entry within the NPS snap-in, and it requires the IP address of the switch or access point.

4. The Network Policy Server and the switch or access point must both be configured with a common "shared secret." If the secrets do not match, they will not be able to correctly communicate.

System Health Validator (SHV) Issues

Some common causes and paths of investigation for System Health Validator errors are as follows:

1. Perhaps the most common cause for System Health Validator failures occurs when the versions of Validator (server side) and System Health Agent (client side) do not match. Always ensure that the SHV/SHA pairs in use are matching versions.

2. Another common cause for System Health Validator–related errors is a failure to correctly register with the Network Policy Server. If this occurs, contact the SHV developer.

3. System Health Validator errors can also appear when the Network Policy Server is unable to load the SHV, or when the SHV terminates unexpectedly. If either of these situations occurs, contact the SHV developer.

Failed Authentications

Failed authentications can occur for a number of reasons, many of which are not specifically related to the NAP portion of the transaction.

Reason #1 – No matching policy

Some common causes and solutions for this reason are:

■ A client request arrived that did not exactly match any of the Network Policies configured on the NPS. Always ensure that you have policies in place that will match all possible client requests. Or you might consider making your existing policies slightly less specific by removing nonrequired conditions from the policies.

- The NPS policy configuration does not include a policy that will match "not NAP capable" clients. When a client machine first boots, the authentication services will start prior to the NAP Agent service, and an authentication will be performed before health information is available. This client will therefore not match any policies with health-based conditions. Whether you grant full access with this policy or not, it still needs to be included in the configuration. Also, know that clients will re-authenticate once the NAP Agent service starts.

Reason #2 – User is denied access

A common cause and solutions for this reason are that, by default, the Network Policy Server will perform an Active Directory account look-up to verify the authenticating user's dial-in privileges. If the user's account does not allow dial-in access, the user will be denied access (regardless of the NPS policy settings). If you want to grant the user access, you can do either of the following things:

- Ensure that the user's account in the Active Directory is set to allow dial-in access.
- Select the Ignore User Account Dial-in Properties box for the policy in NPS, which allows NPS to ignore the dial-in access setting and check only whether the user account is active in Active Directory.

Successful Authentications

Because of the possible complexities of 802.1x and the authentications it allows, there are cases in which clients could be successfully authenticating, yet not gaining the expected level of access.

Problem #1 – Client is NAP enabled but matches the "not NAP capable" policy

Two common reasons and solutions for this problem are:

- Network Policy Server policy evaluation occurs in two stages: Connection Request policies first, and then Network Policies. Because Health is a condition for Network policy evaluation, the health data must be gathered prior to entering the Network Policy stage. Therefore, ensure that the Connection Request Policy being used is configured to Override Authentication and to do PEAP authentication. Also ensure that the PEAP configuration settings include selecting the Perform Quarantine Checks check box. Also ensure that the conditions on the Connection Request Policy are such that only requests from your switches or access points will be matched by that policy.

- At client boot, the authentication services start prior to the NAP Agent. Thus, for the first authentication, there is no health data for evaluation. Therefore, the client will not match any policies in which health criteria are used as conditions. The client will match only policies with the "not NAP capable" condition. However, once the NAP Agent starts, a second authentication will be initiated, and the client will then be able to match the expected policy.

Problem #2 – Client is placed on the wrong VLAN

The solution to this problem will vary, depending upon the switch or access point hardware and sometimes the firmware that you are using. Consult the documentation or support contacts for your hardware, and determine what RADIUS standard or vendor-specific attributes need to be given to that hardware to achieve the functionality you desire. Once you have determined the values that need to be passed to the hardware, ensure that each policy on the Network Policy Server has these values configured in the Profile Settings section.

–Chandra Nukala
Program Manager, Network Access Protection

–Chris Edson
Software Development Engineer in Test, Network Access Protection

Pretty cool stuff, eh? My thanks to the NAP team for contributing these insights. Product teams tend to be especially proud of the features they develop, and NAP is obviously prouder than most because they took the time out of their busy schedule (Ship! Ship!!) to provide this content for my book—thanks, team!

Conclusion

I'm excited about NAP. The days of unrestricted access to Windows networks are coming to an end, and Microsoft has displayed its ongoing commitment to its Trustworthy Computing Initiative by developing the NAP platform that we've described in this chapter. And with industry support by over a hundred different third-party ISVs and IHVs, NAP is likely to be the dominant player in the network access platform marketplace. If you haven't started testing NAP, you should being doing so using the latest build of Windows Server 2008 available to your enterprise because this is one technology you really don't want to be without.

Additional Resources

The best place to start looking for resources about NAP is the Network Access Protection page on TechNet, which can be found at *http://www.microsoft.com/technet/network/nap/default.mspx*. There you'll find overviews, webcasts, Live Meeting presentations, links to Step by Step guides (which go into more detail of how to set up NAP than we could go into in this brief chapter), and more.

The Microsoft Download Center also has great resources on NAP; just go to *http://www.microsoft.com/downloads/* and search for NAP and you'll find many.

There's also a TechNet Forum where you can ask questions and help others trying out NAP; see *http://forums.microsoft.com/TechNet/ShowForum.aspx?ForumID=576&SiteID=17* for this forum (Windows Live registration required).

For ISVs and IHVs who want to NAP-enable their product, the NAP APIs can be found on MSDN at *http://msdn2.microsoft.com/en-us/library/aa369712.aspx*.

And don't forget to check out the NAP blog at *http://blogs.technet.com/nap/default.aspx* as this is a terrific and timely resource for all things NAP.

Finally, be sure to turn to Chapter 14, "Additional Resources," for more sources of information concerning NAP, and also for links to webcasts, whitepapers, blogs, newsgroups, and other sources of information about all aspects of Windows Server 2008.

Well I've been working hard on this chapter, and now it's done. So I better rest a bit and take a nap before I start writing my next chapter. Uh-oh, another bad pun. Better stick to my day job (IT pro) and avoid the nighttime comedy circuit.

Chapter 11

Internet Information Services 7.0

In this chapter:

Understanding IIS 7.0 Enhancements. 341

Conclusion 374

Additional Resources. 375

Watching Microsoft Internet Information Services (IIS) evolve over the last decade or so has been exciting. While a high point for end-user experience was probably the worldwide release of Microsoft Windows 95, for an IT pro like me, one of the high points in Windows platform development was the Microsoft Windows NT 4.0 Option Pack release of IIS 4.0. Since then, as the version numbers have continued to climb, IIS has evolved into the most secure, reliable, and powerful Web application platform around. For instance, since IIS 6.0 was released on Windows Server 2003, there hasn't been a single critical security update for IIS. So what could possibly be new, then, in IIS 7.0? Where can you possibly go if you've already reached the top?

Understanding IIS 7.0 Enhancements

Well, you can always try climbing higher. And that's exactly what the IIS product team has done in version 7 of IIS, which was released with Windows Vista and is being further enhanced and fine-tuned for Windows Server 2008. Compared with the previous version (IIS 6.0), version 7 of IIS has been improved in five main areas:

- Security and patching

- Administration tools

- Configuration and deployment

- Diagnostics

- Extensibility

Let's examine each of these five areas of enhancement, and as we do so we'll get a whirlwind tour of what IIS 7.0 is all about. Sort of like the trip my wife and I made to Europe a few years after we got married—on the left is the Eiffel Tower, on the right is the Matterhorn, over here is the Coliseum, over there is a topless beach near Corfu. Look, the Mona Lisa in the Louvre! Wow, we're at the top of the dome in St. Peter's Basilica! Wow, we're five stories underground in the Catacombs! Look, wow, look at that, wow, look, wow—zoom, we're home!

Sorry but that's a bit what our tour of IIS 7.0 will be like because there's *so* much to learn about that it would really take an entire book to do this feature justice. And we've got only a single chapter to do this—so let's get started! Fortunately, we also have our tour guides (our Microsoft experts) along for the ride to help point out some of the highlights! But like any good tour operator, I want to map out for you where we're going in this chapter. First we'll describe each of these five areas of improvement and note some of the sights worth seeing. Along the way, we'll briefly go inside IIS 7.0 and examine its architecture, which is more interesting than a 16th-century cathedral (well, to a geek, anyway). Then we'll talk about some of the post-Vista improvements that are coming in Windows Server 2008 (though we'll actually mention some of these during the earlier part of our tour). And finally, I'll talk briefly about the Application Server role in Windows Server 2008—summarizing what it's about and how it ties in with IIS. And for those of you who are still unsatisfied at the end of our journey and want to see more, I'll list additional resources you can use to learn more about IIS 7.0 on your own. Sound good? Fasten your seatbelts—we're off!

Security and Patching

One thing I really like about IIS 7.0 is its new modular architecture. What this means is that instead of IIS being a monolithic entity installed by default with only a few features available for optional installation, IIS 7.0 now has more than 40 separate setup components you can choose from and only a small set of these are installed by default. You can now install only IIS features you actually need on your Web server and leave the remaining features uninstalled. The benefits of doing this are fivefold:

- First, your system is more secure. Why? Because the only IIS binaries installed on your system are those you actually need. And the fewer binaries, the less attack surface there is on your machine.

- Second, your system is easier to service. Why? Because maintaining a server involves keeping it patched with the latest critical updates from Microsoft. But if you have only a subset of the available IIS modules installed on your machine, you have to patch only those modules—you don't have to patch modules that aren't installed.

- Third, your system is also easier to manage. For example, as we'll see in a moment, if the component supporting Basic authentication is not installed on your system, the configuration setting for this feature won't be present. And the fewer configuration settings that are surfaced, the less clutter the admin UI has and the easier it is to manage your server.

- Fourth, you can customize your Web server to function in a specific role in your environment.

■ And fifth, you can reduce the memory footprint of your Web server by removing unnecessary modules. As a result, the amount of memory used by worker processes on your machine will be reduced, which can allow you to host more Web sites and Web applications on your machine—something especially valuable in large hosting environments. Reducing the number of installed modules also means that fewer intra-process events are occurring, so this also frees up CPU cycles as well—something that, again, is important in hosting environments.

In addition, you can even create your own custom modules and use these to replace existing modules or add new features to your Web server. We'll talk about this later when we discuss the extensibility of the IIS 7.0 platform.

The following graphic shows the IIS 7.0 components available for you to install when you add the Web Server (IIS) role to your Windows Server 2008 machine. These components are called *modules*, and you can add or remove them from the Web server engine, depending on what you need.

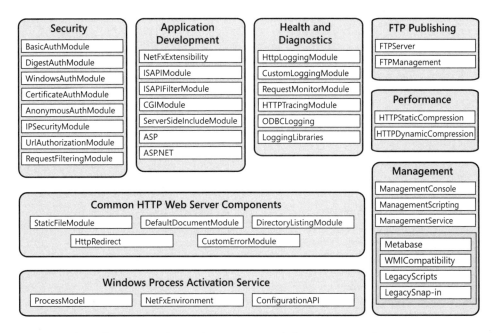

The preceding illustration shows that IIS 7.0 modules are grouped into various categories of functionality. Table 11-1 lists the different modules available in each category and provides a short description of what they do.

Table 11-1   IIS 7.0 Modules and Their Functionality

Module Name	Description
HTTP Modules	
CustomErrorModule	Sends default and configured HTTP error messages when an error status code is set on a response
HttpRedirectionModule	Supports configurable redirection for HTTP requests
OptionsVerbModule	Provides information about allowed verbs in response to OPTIONS verb requests
ProtocolSupportModule	Performs protocol-related actions, such as setting response headers and redirecting headers based on configuration
RequestForwarderModule	Forwards requests to external HTTP servers and captures responses
TraceVerbModule	Returns request headers in response to TRACE verb requests
Security Modules	
AnonymousAuthModule	Performs Anonymous authentication when no other authentication method succeeds
BasicAuthModule	Performs Basic authentication
CertificateMappingAuthenticationModule	Performs Certificate Mapping authentication using Active Directory
DigestAuthModule	Performs Digest authentication
IISCertificateMappingAuthenticationModule	Performs Certificate Mapping authentication using IIS certificate configuration
RequestFilteringModule	Performs URLScan tasks, such as configuring allowed verbs and file extensions, setting limits, and scanning for bad character sequences
UrlAuthorizationModule	Performs URL authorization
WindowsAuthModule	Performs NTLM integrated authentication
Content Modules	
CgiModule	Executes CGI processes to build response output. There's also a FastCGI handler that's installed as part of the CGI install.
DavFSModule	Sets the handler for Distributed Authoring and Versioning (DAV) requests to the DAV handler
DefaultDocumentModule	Attempts to return the default document for requests made to the parent directory
DirectoryListingModule	Lists the contents of a directory
IsapiModule	Hosts ISAPI DLLs
IsapiFilterModule	Supports ISAPI filter DLLs

Table 11-1   IIS 7.0 Modules and Their Functionality

Module Name	Description
ServerSideIncludeModule	Processes server-side includes code
StaticFileModule	Serves static files
Compression Modules	
DynamicCompressionModule	Compresses responses, and applies Gzip compression transfer coding to responses
StaticCompressionModule	Performs precompression of static content
Caching Modules	
FileCacheModule	Provides user-mode caching for files and file handles (required)
HTTPCacheModule	Provides kernel-mode and user-mode caching in HTTP.sys (required)
SiteCacheModule	Provides user-mode caching of site information
TokenCacheModule	Provides user-mode caching of user name and token pairs for modules that produce Windows user principals (required)
UriCacheModule	Provides user mode caching of URL information (required)
Logging and Diagnostics Modules	
CustomLoggingModule	Loads custom logging modules
FailedRequestsTracingModule	Supports the Failed Request Tracing feature
HttpLoggingModule	Passes information and processing status to HTTP.sys for logging
RequestMonitorModule	Tracks requests currently executing in worker processes, and reports information with Runtime Status and Control Application (RSCA) Programming Interface
TracingModule	Reports events to Microsoft Event Tracing for Windows (ETW)

You can install these modules by adding role services and features to the Web Server (IIS) role using Server Manager. (Note that some of these modules cannot be selectively installed or uninstalled unless you uninstall the entire w3svc.) When you add the Web Server (IIS) role to your Windows Server 2008 server, a subset of available role services and features is installed by default (though you can also choose to add role services and features at this time or later).

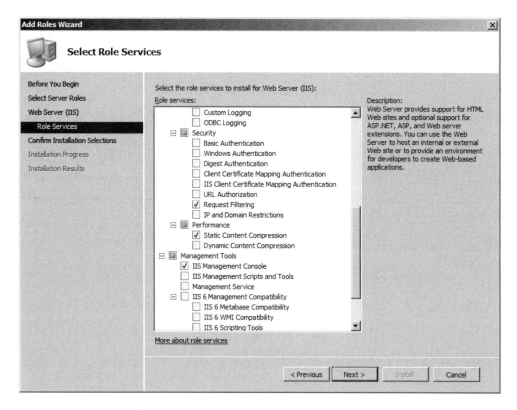

Note in the preceding figure that the Basic Authentication role service (that is, *BasicAuthModule*) is not included in a default install of the Web Server (IIS) role. Keep this in mind, as we'll come back to it later.

To get an idea of how "minimal" IIS 7.0 is out of the box, when you add the Web Server (IIS) role using the defaults already selected for this role, only the following role services and the specified subcomponents (modules) actually get installed:

- Common HTTP
  - ❏ Static Content
  - ❏ Default Document
  - ❏ Directory Browsing
  - ❏ HTTP Errors
- Health and Diagnostics
  - ❏ HTTP Logging
  - ❏ Request Monitor

- Security
  - ❑ Request Filtering
- Performance
  - ❑ Static Content Compression
- Management Tools
  - ❑ IIS Management Console

Look under the Security role service in the preceding list—no Basic authentication, right? Remember that for later.

Windows Process Activation Service

When you add the Web Server (IIS) role to your Windows Server 2008 server, you're also required to install a feature called Windows Process Activation Service (WPAS), together with its three subfeatures: Process Model, .NET Environment, and Configuration APIs. WPAS manages application pools and worker processes running on your machine for both HTTP and non-HTTP requests. For example, when a protocol listener picks up a client request, WPAS determines whether a worker process that can service the request is already running within the application pool. If this is the case, the listener adapter passes the request to the worker process for processing. If there isn't a worker process running in the pool, WPAS starts a new worker process and the listener adapter passes the request to it for processing.

WPAS also functions as a configuration manager that reads and maintains configuration information for sites, applications, and application pools running on IIS, as well as for the global configuration, which includes HTTP central logging and so on. In addition, WPAS maintains the life cycle of worker processes by starting them (for example, when requests come in), stopping them (when they idle out), monitoring their health, and recycling them when needed.

What new functionality does WPAS provide that wasn't there in previous IIS platforms? Let's hear from one of our experts:

From the Experts: Windows Process Activation Service (WPAS)

Windows Process Activation Service, also referred to as WPAS, is a new component in IIS 7.0 that manages application pool configuration and worker processes instead of the WWW process. This enables the same configuration for both HTTP and non-HTTP sites to be used. Thanks to this separation (and in combination with the new modular architecture of IIS 7.0), you can even host non-HTTP sites without the WWW Service even being installed in the first place.

What scenarios does this enable? Because WPAS is not specific to HTTP sites, you can use WPAS to host non-HTTP sites as well. But what do we mean by "non-HTTP sites"?

Well, simply put, WPAS can be used to host sites built on technologies such as Windows Communication Foundation, for example. If you are using WCF with WPAS, are you limited to listening over HTTP? Not at all. In fact, that is the beauty and power of WPAS. You can be hosting a WCF service within WPAS that is using *netTcpBinding*, *netMsm-qBinding*, and so on. As an extension to this, because WPAS supports both HTTP and non-HTTP sites, you can be hosting a service that exposes itself over both HTTP and NET.TCP as well.

–*Jason Olson*
  Technical Evangelist, Windows Server 2008 Developer & Platform Evangelism

Request Processing Pipeline

The modular architecture of IIS 7.0 is also important to the way in which requests are processed by IIS 7.0. By way of comparison, on the previous platform (IIS 6.0), you basically had a monolithic request-processing pipeline that could have its functionality extended through ISAPI. In IIS 7.0, however, you have all these different modules that can be plugged into your generic request pipeline to modify how requests are processed by your server. In addition, you have a public module API that you can use to extend your pipeline by adding your own custom modules.

Another way of comparing the new IIS 7.0 architecture with the old one in IIS 6.0 is by comparing how ASP.NET is integrated with IIS on these two platforms. In IIS 6.0, you basically have IIS and ASP.NET and never the twain shall meet—unless it happens via ISAPI. For example, suppose a request comes in that needs to be processed by ASP.NET. IIS hands it off to ASP.NET via the ISAPI extension aspnet_isapi.dll, which processes the request and returns it to IIS. This mechanism involves feature duplication and is not very efficient. By contrast, IIS 7.0 offers two modes of handling such requests. First, you can use the "classic" mode, where ASP.NET runs as ISAPI just like in IIS 6.0, which is useful for compatibility reasons. And second, you can use the new "integrated" mode, where ASP.NET and IIS are part of the same request-processing pipeline—that is, your .NET modules and handlers plug directly into the generic request-processing pipeline, which is much more efficient than the old model (and provides a far easier extensibility point to program to—ISAPI is so 90s).

Other Security Enhancements

If you thought IIS 6.0 was "secure by default" (and it was, to a large degree), you should take note of some other security enhancements included in IIS 7.0. For example, instead of the IUSR_*computername* local account that was used on previous IIS platforms to provide anonymous access to your server, IIS 7.0 now uses a new built-in anonymous user account for this purpose. To understand the significance of this change, let's hear from one of our experts:

From the Experts: Change with the IIS Anonymous User

The IUSR_*<servername>* account in previous versions of IIS has always been a local account created when IIS was installed on the operating system (unless you install IIS on a domain controller, which is not recommended). Just short of "Internet User," the name that IUSR is often called is *anonymous user*, and it's the identity used to access content on Web sites configured to allow Anonymous authentication. This identity has worked very well to provide unauthenticated access on IIS, but because it is a local account, it has a password and security identity (SID) for NTFS permissions that are unique to the local server. As a result, certain operations involving replication of the configuration system or file permissions (such as restoring from backup or replication between servers in a Web farm) become challenging.

In IIS 7.0, an IUSR_*<servername>* local account has been replaced with the IUSR built-in account. The difference is quite significant. A built-in account cannot be used to log in to the server. In addition, the IUSR account has a well-known SID that is common between all editions of Windows Vista and Windows Server 2008 that have IIS 7.0 installed. If you configure a file to Deny Read for the IUSR account and then xcopy that file to another IIS 7.0 server with permissions, the Deny Read permission is still valid. This is one of the little gems that make a big difference in the life of administrators and security specialists, but it's not as well known as other features of IIS 7.0.

–Brett Hill
IIS Technical Evangelist, Developer and Platform Evangelism

Another security enhancement in IIS 7.0 is built-in URL filtering, which prevents suspicious requests from being serviced by your server. Using the *RequestFilteringModule* module, you can specify allowed verbs and file extensions, set character limits, and scan for bad character sequences within a URL requested by a client. This means you no longer need to install URLScan as a separate add-on for IIS, as this functionality is now available out of the box. Let's hear from another of our experts concerning this enhancement:

From the Experts: What About Using URLScan in IIS 7.0?

You don't need URLScan in IIS 7.0. The core features of URLScan are now built into the new Request Filtering module of IIS. In addition to the core URLScan features, Request Filtering offers new functionality that enables you to deny access to certain segments within the URL.

Unfortunately, there is no user interface for Request Filtering. You have to edit the configuration files directly to use this feature. For more information on how to use Request Filtering, see "How To Use Request Filtering," found at *http://www.iis.net/ default.aspx?tabid=2&subtabid=25&i=1040 on IIS.NET.*

If you have a large library of expressions you want to block and you don't want to add each of these expressions into the new configuration files, you might still want to use URLScan version 2.5 with IIS 7.0. You can do this, but the installer for URLScan version 2.5 does not work on Windows Vista or Windows Server 2008. To work around this issue, copy urlscan.dll and urlscan.ini to the Web Server running IIS 7.0 and then set up urlscan.dll as a global ISAPI filter in IIS.

–Tim Elhajj
  Technical Writer

Another security enhancement is the ability to use .NET role and membership providers for authenticating users trying to access the server. You can also easily enable Forms authentication for any content on your server.

IIS 7.0 also includes an enhanced process model that automatically sandboxes applications on your server. For example, when you create a new Web site on your server, process isolation is enabled for this site by default. In other words, by default each new site you create is assigned to its own unique application pool (see Figure 11-1). By default, these application pools all run as Network Service, and each application pool also has its own separate, scoped configuration file that is created at run time.

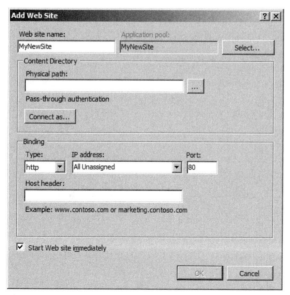

Figure 11-1   Creating a new Web site also creates a new application pool by default

IIS 7.0 also includes a rich delegation infrastructure that lets server administrators create site and application administrators who can administer only designated sites and applications. In addition, you can configure which features of a Web site or Web application to delegate to these different levels of administrators without having to give them full control of the server.

Administration Tools

In addition to having minimized surface area, patching through a componentized architecture, and fully customizable installation options (wow, the Eiffel Tower!), IIS 7.0 also includes a raft of new feature-focused administration tools that can be used to efficiently manage Web servers, sites, and applications—including both IIS and ASP.NET configuration settings from the same place. Let's look at these tools now—but it's only a quick look, so have your cameras ready!

IIS Manager

IIS Manager has been totally revamped in IIS 7.0 to make it more intuitive for those using it. IIS Manager is also more task-oriented than in previous versions of IIS and the "property sheet purgatory" and "tab hell" of IIS 6.0 (actually, it wasn't that bad) has been replaced with icons and a new context-sensitive MMC 3.0 Actions pane (which actually is a lot better!) as you can see in this figure:

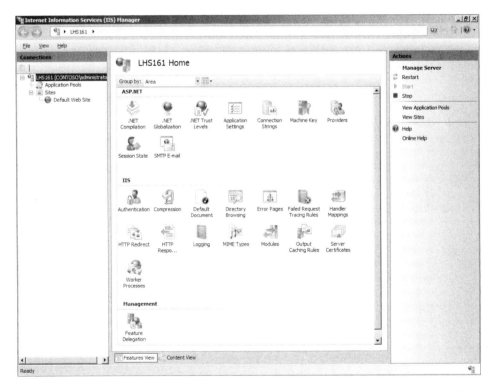

Remember I told you previously that the Basic Authentication module is not installed in a default Web Server (IIS) role installation? Well, if you now select the icon for the Authentication feature (the first one in the IIS section of the Details pane in the preceding figure) and click Open Feature in the Actions pane, you get a list of authentication settings you can configure for your Web server:

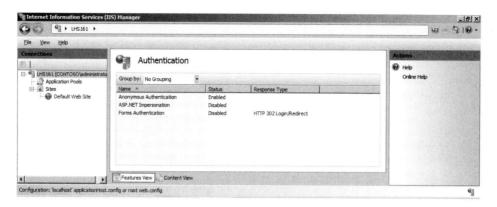

Note that there's no option available for configuring Basic authentication for your Web server. Why not? Because the binaries of that particular component aren't even installed! In other words, the only configuration options you're presented with are those supported by modules already installed on your server. That certainly makes administration a lot easier than the previous platform of IIS 6.0, where you had all those property sheets, tabs, and settings.

How can you make Basic Auth available for applications running on your server? Well, you just go back to Server Manager, right-click on the Web Server (IIS) role, and select Add Role Services to start the Add Role Services Wizard again. Then, in the wizard, you select the check box for Basic Auth and finish the wizard, and the component gets installed. Then, if you open the Authentication feature in IIS Manager, you get this:

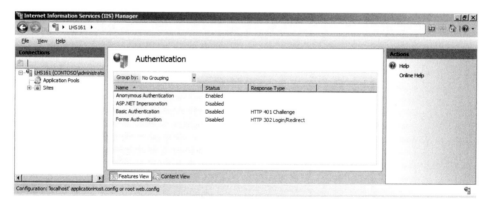

Basic Auth is now installed. Of course, it's also disabled by default and you have to enable it if you want to use it on your server. You might have to restart IIS Manager to make the new setting visible.

The configuration options (icons) you see in IIS Manager depend on the node you select in the console tree in the left pane. For example, if you select a Web site, you get options like these:

If you select any of the icons in the preceding figure, the center Details pane displays settings and might allow you to configure them, while the Action pane at the right gives you a quick way to perform common tasks relating to these settings. For example, if you open the Logging feature, the configuration settings look like this:

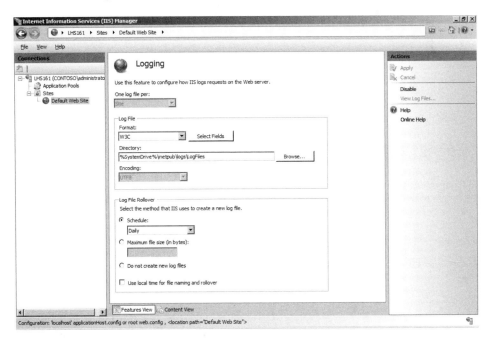

Obviously, we could spend a lot of time exploring all the different settings you can configure and tasks you can perform using IIS Manager, but we need to move on (look, the Coliseum!) and look at some other ways of administering IIS 7.0. But first a quick word from our sponsor—I mean tour guide—I mean expert:

From the Experts: Configuring a UI Feature in IIS 7.0

You might want to configure a UI feature in IIS 7.0 that you don't see in the UI.

There are several possible reasons for this situation. First, if you are running IIS 7.0 on Windows Vista, make sure that the feature you are trying to configure is available. Some features that are available for configuration in Windows Vista do not appear in the UI. You can configure supported features by using other methods—such as appcmd or WMI scripts—or by editing the configuration files directly.

Second, you might not have the feature installed on your Web server. If the feature is not installed, you will not see it in the UI.

Third, if you are running Windows Server 2008 and are connected to a site or an application, you will not see features in the UI unless they have been delegated to that site or application. Additionally, the ability to actually configure a feature that you see in the UI depends on whether the feature was delegated as Read Only or as Read/Write.

For information about IIS 7.0, including additional information about these issues, see *http://www.iis.net*.

—Reagan Templin
 IIS Technical Writer

AppCmd.exe

Remember all the administration scripts that were included with IIS 6.0 so that you could administer it from the command line? These included iisweb.vbs, iisvdir.vbs, iiscnfg.vbs, iisback.vbs, iisext.vbs, and so on. They were a great way of administering IIS 6.0, but they could hardly be called an integrated solution to managing your Web server from the command line.

Well, in IIS 7.0 all those scripts have been done away with (though you can still write your own scripts using the WMI provider for IIS 7.0) and have been replaced by a single command-line tool. AppCmd.exe now gives you a single, unified command-line interface for managing virtually all aspects of your Web server, including sites, applications, application pools, worker processes, and so on. Here's a quick look at the upper-level syntax of this command:

```
C:\Windows\System32\inetsrv>appcmd /?
General purpose IIS command line administration tool.APPCMD (command) (object-type)
<identifier> </parameter1:value1 ...>
Supported object types:
  SITE      Administration of virtual sites
  APP       Administration of applications
  VDIR      Administration of virtual directories
  APPPOOL   Administration of application pools
  CONFIG    Administration of general configuration sections
  WP        Administration of worker processes
  REQUEST   Administration of HTTP requests
  MODULE    Administration of server modules
  BACKUP    Administration of server configuration backups
  TRACE     Working with failed request trace logs

(To list commands supported by each object use /?, e.g. 'appcmd.exe site /?')

General parameters:
/?              Display context-sensitive help message.
/text<:value>   Generate output in text format (default).
                /text:* shows all object properties in detail view.
                /text:<attr> shows the value of the specified
                attribute for each object.
/xml            Generate output in XML format.
                Use this to produce output that can be sent to another
                command running in /in mode.
/in or -        Read and operate on XML input from standard input.
                Use this to operate on input produced by another
                command running in /xml mode.
/config<:*>     Show configuration for displayed objects.
                /config:* also includes inherited configuration.
/metadata       Show configuration metadata when displaying configuration.
/commit         Set config path where configuration changes are saved.
                Can specify either a specific configuration path, "site",
                "app", or "url" to save to the appropriate portion of the
                path being edited by the command, or "apphost", "webroot",
                or "machine" for the corresponding configuration level.
/debug          Show debugging information for command execution.
```

Let's use AppCmd.exe to view a list of Web sites on our server:

```
C:\Windows\System32\inetsrv>appcmd list site
SITE "Default Web Site" (id:1,bindings:http/*:80:,state:Started)
```

There's the Default Web Site running on the machine. Now let's add another site and get it up and running:

```
C:\Windows\System32\inetsrv>appcmd add site /name:"Second Site" /id:2
    /bindings:http://www.woodgrovebank.com:80 /serverAutoStart:true
    /physicalPath:C:\stuff
SITE object "Second Site" added
APP object "Second Site/" added
VDIR object "Second Site/" added
```

Let's see if it worked by checking for all running sites on the machine:

```
C:\Windows\System32\inetsrv>appcmd list sites /state:started
SITE "Default Web Site" (id:1,bindings:http/*:80:,state:Started)
SITE "Second Site" (id:2,bindings:http/*:80:www.woodgrovebank.com,
    state:Started)
```

And sure enough, if we refresh IIS Manager we can see the second site we just created:

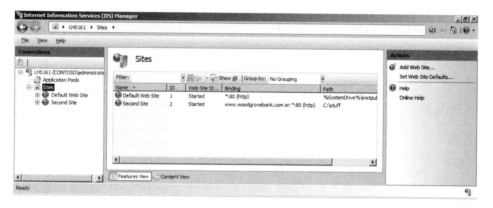

And by the way, we all believe in recycling, don't we? Think globally, act locally (or something like that—I'm a geek so I have tons of pizza cartons lying all over my office—I should recycle them someday). Well, if you've worked much with IIS 6.0, you know about using the iisreset command, which basically shuts down everything on your Web server and restarts it again (everything having to do with IIS that is). You wouldn't use iisreset if you wanted to recycle an application pool in IIS 6.0, so if you wanted to recycle it from the command line you were out of luck. Well guess what—in IIS 7.0 you can do even this from the command line—but using AppCmd.exe of course. Let's learn how:

From the Experts: About iisreset in IIS 7.0

When you use the iisreset command in IIS 7.0, the IIS Admin Service, the Windows Process Activation Service (WAS), and the World Wide Web Publishing Service (W3SVC) are stopped and restarted. You should avoid using iisreset unless absolutely necessary, because the Web server shuts down all applications that depend on these three services until the services successfully restart. This means that you lose the existing state in your applications, your sites and applications become unavailable, and you risk unpredictable results by stopping processes before they finish.

Instead, you can restart an individual site or recycle an application pool that is causing problems. To do this by using IIS Manager, follow these steps:

- To restart an individual site, in the Connections pane, expand the Sites node. In the tree, click the site that you want to restart, and in the Actions pane, click Restart.

- To recycle an application pool, in the Connections pane, click the Application Pools node. On the Application Pools page, select the application pool that you want to recycle, and in the Actions pane, click Recycle.

To do this by using appcmd, use the following commands:

- To restart an individual site, type appcmd stop site "site_name", where *site_name* is the name of the site that you want to restart. Then type appcmd start site "site_name".

- To recycle an application pool, type appcmd recycle apppool "apppool_name", where *apppool_name* is the name of the application pool that you want to recycle.

If you decide to use iisreset, you can include the */noforce* parameter to prevent the services from being forcefully restarted if they cannot do so gracefully, and the */timeout* parameter to specify a number of seconds to wait before the services are restarted. This can help prevent problems that can occur when processes are stopped before they finish.

–Reagan Templin
IIS Technical Writer

Windows PowerShell

Another great tool for managing IIS 7.0 is Windows PowerShell. A great primer on the capabilities of using PowerShell to administer IIS 7.0 is "An Introduction to Windows PowerShell and IIS 7.0," which can be found on the IIS.NET site at *http://www.iis.net/default.aspx?tabid=2&subtabid=25&i=1212&p=1.* We can't get into it any deeper here because the bus is running and the tour has to continue, but let's hear a bit more first from another of our experts:

From the Experts: IIS Managed SDK Inside PowerShell

The Managed SDK for IIS can be used from PowerShell for quick command-line administration. This functionality is handy if you are more familiar with the SDK than with AppCmd.

First, create a script that loads all your IIS Managed SDK assemblies into PowerShell. For instance, create a script named load_iis.ps1 with the following code:

```
$inetsrvDir = (join-path -path $env:windir -childPath "\system32\inetsrv\")
$asmPath =    (join-path $inetsrvDir -childPath "Microsoft.*.dll")
Get-ChildItem -Path $asmPath | ForEach-Object{
    [System.Reflection.Assembly]::LoadFrom(
    (join-path -path $inetsrvDir -childPath $_.Name) )}
```

Save this file, and execute it inside PowerShell by typing ./load_iis.ps1.

PowerShell will load the SDK assemblies from the GAC into the PowerShell environment. You can now use standard PowerShell syntax against the IIS SDK.

For example, if you wanted to list all the Web sites on your server, you could use the New-Object cmdlet in PowerShell to create an instance of the *ServerManager* class as follows:

```
PS C:\> (New-Object Microsoft.Web.Administration.ServerManager).Sites
```

This will list each of your Web sites and public members. You can also get a specific Web site by typing the following:

```
PS C:\> (New-Object Microsoft.Web.Administration.ServerManager).Sites["Default
Web Site"];
```

If you take this concept a step further, you can stop Web sites by using the following code:

```
PS C:\> (New-Object Microsoft.Web.Administration.ServerManager).Sites["Default
Web Site"].Stop();
```

As you use PowerShell more often, you'll find yourself adding more global variables to your assembly load script. For instance, instead of creating a new *ServerManager* on each line, you might want to create a global variable called *$iismgr* that holds your *ServerManager* instance. To add a global alias, put the following at the end of your load_iis.ps1 file:

```
$global:iismgr = (New-Object Microsoft.Web.Administration.ServerManager)
```

Once you have executed this script again, you can type commands like the following inside of PowerShell:

```
PS C:\>$iismgr.Sites.Add("MySite", "http", "*:80:", "c:\inetpub\wwwroot\mysite")
PS C:\>$iismgr.ApplicationPools["DefaultAppPool"].Stop()
PS C:\>$iismgr.WorkerProcesses
```

As time goes on, you'll find that PowerShell can be much more robust for administration than the default AppCmd.exe tool.

–Tobin Titus
Programming Writer, IIS SDK UE

Remote Management

Another way of managing IIS 7.0 is using remote management capability. Before you can do this, you need to run the Add Role Service Wizard for the Web Server (IIS) role in Server Manager, and select the Management Service subcomponent under Management Tools. Remote management provides a secure, firewall-friendly connection to IIS 7.0 over HTTP/SSL, and it can authenticate both Windows and non-Windows credentials.

For more information on enabling and using remote management with IIS 7.0, see the article "How to Enable Remote Administration for IIS Manager," found on IIS.NET at *http://www.iis.net/default.aspx?tabid=2&subtabid=25&i=966.*

WMI Provider

Another great way of managing IIS 7.0 is using WMI scripts. But before you can do this, you need to install the new WMI Provider in IIS 7.0. And to do that, you run the Add Role Service Wizard again for the Web Server (IIS) role in Server Manager, and select the IIS Management Script And Tools subcomponent under Management Tools.

If you want to learn more about managing IIS 7.0 using WMI, a good introduction to the subject is the article "How to Manage Sites using WMI," found on IIS.NET at *http://www.iis.net/default.aspx?tabid=2&subtabid=25&i=961.*

IIS 7.0 API

IIS 7.0 also includes *Microsoft.Web.Administration*, a new a management API that enables editing the XML configuration files for your Web server, sites, and applications. (We'll talk more about configuration files in a moment.) The *Microsoft.Web.Administration* API also provides convenience objects you can use to manage your server and its properties and state.

Again, we don't have time cover this in detail (the bus is running). You can find a great introductory tutorial called "How to Use Microsoft.Web.Administration" on IIS.NET at *http://www.iis.net/default.aspx?tabid=2&subtabid=25&i=952*, but we are blessed by having another of our experts tell us a bit more about this API:

From the Experts: IIS 7.0 Administration API

What is new in IIS 7.0 administration? IIS 7.0 provides a comprehensive managed-code API that, among other things, allows for convenient access to server objects. IIS 7.0 includes *Microsoft.Web.Administration*, which is a new management API for the Web server that enables editing configuration through complete manipulation of the XML configuration files. It also provides convenience objects to manage the server, its properties, and state. The configuration editing aspect of the API provides programmatic access to read and write configuration properties in the IIS configuration file hierarchy and in specific configuration files. The object management aspect of this API provides a series of top-level administration objects for direct management of the server (for example, sites, application pools, worker processes, and so on).

The management classes reside in the *Microsoft.Web.Administration* namespace. The classes provide a weakly typed interface to access configuration sections and convenience objects with properties and methods representing attributes of the configuration (such as the path of a virtual directory) or actions to take on the object (such as recycling an application pool).

–Jason Olson
  Technical Evangelist, Windows Server 2008 Developer & Platform Evangelism

---

Configuration and Deployment

The tour must go on (I wanna see the Matterhorn!), so let's continue and talk briefly about IIS 7.0 configuration and deployment.

Remember the metabase? In IIS 6.0, it was a central, monolithic repository (formatted in XML) that stored pretty much all configuration settings for IIS (although a few were still stored in the registry). Well, in IIS 7.0 the metabase is gone, but that doesn't mean all the scripts you've developed for managing IIS 6.0 via metabase modifications will no longer work. A feature called ABOMapper keeps those scripts working transparently in IIS 7.0. But the metabase is dead in the sense that there is no longer a single, centralized repository for all configuration settings on the Web server. Instead, it's been replaced by a series of .config files of the kind ASP.NET developers will be familiar with.

So what are these different configuration files? Well, first there's a file called applicationHost.config, which resides in the \System32\InetSrv\config directory. The applicationHost.config file is the main configuration file for IIS 7.0, and it contains configuration information concerning sites, applications, virtual directories, logging, and so on. The applicationHost.config file contains two main groups of settings:

- **system.applicationHost**   Includes settings for the activation service, such as the list of application pools, logging settings, listeners, and sites. These settings are centralized and can be specified only in applicationHost.config.

- **system.webServer**   Includes all other settings for the Web server, including the list of modules and ISAPI filters, ASP, CGI, and so on. These settings can be defined here or in any web.config file (if allowed).

Another configuration file is administration.config, which is stored in the same directory and contains things like delegation settings, the list of available modules, the list of administrators, and so on. Then, finally, you have web.config files, which can contain both Web server (or site) settings and ASP.NET settings for applications. These web.config files are generally found in the root directory of a site or application, but they can be located in virtual directories as well (IIS settings are necessarily tied directly to just the app, so they can also reside on vdirs).

Let's take a look at a small snippet from the applicationHost.config file:

```
<security>
    <access sslFlags="None" />
    <applicationDependencies />
    <authentication>
        <anonymousAuthentication enabled="true" userName="IUSR" />
        <basicAuthentication enabled="false" />
        <clientCertificateMappingAuthentication />
        <digestAuthentication />
        <iisClientCertificateMappingAuthentication />
        <windowsAuthentication />
    </authentication>
```

Note that Basic authentication shows up here as disabled, just as it did in IIS Manager earlier. (Flip back a few pages, and you'll see.) What happens if we open the applicationHost.config file in Notepad and edit it by changing "false" to "true" for the <*basicAuthentication*> element? Guess what—if you try this, save the file, and then open IIS Manager and open the Authentication feature, Basic authentication shows up as enabled:

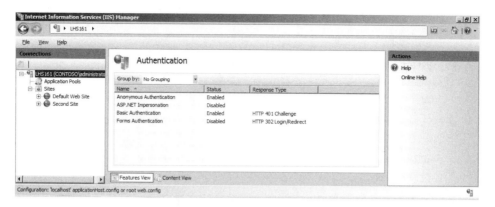

So just like in IIS 6.0, where you could edit the XML metabase in real time, you can do the same with the configuration files here in IIS 7.0. But that's not all. These XML configuration files support inheritance and also additive merging of settings. For example, the settings contained in the applicationHost.config file and in one or more web.config files will merge together to form the actual configuration settings for your site or application.

The fact that configuration settings for IIS 7.0 sites and application can live in different places, including the directories of the site or application itself, also means that distributing the configuration files like this allows you to deploy your sites and applications simply by copying their directory contents using the xcopy command. In other words, the configuration settings for your site live with your site content, so any method for copying files (xcopy, robocopy, FTP, or whatever) can now be used to deploy your site to an IIS machine.

This feature will be really welcome in large hosting environments that have racks of Web servers and thousands of customers, each having one or more Web sites. It's also a terrific way of deploying preconfigured apps to a bunch of stateless front-end Web servers in a Web farm. This is especially true with xcopy because you can include ACLs that are globally unique—NetworkService, application pool identities, the built-in anonymous user account, and so on. And you can even use environment variables to abstract physical paths when you copy files from one server to another. Finally, you can even store your "master" web.config file on a central UNC share so that all your Web servers can share the same configuration file!

Let's learn more about IIS 7.0 configuration from another of our experts:

From the Experts: IIS 7.0 Configuration

One of the most interesting changes in IIS 7.0 is the refactored configuration system. IIS 6 had only one location for configuration settings, metabase.xml. To make changes to it, you needed to be an administrator on the server. Concentrating all the settings in a single store makes it easy for the IIS team to know where to place settings and how to read the configuration. It also makes it easy for administrators to know where to look for problems should they occur. However, it isn't very flexible and doesn't facilitate real-world needs like Web farm replication of settings or empowering server administrators to allow teams or developers to configure their own Web sites on intranet servers. In addition, ASP.NET and IIS 6.0 configuration systems are completely different designs, requiring multiple configuration technologies for a single Web server.

In IIS 7.0, Metabase.xml has been redesigned to become applicationHost.config. The structure of the new applicationHost.config is declared in the IISSchema.xml file, so if you're curious about exactly what options are available for any particular setting, that's the place to look.

The new configuration system provides new choices for how you architect your IIS 7.0 configuration:

- **Single Configuration File**   In this design, all your IIS 7.0 settings are stored in applicationHost.config. To do this, ensure that all IIS 7.0 settings in the IIS Manager, Feature Delegation are set to Read Only. When you make a change to a Web site or applications settings, the updated configuration will be applied using a *<Location>* tag inside applicationHost.config. Benefits to this design are obvious to administrators—total control!

> **Note**   The .NET configuration settings are stored in the root web.config file at microsoft.net\framework\<version>\config\web.config.

- **Delegated Configuration**   Configuration settings that are delegated will be written to web.config between the <system.webserver> entries. Some, but not many, settings are delegated by default. (Review the Feature Delegation page, and click Help for an explanation of what the various settings mean.) To configure a setting to be delegated, you set it to Read/Write. If you do this, understand that if you, the developer, overwrite the web.config with a new web.config, the delegated settings might be affected.

- **Shared Configuration**   This is a new capability of IIS 7.0 that allows you to set up all your IIS 7.0 servers so that they share a single applicationHost.config file. The shared configuration feature is designed to eliminate the need to replicate IIS configuration settings between servers in a Web farm. Specific technical details are posted on IIS.net. You can use this in conjunction with delegated configuration to allow sites or applications to control specific settings

My suggestion is that you take a good look at your Web server, application, and infrastructure design before you deploy IIS 7.0 and determine how to best leverage these new configuration capabilities.

−Brett Hill
IIS Technical Evangelist, Developer and Platform Evangelism

And here's yet another of our experts to explain more about ways you can view and modify your configuration files and the steps you need to follow to do so:

From the Experts: Viewing and Editing Server-Level Configuration Files

Sometimes user accounts that are part of the Administrators group cannot view or edit server-level IIS 7.0 configuration files because they are denied access. In Windows Vista and Windows Server 2008, User Account Control (UAC) requires that all users run in standard user mode unless a task or application requires administrator privileges. The IIS 7.0 server-level configuration files, such as applicationHost.config, require administrator privileges for access. To edit server-level configuration files, you must first elevate your privileges when you open the application that you want to use to view and edit the configuration files.

To open a server-level configuration file, first determine the application that you want to use to view and edit the configuration file, such as Notepad, Microsoft Visual Web Developer Express, or Microsoft Visual Studio. When you open the application, right-click the .exe file and click Run As Administrator. You can then open the configuration file from inside the tool to view and edit configuration settings.

For example, to open applicationHost.config in Notepad with your administrator privileges, complete the following steps:

1. Click Start, click All Programs, and then click Accessories.

2. Right-click Notepad and click Run As Administrator.

3. In the User Account Control dialog box, click Continue to open Notepad using your elevated privileges.

4. In Notepad, click File, and then click Open.

5. Navigate to %windir%\system32\inetsrv\config, and double-click application-Host.config.

> **Note** In the Open dialog box, make sure that you select All Files in the drop-down list to display all file types.

–Reagan Templin
IIS Technical Writer

Diagnostics

We haven't been to that topless beach yet in Corfu, so we'll continue racing ahead with our tour. (Actually, my wife would prefer we see the Louvre instead, so let's forget about the beach.) Another area of enhancement in IIS 7.0 over previous versions is the detailed errors and automatic failure tracing that enables rapid troubleshooting and minimizes downtime. For example, you can view detailed errors in your Web browser, and there are plenty of new error codes that provide prescriptive guidance in various situations.

IIS log files also record more status codes that can help you troubleshoot various problems. For example, when a client's request is denied with a 404 error, the list of sub-status codes shown in Table 11-2 is now supported. (The first three items were supported previously; all the rest are new.)

Table 11-2   Supported 404 Error Sub-Codes

Description	Sub-code
SITE_NOT_FOUND	1
DENIED_BY_POLICY	2
DENIED_BY_MIMEMAP	3
NO_HANDLER	4
URL_SEQUENCE_DENIED	5
VERB_DENIED	6
FILE_EXTENSION_DENIED	7
HIDDEN_NAMESPACE	8
FILE_ATTRIBUTE_HIDDEN	9
REQUEST_HEADER_TOO_LONG	10
URL_DOUBLE_ESCAPED	11
URL_HAS_HIGH_BIT_CHARS	12
CONTENT_LENGTH_TOO_LARGE	13
URL_TOO_LONG	14
QUERY_STRING_TOO_LONG	15

New APIs also expose all runtime diagnostic information in real time, so by programmatically querying IIS, you can see all currently executing requests and other useful information.

Another diagnostic feature is the ability to define failure triggers by error code or time taken, which is configurable per application or per URL. The resulting Failed Request Tracing log contains a chronicle of events for the failed request, and this can quickly help you identify bottlenecks on your server. We'll soon hear from one of our experts concerning Failed Request Tracing. First, let's learn about the details behind failure request tracing trigger conditions:

From the Experts: The Details Behind Failure Request Tracing Trigger Conditions

Failure Request Tracing for IIS 7.0 can trigger failures on three key conditions: Status/Substatus codes, Time Taken, and Event Verbosity. One thing to remember is that the trigger overall is an OR of all the failure conditions defined. If you define all three—say, statusCodes="400-599", timeTaken="00:00:10", and verbosity="Error"—the worker process flushes the trace log for the "failed" request upon reaching the first of those conditions. If your request eventually errors out with an http status code of 500, but it takes 30sec to do that, you'll actually trigger on the *timeTaken* value. The attribute *<failedRequest failureReason="<reason>">* will tell you exactly what failure condition triggered the flush.

The events that make it into the trace log are those that are raised up to the point of the failure. What this means is that only Status/SubStatus code failure conditions (failureReason="STATUS_CODE") capture the entire request from start to end. For *timeTaken* triggers, you see all the events received up to the time limit. In the preceding example, a 10sec failure condition results in IIS capturing the events up to that 10-second limit, and no more. The same thing goes for verbosity triggers: when we receive the first event whose verbosity is equal to or more severe than the current trigger condition, we'll flush all events received up to that point (including the trigger event). So let's say your trigger condition wants to flush for foobar.aspx if verbosity="WARNING". Because verbosity levels are inclusive of the previous error levels, IIS will flush the log for foobar.aspx when it receives the FIRST trace event for a request to that URL whose verbosity level is WARNING, ERROR, or CRITICAL ERROR. If the failure condition verbosity level is ERROR, IIS will flush upon receiving the first ERROR or CRITICAL ERROR trace event.

The goal here is to give you a flexible means of defining failure conditions and flush when a certain condition is reached. Status Code and Time Taken are the most often used currently, but Verbosity is also helpful when you want to capture application failures that result in customized 200 OKs to the client that say, "Sorry, cannot connect to product database." Slap an ERROR trace event in your code, and configure the verbosity failure condition to capture these logs to help diagnose these failures!

—Eric Deily
Senior Program Manager Lead—IIS 7.0, Developer Division

Next, what about your Failed Request Tracing log files? Where are they? Sometimes when you enable Failed Request Tracing, the log files don't appear. Let's learn why:

From the Experts: Where Are My Failed Request Tracing Log Files?

So you've configured Failed Request Tracing, but you cannot find your log files. Now I've got to troubleshoot my troubleshooting feature, eh? Let's start with the basics:

1. Make sure that you've enabled Failed Request Tracing at the site level. Remember that although you can still define failure conditions and what to trace in your web.config files, you still need to have the IIS administrator enable Failed Request Tracing for your site. In the IIS Manager UI, click on the Web site in question, and under Actions select Configure. Then select Failed Request Tracing. This will bring up a dialog that allows you to select Enable Failed Request Tracing, as well as to set the directory to log to and the maximum number of files.

2. Make sure the worker process identity has FULL CONTROL access to the directory in question. You need to do this because the worker process writes out the log files under its own identity, creates the W3SVC# (where # is your site ID) directory, and finally deletes old files.

3. Check the Windows Logs | Application NT Event log for events from the Microsoft-Windows-IIS-W3SVC-WP source. The most typical errors will be permissions errors (as indicated above). Other possible errors include the following:

   ❑ Bad Configuration—This event indicates which configuration is incorrect. This configuration needs to be fixed before that failure condition will be triggered.

   ❑ FileSystem is full—We're writing log files, and XML files at that. Make sure there's space on the volume for writing the log. Though if you hit this error and it's on the system drive, this is probably not the biggest of your worries.

This should help you figure out why you're not getting failure request log files.

−Eric Deily
Senior Program Manager Lead–IIS 7.0, Developer Division

Finally, let's dig a bit deeper into the different conditions that Failed Request Tracing can catch and those it can't catch:

From the Experts: What Conditions Will Failed Request Tracing Not Catch?

Failed Request Tracing is a powerful feature that will really help diagnose problems with Web applications. Unfortunately, there are a few conditions that Failure Request Tracing cannot help with. Those conditions include the following:

■ **Worker process crashes** One thing to remember about Failed Request Tracing is that it buffers the trace events for the requests it's configured to track in process memory. So if that process suffers a failure that causes the process to terminate unexpectedly, the events buffered in that process will be lost.

■ **Failures that happen before any request processing begins** Failure Request Tracing reads the configuration and starts accepting trace events for requests on the Begin Request notification. However, a bit of work happens after the request arrives in the worker process but before this notification occurs. The things that happen to a request that could cause it to fail before Begin Request include the following events:

❑ W3WP fails to load the configuration for the request

❑ URL rewriting failures

If these failures happen, you will *not* get a failed request trace log. The best alternative for you here is to use ETW tracing or check the event log (the Application log again).

–Eric Deily
  Senior Program Manager Lead–IIS 7.0, Developer Division

Extensibility

Your feet are probably tired by now, aren't they? That's what happens when you go on vacation and don't take a good pair of shoes. You should know better than to try and walk 10 miles a day in flip-flops. Well, we're almost there—only a couple more sites to see.

Let's briefly (there's the Mona Lisa!) talk about the extensibility of the IIS 7.0 platform. The core Web server in IIS 7.0 is built on public extensibility APIs, and as we've seen, it has a building-block architecture that allows you to add or remove features, including custom features you've developed. The IIS 7.0 team is excited about the possibilities here. They hope that an entire community of developers will mobilize to build custom modules that will extend the power of IIS 7.0–both as a Web server platform and as a more general application server platform–by adding new authentication/authorization schemes, better directory browsing, new logging capabilities, and just about anything you could conceive of doing with IIS 7.0. Plus you can develop your own modules using either native or managed code. The potential is almost limitless.

We just have time to hear from one more of our experts before we catch the bus to the airport.

From the Experts: Take Your ASP.NET Applications to the Next Level with IIS 7.0

IIS 7.0 takes ASP.NET to the next level by integrating the ASP.NET runtime extensibility model with the core server. This integration allows developers to fully extend the IIS server with the richness of ASP.NET 2.0 and the .NET Framework, instead of using the lower-level IIS C++ APIs. Existing ASP.NET applications also immediately benefit from tighter integration because they can now use existing ASP.NET features such as Forms Authentication, Roles, and Output Caching for all types of content.

Here are some great reasons to take advantage of ASP.NET integration with IIS 7.0:

- **ASP.NET services can be used for all content types**   In the past, ASP.NET functionality—such as Forms Authentication, Roles, URL Authorization, and Output Caching—were available only to ASP.NET content types (.aspx pages, for example). Static files, ASP pages, and other content types could not benefit from these services.

  In IIS 7.0, however, all ASP.NET services can be uniformly provided to all content. For example, you can protect all your Web content, including images and ASP pages, with your existing ASP.NET 2.0 access control solution that uses ASP.NET Forms Authentication, Membership, and Login controls.

- **Fully extend IIS with ASP.NET**   Previous versions of IIS frequently required server extensibility to be developed using the native ISAPI filter or extension extensibility mode because of the runtime limitations of ASP.NET.

  IIS 7.0 allows ASP.NET modules to plug directly into the server pipeline, with the same runtime fidelity as modules developed with the native (C++) server API. ASP.NET modules can execute in all runtime stages of the request-processing pipeline and can be executed in any order with respect to native modules. The ASP.NET API has also been expanded to allow more control over request processing than was previously possible.

- **Unified server runtime**   Tighter ASP.NET integration also allows many of the features between IIS and ASP.NET to be unified.

  IIS 7.0 features unified configuration for IIS and ASP.NET modules and handlers. Many other features, including custom errors and tracing, have been unified to allow better management and cohesive application design.

–Claudia Lake
IIS Technical Writer

What's New in IIS 7.0 in Windows Server 2008

Well, we're in the plane now, and being way up in the sky enables us to see over the horizon. What's on the horizon for IIS 7.0 in Windows Server 2008? Most of what we've discussed so far is already available in IIS 7.0 on Windows Vista (though you probably don't want to run your corporate intranet off a Web server running Windows Vista). Here's a quick overview of what is being enhanced in IIS 7.0 in Windows Server 2008.

Enhanced Application Pool Isolation

We demonstrated earlier that when you create a new site in IIS 7.0 and specify a name for that site, by default the site is assigned its own unique application pool having the same name as the site. A unique application pool SID and AppPool.config file are created as well, to ensure automatic identity isolation for each new application pool. That's actually a feature of IIS 7.0 in Windows Server 2008–in Windows Vista, when you create a new site, the site is assigned to the DefaultAppPool instead. This particular enhancement will be useful in shared-hosting scenarios because sites and applications will be completely isolated from each other for greater security and stability.

Centralized Web Farm Configuration

We also mentioned earlier about storing your configuration files on a central UNC share. Well, IIS 7.0 in Windows Server 2008 lets you share *all* your .config files this way, including the applicationHost.config file, whose location can be configured by editing the registry on your Web server. (In IIS 6.0 you could put your web.config files on a UNC share, but IIS 7.0 also lets you put your applicationHost.config on the share, and this is configured using a redirection.config file in the inetsrv\config directory.) That's a pretty cool enhancement, and it will be greatly appreciated for Web-farm scenarios, as it will make management of a Web farm a lot easier!

Delegated Remote Administration

Another feature of IIS 7.0 that will be available in Windows Server 2008 is the ability to enable remote management for both Administrators and Delegated Site Owners. Firewall-friendly remote management using HTTP/SSL and authenticating both Windows and non-Windows credentials are also new in Windows Server 2008, as is support for auto-deployment of new Administration features from server to client. What this means is that if you add new management capabilities to the UI (since it's extensible), those new capabilities will be downloaded to the remote administration tool. (Note that this tool is an out-of-band release to allow Windows XP users to manage their IIS 7.0 servers also.) This feature allows IIS 7.0 to be implemented in a self-service config scenario, where your machine admin might be remotely managing the server from inside your company firewall while a remote site admin manages a scoped-out configuration for a single site on the server from a location outside your firewall.

FastCGI Support for PHP and Other Languages

Another new feature of IIS 7.0 in Windows Server 2008 is built-in support for FastCGI applications. CGI was the first Web application paradigm and was popular in the '90s on UNIX platforms, but it suffered from a lot of overhead that made it impractical in many situations. In Windows Server 2008, however, FastCGI is optimized for high performance and reliability and can reuse CGI processes for servicing multiple requests. The result is that FastCGI is something like 25 times faster than regular CGI, making FastCGI a viable way of hosting Web applications on IIS. So this means you can now run PHP apps, Perl scripts, and Ruby applications on IIS—with a level of performance and stability that previously was available only for ISAPI applications. Clearly, this is another great driver for hosting companies to upgrade or migrate their Web servers to IIS 7.0.

Modern FTP Server with FTP/SSL

A much-requested feature has finally arrived (well, almost—see end of paragraph) in IIS 7.0 on Windows Server 2008—a secure FTP server that supports FTP over SSL. The new FTP server being developed for Windows Server 2008 will have a modern code base that supports UTF8 throughout and includes full IPv6 support, COM and .NET extensibility, and .NET membership integration with SQL Server and other repositories. This new FTP server makes IIS 7.0, with its XML configuration files, into a fully integrated Web publishing system—secure Web publishing at last! Well, in point of fact this particular feature doesn't ship in-box but instead will ship out-of-band at the same time Windows Server 2008 RTM's.

Advanced Schema Extensibility

Finally, IIS 7.0 in Windows Server 2008 will have a single XML schema for both config and dynamic data, and it will support the plugging in of new or merged configuration sections, dynamic properties, and methods.

A few other improvements are also coming, but we'll move forward to the last part of our trip, which is the airport in my home town of Winnipeg. Just don't visit Winnipeg in the middle of winter, unless you enjoy freezing your nose off.

The Application Server Role

We need to finish by talking briefly about the Application Server role, one of the many roles you can install on Windows Server 2008 using Server Manager.

So what is it?

You can think of the Application Server role as a kind of superset of IIS functionality. For example, say you're a customer who wants to serve Web content and you want an HTTP engine to do this. It doesn't matter whether you're a corporate customer, a hoster, or whatever—you just need an engine to pump out HTTP. Clearly IIS 7.0 can do that, but the Application Server role on Windows Server 2008 can do even more.

For instance, what if you want to host a Web service implemented using Windows Communication Foundation instead of a Web site or Web application? Web services (that is, WCF apps) are basically services that listen on HTTP, TCP, named pipes, or whatever for clients to make requests from them. For example, say you've got a WCF app that is listening for requests. A request comes in, and the app does some stuff in response—maybe it accesses a database, does some computations, generates some graphics, kicks off a workflow, or whatever. It just does something in response to the request. But it has no visible Web page that a user can see—it just listens like a service, hiding beneath the surface (the UI) of the system.

Or maybe your Web service isn't based on a request/response model at all. Maybe it just uses a scheduler to kick off a batch job at various times of the day, perhaps to perform some computations in a database or generate a report.

The point is, these apps are running on IIS 7.0, so you've got all the same management tasks to perform: configuring your application pools, delegating administration, monitoring worker process activity, and so on. In fact, you can (but don't need to) use the same tools—such as IIS Manager and AppCmd.exe—to manage your Web service as you would to manage a Web site or Web application.

So how do you turn your Windows Server 2008 machine into an Application Server? You install the Application Server role, which also requires you to install the .NET Framework 3.0 on your machine. The .NET Framework 3.0 is built on top of the earlier .NET Framework 2.0 and includes the following components:

- **Windows CardSpace**   Formerly code-named "InfoCard," this component provides the consistent user experience required by the identity metasystem. It's hardened against tampering and spoofing to protect the end user's digital identities and maintain end-user control.

- **Windows Communication Foundation**   Formerly code-named "Indigo," this component is a set of .NET technologies for building and running connected systems. It provides a communications infrastructure built around the Web services model.

- **Windows Presentation Foundation**   Formerly code-named "Avalon," this component provides a foundation for building Windows Server 2008 applications and experiences. It also lets you blend together the application UI, documents, and media content.

- **Windows Workflow Foundation**   Formerly named "WinFX," this is the programming model, engine, and tools for building workflow-enabled applications. It consists of a .NET namespace, an in-process workflow engine, and designers for Visual Studio 2005.

So all this gets installed when you add the Application Server role, and you also get a choice of which role services and subcomponents you want to install:

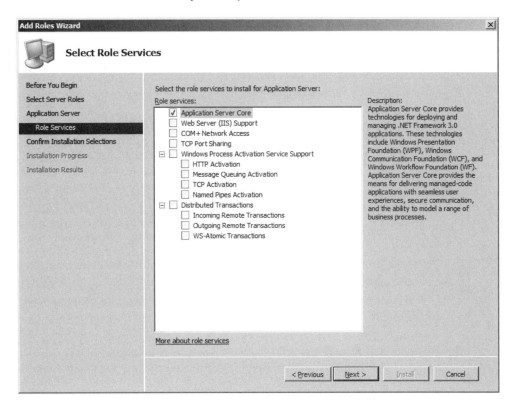

Unfortunately, we can't go any deeper into this role right now because our plane is landing and we have to extinguish all cigarettes (shhh!) and fasten our seatbelts again. But we'll close with our Captain speaking (one of our experts, actually), who will say a few words about managing Application Servers using PowerShell. Listen up, everybody—the Captain is speaking:

From the Experts: PowerShell as a Multitool for Administering Application Servers

Microsoft Windows PowerShell provides a command-line shell and scripting language that helps IT Professionals achieve greater productivity. With a new administrator-focused scripting language, more than 130 standard command-line tools, and consistent syntax and utilities, Windows PowerShell allows IT Professionals to more easily perform and automate system administration tasks. To gain some additional background on PowerShell, see the PowerShell page at *http://www.microsoft.com/windowsserver2003/technologies/management/powershell/default.mspx*.

Windows PowerShell 1.0 was introduced in November 2006 as a downloadable tool, suitable for use on Windows XP, Windows Vista, and Windows Server 2003. It also runs on Windows Server 2008.

For the administrator who is responsible for managing Windows Server 2008 servers in a distributed environment, PowerShell is a multitool: it can be applied in numerous ways to perform many different tasks. PowerShell will work with Windows Server 2008 servers in various workloads, but it particularly applies to Application Servers, which are typically managed in sets and need to have similar configurations, with semi-regular changes and updates.

For example, consider the task of verifying the Service Pack level or the network configuration of each machine under management. These are the kinds of things that might be mandated by an IT policy. An administrator needs an efficient and automatic way to query each machine and generate a quick and dirty report, periodically. This is an ideal job for a PowerShell script. Or consider the job of verifying the signatures on various application artifacts deployed to all members of a farm of servers.

Of course, a script running under the Windows Scripting Host can do these things, too. What makes PowerShell better for these tasks? PowerShell supports better handling of the query output, and includes sorting, filtering, reformatting (for example, to generate a .csv file suitable for import into an Excel spreadsheet), and pipelines for post-processing of the data. Combined with a visualization toolkit such as PowerGadgets (which is described in detail at *http://www.powergadgets.com*) or Microsoft Excel charting, PowerShell can be a real boon to administrators of application server farms.

–*Dino Chiesa*
  Director in the Application Platform Marketing organization at Microsoft

Conclusion

I'm sure you're as tired as my travel metaphor by now, as if you'd actually been traveling and seeing all those great sites we pretended to have seen on our journey. But I hope you're not tired with IIS 7.0–the journey from first release of the IIS platform to today's version has been almost as exciting to me as a real vacation overseas. (My wife will take the real trip any day over IIS.) It's time to move on to our next chapter, where we'll touch upon a whole bunch more new features and enhancements in Windows Server 2008.

Additional Resources

The hottest place to start looking for resources about IIS 7.0 is IIS.NET, the public-facing home of the IIS 7.0 team. Just go to *http://iis.net*, and you'll find the latest news about IIS 7.0; a TechCenter full of articles, blogs, videos, and other stuff; a forum where you can post your questions or help others; and lots more.

The Windows Server TechCenter on Microsoft TechNet also has an IIS 7.0 technical library, which can be found at *http://technet2.microsoft.com/WindowsServer/en/library/ 9d93db52-0855-4161-b1d3-8581a8385f1f1033.mspx?mfr=true*. This site has steadily growing content (though it's still based on a pre-release version of Windows Server 2008).

And, of course, be sure to turn to Chapter 14, "Additional Resources," for more sources of information concerning NAP, and also for links to webcasts, whitepapers, blogs, newsgroups, and other sources of information about all aspects of Windows Server 2008.

Chapter 12
Other Features and Enhancements

In this chapter:

Storage Improvements 378

Networking Improvements 402

Security Improvements. 407

Other Improvements. 414

Conclusion 419

Additional Resources. 419

In the last several chapters, we've highlighted some of the exciting new features and enhancements that are included in Microsoft Windows Server 2008. We've examined improvements to Active Directory and Terminal Services, the new Network Access Protection platform, the all new Microsoft Internet Information Services 7.0, improvements to Failover Clustering, the new Windows server core installation of Windows Server 2008, the Windows Server Virtualization architecture, and various new and improved management tools.

Obviously there's more. What about core networking improvements? New and enhanced security features? New storage features and enhancements? New tools for deployment? Volume activation and licensing changes? We haven't talked about these yet, so let's discuss them now. You can think of this chapter as a general grab bag of features we haven't talked about before now. Lumping them together in this chapter in no way is intended to suggest that these features are less important than features that were given an entire chapter of their own. It's just that this book was never intended as a comprehensive, systematic guide to all of Windows Server 2008—that would take at least 1500 pages to achieve. But I was told by Microsoft Press to keep the page count down to around 400 pages max, and I've written a lot about some topics either because I know a lot about them or the product team helped out a lot. That means I'll have to finish up my roundup of feature discussions with the whirlwind tour you'll be presented with in this chapter.

But this chapter won't be just a bunch of bullet points. In fact, most of this chapter has been written by various members of Windows Server 2008 feature teams. As a result, I'll keep out of their way most of the time and let them do the talking. Feature teams are justifiably very proud of what they accomplish, so I wanted to give them the maximum opportunity to describe their new features and how they work, how to implement them, and how to troubleshoot them.

Don't expect coverage in this chapter, however, of every remaining new feature or enhancement of Windows Server 2008. Remember, this book is based on Beta 3 (with some chapters focusing on near-Beta 3 because of the time constraints of getting this book done in time for TechEd) and that means some features are not fixed yet while others might not even be revealed until the Release Candidate stage of development. So if I miss discussing some feature you'd love to hear about, forgive me—with luck, the depth of information provided about other features will make up for any omissions.

Note that one topic I'll defer until later is deploying Windows Server 2008. We'll cover that topic briefly in Chapter 13, "Deploying Windows Server 2008," where it will fit in better with some practical advice on testing Windows Server 2008 for your environment. We'll also cover Volume Activation 2.0 in Chapter 13 because licensing and activation are closely related to the topic of deployment.

Storage Improvements

Let's begin by examining some of the storage improvements found in Windows Server 2008. We'll key in on and briefly describe the following features:

- File Server role
- Windows Server Backup
- Storage Explorer
- SMB 2.0
- Multipath I/O (MPIO)
- iSCSI Initiator
- Remote Boot
- iSNS Server

File Server Role

As we saw previously in Chapter 5, "Managing Server Roles," one of the roles you can add to a Windows Server 2008 server is the File Server role. And as we also saw in Chapter 5, when you add this particular role, there are also several optional role services you can install on your machine. Beta 3 of Windows Server 2008 includes a new tool for managing the File Server role—namely, the Share And Storage Management MMC snap-in. This new snap-in presents a unified overview of the File Server resources within a given system, including separate tabs for shared directories and storage volumes, and two new provisioning wizards that are designed to assist you in configuring shares and storage for the File Server role. The main console of the Share And Storage Management snap-in displays a tabbed overview of shares and volumes with key properties, and it exposes the following management actions:

- Volume actions: extend, format, delete, and configure properties

- Share actions: stop sharing and configure properties

Let's look at a few screen shots of this new snap-in. First, here's the Share And Storage Management node selected with the focus on the Shares tab, which shows all the shared folders managed by the server:

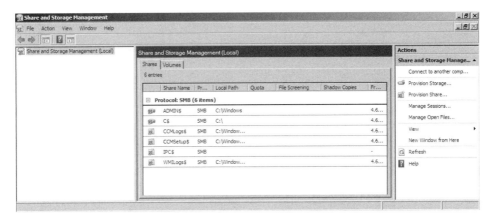

And here's the same snap-in with the focus on the Volumes tab:

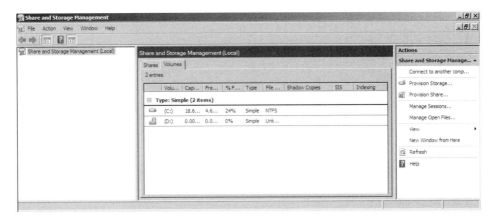

The Share And Storage Management snap-in also provides you with two easy-to-use wizards for managing your file server: the Provision A Shared Folder Wizard and the Provision Storage Wizard.

The Provision Storage Wizard provides an integrated storage provisioning experience for performing tasks such as creating a new LUN, specifying a LUN type, unmasking a LUN, and creating and formatting a volume. The wizard supports multiple protocols, including Fibre Channel, iSCSI, and SAS, and it requires a VDS 1.1 hardware provider. Here's a screen shot showing the Provision Storage Wizard and displaying on the left the various steps involved in running the wizard:

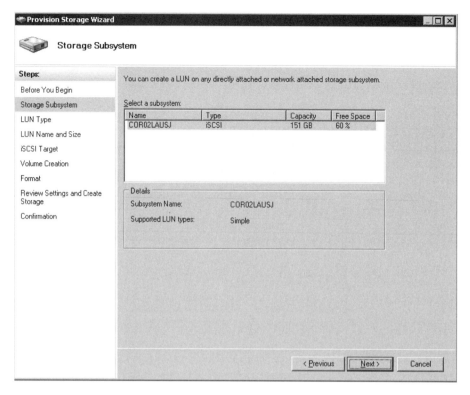

The Provision A Shared Folder Wizard provides an integrated file share provisioning experience that lets you easily select sharing protocols (SMB or NFS). Depending on your protocol selection, the wizard lets you configure either SMB or NFS settings. The following SMB settings can be configured:

- User limit
- Access-based enumeration
- Offline settings
- NTFS and share permissions

Or you can specify NFS settings such as these:

- Allow anonymous access
- Client groups and host permissions

In addition, the wizard lets you specify a quota or file screen template and add or publish your share to a DFS namespace. Here's a screen shot showing the Provision A Shared Folder Wizard and displaying on the left the various steps involved in running the wizard:

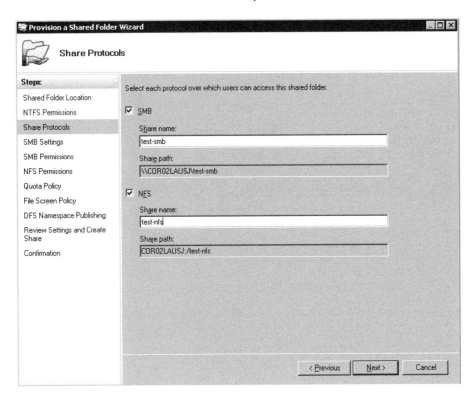

Windows Server Backup

Windows Server Backup is the replacement for the NTBackup.exe tool found on previous versions of Windows Server. It's implemented as an optional feature you can install using Server Manager, the Initial Configuration Tasks screen, or the ServerManagerCmd.exe command. Windows Server Backup uses the Volume Shadow Copy Service first included in Windows Server 2003. Because of this, Windows Server Backup takes a snapshot of any volume and backs the volume up without having to take the server down because of applications or services that are running. The result of this is that you no longer need to worry about scheduling backups during downtimes when the system is idle.

Windows Server Backup was basically designed to target the single-server backup needs for DIYs (do-it-yourselfers) because most small organizations don't bother to back up until a disaster strikes. Additionally, Microsoft studies revealed that the NTBackup.exe tool found in previous versions of Windows Server was generally too complex for this market segment to use effectively. Windows Server Backup is not targeted toward typical mid- and large-sized organizations, as they typically use third-party backup solutions from vendors.

In a nutshell, here's what Windows Server Backup is all about: Windows Server Backup is an in-box backup and recovery tool in Windows Server 2008 that protects files, folders, volumes, application data, and operating system components. It provides recovery granularity for everything from full servers to data pertaining to individual files or folders, applications, or system state information. It is not, however, intended as a feature-by-feature replacement for NTBackup.exe. The focus of the tool's design is simplicity, reliability, and performance so that the IT generalist can use it effectively. The tool has minimal configuration requirements and provides a wizard-driven backup/recovery experience. Figure 12-1 shows the new Windows Server Backup MMC snap-in, which can be used to perform either scheduled or ad hoc backups on your server.

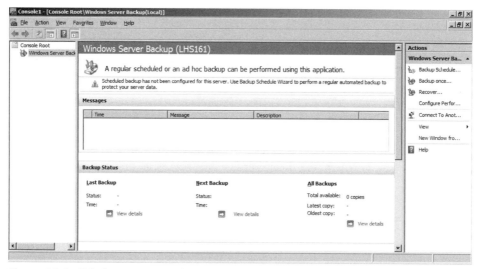

Figure 12-1   Windows Server Backup MMC snap-in

Windows Server Backup uses the same block-level image-based backup technology that is used by the CompletePC Backup And Recovery feature in Windows Vista. In other words, Windows Server Backup backs up volumes using the Microsoft Virtual Server .vhd image file format just like CompletePC does on Windows Vista. Using snapshots on the target disk optimizes space and allows for instant access to previous backups when needed, and block-level recovery can be used to restore a full volume and for *bare-metal restore (BMR)*. This improved bare-metal restore (which builds on the ASR of NTBackup.exe in Windows Server 2003) means also that no floppy disk is needed anymore to store disk configuration information. In addition, you can perform recovery from the Windows Recovery Environment (WinRE) using single-step restore, where only one reboot is required. You can also mount a snapshot of a .vhd file as a volume for performing file, folder, and application data recovery. Note that Windows Server Backup takes only one full snapshot of your volume—after that it's just differentials that are captured.

An important point is that Windows Server Backup is optimized for backing up to disk, not tape. You can also use it for backing up servers to network shares or DVD sets, but there is no tape support included. Why is that? Well, just consider some of the trends occurring in today's storage market that are beginning to drive new backup practices. For example, one strong trend is the movement toward disk-based archival storage solutions. The cost of disk storage capacity was originally around ten times the cost of tape, but with massive consumer adoption of small form-factor devices that include hard drives in them, the cost of disk storage capacity has dropped precipitously to about twice the cost of tape. As a result, many admins are now implementing "disk to disk to tape" backup solutions, which leverage the low latency of disk drives to provide fast recoveries when needed. And with Windows Server Backup on Windows Server 2008, an admin can quickly mount a local (SATA, USB, or FireWire) disk or a SAN (iSCSI or FC) disk and seamlessly schedule regular backup operations.

Finally, Windows Server Backup also includes a command-line utility, Wbadmin.exe, that can be used to perform backups and restores from the command line or using batch files or scripts. Here's a quick of example of how you can use this new tool. Say that you're the administrator of a mid-sized company with a dozen or so Windows Server 2008 servers that you need to have backed up regularly. Instead of purchasing a backup solution from a third-party ISV, you decide to use the Wbadmin.exe tool to build your own customized backup solution. You've installed the Windows Server Backup feature on all your servers, and they have backup disks attached. You want to ensure that the C and E drives on your servers are being backed up daily at 9:00 PM. Here's a command you can run to schedule such backups:

```
Wbadmin get disks
Wbadmin enable backup -addtarget:<disk identifier> -schedule:21:00 -include:c:,e:
```

Say that you then get a call from one of your users informing you that some important documents were accidentally deleted from d:\users\tallen\business and need to be recovered. You can try recovering these documents from the previous evening's backup by doing this:

```
Wbadmin get versions
Wbadmin start recovery -version:<version-id> -itemtype:file -items:
    d:\users\tallen\business -recursive
Wbadmin start recovery -version:<version-id> -itemtype:file -items:
    d:\users\tallen\business -recoverytarget: d:\AlternatePath\ -recursive
```

What if a server failed and you had to do a bare-metal recovery? To do this, just use the Windows Server 2008 media to boot in to the WinRE environment and choose the option to perform a recovery of your entire server from the backup hard disk onto the current hard disk. To do this, once you're in the WinRE environment, launch a command prompt and type this:

```
Wbadmin get versions -backuptarget:<drive-letter>
Wbadmin start BMR -version:<version-id> -backuptarget:<drive-letter> -
    restoreAllVolumes -recreateDisks
```

Finally, for those of you who are still not convinced that Windows Server Backup is better than the NTBackup.exe tool in the previous platform (and I know you're out there somewhere, griping about "No tape support"), Table 12-1 provides a comparison of features for the two tools. Guess which one has the most supported features?

Table 12-1   Comparison of Windows Server Backup with NTBackup.exe

Feature	NT Backup	Server Backup
User Data Protection	Yes	Yes
System State Protection	Yes	Yes
Disaster Recovery Protection	Yes	Yes
Application Data Protection	No	Yes
Disk Media (not VTL) Storage	Yes	Yes
DVD Media Storage	No	Yes
File Server Storage	Yes	Yes
Tape Media Storage	Yes	No
Remote Administration	No	Yes

Storage Explorer

Storage Manager for SANs (SMfS) was available in Windows Server 2003 R2 as a tool to help you create and manage logical unit numbers (LUNs) on Fibre Channel (FC) and iSCSI disk drive subsystems that support the Virtual Disk Service (VDS) in your storage area network (SAN). Windows Server 2008 builds on this by providing a new tool called Storage Explorer, an MMC snap-in that provides a tree-structured view of detailed information concerning the topology of your SAN.

Storage Explorer uses industry-standard APIs to gather information about storage devices in FC and iSCSI SANs. With Storage Explorer, the learning curve for Windows admins is much easier than traditional proprietary SAN management tools because it is implemented as an MMC snap-in and therefore looks and behaves like applications that Windows admins are already familiar with. The Storage Explorer GUI provides a tree-structured view of all the components within the SAN, including Fabrics, Platforms, Storage Devices, and LUNs. Storage Explorer Management also provides access to the TCP/IP management interfaces of individual devices from a single GUI. By combining Storage Explorer and SMfS, you get a full-featured SAN configuration management system that is built into the Windows Server 2008 operating system.

Let's now take a look at a few screen shots showing Storage Explorer at work. First, here's a shot of the overall tree-structured view showing the components of the SAN, that is Windows servers, FC Fabrics, and iSCSI Fabrics:

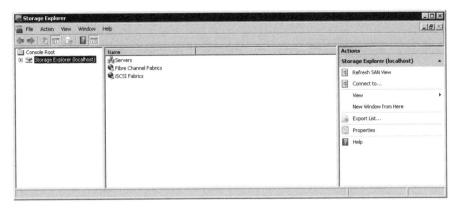

Let's drill down into each of these three subnodes. Here's a shot of the Servers node showing various servers (these shots were taken using internal test servers at Microsoft, so their names have been obfuscated):

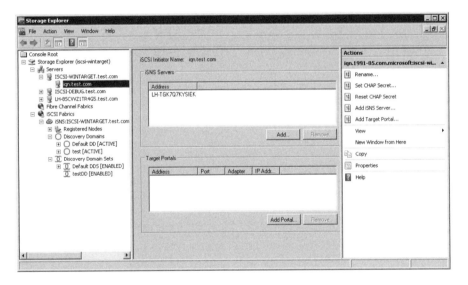

And here's a screen capture displaying details under the Fibre Channel Fabrics subnode:

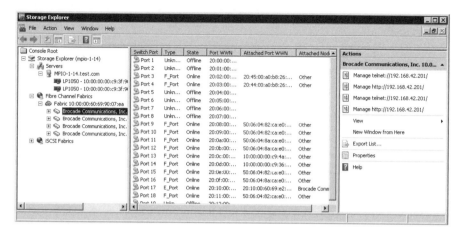

Finally, this one shows details under the iSCSI Fabrics subnode:

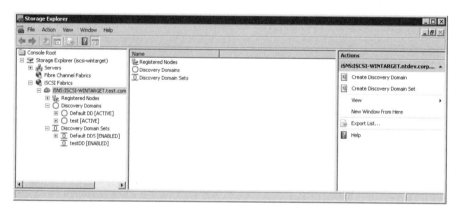

SMB 2.0

Another enhancement in Windows Server 2008 (and in Windows Vista) is version 2 of the Server Message Block (SMB) protocol. SMB is used by client computers to request file services from servers over a network. SMB is also used as a transport protocol for remote procedure calls (RPCs) because it supports the creation and use of named pipes. Unfortunately, SMB 1.0 on previous Windows platforms is considered overly "chatty" as a protocol—that is, it generates too much network traffic, especially for use over slow or congested WAN links. In addition, SMB 1.0 has some restrictive constants regarding the number of open files and the total number of shares it can support and it doesn't support durable handles or symbolic links. Finally, the signing algorithms used by SMB 1.0 are cumbersome to use.

As a result of these considerations, Microsoft introduced SMB 2.0 in Windows Vista and includes support for this protocol in Windows Server 2008. The benefits of the new protocol include less restrictive constants for file sharing, packet compounding to reduce chattiness, improved message signing, and support for durable handles and symbolic links.

Note that Windows Server 2008 and Windows Vista support both SMB 1.0 and SMB 2.0. The version of SMB that is used in a particular file-sharing scenario is determined during the SMB session negotiation between the client and the server, and it also depends on the operating system on the client and server as well—see Table 12-2 for details.

Table 12-2   SMB 1.0 and 2.0 Support for Various Windows Operating Systems

Client	Server	Version of SMB used
Windows Server 2008 or Windows Vista	Windows Server 2008 or Windows Vista	SMB 2.0
Windows Server 2008 or Windows Vista	Windows XP, Windows Server 2003, or Windows 2000	SMB 1.0
Windows XP, Windows Server 2003, or Windows 2000	Windows Server 2008 or Windows Vista	SMB 1.0
Windows XP, Windows Server 2003, or Windows 2000	Windows XP, Windows Server 2003, or Windows 2000	SMB 1.0

Multipath I/O

When you think of high-availability storage for your organization, you might think of using RAID to provide disk redundancy and fault tolerance. Although this is a good solution, it protects only your disks. Also, if there's only one path from your server to your storage device and any component in that path fails, your data will be unavailable—no matter how much disk redundancy you've implemented.

A different approach to providing high-availability storage is to use *multipathing*. A multipathing (or multipath I/O) solution is designed to provide failover using redundant physical path components, such as adapters, cables, or switches that reside on the path between your server and your storage device. If you implement a multipath I/O (MPIO) solution and then any component fails, applications running on your server will still be able to access data from your storage device. In addition to providing fault tolerance, MPIO solutions can also load-balance reads and writes among multiple paths between your server and your storage device to help eliminate bottlenecks that might occur.

MPIO is basically a set of multipathing drivers developed by Microsoft that enables software and hardware vendors to develop multipathing solutions that work effectively with solutions built using Windows Server 2008 and vendor-supplied storage hardware devices. Support for MPIO is integrated into Windows Server 2008 and can be installed by adding it as an optional feature using Server Manager. To learn more about MPIO support in Windows Server 2008, let's hear now from a couple of our experts at Microsoft:

From the Experts: Multipathing Support for High Availability

Windows Server 2008 includes many enhancements for the connectivity of Windows Server servers to SAN devices. One of these enhancements, which enables high availability for connecting Windows Server servers to SANs, is integrated Microsoft MPIO support. The Microsoft MPIO architecture supports iSCSI, Fibre Channel, and Serial Attached SCSI (SAS) SAN connectivity by establishing multiple sessions and connections to the storage array. Multipathing solutions use redundant physical path components—adapters, cables, and switches—to create logical paths between the server and the storage device. If one or more of these components fail and cause the path to fail, multipathing logic uses an alternate path for I/O so that applications can still access their data. Each NIC (in the case of iSCSI) or host bus adapter (HBA) should be connected through redundant switch infrastructures to provide continued access to storage in the event of a failure in a storage fabric component. Failover times will vary by storage vendor and can be configured through timers in the parameter settings for the Microsoft iSCSI Software Initiator driver, the Fibre Channel host bus adapter driver, or both.

New Microsoft MPIO features in Windows Server 2008 include a native Device Specific Module (DSM) designed to work with storage arrays that support the Asymmetric logical unit access (ALUA) controller model (as defined in SPC-3) as well as storage arrays that follow the Active/Active controller model. The Microsoft DSM provides the following load balancing policies (note that load balancing policies are generally dependent on the controller model—ALUA or true Active/Active—of the storage array attached to Windows):

- **Failover**   No load balancing is performed. The application will specify a primary path and a set of standby paths. Primary path is used for processing device requests. If the primary path fails, one of the standby paths will be used. Standby paths must be listed in decreasing order of preference (that is, most preferred path first).

- **Failback**   Failback is the ability to dedicate I/O to a designated preferred path whenever it is operational. If the preferred path fails, I/O will be directed to an alternate path until but will automatically switch back to the preferred path when it becomes operational again.

- **Round Robin**   The DSM will use all available paths for I/O in a balanced, round robin fashion.

- **Round Robin with a Subset of Paths**   The application will specify a set of paths to be use in Round Robin fashion, and a set of standby paths. The DSM will use paths from primary pool of paths for processing requests as long as at least one of the paths is available. The DSM will use a standby path only when all the primary paths fail. Standby paths must be listed in decreasing order of preference (that is, most preferred path first). If one or more of the primary paths become available,

DSM will start using the standby paths in their order of preference. For example, given 4 paths—A, B, C, and D, A, B, and C are listed as primary paths and D is standby path. The DSM will choose a path from A, B, and C in round robin fashion as long as at least one of them is available. If all three fail, the DSM will start using D, the standby path. If A, B, or C become available, DSM will stop using D and switch to the available paths among A, B, and C.

■ **Dynamic Least Queue Depth**   The DSM will route I/O to the path with the least number of outstanding requests.

■ **Weighted Path**   Application will assign weights to each path; the weight indicates the relative priority of a given path. The larger the number the lower the priority. The DSM will choose a path, among the available paths, with least weight.

The Microsoft DSM remembers Load Balance settings across reboots. When no policy has been set by a management application, the default policy that will be used by the DSM will be either Round Robin, when the storage controller follows the true Active-Active model, or simple Failover in the case of storage controllers that support the SPC-3 ALUA model. In the case of simple Failover, any one of the available paths could be used as primary path, and the remaining paths will be used as standby paths.

Microsoft MPIO was designed specifically to work with the Microsoft Windows operating system, and Microsoft MPIO solutions are tested and qualified by Microsoft for compatibility and reliability with Windows. Many customers require that Microsoft support their storage solutions, including multipathing. With a Microsoft MPIO-based solution, customers will be supported by Microsoft should they experience a problem. For non-Microsoft MPIO multipathing implementations, Microsoft support is limited to best-effort support only, and customers will be asked to contact their multi-path solution provider for assistance. Customers should contact their storage vendor to obtain multipathing solutions based on Microsoft MPIO.

Microsoft MPIO solutions are also available for Windows Server 2003 and Windows 2000 Server as a separately installed component.

Adding MPIO Support

To install MPIO support on a Windows Server 2008 server, do the following:

1. Add the Microsoft MPIO optional feature by selecting the Add Features option from Server Manager.

2. Select Multipath I/O.

3. Click Install.

4. Allow MS MPIO installation to complete and initialize.

5. Click Finish.

Configuration and DSM Installation

Additional connections through Microsoft MPIO can be configured through the GUI configuration tool or the command-line interface. MPIO configuration can be launched from the control panel (classic view) or from Administrative Tools.

Adding Third-Party Device-Specific Modules

Typically, storage arrays that are Active/Active and SPC3 compliant also work using the Microsoft MPIO Universal DSM. Some storage array vendors provide their own DSMs to use with the Microsoft MPIO architecture. These DSMs should be installed using the DSM Install tab in the MPIO properties Control Panel configuration utility:

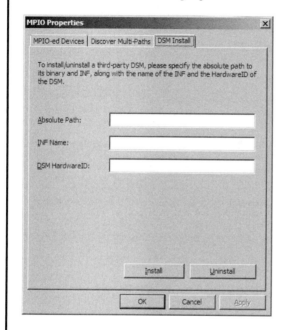

–Suzanne Morgan
   Senior Program Manager, Windows Core OS

–Emily Langworthy
   Support Engineer, Microsoft Support Team

iSCSI Initiator

iSCSI, which stands for *Internet Small Computer System Interface*, is an interconnect protocol based on open standards that is used for establishing and managing connections between TCP/IP-based storage devices, servers, and clients. iSCSI was designed as an alternative to Fibre Channel (FC) for deploying SANs, and it supports the block-based storage needs of database applications. Advantages of iSCSI over FC include lower cost and a more flexible topology, the ease of scaling up (more devices) and across (devices from different vendors), and virtual lack of inherent distance limitations on the protocol's operations.

Although the need for SANs in large enterprises continues to grow, organizations often find them difficult and expensive to implement or become locked into a single storage vendor's solution. By contrast, iSCSI SANs are easier to implement and can leverage your existing TCP/IP networking LAN/WAN infrastructure instead of requiring the building of a separate FC infrastructure. iSCSI SANs can also be implemented using lower-cost SATA disks instead of proprietary high-end storage devices. And by using iSCSI hardware that is certified by the Windows Logo Program, you can deploy Microsoft Exchange Server, SQL Server, and Windows SharePoint Services on iSCSI SANs.

iSCSI solutions are simple to implement. You just install the Microsoft iSCSI Initiator (which was an optional download for Windows Server 2003 but is now a built-in component in Windows Server 2008) on the host server, configure a target iSCSI storage device, plug everything into a Gigabit Ethernet switch, and bang—you've got high-speed block storage over IP. Provisioning, configuring, and backing up iSCSI devices is then done basically the same way you do these operations for any direct-attached storage devices.

Let's hear now from another of our experts concerning the inbox support for iSCSI SANs in Windows Server 2008:

From the Experts: Inbox iSCSI SAN Support

The Microsoft iSCSI Software Initiator is integrated into Windows Server 2008. Connections to iSCSI disks can be configured through the control panel or the command-line interface (iSCSICLI). The Microsoft iSCSI Software Initiator makes it possible for businesses to take advantage of existing network infrastructure to enable block-based storage over wide distances, without having to invest in additional hardware. iSCSI SANs are different from Network-Attached Storage (NAS). iSCSI SANs connect to storage arrays as a block interface while NAS appliances are connected through CIFS or NFS as a mapped network drive. Many applications, including Exchange Server 2007, require block-level connectivity to the external storage array. iSCSI provides lower-cost SAN connectivity and leverages the IP networking expertise of IT administrators. (See Figure 12-2.) These days, many customers are migrating their direct-attached storage (DAS) to SANs.

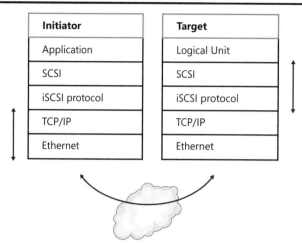

Figure 12-2   iSCSI protocols stack layers

Once the disks are configured and connected, they appear and behave just like local disks attached to the system. Microsoft applications supported on Windows with local disks that are also supported with iSCSI disks include Exchange, SQL Server, Microsoft Cluster Services (MSCS), and SharePoint Server. Most third-party applications for Windows are also supported when used with iSCSI disks.

Performance-related feature enhancements new to Windows Server 2008 in the iSCSI Software Initiator include implementation of Winsock Kernel interfaces within the iSCSI driver stack, as well as Intel Slicing by 8 Algorithm for iSCSI digest calculation.

Additional features that are also supported in previous Windows versions include the following:

- Support for IPV6 addressing
- IPSec support
- Microsoft MPIO support
- Multiple connections per session (MCS)
- Error Recovery Level 2

Advantages of iSCSI SAN connected storage include:

- Leverages existing Ethernet infrastructures
- Provides the interoperability and maturity of IP
- Has dynamic capacity expansion
- Provides for simpler SAN configuration and management
- Provides centralized management through consolidation of storage
- Offers scalable performance
- Results in greater storage utilization

iSCSI components offer higher interoperability than FC devices, including use in environments with heterogeneous storage. iSCSI and FC SANs can be connected using iSCSI bridge and switch devices. When using these components, it's important to test whether the Fibre Channel storage on the other side of the iSCSI bridge meets interoperability requirements. Because a Windows host connects to iSCSI bridges through iSCSI, adherence to iSCSI and SCSI protocol standards is assumed and FC arrays that do not pass the Logo tests (especially SCSI compliance) can cause connectivity problems. Ensure that each combination of an iSCSI bridge and Fibre Channel array has passed Logo testing and is specifically supported by the storage vendor.

Some considerations and best practices for using iSCSI storage area networks are detailed in the following sections.

Performance Considerations

Ensure that your storage array is optimized for the best performance for your workload. Customers should choose iSCSI arrays that include RAID functionality and cache. For Exchange configurations and other I/O throughput applications that are sensitive to latency, it's especially important to keep the Exchange disks in a separate pool on the array

One common misconception about iSCSI is that throughput or IOPS on the host is the limiting factor. The most common performance bottleneck for storage area networks is actually the disk subsystem. For best results, use storage subsystems with large numbers of disks (spindles) and high RPM drives to address high-performance application requirements. Maximize the number of spindles available on the iSCSI target to service incoming requests. On the host, the Microsoft iSCSI software initiator typically offers the same IOPS and throughput as iSCSI hardware HBAs, however, CPU utilization will be higher. An iSCSI HBA can be used to reduce CPU utilization or additional processors can be added to the system. Most customers implementing iSCSI solutions don't experience higher than 30 percent CPU utilization. To prevent bottlenecks on the bus, use PCI-Express based NICs vs. standard PCI. In addition, 10-GB NICs can be used for high transaction-based workloads including streaming backup over iSCSI SANs.

For applications that don't have low latency or high IOPS requirements, iSCSI storage area networks can be implemented over MAN or WANs links as well, allowing global distribution. iSCSI eliminates the conventional boundaries of storage networking, enabling businesses to access data worldwide and ensuring the most robust disaster protection possible.

Follow the storage array vendor's best practice guides for configuring the Microsoft iSCSI Initiator timeouts.

Here's some expert advice: Be sure to use a 512-KB block size when creating iSCSI targets through a storage array or manufacturer's setup utilities. Use of a block size other than 512 KB can cause compatibility problems with Windows applications.

Security Considerations

The iSCSI protocol was implemented with security in mind. In addition to segregating iSCSI SANs from LAN traffic, you can use the following security methods, which are available using the Microsoft iSCSI Software Initiator:

- One-way and mutual CHAP

- IPSec

- Access control

Access control to a specific LUN is configured on the iSCSI target prior to logon from the Windows host. This is also referred to as *LUN masking*.

The Microsoft iSCSI Software Initiator supports both one-way and mutual CHAP as well as IPSec.

Networking Best Practices

Following is a list of best practices for using iSCSI storage area devices:

- Use nonblocking switches, and disable unicast storm control on iSCSI ports. Most switches have unicast storm control disabled by default. If your switch has this setting enabled, you should disable it on the ports connected to iSCSI hosts and targets to avoid packet loss.

- Segregate SAN and LAN traffic. iSCSI SAN interfaces should be separated from other corporate network traffic (such as LAN traffic). Servers should use dedicated NICs for SAN traffic. Deploying iSCSI disks on a separate network helps to minimize network congestion and latency. Additionally, iSCSI volumes are more secure when you segregate SAN and LAN traffic using port-based VLANs or physically separate networks.

- Set the negotiated speed, and add more paths for high availability. Use either Microsoft MPIO or MCS (multiple connections per session) with additional NICs in the server to create additional connections to the iSCSI storage array through redundant Ethernet switch fabrics. For failover scenarios, NICs should be connected to different subnets. For load balancing, NICs can be connected to the same subnet or different subnets.

- Enable flow control on network switches and adapters.

- Unbind file and print sharing on the NICs that connect only to the iSCSI SAN.

- Use Gigabit Ethernet connections for high-speed access to storage. Congested or lower-speed networks can cause latency issues that disrupt access to iSCSI storage and applications running on iSCSI devices. In many cases, a properly designed IP-SAN can deliver better performance than internal disk drives. iSCSI is suitable for WAN and lower-speed implementations, including replication where latency and bandwidth are not a concern.

- Use server-class NICs that are designed for enterprise networking and storage applications.

- Use CAT6-rated cables for gigabit network infrastructures. For 10-gigabit implementations, Cat-6a or Cat-7 cabling is usually required for use with distances over 180 feet (55 meters).

- Use jumbo frames, as these can be used to allow more data to be transferred with each Ethernet transaction. This larger frame size reduces the overhead on both your servers and iSCSI targets. It's important that every network device in the path, including the NIC and Ethernet switches, support jumbo frames.

Common Networking Problems

Common causes of TCP/IP problems include duplicate IP addresses, improper subnet masks, and improper gateways. These can all be resolved through careful network setup. Some common problems and resolutions to them are detailed in the following list:

- **Adapter and switch settings**   By default, the adapter and switch speed is selected through auto-negotiation and might be slow (10 or 100 Mbps). You can resolve this by setting the negotiated speed.

- **Size of data transfers**   Adapter and switch performance can also be negatively affected if you are making large data transfers. You can correct this problem by enabling jumbo frames on both devices (assuming both support jumbo frames).

- **Network congestion**   If the network experiences heavy traffic that results in heavy congestion, you can improve conditions by enabling flow control on both the adapter and the switch.

Performance Issues

IOPS and throughput are typically the same for hardware and software initiators; however, using a software initiator can create higher utilization of the CPU. Most customers do not experience CPU utilization above 30 percent in servers using the Microsoft iSCSI Software Initiator with 1 Gigabit networks. Customers can set up initial configurations using the Microsoft iSCSI Software Initiator and measure CPU utilization. If CPU utilization is consistently high, a TCP/IP offload NIC that implements Receive Side Scaling (RSS) or Chimney Offload can be evaluated to determine the benefit of lowered CPU utilization on the server. Alternatively, additional CPUs can be added to the server. Some enterprise class NICs include RSS as part of the base product, so additional hardware and drivers to use RSS are not needed.

Here's some expert advice: Windows Server 2008 includes support for GPT disks, which can be used to create single volumes up to 256 terabytes in size. When you are using large drives, the time required to run chkdsk.exe against the drive should be considered. Many customers opt to use smaller LUNs to minimize chkdsk.exe times.

Improving Network and iSCSI Storage Performance

Network performance can be affected by a number of factors, but generally incorrect network configuration or limited bandwidth are primary causes.

Additional items to check include the following:

- Write-through versus write-back policy
- Degraded RAID sets or missing spares

Performance Monitor/System Monitor

A Performance Monitor log can give clues as to why the system is hanging. Look for the system being I/O bound to the disk as demonstrated by a high "disk queue length" entry. Keep in mind that the disk queue length for a given SAN volume is the total number divided by number of disk spindles per volume. A sustained reading over 2 for "disk queue length" indicates congestion.

Also, check the following counters:

- Processor \ DPCs queued/sec
- Processor \ Interrupts/sec
- System \ Processor queue length

There are no magic numbers that you look for, but there are deviations that you should look for. The counters just listed help check for hardware issues such as a CPU-bound condition, high interrupt count, and high DPC count, which could indicate stalling at the driver queue.

Deployment

Using Windows as an iSCSI host is also supported with Windows 2000, Windows Server 2003, and Windows XP as a separate download from *http://www.microsoft.com/downloads.*

iSCSI Configuration

iSCSI initiator configuration can be launched from the control panel (classic view) or from Administrative Tools. iSCSI is supported with all SKUs and versions of Windows Server 2008, including the Windows server core installation option. When using the Windows server core installation option, iSCSICLI must be used to configure connections to iSCSI targets:

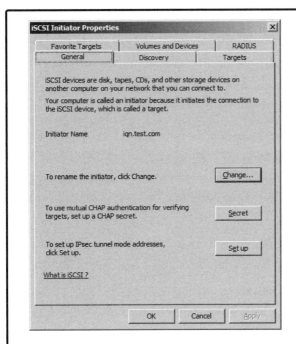

More information on iSCSI support in Windows is available at *http://
www.microsoft.com/WindowsServer2003/technologies/storage/iscsi/default.mspx.* More
information on the IETF iSCSI Standard is available from the IETF (*www.ietf.org*).

–Suzanne Morgan
 Senior Program Manager, Windows Core OS

–Emily Langworthy
 Support Engineer, Microsoft Support Team

iSCSI Remote Boot

Beginning with Windows Server 2003, you could also use iSCSI in "boot-from-SAN"
scenarios, which meant that you no longer had to have a directly attached boot disk to load
Windows. Being able to boot over an IP network from a remote disk on a SAN lets organizations centralize their boot process and consolidate equipment resources—for example, by
deploying racks of blade servers.

Booting from SAN

To boot from SAN over an IP network on Windows Server 2003, you needed to install an
iSCSI HBA that supported iSCSI boot on your server. This is because the HBA BIOS contains

the code instructions that make it possible for your server to find the boot disk on the SAN storage array. The actual boot process works something like this:

1. The iSCSI Boot Firmware (iBF) obtains network and iSCSI values from a DHCP Server configured with a DHCP reservation for the server, based on the server NIC's MAC address.

2. The iSCSI boot firmware then reads Master Boot Record (MBR) from the iSCSI target and transfers control. Then the boot process proceeds.

3. Windows start=0 drivers then load.

4. The Microsoft BIOS iSCSI parameter driver then imports configuration settings used for initialization (including the IP address).

5. An iSCSI login establishes the "C:\" drive.

6. The boot proceeds to its conclusion, and Windows then runs normally.

In addition to now having the iSCSI Software Initiator integrated directly into the operating system, Windows Server 2008 also includes new support for installation of the operating system directly to the iSCSI volume on the SAN. This means you can boot from your Windows Server 2008 media, and the iSCSI connected disk now automatically shows up in the list of connected disks that you can install the operating system onto. This provides the same kind of functionality as the iSCSI HBA that was needed in Windows Server 2003 while reducing your cost because you're able to use commodity NICs. In addition, Windows Server 2008 can be used in conjunction with System Center Configuration Manager 2007 to easily manage your boot volumes on the SAN.

Our experts will now give us more details on booting Windows Server 2008 from a SAN:

From the Experts: Booting Windows Server 2008 Remotely

Windows Server 2008 adds support to natively boot Windows remotely over a standard Ethernet interface. This enables Windows servers, including blade servers with no local hard drive, to boot from images consolidated in a data center or centralized storage location on an IP network.

Parameters needed to boot Windows are stored in low-level memory by the server option ROM, NIC option ROM, or PXE. They are used by the Windows Boot Manager to bootstrap Windows using standard Interrupt 13 calls and the iSCSI protocol. Customers who want to remotely boot their servers using iSCSI should look for servers or network interface cards that implement the iBFT (ISCSI BIOS Firmware Table) specification, which is required for iSCSI boot using the Microsoft iSCSI Software Initiator. The remote boot disk appears to Windows as a local drive. Boot parameters for the boot disk can be configured statically in the NIC or server option ROM or via a Dynamic Host Control Protocol (DHCP) reservation. Configuration through a DHCP reservation for the server based on a MAC address allows for the most flexibility to dynamically point the server to alternate boot images. Previously, booting a Windows server required an expensive and specialized HBA.

iSCSI provides lower-cost SAN connectivity and leverages the IP networking expertise of IT administrators. Many customers these days are migrating their DAS to storage area networks. Migrating boot volumes to a central location offers similar advantages for data volumes.

Examples of new hardware products that support iSCSI boot natively via the iBFT in firmware or option ROMs include the following:

- IBM HS20 Blade Server

- Intel Pro/1000 PF and PT network adapters

- Additional products to be announced this year

Examples of products that support iSCSI boot natively via PXE ROM implementation and can be used with existing hardware include the following:

- EmBoot Winboot/i

Installation Methods

For rapid deployment, Windows Server 2008 can be directly installed to a disk located on an iSCSI SAN. A bare-metal system with native iSCSI boot support can be installed using the following methods:

- Boot from Windows Server 2008 Setup Installation media (DVD)

- Boot from WinPE, and initiate installation from directory on a network-connected drive

- Windows Deployment Services (included in the box in Windows Server 2008)

- System Center Configuration Manager 2007

- Third-party deployment tools

Scripts and automated installation tools (including unattend.xml) typically used with locally attached drives can also be used with iSCSI-connected disks.

Once Windows Server 2008 is installed, the boot image can be set as a master boot image using Sysprep. Customers should use the LUN-cloning/image-cloning feature available in most iSCSI storage arrays to create additional copies of images quickly. Using LUN cloning allows the image to be available almost immediately and booted even before the copy is complete.

Windows Deployment Services (WDS) assists with the rapid adoption and deployment of Windows operating systems. Windows Deployment Services allows network-based installation of Windows Vista and Windows Server 2008 to deploy Windows Server 2008 to systems with no operating system installed.

Installation to an iSCSI Boot LUN

The following steps are used to install Windows Server 2008 directly to an iSCSI boot LUN:

1. Configure iSCSI target according to the manufacturer's directions. Only one instance of the boot LUN must be visible to the server during the installation. The installation might fail if multiple instances of the boot LUN are available to the server. It is recommended that the Spanning Tree Protocol be disabled on any ports that are connected to Windows Server 2008 hosts booting via iSCSI. The Spanning Tree Protocol is used to calculate the best path between switches where there are multiple switches and multiple paths through the network.

2. Configure iSCSI pre-boot according to the manufacturer's directions. This includes configuring the pre-boot parameters either statically or via DHCP. If iSCSI is configured properly, you get an indication during boot time that the iSCSI disk was successfully connected.

3. Boot the system from the Windows Server 2008 Setup DVD, or initiate installation from a network path containing the Windows Server 2008 installation files.

4. Enter your Product Key.

5. Accept the EULA.

6. Select Custom (Advanced).

7. Select the iSCSI Disk. You can distinguish the iSCSI boot disk from other disks connected to the system by checking the size of the disk, which will map to the size of the disk you created in step 1.

8. Windows will complete installation and automatically reboot.

The ability to boot a Windows Server using the Microsoft iSCSI Software Initiator is also available for Windows Server 2003 as a separate download. Windows Server 2008 provides this capability out of the box and provides more direct integration with Windows Server 2008 Setup.

Windows Server 2008 and previous versions of Windows continue to support booting from a remote drive on SAN using a more expensive/specialized HBAs, including iSCSI or Fibre Channel HBAs. The Microsoft iSCSI Architecture integrates the use of iSCSI HBAs (host bus adapters) within Windows. Only HBAs that integrate with the Microsoft iSCSI Initiator service to complete login and logout requests are supported by Microsoft. For a list of supported HBAs, see the Windows Server Catalog of Tested Products at *http://www.windowsservercatalog.com*.

–Suzanne Morgan
Senior Program Manager, Windows Core OS

–Emily Langworthy
Support Engineer, Microsoft Support Team

iSNS Server

Finally, the Internet Storage Naming Service (iSNS) is another optional feature in Windows Server 2008. This naming service assigns iSCSI initiators to iSCSI targets (storage systems). In Fibre Channel SANs, this functionality is in the FC switch. By providing this functionality as an optional component of Windows Server 2008, you can avoid the expense of a managed switch having name-server functionality. iSNS is usually deployed to help manage larger iSCSI SAN environments that include multiple initiators and multiple targets.

Let's hear once again from our experts concerning this feature to learn more about it:

From the Experts: iSNS Server

The Microsoft Internet Storage Name Service (iSNS) Server included in Windows Server 2008 adds support to the Windows operating system for managing and controlling iSNS clients. More information on the iSNS Standard is available from the IETF (*www.ietf.org*).

Microsoft iSNS Server is a Microsoft Windows service that processes iSNS registrations, deregistrations, and queries via TCP/IP from iSNS clients. It also maintains a database of these registrations. The Microsoft iSNS Server package consists of Windows service software, a control-panel configuration tool, a command-line interface tool, and WMI interfaces. Additionally, a cluster resource DLL enables a Microsoft Cluster Server to manage a Microsoft iSNS Server as a cluster resource.

A common use for Microsoft iSNS Server is to allow iSNS clients—such as the Microsoft iSCSI Initiator—to register themselves and to query for other registered iSNS clients. Registrations and queries are transacted remotely over TCP/IP. However, some management functions, such as discovery-domain management, are restricted to being transacted via WMI.

Microsoft iSNS Server facilitates automated discovery, management, and configuration of iSCSI and Fibre Channel devices (using iFCP gateways) on a TCP/IP network, and it stores SAN network information in database records that describe currently active nodes and their associated portals and entities. The following are some key details about how iSNS Server operates:

- Nodes can be initiators, targets, or management nodes. Management nodes can connect to iSNS only via WMI or the isnscli tool.

- Typically, initiators and targets register with the iSNS Server, and initiators query the iSNS Server for a list of available targets.

- A dynamic database stores initiator and target information. The database aids in providing iSCSI target discovery functionality for the iSCSI initiators on the network. The database is kept dynamic via the Registration Period and Entity Status Inquiry features of iSNS. Registration Period allows the server to automatically deregister stale entries. Entity Status Inquiry provides the server a pinglike functionality to determine whether registered clients are still present on the network, and it allows the server to automatically deregister clients that are no longer present.

- The State Change Notification Service allows registered clients to be made aware of changes to the database in the iSNS Server. It allows the clients to maintain a dynamic picture of the iSCSI devices available on the network.

- The Discovery Domain Service allows an administrator to assign iSCSI nodes and portals into one or more groups, called Discovery Domains. Discovery Domains provide a zoning functionality, where an iSCSI initiator can discover only iSCSI targets that share at least one Discovery Domain in common with it.

–Suzanne Morgan
Senior Program Manager, Windows Core OS

–Emily Langworthy
Support Engineer, Microsoft Support Team

Networking Improvements

One area in which networking has been improved in Windows Server 2008 is its implementation of DHCP. The following sidebar has been excerpted with permission from a couple of posts on the Microsoft Windows DHCP Team Blog found at *http://blogs. technet.com/teamdhcp/*. It provides an overview of DHCPv6 support in both Windows Server 2008 and Windows Vista:

From the Experts: DHCPv6 Support in Windows Vista and Windows Server 2008

Windows Vista introduces support for DHCPv6. The DHCPv6 client implementation in Windows Vista is compliant with RFC 3315. It supports two modes of operation: Stateless and Stateful.

- **DHCPv6 Stateless mode**   is the mode in which the host uses a non-DHCPv6 method to obtain an IPv6 address and uses DHCPv6 only to obtain other configuration parameters, such as the IPv6 address of the DNS server. Typically, in this mode, clients use the IPv6 prefix from a router advertisement to auto-configure an IPv6 address for the network interface.

- **DHCPv6 Stateful mode**   is the mode in which a client uses DHCPv6 to obtain an IPv6 address from the DHCPv6 server along with other configuration parameters.

The DHCPv6 client mode of operation in Windows Vista is controlled by router advertisements. When the TCP/IP stack in Windows Vista receives a Media Connect event on a network interface, it sends a router solicitation. The router advertisement received in response determines the behavior of the DHCPv6 client on that interface. If both the M and O flags in the router advertisement are set, the client assumes that it should use DHCPv6 Stateful mode. If the O flag is set but the M flag is not set, the DHCPv6 client uses the Stateless mode of operation.

DHCPv6 Stateless and Stateful Servers in Windows Server 2008

In Windows Server 2008, Microsoft has also introduced DHCPv6 functionality to the DHCP server. The Windows Server 2008 DHCP server includes support for both the DHCPv6 Stateless and the DHCPv6 Stateful Server functionality. In the DHCPv6 stateless mode, clients use DHCPv6 only to obtain network configuration parameters other than the IPv6 address. In this scenario, clients configure an IPv6 address through a non-DHCPv6-based mechanism (possibly through IPv6 address auto-configuration based on the IPv6 prefixes included in router advertisements, or through static configuration). In DHCPv6 Stateful mode, clients acquire both the IPv6 address and other network configuration parameters through DHCPv6.

In Windows Server 2008 Beta 3, Microsoft has now included the following DHCPv6 features:

- Administrators can create IPv6 address scopes by simply specifying an IPv6 subnet prefix. The Windows DHCPv6 Stateful server automatically generates an IPv6 address for allocation to the client.

- The addresses generated by the DHCPv6 server are sparsely distributed over the available address space for that subnet. By randomly distributing the address over the large address range made available by a 64-bit IPv6 prefix, the Windows DHCP server makes it much harder to guess IPv6 network addresses.

- Clients can acquire a nontemporary address and a temporary address through DHCPv6. A nontemporary IPv6 address can be used for Dynamic DNS registration so that the client is "known" by that address. A temporary IPv6 address, on the other hand, can be used for establishing outgoing connections in scenarios where the client needs privacy for its nontemporary address.

- Administrators can simplify the deployment by using the router advertisements to provide hints on whether to use DHCPv6 in Stateless or Stateful mode.

- The Windows DHCPv6 server provides support for server authorization in Active Directory. This helps reduce the possibility of a rogue server in managed domain environments.

- Microsoft recommends that administrators add reservations for clients with statically configured IPv6 addresses so that those addresses are not inadvertently allocated to clients. In addition, administrators can configure a certain range of addresses as exclusions to ensure that these addresses are not assigned to clients.

■ Administrators also have access to other DHCP server functionality, such as the capability for audit logging and use of the export/import commands to migrate DHCP server configuration and state information.

DHCPv6 Deployment Considerations

In the use of IPv6 address auto-configuration, the administrator has no control over the actual IPv6 addresses being used by the client. DHCPv6 Stateless deployment in conjunction with IPv6 address auto-configuration may hence be suitable for scenarios where there are no requirements to audit the use of addresses by clients, such as on public networks and in home scenarios. With DHCPv6 Stateful deployments, the administrator has control over the IPv6 address used by the client and can audit the IPv6 addresses being used by the clients on the network. A DHCPv6 Stateful deployment may hence be more appropriate in scenarios where such logging/auditing capability is needed, such as in Enterprise deployments.

–Santosh Chandwani
Windows Enterprise Networking

Another networking improvement in Windows Server 2008 (one that will also be included in Windows Vista Service Pack 1) is in the area of virtual private networking and remote access. I'll bet there have been times when you've been at a hotel somewhere and your PPTP-based or L2TP-based VPN connection couldn't go through, either because of a PPTP GRE port-blocking or an L2TP ESP port-blocking issue caused by some firewall or NAT router along the path between your client computer and the remote VPN server you were trying to connect to. And I'll bet you probably muttered something like, "Why can't IP-based VPN connections just work?" Well guess what–your wish has been granted!

Windows Server 2008 and Windows Vista SP1 will include a new type of VPN tunnel called Secure Socket Tunneling Protocol (SSTP), which enables VPN tunnel connectivity across any scenario. For example, if your client computer or the remote server is behind NAT routers, firewalls, or Web proxies, SSPT will make your VPN connection just work. Plus, it will work just the same as before–that is, it will have the same end-user remote-access experience (such as using a RAS dialer) and also the same network administration experience (such as using a RRAS server).

This an exciting new feature, so we're going have two sidebars on this topic. The first sidebar provides an overview of what SSTP is and what it can do:

From the Experts: What Is Secure Socket Tunneling Protocol?

A virtual private network (VPN) provides a way of connecting to your corporate network remotely over the Internet. Prior to SSTP, Windows 2003 Server included support for PPTP-based and L2TP/IPSec-based VPN tunnels. If the remote access user is behind a firewall, these VPN tunnels require specific ports to be opened inside the firewalls (such as TCP port 1723 and IP protocol type GRE for allowing PPTP connection). There are scenarios (like visiting a customer, partner site, or hotel) where only Web access (TCP port 80 and 443) is given and all other ports are blocked. As a result, remote users in these scenarios run into VPN connectivity issues, thereby increasing help desk calls and reducing productivity for the employees.

Secure Socket Tunneling Protocol (SSTP) is a new VPN tunnel introduced in Windows Server 2008 that solves these VPN connectivity problems. It does this by using HTTPS as the transport layer so that VPN connections can traverse commonly configured firewalls, NATs, and Web proxy servers. Because an HTTPS connection (that is, TCP port 443) is normally used for accessing protected Internet sites such as Internet commerce sites, it is normally opened on firewalls and can traverse Web proxies and NAT routers.

A computer running Windows Server 2008 and Routing and Remote Access is an SSTP-based VPN server listening for SSTP connections. The SSTP server must have a computer certificate with the Server Authentication Enhanced Key Usage (EKU) property installed. This computer certificate is used to authenticate the SSTP server to the SSTP client during the establishment of an SSL session. The SSTP client validates the computer certificate of the SSTP server. To trust the computer certificate, the root Certification Authority (CA) of the issuing CA of the SSTP server's computer certificate must be installed on the SSTP client.

From a protocol-layering perspective, an SSTP-based VPN tunnel acts as a peer-to-L2TP and PPTP-based VPN tunnel. This means PPP is encapsulated over SSTP, which then sends the traffic over HTTPS connections. As a result of this, all the other features of the VPN tunnel—such as the NAP-based health check, carrying IPv6 traffic on top of the VPN tunnel, different authentication algorithms such as username and smartcard, integrated VPN client, and connection manager–based VPN client—remain the same for SSTP, PPTP, and L2TP. This gives the administrator a good migration path for moving from L2TP/PPTP to SSTP.

–Samir Jain
  Lead Program Manager, Windows Enterprise Networking (RRAS)

–Kadirvel C. Vanniarajan
  Software Design Engineer, Windows Enterprise Networking (RRAS)

And now in our second sidebar, our experts from the product team are going to dig deeper and provide us with an explanation of how this new feature works:

From the Experts: How Does Secure Socket Tunneling Protocol Work?

SSTP works on top of HTTPS, which amounts to nothing but HTTP using Secure Socket Layer (SSL) for information confidentiality. SSL also provides the mechanism to authenticate the endpoints as required when using Public Key Infrastructure (PKI). SSTP uses the SSL for authenticating the server to the client, and it relies on PPP running on top of it for authenticating the client to the server. That is, the server gets authenticated by the client by means of certificates, and the client gets authenticated by the server through the existing suite of authentication protocols supported by PPP. The information confidentiality is provided by the SSL.

When a client connects to the Remote Access Server using SSTP as the tunneling protocol, SSTP establishes the HTTPS session to the remote server at port 443 at a specific URL. The HTTP proxy settings configured through Internet Explorer will be used for establishing this connectivity. As with any HTTPS sessions, this involves the client trusting the certificate provided by the server. For this to happen, the appropriate trusted root certificate should be present in the machine certificate store. Once the certificate validation completes, the SSL handshake is complete and the HTTP session is established on top of it. After this, the SSTP layer is used to negotiate parameters between the client and the server. Once the SSTP layer is also established, the PPP negotiation starts on top of this, which provides the mechanism to authenticate the client to the server and also to tunnel the data. From this point on, the steps involved are just like PPP over PPTP/L2TP. A tunnel interface gets created on the client, and packets routed through this tunnel interface travel over the SSTP tunnel to the network beyond the Remote Access Server.

Let's take a closer look at the steps involved by using the following scenario.

A client with IP address 192.168.0.100 is behind a Web proxy with IP address 192.168.0.10:8080. It is trying to establish an SSTP tunnel to a Remote Access Server (supporting SSTP) that has the public IP address 202.54.175.68. This server is published with the domain contoso.com, and the client has a trusted root certificate that trusts this domain in its machine certificate store. Let 172.23.0.0/24 be the subnet address that will be shared between the SSTP clients and the intranet.

Following are the steps that occur when setting up the tunnel:

1. The client connects to the Remote Access Server as https://contoso.com/sra_{BA195980-CD49-458b-9E23-C84EE0ADCD75}/.

2. This request is sent through the Web proxy. A CONNECT request is sent to the proxy server with the server name and URI noted in step 1. The proxy server establishes the TCP connection to port 443 of the server.

3. The SSL handshake happens on top of this. While this is happening, the server provides its certificate to the client and the client validates it against the trusted root certificates present in the machine certificate store.

4. The client sends the HTTP request to the server to establish the HTTPS session.

5. SSTP negotiates parameters on top of the HTTPS session.

6. PPP starts on top of SSTP, providing the client authentication and negotiation of other parameters such as the tunnel IP address and so on.

7. A virtual interface gets created on the client machine with the IP address from the pool 172.23.0.0/24. This address is allocated by the Remote Access Server as a part of the PPP's NCP phase.

8. Any data traffic destined to travel over the aforementioned virtual interface is tunneled to the Remote Access Server and reaches the intranet.

For SSTP also, the PPP and the stack above it remains the same as that of PPTP/L2TP-based VPN tunnels.

–Kadirvel C. Vanniarajan
Software Design Engineer, Windows Enterprise Networking (RRAS)

–Samir Jain
Lead Program Manager, Windows Enterprise Networking (RRAS)

For additional information on networking enhancements in Windows Vista and Windows Server 2008, see the page titled "New Networking Features in Windows Server "Longhorn" and Windows Vista" found on Microsoft TechNet at *http://www.microsoft.com/technet/ network/evaluate/new_network.mspx*. Note that this page has been updated since its original version was posted, so it should be an up-to-date source of information on networking improvements in these platforms.

Security Improvements

In addition to networking enhancements, Windows Server 2008 also includes a number of security improvements beyond those included in the Windows Vista platform. Again, I won't be able to describe all these in detail, so I'll just let our experts at Microsoft fill us in.

Let's start with BitLocker Drive Encryption, a data protection feature available in Windows Vista Enterprise and Windows Vista Ultimate for client computers and also available in Windows Server 2008. BitLocker provides enhanced protection against data theft and exposure for computers that are lost or stolen, and it provides more secure data deletion when BitLocker-protected computers are decommissioned. BitLocker helps mitigate such unauthorized data access on lost or stolen computers through two major data-protection features: by encrypting the entire Windows operating system volume on the hard disk (including the swap and hibernation files), and by checking the integrity of early boot components and boot configuration data on computers that support Trusted Platform Module (TPM) version 1.2.

The main difference between BitLocker on Windows Server 2008 and its implementation on Windows Vista is the inclusion of support for data volumes. Other changes include EFI support and a new multifactor authenticator. Let's now hear from one of our experts at Microsoft concerning each of these improvements:

From the Experts: BitLocker Enhancements in Windows Server 2008

BitLocker Drive Encryption (BDE) on Windows Server 2008 is an optional component that needs to be installed using Server Manager. BDE on Windows Server 2008 now supports the following:

- Data volumes: any number of volumes other than the OS or system volume

- A new authenticator: TPM+USB+PIN

- EFI support

Data Volumes

This new feature extends BitLocker encryption support to volumes other than bootable volumes in the Windows Vista client (Enterprise and Ultimate SKUs). These volumes are called *data volumes*. A data volume is any locally created internal volume exposed by Plug and Play in the context of a booted operating system that isn't the volume that was booted. Any nonactive volume exposed by Plug and Play that contains only data or a different instance of an OS other than the currently booted/running OS is considered a data volume. An encrypted volume the user wants to access that is not already unlocked by the BitLocker code that is executed in the boot manager is considered a data volume.

New Authenticator

This authenticator was added in response to numerous requests from partners to improve the level of security. An additional multifactor authentication method is offered that combines a key protected by the TPM with a Startup Key (SK) stored on a USB storage device and a user-generated personal identification number (PIN). This allows customers to implement a simpler security policy and the development team believes that this will lead to a higher rate of adoption of BitLocker in governmental organizations.

EFI

Today most computers rely on the PC/AT (or INT 19 style) BIOS architecture. However, a replacement technology is under way: the Extensible Firmware Interface (EFI). The Trusted Computing Group (TCG, the industry-standard group defining the TPM and related technologies) and Intel are working to provide firmware feature parity with PC/AT trusted platform BIOSs. This new feature provides associated feature support in the Windows Vista loader to use this functionality and provide feature parity (including PPI) with BIOS-based machines.

–Tony Ureche
* Program Manager, Windows Security, Core Operating Systems Division*

Crypto Next Generation (CNG), which was first introduced in Windows Vista, has also been enhanced in Windows Server 2008. The CNG API is the long-term replacement for the CryptoAPI of previous Windows platforms and is designed to be extensible at many levels and cryptography-agnostic in its behavior. Let's hear from another of our experts concerning the improvements to CNG in Windows Server 2008:

From the Experts: Enhancements to Crypto Next Generation in Windows Server 2008

Within Microsoft, specific support for the SSL protocol was first added to Internet Explorer 2.0 in 1995. Along with this, development began on a general-purpose application programming interface (API) for symmetric and public-key cryptography. This API, called *CryptoAPI* or *CAPI1*, provided a common interface abstraction, in user mode, for cryptographic algorithms (sometimes called the "pluggable" provider model) for Microsoft and third-party applications.

CNG is Microsoft's new core cryptographic API, first shipping in Windows Vista. CNG is positioned to replace existing uses of CryptoAPI throughout the Microsoft software stack. Third-party developers will find lots of new features in CNG, including the following ones:

- A new crypto configuration system, supporting better crypto agility
- Finer-grained abstraction for key storage (and separation of storage from algorithm operations)
- Process isolation for operations with long-term keys
- Pluggable random number generators
- Relief from export-signing restrictions
- Thread safety throughout the stack
- Kernel-mode cryptographic API

In addition, CNG includes support for all required Suite-B algorithms, including ECC. The existing CAPI (CryptoAPI) programs will continue to work as CNG becomes available. CNG Microsoft-provider and legacy CAPI1 CSPs are in the FIPS 140-2 process at target level 1.

–Tolga Acar
* Senior Program Manager, Cryptography, Windows Core Security*

Another new Windows Vista feature that will see extended use in Windows Server 2008 deployments is called *Owner Access Restriction*. This is a new feature in the ACL model that helps in diverse scenarios, including compliance, service hardening, and Active Directory management. Let's hear from another of our experts describing what this is all about:

From the Experts: Owner Access Restriction

In Windows Vista and Windows Server 2008, the ACL model provides a new mechanism that gives administrators more control over the rights of a resource's owner. Administrators can use a new feature in the ACL model called Owner Access Restriction (OAR) for this purpose. Using a new well-known SID, OwnerRights (S-1-3-4), the DACL can now contain ACEs that limit the rights of the owner. There are several scenarios where OAR might be useful, and they span service hardening, file management, and system file protection. Here is a walkthrough of a typical scenario—the group removal scenario:

1. A user, as a member of a group, has the right to create a resource within a container (for example, a file within a folder).

2. He creates such a resource within the container.

3. The application does not want him to be able to write to or delete the resource after he is removed from the group.

4. But he can perform these functions because he is the owner of the resource, regardless of the ACL on the resource

Or in other words:

ALLOW OWNER_RIGHTS READ_CONTROL CONTAINER_INHERIT, OBJECT_INHERIT

In step 2, the inheritable ACE propagates to the newly created container. Consequently, step 4 is no longer possible—the owner cannot write the resource.

This is an important scenario for Active Directory, where the user is the owner of the *Computer* object when he joins a machine to a domain. With OAR, Active Directory can ensure that the owner of the *Computer* object has a necessarily limited set of rights.

—Satyajit Nath
Program Manager, Windows Core Operating System Security

Windows Auditing is another area in which there have been significant improvements in Windows Server 2008. When auditing is enabled on a Windows computer, Success or Failure events can be logged in the Security log to provide a trail for forensic analysis and archival purposes. Implementing an audit policy is an important facet of overall security, as monitoring the creation or modification of objects gives you a way to track potential security problems. It also helps to ensure user accountability and provides evidence in the event of a security breach. Let's hear about the auditing improvements in Windows Server 2008 from another of our experts at Microsoft:

From the Experts: Auditing Improvements in Windows Server 2008

In Windows Server 2008, the auditing feature has been improved to provide an audit trail that is both more comprehensive and easier to interpret. The event records in the security event log have been reformatted to make them easier to understand and to include more relevant information. Also, many new events have been added.

Some highlights of the enhancements are listed here:

- New events have been added for Directory Service changes, indicating old and new values of changed attributes.

- Registry changes now include old and new values.

- There are events for changes to security descriptors (permissions) on objects.

- There are new events for IPSec.

- There are events for access to shares and RPC interfaces.

Audit policy has been dramatically improved as well, and it now includes the ability to turn sets of events on and off at a very granular level. To use this feature, you have to use the command-line tool auditpol.exe.

Here are a few examples:

```
auditpol.exe -list -subcategory:*
auditpol.exe -set -subcategory:"Account Lockout" -success:enable
```

To use the new granular audit policy feature with Group Policy, you must use it in a script. Microsoft Knowledge Base article 921469 discusses how to accomplish this; the article can be found at *http://support.microsoft.com/kb/921469*.

There are also many new Security events in Windows Server 2008–in fact, 340 such events in total. Here is the prototype for the new event when you move an AD object to a new place in the directory:

```
A directory service object was moved.
    Subject User SID: <security ID of the user that moved the object>
    Subject User Name: <sAMAccountName of the user that moved the object>
    Subject Domain: <domain name of the user that moved the object>
    Subject Logon ID: <logon ID of the user that moved the object>
    Directory Service Name: <Active Directory domain name>
    Directory Service Type: <type of AD installation>
    Old Object DN: <original distinguished name of the object before the move>
    New Object DN: <new DN of the object after the move>
    Object Type: <schema class name of the object>
```

Here is a sample registry value change audit:

```
Log Name:       Security
Source:         Microsoft-Windows-Security-Auditing
Date:           3/23/2007 5:49:06 PM
Event ID:       4657
Task Category: Registry
Level:          Information
Keywords:       Audit Success
User:           N/A
Computer:       erics-workstation.microsoft.com
Description:
A registry value was modified.

Subject:
            Security ID: MICROSOFT\ericf
            Account Name: ericf
            Account Domain: MICROSOFT
            Logon ID: 0x2e454cd

Object:
            Object Name:
    \REGISTRY\MACHINE\SOFTWARE\Microsoft\Windows\CurrentVersion\Run
            Object Value Name:  Malware
            Handle ID: 0x124
            Operation Type: Existing registry value modified

Process Information:
            Process ID: 0x550
            Process Name: C:\Windows\regedit.exe

Change Information:
            Old Value Type: REG_SZ
            Old Value:
            New Value Type: REG_SZ
            New Value: virus.exe
```

In this case, *Old Value* is blank because there wasn't originally a value–I created it.

Events are also available to applications as XML. Here is the text of the second event written as XML:

```
<Event xmlns="http://schemas.microsoft.com/win/2004/08/events/event">
  <System>
    <Provider Name="Microsoft-Windows-Security-Auditing" Guid="{54849625-5478-
4994-a5ba-3e3b0328c30d}" />
    <EventID>4657</EventID>
    <Version>0</Version>
    <Level>0</Level>
    <Task>12801</Task>
    <Opcode>0</Opcode>
    <Keywords>0x8020000000000000</Keywords>
    <TimeCreated SystemTime="2007-03-24T00:49:06.763Z" />
    <EventRecordID>945778</EventRecordID>
    <Correlation />
    <Execution ProcessID="4" ThreadID="52" />
    <Channel>Security</Channel>
    <Computer> erics-workstation.microsoft.com</Computer>
    <Security />
  </System>
  <EventData>
    <Data Name="SubjectUserSid">S-1-5-21-390000000-620000000-180000000-290000</
Data>
    <Data Name="SubjectUserName">ericf</Data>
    <Data Name="SubjectDomainName">NTDEV</Data>
    <Data Name="SubjectLogonId">0x2e454cd</Data>
    <Data
Name="ObjectName">\REGISTRY\MACHINE\SOFTWARE\Microsoft\Windows\CurrentVersion\Run
</Data>
    <Data Name="ObjectValueName">Malware</Data>
    <Data Name="HandleId">0x124</Data>
    <Data Name="OperationType">%%1905</Data>
    <Data Name="OldValueType">%%1873</Data>
    <Data Name="OldValue">
    </Data>
    <Data Name="NewValueType">%%1873</Data>
    <Data Name="NewValue">virus.exe</Data>
    <Data Name="ProcessId">0x550</Data>
    <Data Name="ProcessName">C:\Windows\regedit.exe</Data>
  </EventData>
</Event>
```

–Eric Fitzgerald
Senior Program Manager, Windows Core Operating System Security

For additional information concerning security enhancements in Windows Vista and Windows Server 2008, see the "Security and Protection" section in the Windows Vista TechCenter Library found on Microsoft TechNet at *http://technet.microsoft.com/en-us/windowsvista/aa905062.aspx.*

Other Improvements

Finally, here are a couple more improvements you might be interested in hearing about. The first concerns some enhancements that have been made to the Fax Server role in Windows Server 2008. A lot of what is shipping in Windows Server 2008 for this role is based on Windows Server 2003. However, Windows Server 2008 has some major new features for this role, including a new accounts infrastructure and a new feature called *Reassign*, which allows a company to route faxes to individual recipients. Let's now hear from one of our experts on the product team, first concerning the new Reassign function:

From the Experts: Public and Private Mode in Windows Fax Server

Fax Server in Windows Server 2008 supports two different operating modes, which are governed by the Reassign Setting for the fax server. These two modes, described in the following list, apply only to incoming fax messages:

- **Public Mode**   In this mode, all fax messages are received in a central Server Inbox, and these are visible and available to all users of the fax server.

- **Private Mode**   In this mode, all fax messages are received in a central Server Inbox, but this is hidden from individual users, and they cannot access these fax messages until they are assigned to the mailboxes of the individual users.

Configuring the fax server in public mode is recommended for small businesses that do not have a dedicated fax administrator or routing assistants and are comfortable with having the incoming faxes available to all users of the fax server. For example, a travel agency might configure its fax server in public mode so that all the travel agents are able to view incoming faxes and work with them. This mode does not require a large administration overhead, and it's easy to configure and use. In this mode, when an authenticated user launches her Windows Fax and Scan application, she will have access to all the received faxes on the server.

Configuring the fax server in private mode is recommended for businesses that might have either a dedicated fax administrator or an IT generalist who manages the fax server along with other server roles such as file and print. This mode is recommended for the usage scenario where individual faxes need to be kept private and made available only to the intended recipient. This setting requires that the business employ routing assistants who have access to the protected server inbox, go through the received faxes manually, and assign them to the intended recipient. In this mode, when an authenticated user launches her Windows Fax and Scan application, the faxes that are assigned to her account show up in her Inbox.

The default setting in Windows Server 2008 is public mode. To configure this setting, the fax administrator does the following:

1.   Launch the fax service manager.

2.   Right-click on the root node.

3.   Launch the Properties dialog.

4.   Navigate to the Accounts tab.

5.   Choose whether the Reassign Setting is On or Off.

When using private mode, the administrator has to designate certain users as routing assistants. These users have access to the server inbox and do the actual reassign operation. To designate a particular user as a routing assistant, the fax administrator does the following:

1.   Launch the fax service manager.

2.   Right-click on the root node.

3.   Launch the Properties dialog.

4.   Navigate to the Security tab.

5.   Click the Advanced button.

6.   Choose the particular user who needs to be designated as the routing assistant.

7.   Click Edit.

8.   Select the Allow check-box for the Manage Server Receive Folder setting.

As mentioned earlier, assigning a fax is permissible only in private mode. If a server has been set up in private mode, the routing assistants launch the Windows Fax and Scan application to assign faxes to the ultimate recipients. The routing assistants have access to the private server inbox that contains the unassigned faxes. If there are any unassigned faxes, the routing assistants can right-click the fax message and choose the Reassign task. Doing this displays a dialog box in which the user can choose the fax accounts to which the fax has to be assigned. The routing assistant can also optionally add some fax message metadata such as the subject and the sender, if that is displayed on the cover page. When the routing assistant completes the assign operation, the fax is marked as assigned and delivered into the Inbox of the intended recipient.

Also, the fax server can be made to operate in either of the modes by choosing the On/Off option for Reassign Setting. This new feature in Windows Server 2008 makes the management of received faxes easy and efficient, and it can be tailored to the requirements of the business.

–*Suryanarayana Shastri*
Program Manager, Windows Experience Documents and Printing

Next, let's hear from the same expert as he explains the new accounts model for the Fax Server role in Windows Server 2008:

From the Experts: Accounts Model in Windows Fax Server

Fax Server in Windows Server 2008 introduces the concept of *Accounts*. An account can be briefly described as a registration between an authenticated user and the fax server.

All clients connecting to a Windows Server 2008 Fax Server need to have an account with the fax server. If the account already exists, the server authenticates the user and establishes the connection. If the account does not exist, the server either automatically creates the account or, if not permitted to do so, denies the connection to the client. An account is the same as the end user's Windows credentials, and it is tied to Windows authentication. So an administrator creating an account for an end user allows the Windows authenticated user to access only the fax server.

The first configuration setting that the fax administrator needs to consider is whether the server supports auto-creation or accounts. This scenario works as follows: In an auto-create environment, the server automatically creates an account for an authenticated user if it does not exist. If the setting is turned off, the server does not create the account and denies the connection. The administrator can choose this setting by taking the following steps:

1. Launch the fax service manager.

2. Right-click on the root node.

3. Launch the Properties dialog.

4. Navigate to the Accounts tab.

5. Choose whether the Auto-Create Accounts On Connection option is On or Off.

If auto-create is Off, the fax administrator has to manually manage the accounts on the fax server. If a user needs to work with the fax server, the administrator creates the account manually and then asks the user to try connecting to the fax server. To create an account, the fax administrator takes the following steps:

1. Launch the fax service manager.

2. Navigate to the Accounts node.

3. Choose Action | New | Account....

4. Enter the username and the domain for the account.

5. Click Create, and create the new account.

The default setting in Windows Server 2008 is that the auto-creation of accounts is turned on.

The administrator can use the same Accounts node to delete an existing account.

When an end user launches Windows Fax and Scan to work with a Windows Server 2008 Fax Server, the server authenticates whether he has an account or not. The connection is established only if the particular user has a valid account on the fax server.

The accounts model in fax server allows a higher degree of control for the fax administrator, and it enforces better security on the fax server.

–Suryanarayana Shastri
Program Manager, Windows Experience Documents and Printing

Finally—and this might sound more like a regression than an improvement (though it's not)—administrators need to know about the removal of third-party display drivers from Windows Server 2008 as of Beta 3. Let's hear from another of our experts at Microsoft concerning these changes:

From the Experts: Display Driver Support in Windows Server 2008

Windows Server 2003 shipped with many third-party display devices supported. This support was different based on the product SKU—for example, Standard edition vs. Enterprise edition. On Standard edition, third-party drivers were present and fully supported to enable full support if the system was going to be used as a client or in a workstation environment or role. On Enterprise edition, the development team decided to have *no* third-party display driver support, Direct3D was disabled by default via registry settings, and only the Microsoft-owned VGA drivers for base display support were shipped.

Windows Server 2008 pre-Beta3 had the same display device support that was in the Windows Vista client release. The code base used for the Windows Server 2008 release was carried forward from Windows Vista and, along with this, all the client-level device support. Windows Server 2008 does not have the ability to differentiate device support on a per-SKU or edition basis as did Windows Sever 2003. So the only differentiating mechanism available is the product type decoration in the driver INFs, which are documented on MSDN at *http://msdn2.microsoft.com/en-us/library/ms794359.aspx*.

The Windows graphics team reviewed the current limitations within per-SKU differentiation, and they discussed many options with our hardware and OEM partners. The decision was to mark all inbox third-party display drivers as Workstation only, thereby not enabling them on any Windows Server 2008 SKU. Starting with the Beta3 release of Windows Server 2008, the default user experience upon installing the operating system is that the user will boot the machine with the Microsoft-supplied VGA driver. Some of the specifics of this include the following:

- The VGA driver always assumes that a monitor is connected even if it cannot detect one.

- The default display resolution for the VGA driver is 800 x 600. There is logic to choosing a higher resolution, but that is bypassed for the VGA driver because we cannot determine the frequency it will use for resolutions set through the VESA BIOS.

- The frequency of modes for the VGA driver is chosen by the video BIOS, but for 800 x 600 we have yet to encounter a BIOS that defaults to anything other than 60 Hz. The reason we use 800 x 600 as the default mode is that we found a few BIOSes that choose unusual timings for higher resolutions.

- Regarding color depth, the default color depth is 32 bits per pixel at 800 x 600. If this mode is not supported, we try the highest color depth available for 800 x 600, and in the very rare cases where none is available, we take the best 640 x 480 color depth mode available.

- Regarding the maximum display resolutions available when running the VGA driver, this is based on what the display device reports as available VESA modes listed in their video BIOS. Most devices since 2004 should properly support 640 x 480, 800 x 600, 1024 x 768, and 1200 x 1024 at good color depths, either 16 or 32 bpp.

- With the VGA driver installed, only system hibernation is supported. You cannot enter any sleep states outside of S4 (hibernation) and S5 power off.

With the removal of third-party display drivers in the Windows Server 2008 release, the core graphics infrastructure is still available to re-enable full display functionality. You need to go through Windows Update or your system provider to obtain display drivers for your hardware and install them to regain functionality.

Figure 12-3 shows a snapshot of a known behavior issue with respect to VGA running on some hardware vendor devices—for example, Intel-integrated and ATI discrete graphics adapters have been known to show the VGA driver as "!" that is, banged out in the Device Manager. This is known as a "Won't Fix OS" issue. The result is that the device is reported as Code 10; however, the VGA driver is still loaded and functioning properly.

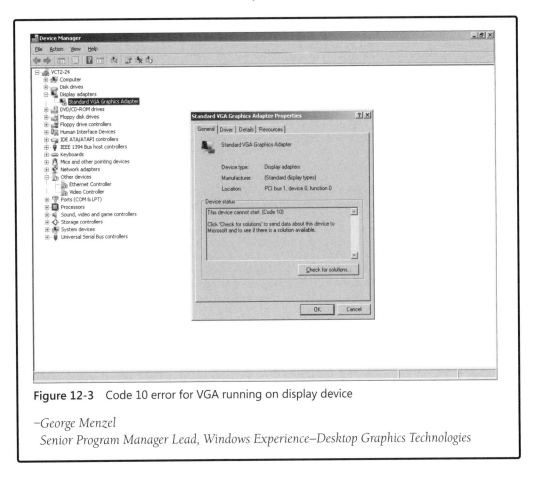

Figure 12-3   Code 10 error for VGA running on display device

–George Menzel
    Senior Program Manager Lead, Windows Experience–Desktop Graphics Technologies

Conclusion

Well, that's certainly a whole lot of new features and enhancements in Windows Server 2008, isn't it? Gee, I hope I didn't miss anything important. By the way, did I tell you about the free Microsoft Easy Grill Oven included with every seventh license you purchase? Oh no, I wasn't supposed to mention that! Wait a moment, someone's knocking at my front door.... Oh no, it's the Marketing Police, they've come to get me! I'm going to jail!! I sure hope they'll let me take my Tablet PC along–I wonder if I'll have wireless Internet access in my cell?

Additional Resources

The starting point for finding information about all things storage on Microsoft platforms is *http://www.microsoft.com/storage/*. Although this link currently redirects you to *http://www.microsoft.com/windowsserversystem/storage/default.mspx*, I have a feeling this will change as Windows Server 2008 approaches RTM.

If you have access to the Windows Server 2008 beta program on Microsoft Connect (*http://connect.microsoft.com*), you can get the Microsoft Windows Server "Longhorn" Beta 2 Storage Manager for SANs Step-by-Step Guide.

Finally, be sure to turn to Chapter 14, "Additional Resources," for more sources of information concerning the Windows server core installation option, and also for links to webcasts, whitepapers, blogs, newsgroups, and other sources of information about all aspects of Windows Server 2008.

Chapter 13
Deploying Windows Server 2008

In this chapter:

Getting Windows Server 2008. 421

Installing Windows Server 2008 422

Using Windows Deployment Services 423

Understanding Volume Activation 2.0 432

Conclusion 439

Additional Resources. 440

Now that we've examined most of the new features and enhancements that are found in Microsoft Windows Server 2008, it's time to roll up your sleeves and start putting it through its paces. This chapter talks about playing around with Windows Server 2008–how you can get it, and how to install and deploy it for testing and evaluation purposes. After all, you can't learn about something just by reading about it–you have to get your hands dirty playing with the thing to really understand how it works and what its capabilities are.

Getting Windows Server 2008

How do you get hold of Windows Server 2008 so that you can try it out? You can use a number of channels, but the first place you should go to is TechNet Beta Central–your one-stop location for acquiring public betas and resources for deploying and testing them. At the time of writing this chapter, Windows Server 2008 has almost reached the Beta 3 release milestone, and plans are for Beta 3 to be a public beta that you can download from Beta Central. So to get the latest public release of Windows Server 2008, go to Beta Central, download it, install it, and give it a test drive to see how it handles.

If you have an MSDN or TechNet subscription, you have another avenue for obtaining the bits to play with. In fact, with these subscriptions you can get builds more frequently than you can with the public beta program. If you have an MSDN or TechNet subscription, however, you've already had access to several Community Technology Preview (CTP) builds of Windows Server 2008 through the Subscriber Download Center.

Another source of Windows Server 2008 builds is Microsoft Connect, where you can sign up to beta-test various Microsoft products before they're released to the public. Microsoft Connect not only gives you access to CTP, Beta, and RC builds, it also gives you access to pre-release documentation, private newsgroups, and private Live Meeting events and chats. Microsoft Connect does more than connect you with Microsoft and its upcoming products; it also connects you with a whole community of beta testers around the world. Try it out today. If you haven't seen it, just go to *http://connect.microsoft.com* and log on with your Windows Live ID.

Finally, if you're part of a mid- or large-sized organization and want to test pre-release, upcoming Microsoft platforms with a view to deploying them in your environment, Microsoft's Technical Adoption Program (TAP) is the way to go. Unfortunately, you usually have to get involved in TAP very early in the development life cycle for a product, so the TAP for Windows Server 2008 is probably already closed as you read this. It's not too late to start asking about getting on TAP for Windows 7, however! For more information about TAP and other early adopter programs at Microsoft, see *http://msdn2.microsoft.com/en-us/isv/bb190411.aspx*.

Installing Windows Server 2008

OK, now that you've got the bits, how do you install them? First of all, remember that we're talking about a beta product (assuming you're reading this around the time of publication of this book), so don't try to use Windows Server 2008 in a production environment. At least, not until the RC stage—unless you're in TAP. In that case, you've probably been using it for a while now on your production network because you get a lot of support from Microsoft when you're part of that program.

What should you install Windows Server 2008 on, then, if you're going to be testing it? Well, you could build a test network with a few spare boxes if you have some kicking around. Or you could use Microsoft Virtual Server 2005 R2 to create a virtual test environment and try out Windows Server 2008 there. I've even got Windows Server 2008 running in a virtual machine in Microsoft Virtual PC 2007, and it runs fine. I can install Active Directory on it, join a Windows Vista client (also running in a VM) to the domain, and test various features and enhancements of Windows Server 2008 quite easily. Just make sure you've got lots of RAM in your testing machine because Windows Server 2008 VMs that are running well eat up a lot of RAM (at least in the beta stage they do).

Manual Installation

So you've downloaded an .iso image of Windows Server 2008 from one of the sources I mentioned earlier, you've burned it to DVD (or mounted the .iso using some utility), and you're ready to install it. What should you do next?

First of all, don't try upgrading from a previous platform such as Windows Server 2003—at least, not just yet. Once Windows Server 2008 reaches the RC stage it might support upgrades, but Beta builds rarely support upgrading from previous versions of a platform. Perform a clean install instead. The easiest way to do this is by using the manual approach. Pop your Windows Server 2008 DVD into your machine, boot from the DVD, and the setup process begins. Choose a drive to install it on, enter your product key (obtained from Microsoft Connect, MSDN, or whatever), and then choose the kind of installation you want to perform. That is, perform either a full installation of Windows Server 2008 or a Windows server core installation.

Be sure you don't neglect trying out the Windows server core installation option. As we saw in Chapter 6, "Windows Server Core," it's pretty cool. And it's something that larger customers have been frequently requesting—you know, the kind of customer that needs to deploy racks of domain controllers, racks of file servers, and so on. They want low-footprint, low-attack-surface, fixed-function solutions that are stripped down and have no nonessential components. You could be one of those customers some day, or maybe you are now. So try the Windows server core installation option, and put it through its paces. It'll be worth the effort.

Unattended Installation

Another way you can try installing Windows Server 2008 is by performing an unattended installation. To do this, you can download the Windows Automated Installation Kit (Windows AIK) from the Microsoft Download Center. Then use one of its core components, the Windows System Image Manager (Windows SIM), to create a distribution share and an unattend.xml answer file for unattended installation. The unattend.xml settings for Windows Server 2008 are a superset of those for Windows Vista, and you should take time to explore what these settings do and how you can install Windows Server 2008 from a network share with minimal user intervention.

The "Step-by-Step Guide" for the Windows server core installation option of Windows Server 2008 even has an appendix with a sample unattend.xml file you can use or customize to perform an unattended installation of the Windows server core option on a machine. Customizing this file is a good way to get introduced to the XML syntax used in answer files for deploying both Windows Vista and Windows Server 2008.

Using Windows Deployment Services

A powerful tool for deploying Windows Vista and Windows Server 2008 in mid- and large-sized organizations is Windows Deployment Services, an updated and redesigned version of the Remote Installation Services (RIS) feature found in Windows Server 2003 and Windows 2000 Server. Windows Deployment Services enables enterprises to rapidly deploy Windows operating systems using network-based installation that doesn't require you to be present at each target computer or to install directly from DVD media. Windows Deployment Services has three types of components:

- **Server components**   These include a Preboot Execution Environment (PXE) server and Trivial File Transfer Protocol (TFTP) server to enable network booting of clients so that they can load and install an operating system on a machine. Other server components include a shared folder and image repository containing boot images, your installation images, and various files you need to support network boots.

- **Client components**   These include a GUI that runs within the Windows Pre-Installation Environment (Windows PE) and communicates with the server components to select and install an operating system image on a machine.

- **Management components**   These include various tools you use to manage your Windows Deployment Services server, operating system images, and client computer accounts.

The first release of Windows Deployment Services was the Windows Deployment Services update for Windows Server 2003. This version of Windows Deployment Services is included in both the Windows AIK and in Service Pack 2 for Windows Server 2003. It has a number of enhancements to the original RIS feature set, including the following:

- A new Windows Deployment Services MMC snap-in and the wdsutil.exe command-line tool

- Native support for Windows PE as a boot operating system and for the new Windows Imaging (WIM) file format used by Windows Vista and Windows Server 2008

- An extensible PXE server component, plus a new client menu for selecting boot operating systems

The upcoming Windows Server 2008 release of Windows Deployment Services will include several additional enhancements, including multicast deployment, TFTP windowing, and EFI x64 network boot support. Let's look briefly at each of these improvements in turn.

Multicast Deployment

Today organizations can use the Windows Deployment Services update for Windows Server 2003 to deploy Windows Vista to client machines on your network. On a Gigabit Ethernet network, this scenario scales well up to about 75 client machines, but not much further because of the large size of the images and because unicast transmission is used to transfer these images over the network. You can get around this limit by batching your client machines into bunches of 75. But what if you have a lab environment where you have a lot of clients that need to receive images concurrently and only a limited amount of time available for imaging all of them? Or what if your corporate environment requires that images be installed on demand while not slowing down other network functions on your production network because of excessive bandwidth usage by image transfers?

Multicasting would be a big plus in these scenarios, and some third-party deployment products have supported multicast deployment where you configure your image for multicast, stage a bunch of clients, click a button, and your deployment kicks off. Well, the enhanced Windows Deployment Services in Windows Server 2008 can do this and more. Imagine an always-on deployment solution where a client can request an image at any time to trigger a new multicast deployment. Or imagine an always-on solution where a client can join an existing multicast deployment in midstream and still receive the entire image instead of just the last part of it. Well, you've just imagined Windows Deployment Services in Windows Server 2008! In fact, here are some things you can do using the Windows Deployment Server role in Windows Server 2008 (and most of these features are supported now in Beta 3):

- Support for multicast deployment of both Windows Server 2008 and Windows Vista (with Service Pack 1, actually—plus, don't forget your routers have to be multicast-enabled as well).

- Support for both automatic (AutoCast) multicast deployment and manually initiated (ScheduledCast) multicast deployment.

- Support for both Windows PE–based multicast deployment and ImageX multicast deployment, and without the need of even having Active Directory deployed on your network.

- Real-time progress monitoring of multicast transmission using either the Windows Deployment Services snap-in or the wdsutil.exe command-line tool.

- Logging of every installation stage to the application logs on your Windows Deployment Server using the Windows infrastructure. This means you can now track the progress of your installations and gather metrics for later analysis.

- A new client UI page that indicates multicast transmission and new management features in the Windows Deployment Services snap-in and the wdsutil.exe command-line tool.

This is really good news for organizations planning to use Windows Deployment Services to undertake large deployments of Windows Vista clients and Windows Server 2008 servers. Let's hear more about multicast deployment from one of our experts at Microsoft:

From the Experts: Using Custom Network Profiles with WDS Multicast

The multicast feature set of Windows Deployment Services (WDS) supports the notion of network profiles, which are groups of parameters that dictate the low-level performance and functionality of the underlying transport protocol. WDS ships with three standard profiles, optimized for particular network bandwidth configurations: 10 Mb, 100 Mb, and 1 Gb. Although any of the aforementioned profiles work on any network configuration with links above 10 Mb, the transport protocol might not necessarily perform optimally on your particular networking topology. The custom multicast network profile provides a mechanism to tweak multicast protocol parameters so that you can achieve the best transfer performance with the least impact to your network.

To enable the custom network profile, run the command **WDSUTIL /set-server / transport /profile:custom**.

You can adjust the network profile parameter values by editing the registry keys at the following location:

```
HKEY_LOCAL_MACHINE\System\CurrentControlSet\Services\WDSServer\Providers\WDSMC\
Profiles\Custom
```

Common Parameters to Adjust

Following is a list of the parameters that most often need to be adjusted:

- **Bandwidth Utilization**   Name = TpMaxBandwidth

  The value equals the percentage of bandwidth multicast traffic that should be used on each NIC. For example, suppose you have a server with two network interfaces: one connected to a 1-Gb network, and the other connected to a 100-Mb network. Setting this value to 80 specifies that the maximum bandwidth used by multicast is 80 percent of the available bandwidth on the first interface (1 Gb) and 80 percent of the available bandwidth on the second interface (100 Mb).

- **Block Size**   Name = ApBlockSize

  The value equals the block size in bytes. A larger block size generally results in faster transfers, but it can cause issues if packet loss is high on the network (because there will be more data to retransmit as acknowledgment occurs at the block level). It is recommended to set this value in 4-KB increments—for example, 1 KB (1024 bytes), 4 KB (4096), 8 KB (8192), 16 KB (16384).

- **Packet Time To Live (TTL)**   Name = TpMulticastTTL

  The TTL value determines the maximum number of network hops a multicast packet can traverse before being dropped by the devices on the network. You can use this value to restrict which clients can receive multicast content. For example, if your multicast server is in a hub office and you want to restrict clients from a branch office that is five network hops away from receiving multicast content, set the TTL to a very low value (for example, 3).

Best Practices

Following is a list of best practices to follow when working with WDS multicast:

■   Adjust parameter values only in the custom profile. Never adjust parameter values in the default profiles. The custom profile is prepopulated with parameter values identical to that of the 100-Mb profile. If you need to return to the default values, set all parameters to mirror the 100-Mb values.

■   Before switching to the custom network profile, perform sample deployments using each of the default profiles to determine which of the three (10 Mb, 100 Mb, or 1 Gb) performs best in your network topology. Take the parameter values of the identified default profile, and use those as starting points in the custom profile.

■   Change only one parameter value at a time. Perform controlled tests after each change to assess the impact.

–Scott Dickens
Lead Program Manager, Windows Deployment Team

TFTP Windowing

TFTP windowing is another enhancement to Windows Deployment Services in Windows Server 2008. TFTP is a simplified form of FTP that's been around since about 1980. Its use on Microsoft Windows platforms today is restricted to downloading Windows PE from your Windows Deployment Server so that a network boot can be performed on your client machine to download an image and kick off the installation process. TFTP was used in a similar way in RIS on Windows Server 2003 and Windows 2000 Server.

The main problem with TFTP for use in deployment is that it uses the connectionless UDP as its network transport, and each time the client receives a packet it has to send an ACK to the server to indicate success. This has two disadvantages: First, it slows down the transmission process because of all the ACKs that need to be sent and received, and this eats up network bandwidth also. And second, if your network link is slow, this ACKing can slow down your deployment even more.

Rather than try and rewrite the TFTP daemon from scratch, the product team instead decided to modify TFTP by adding a new feature called *TFTP windowing*, which is similar in some respects to the TCP windowing used by the TCP/IP network stack on Windows computers. What TFTP windowing involves is this: You define a window size that indicates how many UDP packets it takes to fill up the window. As packets arrive, the window starts filling up, but no ACK is transmitted until the entire window has been filled. The result is a lot fewer ACKs, and therefore, faster downloading of Windows PE from your Windows Deployment Server to your client computers, which can be server boxes on which you want to install Windows Server 2008 or client boxes on which you want to install Windows Vista.

A side effect of this change is that you can now use Windows Deployment Services to easily deploy Windows Vista or Windows Server 2008 to dual-homed machines, a scenario that was difficult to support using the initial release of Windows Deployment Services. Let's hear from another of our experts, this time concerning TFTP windowing:

From the Experts: Using TFTP Windowing with WDS TFTP Server for Improved Performance

Windows Deployment Services uses TFTP to download all files in the pre-OS environment. TFTP is a UDP-based protocol that was designed to be simple; it does not have any security or authentication built in. The client requests a specific file from the TFTP server; the server divides the file into equal data blocks and sends it to the client. The client needs to acknowledge each data packet before the next data packet is sent by the server. This process works great if the server is not overloaded, but it starts to fall apart as network load increases and roundtrip time increases.

TFTP in Windows Server 2003

In Windows Server 2003, the WDS team added support for configurable data block sizes. The goal was to get as much data to the client before requiring an acknowledgment from the client. To configure the block size, administrators have to edit the BCD file generated for each architecture. The following steps demonstrate how this is done:

1. Go to the appropriate architecture directory, REMINST\Boot\<architecture>.

2. Use the BcdEdit.exe tool to add or edit the block size:

    ```
    BcdEdit -store default.bcd -set {68d9e51c-a129-4ee1-9725-2ab00a957daf}
       ramdisktftpblocksize <block size>
    ```

3. Inform the WDS server that configuration has changed so that it can apply the changes:

    ```
    sc control wdsserver 129
    ```

Limitations of This Approach

This feature enables the transferring of more data per packet, but it has its own limitations:

■ The TFTP transfer is done using services provided by the BIOS, so the BIOS implementation on the client must be capable of picking up fragments of the UDP packet and assembling them into a full packet. In our testing, it was discovered that some BIOS implementations do not support this and thus TFTP download fails.

- On a lossy or congested network, if a single UDP fragment is lost, the whole UDP becomes useless.

- The maximum data that can be transferred in is restricted by the maximum size of the UDP packet, which is 65,535 bytes.

- Some network switches apply ACLs on the UDP fragments as well and might discard UDP fragments if the fragments match their ACL.

TFTP in Windows Server 2008

Although the changes mentioned earlier in this sidebar do help to improve the download times, it was evident that we needed more for Windows Server 2008. So the WDS team added support for windowing in Windows Server 2008. The idea is that instead of the server sending one data packet and then waiting for acknowledgment from the client, the server now has a window of multiple data packets that are sent back-to-back without any acknowledgment from client. The client receives all data packets and then sends an acknowledgment. This mechanism also improves performance in high-latency networks.

The number of packets the server should send without acknowledgment is configurable:

1. Go to the appropriate architecture directory, REMINST\Boot\<architecture>.

2. Use the BcdEdit.exe tool to add or edit the window size:

   ```
   BcdEdit -store default.bcd -set {68d9e51c-a129-4ee1-9725-2ab00a957daf}
       ramdisktftpwindowsize <window size>
   ```

3. Inform the WDS server that the configuration has changed so that it can apply the changes:

   ```
   sc control wdsserver 129
   ```

Best Practices

Following is a list of best practices to follow when working with TFTP windowing:

- Change one parameter at a time, and perform testing in a controlled environment to assess the impact.

- If network switches in your environment enforce ACLs, set the block size to 1024 bytes and tweak the window size.

–Asad Yaqoob
Software Design Engineer, Windows Deployment Team

EFI x64 Network Boot Support

Finally, a third enhancement to Windows Deployment Services in Windows Server 2008 is the support for x64 EFI network boot. Extended Firmware Interface (EFI) is the next-generation firmware model and is likely to replace the legacy BIOS in the next few years. Overall, the enterprise hardware landscape is quickly moving toward EFI, particularly on x64 server hardware. Unfortunately, no network boot support for x64 EFI exists on Windows Server 2003—only IA64 hardware supports EFI for Windows Server 2003. And although the initial release of Windows Vista didn't include x64 EFI support, future releases of this platform will likely do so. But Windows Server 2008 does include x64 EFI support, though it's limited in scope to supporting basic network boots and has no support for architecture discovery, pending devices, or PXE referral. Still, it's a good start, and it makes deploying Windows Server 2008 to x64 EFI hardware a reality today using Windows Deployment Services.

Before we leave the topic of Windows Deployment Services, let's hear once again from one of our experts, this time talking about how to upgrade your old RIS server to a Windows Deployment Server running Windows Server 2008:

From the Experts: Upgrading Your Old RIS Server to a Windows Server 2008 WDS Server

Windows Deployment Services is a replacement of the Remote Installation Services optional component in Windows Server 2003. However, the two services use different operating system image formats: RIS uses RIPREP and RISETUP images, while WDS uses WIM images, as found on the Windows Vista and Windows Server 2008 DVDs. Because of this, a Windows Server 2003 server running RIS cannot be directly upgraded to a Windows Server 2008 server—the data in these images would be lost. The upgrade path, therefore, requires the following process to be completed:

1. Update RIS to WDS. There are two ways to do this: either apply Service Pack 2 to the server, or install the hotfix update included in the Windows AIK. Speaking of which...

2. Install the Windows AIK. It contains necessary support files for image conversion.

3. Update the path environment variable to include the Windows AIK install directory.

4. Initialize the WDS server. This can be done either through the WDS MMC Wizard or by running **WDSUTIL /Initialize-Server /RemInst:D:\RemoteInstall**, where *D:\RemoteInstall* is the path to the REMINST shared directory used by RIS. This places the server into Mixed Mode.

5. Convert the RIS images to WIM. There are two ways to do this:

   ❏ Deploy them to a reference PC, run sysprep to generalize them, and then use the WDS Capture tool to capture them as a WIM and upload them to the WDS server.

   ❏ Convert them offline on the WDS server. To do this from the WDS MMC, open the Legacy Images node on the server, right-click on an image, and select Convert To WIM. Alternatively, at a command prompt, run **WDSUTIL /Convert-RIPREPImage /FilePath:<path1> /DestinationImage /FilePath:<path2>**, where *path1* is the full path to the riprep.sif file and *path2* is the full path and file name of the new WIM file. Note that offline conversion works only on RIPREP images, not on RISETUP images.

6. Force the server into Native mode by running **WDSUTIL /Set-Server /ForceNative**.

7. Upgrade the server to Windows Server 2008.

–Jez Sadler
Program Manager, Windows Deployment Team

Solution Accelerator for Windows Server Deployment

If you've begun deploying Windows Vista within your organization, you've probably been using the Microsoft Solution Accelerator for Business Desktop Deployment (BDD) 2007, a set of comprehensive guidance and tools from Microsoft that you can use to optimally deploy Windows Vista and the 2007 Office system. BDD 2007 is the deployment story Microsoft has for Windows Vista, so it make sense that Microsoft is also developing a similar story for the Windows Server 2008 platform. The Microsoft Solution Accelerator for Windows Server Deployment will provide role-based deployment and purposing of Windows Server 2008 servers through automation tools and guidance. The Solution Accelerator for Windows Server Deployment will leverage the Microsoft System Center Configuration Manager 2007 Operating System Deployment (OSD) Package and the Microsoft Systems Management Server V4 Task Sequencer for its infrastructure. Core deployment scenarios for using the Solution Accelerator for Windows Server Deployment include performing clean installs of Windows Server 2008 using Lite Touch Installation (LTI) and Zero Touch Installation (ZTI), upgrading Windows Server 2003 to Windows Server 2008 using LTI and ZTI, and performing clean installs of Windows Server 2003 using LTI and ZTI. In addition, current plans are for you to be able to deploy Windows Server 2008 with a subset of available roles, including the AD, DNS, DCHP, File and Print, and IIS roles.

All I can say is this: if BDD is terrific, then the Solution Accelerator for Windows Server Deployment will likely be absolutely outstanding and will end up being the best-practice solution for deploying Windows Server 2008 for mid- and large-sized organizations. So stay tuned!

Understanding Volume Activation 2.0

Finally, it's not enough to deploy Windows Server 2008—you also have to ensure that the product is properly licensed and activated. Microsoft products sold through OEM, retail, and Volume Licensing channels now include product activation technology to reduce software piracy and ensure that your copies of the products are genuine. Windows Server 2008 uses the same type of activation that was first introduced in Windows Vista—namely, Volume Activation (VA) 2.0. (Previous versions of Microsoft operating systems such as Windows XP and Windows Server 2003 use VA 1.0.) VA 2.0 uses two types of keys:

- **Multiple Activation Keys (MAKs)**   In this scenario, your product keys activate either individual computers or a group of computers by connecting over the Internet to special servers at Microsoft. (You can also activate your computers by telephone if needed.) MAKs can be used only a limited number of times, though the activation limit can be increased by calling your Microsoft Activation Center. Computers running Windows Vista or Windows Server 2008 can be activated with a MAK either by having each computer connect directly to Microsoft servers (something called *individual activation*) or by having multiple computers activated simultaneously using a single connection to Microsoft (called *proxy activation*, which is similar to how VA 1.0 works).

- **Key Management Service (KMS)**   In this scenario, your organization hosts its own internal KMS running on Windows Server 2008, Windows Vista, or Windows Server 2003. This KMS is used to automatically activate Windows Vista and Windows Server 2008. Computers that have been activated using KMS are required to reactivate by connecting to your KMS host at least once every six months.

VA 2.0 has been modified and enhanced in Windows Server 2008 in several ways:

- Windows Server 2008 currently requires only a KMS count of 5 to activate, compared with the 25 required for Windows Vista activation. (This behavior might change before RTM, however.)

- There are multiple KMS keys and a new Hierarchical KMS activation structure. These are described by one of our experts in the sidebar that follows.

From the Experts: Volume Activation 2.0 and Windows Server 2008

The following sidebar explains Volume Activation 2.0 in Windows Server 2008 and provides technical insight and recommendations for deploying a VA 2.0 solution.

Knowledge and Strategies for a Successful Deployment

Volume Activation 2.0 is a solution that helps IT Pros automate and manage the activation of volume editions of Windows Vista and Windows Server 2008. Product activation is a new requirement for each installed system covered under a Volume License agreement. Using volume activation can greatly speed up and simplify the deployment process, but it requires some planning up front.

There are multiple activation methods available, and they use two types of customer-specific keys—namely, Multiple Activation Key (MAK) and the Key Management Service (KMS). A MAK is a product key that can be installed on multiple computers and that activates a predefined number of times. Each MAK-activated computer must independently activate by phone or over the Internet, or be proxy activated over the Internet using the Volume Activation Management Tool (VAMT) found at *http://go.microsoft.com/fwlink/ ?LinkID=77533*. It should be noted that an update to VAMT will be required at Windows Server 2008 RTM for VAMT to function with Windows Server 2008 Volume Licensing. VAMT is currently available for use with Vista Volume Licensing at the link just mentioned.

The alternative method—KMS activation—is often the least understood aspect of VA 2.0. KMS is a trusted mechanism that, once the KMS host is activated, allows volume client computers within the enterprise to activate themselves without any interactions with Microsoft. The following section describes KMS functionality and strategies that can ensure a successful Windows Server 2008 KMS deployment.

For a complete description of Volume Activation 2.0, including both MAK and KMS activation, see the "Windows Vista Volume Activation 2.0 Step-by-Step Guide" found at *http://go.microsoft.com/fwlink/?LinkID=76704*.

Volume Licensing Changes

Windows Vista introduced VA 2.0, which represents a significant change from previous Volume Licensing (VL) solutions. Windows Server 2008 includes several changes and refinements in the implementation of VA 2.0. Under VA 2.0, volume clients do not need a product key during installation. By default, VL editions of Windows Server 2008 and Windows Vista install as KMS clients. With a properly configured KMS infrastructure, these clients automatically discover the KMS hosts on the network and activate themselves without administrative or user intervention. This can equate to a huge deployment savings, both in time and effort. However, organizations must also secure their KMS hosts from a public access point to comply with Microsoft product usage policies.

An important concept to understand about KMS activation is that the KMS returns only a count to the KMS clients. The client reads the count and decides whether or not the count is high enough for the client to activate. As of this writing, Windows Server 2008 KMS clients will activate if the count is 5 or higher. Windows Vista KMS clients require a count of 25.

There are many editions of Windows Server 2008. To simplify these for the purpose of Volume Licensing, they have been combined into three product groups: Group_A, Group_B, and Group_C. Product Group A includes Storage Server, Web Server, and Compute Cluster Editions. Product Group B includes Storage Server Enterprise and

Windows Server 2008 Standard and Enterprise Editions. Product Group C includes Datacenter and Itanium Editions. MAK and KMS keys are associated with each product group. This is illustrated in Table 13-1. Specific attention should be paid to this key matrix to ensure that the proper keys are used so that all deployed systems will activate properly.

Table 13-1   Product Groups and Server Editions for Windows Server 2008

Product group	Server editions
Group A	Storage Server
	Web Server
	Compute Cluster
Group B	Storage Server Enterprise
	Standard
	Enterprise
Group C	Datacenter
	Itanium

Note that Windows Server 2008 Storage Server editions can be activated by KMS, but they cannot host KMS.

The volume keys available for Windows Server 2008 follow the product grouping. For MAK, this is fairly intuitive, as shown in Table 13-2.

Table 13-2   MAK Keys Available for Windows Server 2008

Product group	MAK used to activate
Group A	MAK_A
Group B	MAK_B
Group C	MAK_C

To ensure that organizations don't need multiple KMS hosts to support the deployment of mixed Windows Server 2008 editions, KMS activation of Windows Server 2008 follows a hierarchical structure. Each successive product group can activate all the groups below it, and the KMS can be hosted on any edition that it can activate. Additionally, Windows Server 2008 KMS keys can be used with KMS for Windows Server 2003. Installing Windows Server 2008 keys in KMS for Windows Server 2003 requires an update at Windows Server 2008 RTM.

As detailed in Table 13-3, a KMS_A key can activate only product Group A and Windows Vista. A KMS_C key, on the other hand, can activate all three Windows Server 2008 product groups and Windows Vista. This same KMS_C key can be hosted on any edition of Windows Server 2008 listed in the three product groups, as well as on KMS for Windows Server 2003. Table 13-3 lists the KMS keys, the OS editions that can host a given KMS, and the KMS clients that key can activate.

Table 13-3   KMS Keys vs. Supported Hosts and Clients Activated

KMS key	Hosts that support this KMS key	KMS clients activated by this key
Vista KMS keys	KMS for Windows Server 2003 Windows Vista	Windows Vista
KMS_A	KMS for Windows Server 2003 Windows Server 2008 Web Server Windows Server 2008 Compute Cluster	Windows Vista Windows Server 2008 Storage Server Windows Server 2008 Web Server Windows Server 2008 Compute Cluster
KMS_B	KMS for Windows Server 2003 Windows Server 2008 Web Server Windows Server 2008 Compute Cluster Windows Server 2008 Standard Edition Windows Server 2008 Enterprise Edition	Windows Vista Windows Server 2008 Storage Server Windows Server 2008 Storage Server Enterprise Windows Server 2008 Web Server Windows Server 2008 Compute Cluster Windows Server 2008 Standard Edition Windows Server 2008 Enterprise Edition
KMS_C	KMS for Windows Server 2003 Windows Server 2008 Web Server Windows Server 2008 Compute Cluster Windows Server 2008 Standard Edition Windows Server 2008 Enterprise Edition Windows Server 2008 Datacenter Windows Server 2008 Server Itanium	Windows Vista Windows Server 2008 Storage Server Windows Server 2008 Storage Server Enterprise Windows Server 2008 Web Server Windows Server 2008 Compute Cluster Windows Server 2008 Standard Edition Windows Server 2008 Enterprise Edition Windows Server 2008 Datacenter Windows Server 2008 Server Itanium

Always use the highest KMS key available to your organization. This ensures that the later installations of Windows Server 2008 KMS clients will be able to activate. If you later purchase a license from a higher product group, install that KMS key on the existing KMS hosts using **slmgr /ipk <KMS Key>** and then reactivate the KMS with Microsoft (by Internet or telephone). This process replaces the lower KMS key. KMS clients will pick up the new key the next time they renew their activation.

KMS Auto-Discovery

To get the greatest value from volume activation, KMS auto-publishing and KMS auto-discovery should be used as much as possible. This requires a working understanding of KMS interaction with DNS.

KMS clients query DNS automatically to locate KMS hosts, looking specifically for SRV records named _VLMCS._TCP. These SRV records identify KMS hosts on the network.

When a KMS key is installed on a KMS host, the host publishes an SRV record to the DNS zone identified in its Primary DNS Suffix (by default). (This requires Dynamic DNS, and the host must have write permissions. This is discussed in depth in the "Windows Vista Volume Activation 2.0 Step-by-Step Guide" mentioned earlier.)

However, a KMS host can be configured to publish to multiple domains by listing the domains in the following registry key. If you use this approach, make sure that all desired zones are listed—setting this value overrides the default publishing behavior:

```
HKLM\SOFTWARE\Microsoft\Windows NT\CurrentVersion\SL
Value Name: DnsDomainPublishList
Type: REG_MULTI_SZ
```

When a KMS client successfully contacts a KMS, the KMS host name is cached in the registry. As shown in Figure 13-1, when a KMS client attempts to activate or renew its activation, it first checks the registry for a cached KMS host. If no name is cached or if an activation attempt against a cached KMS host fails, the client queries the DNS zone specified in the Primary DNS Suffix. If no KMS SRV records are found or if the Primary DNS Suffix is empty, the KMS client determines whether or not the system is domain joined. KMS clients joined to an Active Directory domain query the DNS zone specified by Active Directory. Non-domain-joined computers query the DNS Suffix specified by DHCP Option 15. If no KMS SRV records are found, the KMS client attempts to activate again in two hours by default.

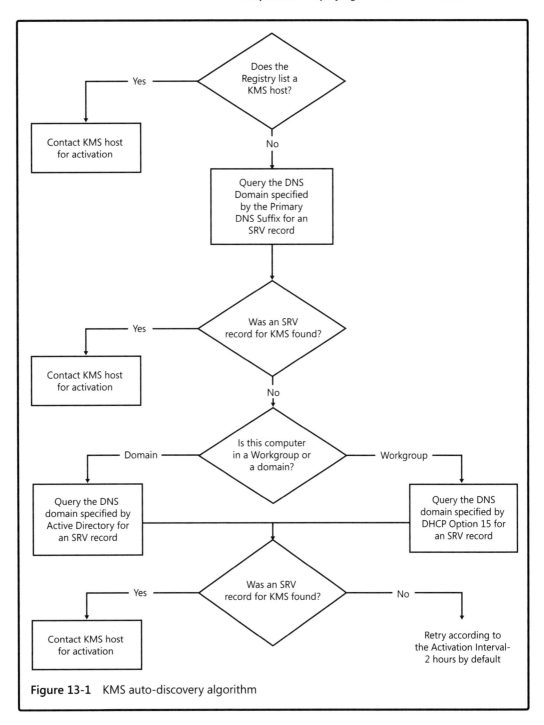

Figure 13-1   KMS auto-discovery algorithm

KMS Deployment Strategies

By understanding the KMS auto-discovery process and your DNS architecture, you can better plan the deployment of KMS hosts and minimize KMS client issues.

Following these steps and using the KMS ability to publish to multiple domains should ensure that KMS clients can locate your KMS hosts and activate without further administrative interaction:

1. **Primary DNS Suffix** One of the following steps will be appropriate for your deployment:

    ❑ If a Primary DNS Suffix exists on your volume clients, ensure that a KMS exists in the specified DNS zone.

    ❑ If the KMS cannot be placed in the zone specified by the Primary DNS Suffix, ensure a KMS SRV record is published in that DNS zone.

2. **DHCP** Ensure that Option 15 in all DHCP servers contains a DNS zone in which a KMS SRV record is published.

3. **Active Directory** If Active Directory exists in the organization, ensure that a KMS SRV record exists in the AD domain.

4. **Network Access** KMS clients contact the KMS using RPC over TCP. By default, the clients use Port 1688, but this is configurable. When planning the activation infrastructure, remember that not only do the clients need to find the KMS, they must be able to communicate with it and receive its response.

Summary

Windows Server 2008 and Windows Vista deployments can be simplified by creating an effective KMS infrastructure. Use the KMS key for the highest Windows Server 2008 product group you have licensed, and upgrade your KMS if you purchase a Volume License for a higher product group. This ensures that your high-end servers can activate. Take the time to fully understand KMS auto-discovery; this is the most important step in this process. In Windows Vista and Windows Server 2008, multilevel name searches do not use the DNS Suffix search list. Therefore, properly positioning the KMS SRV resource records in DNS is critical to a successful KMS client deployment.

Finally, though it has not been described previously in this sidebar, always monitor your deployment for issues. Confirm that KMS SRV records exist in each identified DNS zone. Make sure that the volume clients in each subnet and site can locate the KMS and successfully contact it. Use the activation-related tools and methods described in the "Windows Vista Volume Activation 2.0 Step-by-Step Guide," including the remote WMI functionality built into slmgr.vbs. Use VAMT, SMS-SP3, and the KMS Management Pack for MOM 2005 found at *http://go.microsoft.com/fwlink/?LinkID=83216*.

Additional Resources

I cannot recommend strongly enough that anyone planning or implementing a volume deployment of Windows Server 2008 or Windows Vista should read and understand the "Windows Vista Volume Activation 2.0 Step-by-Step Guide." Afterward, use these links to find additional Volume Activation resources, documentation, and tools:

- For answers to frequently asked questions about Windows Vista Volume Activation 2.0, refer to the Volume Activation 2.0 FAQ found at *http://go.microsoft.com/fwlink/?LinkId=76702.*

- For a list of WMI methods, KMS registry keys, KMS events, KMS error codes, and KMS RPC messages, refer to the "Volume Activation 2.0 Technical Attributes" found at *http://go.microsoft.com/fwlink/?LinkId=76703.*

- For the "Volume Activation 2.0 Troubleshooting Guide by Error Code," go to *http://go.microsoft.com/fwlink/?LinkID=83724.*

- For documentation and to download the Volume Activation Management Tool (VAMT), go to *http://go.microsoft.com/fwlink/?LinkID=77533.*

- For documentation and download information on KMS for Windows Server 2003, go to *http://go.microsoft.com/fwlink/?LinkID=82964* (for an x86 platform) or *http://go.microsoft.com/fwlink/?LinkId=83041* (for x64).

- For documentation and to download the KMS Management Pack for MOM 2005, go to *http://go.microsoft.com/fwlink/?LinkID=83216.*

- For information about the Microsoft Solution Accelerator for Business Desktop Deployment (BDD), go to *http://go.microsoft.com/fwlink/?LinkId=76620.*

- For a list of Volume License products available, go to *http://www.microsoft.com/licensing/default.mspx.*

–Aaron J. Smith
Excell Data Corp

Conclusion

You're near the end of the book. You've learned a lot about Windows Server 2008 and its new features and enhancements. And you've deployed it in your test environment so that you can start putting to work the things you've learned. But short of trial and error, are there any other sources of good information out there for learning more about Windows Server 2008? You bet! Turn now to the last chapter and find out more.

Additional Resources

If you have access to Microsoft Connect, you'll be able to download the "Windows Server 2008 Windows Deployment Services Step-by-Step Guide." By working through this guide, you can learn a lot about configuring and using Windows Deployment Services in Windows Server 2008. This guide might also be available from the Microsoft Download Center by the time you read this. So go to *http://www.microsoft.com/downloads* and search for the guide—hopefully, you'll find it.

There's also a TechNet Forum where you can ask questions and help others who are trying to deploy Windows Server 2008. See *http://forums.microsoft.com/TechNet/ShowForum.aspx? ForumID=579&SiteID=17* for this forum. (Windows Live registration is required.)

There's also a Windows Deployment Services whitepaper that should be available from the Microsoft Download Center by the time you're reading this. It describes in detail how Windows Deployment Services works. Go to *http://www.microsoft.com/downloads* and search for "Windows Deployment Services."

Finally, be sure to turn to the next chapter for more sources of information about deploying Windows Server 2008 and for links to webcasts, whitepapers, blogs, newsgroups, and other sources of information about all aspects of Windows Server 2008.

Chapter 14
Additional Resources

In this chapter:

Product Home Page 441

Microsoft Windows Server TechCenter 442

Microsoft Download Center. 442

Microsoft Connect. 443

Microsoft TechNet. 445

MSDN 451

Blogs 452

Channel 9 454

Microsoft Press Books. 454

Conclusion 455

For my final chapter, I'll list various resources you can use to learn more about Windows Server 2008. A couple of caveats before I begin, however. First, all URLs are subject to change, and specific resources such as whitepapers and Step-by-Step Guides themselves might come and go as they're updated for each successive release of Windows Server 2008. And second, I wrote this chapter just before the Beta 3 release of Windows Server 2008—as a result, some of the main Web sites such as the Windows Server 2008 home page and the Windows Server 2008 section on TechNet were still in their preliminary form and had limited content. I've been told by various teams inside Microsoft, however, that as of Beta 3 these sites will not only be reorganized and restructured, but they'll also have a lot more technical content added to them. Fortunately, the teams also gave me some forward links that you can use to redirect your browser to the final location of this content.

Product Home Page

The product home page for Windows Server 2008 is currently found at *http://www.microsoft.com/windowsserver/longhorn*. As of Beta 3, it will include an updated product overview, a more comprehensive features list, links to where you can get the Beta 3 eval bits, TechCenter, and more. The goal of the product site is to help build awareness of Windows Server 2008 among Microsoft customers, so start there if Windows Server 2008 is new to you and you want to find out more. Unfortunately, I can't describe it more right now because the site is still being baked and I have to finish this book quickly so that it can be published in time for TechEd 2007.

Microsoft Windows Server TechCenter

Microsoft Windows Server TechCenter is the place for you to connect with Windows Server–related resources within Microsoft and the broader Windows Server community. I've been told by internal teams that the TechCenter home page for Windows Server 2008 will initially be located at *http://www.microsoft.com/technet/windowsserver/longhorn/default.mspx* and that this will then later redirect to the final location for this section. Here's what I've been told about the organization of the sections of the coming TechCenter for Windows Server 2008:

- The Evaluation section home will be at *http://www.microsoft.com/technet/windowsserver/longhorn/evaluate/default.mspx.*

- The Reviewer's Guide will be at *http://www.microsoft.com/technet/windowsserver/longhorn/evaluate/review-guide.mspx.*

- System Requirements will be outlined at *http://www.microsoft.com/technet/windowsserver/longhorn/evaluate/system-requirements.mspx.*

- The FAQ will be at *http://www.microsoft.com/technet/windowsserver/longhorn/evaluate/faq.mspx.*

There will also be short Server Role landing pages on the TechCenter so that you can find out more about the Terminal Services role, the Network Policy And Access Services role, the Web Server (IIS) role, and so on. These landing pages will be in the Windows Server 2008 Technical Library and will have more of the kind of deep, technical info that IT pros like us crave. Wait—some more late-breaking news! I've just been told that the landing page for the Windows Server 2008 Technical Library will be *http://technet2.microsoft.com/WindowsServerLonghorn/en/library/bab0f1a1-54aa-4cef-9164-139e8bcc44751033.mspx* and that you'll find lots of technical content there covering server roles, services, components, technologies, and so on. This site will include Changes In Functionality documentation—that is, what's new in Windows Server 2008 compared with previous Windows Server versions.

Anyway, be sure to check out the TechCenter for Windows Server 2008 once it's live. I'm sure you'll find a ton of information there about Windows Server 2008. I wish I could describe what's there, but it's not up yet and I get a 404 when I go there.

Microsoft Download Center

The Microsoft Download Center (*http://www.microsoft.com/downloads*) has a growing number of whitepapers available concerning different aspects of Windows Server 2008. The following is a sampling of these resources at the time of this writing, but I expect that a whole lot more will be available to you by the time you're reading this:

- Active Directory Certificate Server Enhancements in Windows Server Code Name "Longhorn"

- Introduction to Network Access Protection

- Network Access Protection Platform Architecture

- Configuring Network Access Protection Policies in Windows Server "Longhorn"

- 802.1X NAP Enforcement Step-by-Step Guide

- Internet Protocol Security Enforcement in the Network Access Protection Platform

- Cisco Network Admission Control and Microsoft Network Access Protection Interoperability Architecture

- System Center Configuration Manager Network Access Protection Process Flow

- Setting Up Virtual Private Network Enforcement for Network Access Protection in a Test Lab

- Setting Up Dynamic Host Configuration Protocol Enforcement for Network Access Protection in a Test Lab

- Setting Up Internet Protocol Security Enforcement for Network Access Protection in a Test Lab

Note that it's usually a good idea after you've searched the Download Center for resources on a particular topic to sort those resources by date to list the most recent ones first. Some resources might have been written specifically for earlier Beta versions of Windows Server 2008 and might not have been updated yet for the latest available version of the product.

Wait—more late-breaking news from the product team! I've just been told that the Microsoft Download Center will have downloadable versions of content contained in the Windows Server 2008 Technical Library and that this will include updated versions of documentation currently found on Microsoft Connect and also some additional content. (See the next section for what's on Microsoft Connect.) And while I don't have a complete list of this documentation, I've been told that the following forward link will take you there by the time you're reading this: *http://go.microsoft.com/fwlink/?LinkId=86807*.

Microsoft Connect

Microsoft Connect (*http://connect.microsoft.com*) is the place to go if you want to join and participate in beta testing various Microsoft products, including Windows Server 2008. Connect is also a great source of pre-release documentation on the product, though as I said above, this documentation should also be available from the Download Center by the time you read this.

There are two special types of documentation currently on Connect that I want to highlight for you. First, there's the "Changes in Functionality in Windows Server Code Name Longhorn" document that is updated every few months with more detailed information concerning the new features and enhancements of the platform. This doc and the book you're holding in your hands provide a very comprehensive overview of Windows Server 2008 as of Beta 3. And while this book will not be updated for RTM—as Microsoft Press will be releasing other (bigger and fatter) books about Windows Server 2008—the "Changes in Functionality" doc will continue to be updated until it's released in final form at RTM. So keep an eye on this doc as it develops.

The other type of documentation on Connect (and soon to be on the Download Center) is the Step-by-Step Guides, which are hands-on tutorials for testing various Windows Server 2008 features. These Step-by-Step Guides are a gold mine for those interested in getting hands-on experience with the product, and the following list shows the titles currently available at the time of writing this chapter:

- Step-by-Step Guide for Windows Server "Longhorn" Active Directory Domain Services Backup and Recovery

- Step-by-Step Guide for Windows Server "Longhorn" AD DS Installation and Removal

- Step-by-Step Guide for Active Directory Federation Services in Windows Server "Longhorn"

- Windows Server Active Directory Rights Management Services Step-by-Step Guide

- Windows Server "Longhorn" Auditing AD DS Changes Step-by-Step Guide

- Windows Server "Longhorn" Backup and Recovery Step-by-Step Guide

- Windows Server "Longhorn" Certificate Settings in Group Policy Step-by-Step Guide

- Step-by-Step Guide for Configuring a Two-Node File Server Failover Cluster in Windows Server "Longhorn"

- Step-by-Step Guide for Configuring Network Load Balancing with Terminal Services: Windows Server "Longhorn"

- Step-by-Step Guide to Controlling Device Installation Using Group Policy

- Microsoft Windows Server Code Name "Longhorn" Server Core Step-by-Step Guide

- Windows Server Code Name "Longhorn" Step-by-Step Guide to Distributed File System

- Using Identity Federation with Active Directory Rights Management Services Step-by-Step Guide

- Microsoft Windows Server "Longhorn" Initial Configuration Tasks Step-by-Step Guide

- Installing, Configuring, and Troubleshooting Microsoft Online Responder

- Managing Group Policy ADMX Files Step-by-Step Guide

- Windows Server "Longhorn" Network Access Protection and DHCP Step-by-Step Guide

- Windows Server "Longhorn" Network Access Protection and IPSec Step-by-Step Guide

- Windows Server "Longhorn" Network Access Protection Using VPN (RRAS) Step-by-Step Guide

- Windows Server "Longhorn" NFS Step-by-Step Guide

- Microsoft Windows Server Code Name "Longhorn" Offline Files Step-by-Step Guide

- Windows Server "Longhorn" Performance and Reliability Monitoring Step-by-Step Guide

- Step-by-Step Guide for Planning, Deploying, and Using a Windows Server "Longhorn" Read-Only Domain Controller

- Microsoft Windows Server "Longhorn" Print Management Step-by-Step Guide

- Windows Server "Longhorn" Restartable Active Directory Step-by-Step Guide

- Microsoft Windows Server Code Name "Longhorn" Server Core Step-by-Step Guide

- Microsoft Windows Server "Longhorn" Storage Manager for SANs Step-by-Step Guide

- Windows Server "Longhorn" Terminal Services Remote Programs Step-by-Step Guide

- Windows Server "Longhorn" TS Gateway Server Step-by-Step Setup Guide

- Windows Server "Longhorn" Release TS Licensing Step-by-Step Setup Guide

- Windows Server "Longhorn" Windows Deployment Services Step-by-Step Guide

- Microsoft Windows Server "Longhorn" Windows System Resource Manager Step-by-Step Guide

Finally, in addition to the "Changes in Functionality" doc and the Step-by-Step Guides, Connect also has chat transcripts, Live Meeting recordings, and other useful information to those who are beta testing Windows Server 2008.

Microsoft TechNet

The Microsoft TechNet home page at *http://technet.microsoft.com/en-us/default.aspx* is another launching point you can use to explore different resources that can help you learn more about Windows Server 2008. Let's briefly touch on some of the ones currently available at the time of this writing.

Beta Central

Want to test drive Windows Server 2008? Go to TechNet's Beta Central at *http://www.microsoft.com/technet/prodtechnol/beta/betacentral.mspx*, where you can download Beta 3, install it in your test environment, and start getting familiar with it today.

TechNet Events

On the TechNet IT Events And Webcasts page at *http://www.microsoft.com/technet/community/events/default.mspx*, you'll find information about live and on-demand webcasts you can watch and also in-person events you can attend in or near your city. Using your Windows Live ID, you can log in to the site, register for events, and manage your event registrations. The Microsoft Events And Webcasts home page at *http://www.microsoft.com/events/default.mspx* is another launching place for finding this information, as well as more information, such as MSDN webcasts and events for developers.

Webcasts

TechNet offers both live and on-demand webcasts, and these are a terrific way to learn more about Windows Server 2008. Live webcasts use Microsoft Live Meeting, and you usually have an opportunity to ask the speaker questions at the end of the webcast (time permitting). On-demand webcasts are recorded sessions of live webcasts that you can play back using the Live Meeting Player.

Webcasts usually take about an hour. Topics range from basic overviews of platforms and their features to more technical sessions (level 200) and technical deep-dives (level 300). IT pros will be most interested in viewing or participating in the TechNet webcasts, but there are also MSDN webcasts for developers and more general webcasts for business decision makers. A seasoned IT pro can learn from them all.

At the time of this writing, these are some of the TechNet webcasts that cover different aspects of Windows Server 2008 (and they're ordered roughly in the same order as features are presented in this book):

- Introducing Windows Server Code-Named "Longhorn" (Level 200)
- Ten Reasons to Prepare for Windows Server Code-Named "Longhorn" (Level 200)
- Windows Server "Longhorn" and Windows Vista: Better Together (Level 200)
- Understanding Windows Hypervisor and Virtualization in Windows Server Codenamed "Longhorn" (Level 200)
- Transitioning to Windows Virtualization (Level 300)
- Installing, Configuring, and Managing Server Roles in Windows Server "Longhorn" (Level 300)
- Identity and Access Solutions in Windows Server "Longhorn" (Level 300)
- Public Key Infrastructure Enhancements in Windows Vista and Windows Server Code-Named "Longhorn" (Level 300)
- Introduction to Terminal Services in Windows Server Code-Named "Longhorn" (Level 200)

- Introduction to Terminal Services in Windows Server Code-Named "Longhorn" (Level 300)

- Achieving High Availability with Windows Server "Longhorn" Clustering (Level 200)

- A Sneak Peak at the Future of Server Clustering (Level 300)

- Network Access Protection for Windows Server Code-Named "Longhorn" and Windows Vista (Level 200)

- Enabling Trusted Communications and Health Policy Enforcement with Network Access Protection (NAP) (Level 300)

- Security Matters: Network Access Protection (Level 300)

- Exploring the Future of Web Development and Management with Internet Information Services (IIS) 7.0 (Level 200)

- Overview of Networking in Windows Vista and Windows Server "Longhorn" (Level 200)

- Next-Generation Networking with Windows Server "Longhorn" (Level 200)

- Next Generation Networking with Windows Vista and Windows Server Code Named "Longhorn" (Level 300)

- Overview of Windows Deployment Services (Level 200)

- Windows Deployment Services Overview (Level 200)

And here are a few other webcasts about Windows Server 2008 that an IT pro like you might find useful and interesting:

- Microsoft Webcast: Longhorn Server Preview

- Microsoft Webcast: How Microsoft Maximizes Its IT Investment Through Infrastructure Optimization

- Microsoft Webcast: Overview and Road Map of the Microsoft Virtualization Strategy

- MSDN Webcast: Digital Certificate Enhancements in Windows Vista and Windows Server Code-Named "Longhorn" (Level 200)

- Live From Redmond: Putting the Lego set together: Inside IIS 7.0's Componentization

- TechNet Webcast: How Microsoft IT Manages Active Directory Infrastructure (Level 300)

As you can see, these webcasts are a tremendous resource and a great learning opportunity, so be sure to check them out soon.

In-Person Events

Microsoft offers a variety of types of in-person events in various cities at different times. These events include TechNet events, MSDN events, Microsoft Dynamics events, and Microsoft Connections events—though as IT pros, you're probably most interested in the TechNet events such as TechEd. To find out about upcoming events in your area, go to *http://msevents.microsoft.com/CUI/default.aspx?culture=en-US*. Log on using your Windows Live ID, and search for events happening near you. Yet another way to find TechNet events is to use *http://www.technetevents.com*.

TechNet Virtual Labs

TechNet Virtual Labs are a great way of getting hands-on experience with Windows Server 2008 if you don't have the hardware, time, or inclination to install it yourself. Virtual labs are remote Terminal Services sessions in which you can try out products in a virtual online environment. In 90 minutes or less, you can evaluate and test some of Microsoft's newest products through a series of guided, hands-on labs that include a manual you can download. At the time of this writing, the following virtual labs are available at *http://www.microsoft.com/ technet/traincert/virtuallab/default.mspx* for learning about Windows Server 2008:

- Microsoft Windows Server "Longhorn" Server Core Virtual Lab

- Microsoft Windows Server "Longhorn" Server Manager Virtual Lab

- Microsoft Windows Server "Longhorn" Terminal Services Gateway and Remote Programs Virtual Lab

- Windows Vista: Managing Windows Longhorn Server and Windows Vista Using Group Policy Virtual Lab

- Managing Windows Vista and Windows Server 2008 Network Bandwidth with Policy-Based Quality of Service Virtual Lab

You can probably expect more virtual labs to be available by the time you read this,.

TechNet Community Resources

Got a question about Windows Server 2008? Try out the various TechNet Community resources to get your question answered by your peers and also by experts at Microsoft. Let's take a look at some of these community resources and how you can use them.

TechNet Chats

TechNet chats are a great source of informational tidbits about Windows Server 2008 and other Microsoft products. These chats take place regularly (more or less) and allow interaction between Microsoft's customers and the product development team members, product support staff, and other technology experts at Microsoft. You can find a schedule for upcoming chats at *http://www.microsoft.com/technet/community/chats/default.mspx*. What's really valuable, however, is that all chat sessions are archived so that you can read them offline at your convenience to troll them for tips, tricks, and insights. The chat archive page can be found at *http://www.microsoft.com/technet/community/chats/trans/default.mspx*. Here's a quick list of some of the Windows Server 2008 chat transcripts located there that you might be interested in reading:

- Deploying NAP End to End in your Enterprise (March 13, 2007)

- Identity and Access Technology and Windows Server "Longhorn" (March 01, 2007)

- Documentation: What's New in Vista and What's Coming in Longhorn (February 20, 2007)

- Network Access Protection (NAP) System Health Agent/Validator (February 12, 2007)

- EAPHost in Windows Vista and Longhorn (December 18, 2006)

- DHCP enhancements in Windows Vista: NAP enforcement and DHCPv6 (December 14, 2006)

- Windows PowerShell, Internet Information Services (IIS) 7.0 and Windows Server "Longhorn" (December 4, 2006)

- Network Access Protection in Windows Vista and Windows Server 2008 (September 14, 2006)

I'm sure that by the time you're reading this book, there will be many more chat transcripts available on this site, so be sure to check it out.

TechNet Forums

TechNet also hosts a number of Web-based forums that you can participate in (and which require a Windows Live ID for access) by posting comments, asking questions, or helping others. At the time of this writing, the following forums are available for discussing issues relating to Windows Server 2008:

- General

- Directory Services

- File Services and Storage

- Migration

- Management

- Network Access Protection

- Platform Networking

- Print/Fax

- Setup and Deployment

- Terminal Services

- Security

- Server Core

- Server Virtualization

- Failover Clustering

These forums can be accessed from the TechNet Forums main page found at *http://forums.microsoft.com/TechNet/default.aspx?SiteId=17*. By the way, you might have noticed that there is no forum for discussing IIS 7.0 in the preceding list. That's because IIS 7.0 has its own set of forums hosted on IIS.NET at *http://forums.iis.net*.

TechNet Newsgroups

Another great way of asking questions and discussing issues concerning Microsoft products is to use the TechNet newsgroups. These newsgroups can be accessed either by using your Web browser from *http://www.microsoft.com/technet/community/newsgroups/default.mspx* or using your favorite NNTP newsreader by downloading a list of newsgroups from *news://msnews.microsoft.com*. At the time of this writing, there are newsgroups for Windows Vista but none yet for Windows Server 2008.

By the way, what's really great about these newsgroups is that they are haunted by the spirits of Microsoft Most Valuable Professionals (MVPs), who spend their days idly trolling newsgroups to find newbies they can initiate into the mysteries of how Microsoft products do their magic. Just kidding—MVPs are anything but idle, as many of them hold down full-time jobs while still managing to spend a few hours or more a week patiently answering questions posted to these newsgroups. I'm an MVP myself, and I know the late-night effort this involves. But I'm also aware of the reward—that is, helping others. We also get a few nice perks from Microsoft when we're awarded MVP recognition, but most of us are in it because we enjoy voluntarily sharing our knowledge of and experience with Microsoft products with the larger user community around the world.

TechNet User Groups

Microsoft has been aggressively sponsoring and supporting IT pro user groups in the last few years, and the result has been impressive. In my own hometown of Winnipeg, Canada, we have an IT pro user group that meets monthly to do presentations, share insights, ask questions, and more. How do you find an IT pro user group in your area? Start with Culminis (*http://www.culminis.com*), which at the time of this writing includes over 836 member organizations, representing 2,117,426 IT professionals worldwide! Culminis is an international non-stock corporation whose goal is to facilitate the growth of IT pro user groups interested in Microsoft IT products and solutions. Microsoft lists Culminis and several other similar organizations on their TechNet Community site, at *http://www.microsoft.com/technet/community/usergroup/default.mspx*, as a good place to start if you're looking for a local user group or association to get involved in.

TechNet Columns

TechNet also has a series of different columns of interest to IT pros. For instance, there's The Cable Guy at *http://www.microsoft.com/technet/community/columns/cableguy/default.mspx*. The Cable Guy is indeed a real person, Joseph Davies. He's a technical writer and networking expert at Microsoft who has also written several books for Microsoft Press and numerous whitepapers that are available from the Microsoft Download Center. If you want to get brief but technically deep overviews of different networking features in Windows Vista and Windows Longhorn Server, this is a great place to start. Other columns such as "IIS Insider" and "Security Management" might be of interest to you as well.

TechNet Magazine

Free to individuals in the United States and also available online is TechNet Magazine, Microsoft's own IT pro magazine, which is packed with terrific articles written by experts who really know their stuff. Find out more about this magazine and subscribe to it at *http://www.microsoft.com/technet/technetmag*, as there's bound to be more and more Windows Server 2008 content in it over the coming months.

TechNet Flash Newsletter

Finally, a great way of hearing about all the latest and greatest resources for Windows Server 2008 on TechNet is to subscribe to the TechNet Flash newsletter, which is published every other week and offers free technology information and updates, expert insight, special offers, and other information for IT professionals. To subscribe to TechNet Flash, go to *http://www.microsoft.com/technet/abouttn/subscriptions/flash_register.mspx* right away.

MSDN

The Microsoft Developer Network (MSDN) at *http://msdn.microsoft.com* will be another valuable resource concerning Windows Server 2008, but it's targeted at a developer audience instead of IT pros like ourselves, who generally spend most of our time on TechNet instead. Developers can find programming guides on MSDN for the various new and enhanced Active Directory features and components in Windows Server 2008. For example, at the time of this writing the following programming guides seem to be available:

- The Active Directory Domain Services (AD DS) programming guide is located at *http://msdn2.microsoft.com/en-us/library/aa362244.aspx*.

- The Active Directory Lightweight Directory Services (AD LDS) programming guide is located at *http://msdn2.microsoft.com/en-us/library/aa705886.aspx*.

- The Active Directory Federation Services (AD FS) programming guide is located at *http://msdn2.microsoft.com/en-us/library/bb267808.aspx*.

- The Active Directory Rights Management Services (AD RMS) SDK is located at *http://msdn2.microsoft.com/en-us/library/aa362715.aspx.*

I'm sure there's more, but because I'm an IT pro and not a developer, I'll leave it at that.

Blogs

Blogs are a great way to feed your understanding of different Windows Server 2008 technologies and features. Here's a short list of blogs by product teams and experts at Microsoft. Because they're insiders, they obviously know what they're talking about—at least we hope so! The following blogs are listed in no particular order. Some of them deal specifically with Windows Server 2008, while others cover related technology areas like networking or performance. Here you go:

Group Policy Team Blog, which can be found at *http://blogs.technet.com/grouppolicy/default.aspx,* has a lot of helpful articles on how Group Policy works in Windows Vista and Windows Server 2008.

Routing and Remote Access Blog, found at *http://blogs.technet.com/rrasblog/default.aspx,* includes some tips and insights concerning how to use RRAS for VPN/dial-up scenarios in Windows Vista and Windows Server 2008.

Windows PowerShell is a blog about (duh) Windows PowerShell, posted by the (you guessed it) Windows PowerShell team at Microsoft. Because PowerShell is going to be included in Windows Server 2008, you need to start learning about this fantastic command-line management platform. So go to *http://blogs.msdn.com/powershell/default.aspx* right now and get cracking! By the way, I love blogs that have creative titles like this.

Ask The Performance Team is where you should point your newsreader to if you want to (smile) ask the Windows Performance Team anything about Windows Longhorn Server or Windows Vista performance issues. The blog can be found at *http://blogs.technet.com/askperf/default.aspx.*

Server Core is another aptly (if boringly) named blog, but the content you'll find there is anything but boring. Andrew Mason, a Program Manager who has worked on developing the Windows server core installation option of Windows Server 2008, has posted a series of terrific articles that will get you deep inside how to configure and manage a server running the Windows server core installation option. Check out this blog at *http://blogs.technet.com/server_core.*

Michael Howard's Web Log is subtitled, "A Simple Software Security Guy at Microsoft!" If you're looking for blog content on the security end of things, this is a good place to begin. Michael's blog is at *http://blogs.msdn.com/michael_howard/default.aspx.*

Windows Server Division Weblog is a good blog whose feed you can subscribe to if you want to get general announcements and participate in discussions concerning Windows Server 2008 and other Microsoft server platforms and products. This blog can be found at *http://blogs.technet.com/windowsserver/default.aspx.*

Adventures in Server Land is a blog by Jason Olson, a Technical Evangelist and member of the Developer and Platform Evangelism team. Jason's blog can be found at *http://blogs.msdn.com/jolson/about.aspx.* He bills his blog as, "The adventures and life of a Technical Evangelist as he digs through the latest core technologies in Longhorn Server."

ScottGu's Blog is subtitled with, "Scott Guthrie lives in Seattle and builds a few products for Microsoft." Scott is more than that, however—he's a General Manager within the Microsoft Developer Division and runs the development teams that build IIS 7.0, the common language runtime (CLR), the .NET Compact Framework, ASP.NET/Atlas, the Windows Presentation Foundation, and more. So if you're interested in any of these technologies and how they apply to Windows Server 2008, check out his blog at *http://weblogs.asp.net/scottgu/default.aspx.*

Terminal Services Team Blog is the starting place if you're interested in anything that has to do with Terminal Services in Windows Server 2008. Lots of excellent stuff here. Check it out at *http://blogs.msdn.com/ts/default.aspx.*

The Filing Cabinet is subtitled as, "An IT Pro blog about file services and storage features in Windows Server, Windows XP, and Windows Vista." I expect the blog will also include similar content concerning Windows Server 2008 by the time you're reading this. You can find this blog at *http://blogs.technet.com/filecab/default.aspx.*

Windows Core Networking is subtitled, "Windows Core Networking APIs and technologies such as Winsock, TCP/IP stack, WFP, IPsec, IPv6, WSK, WinINet, Http.sys, WinHttp, QoS, and System.Net." Great subtitle! It's a good place to feed from if you want to learn more about networking in Windows Vista and Windows Server 2008. Just go to *http://blogs.msdn.com/wndp/default.aspx.*

Windows Virtualization Team Blog is a blog by John Howard, a Program Manager for Windows Virtualization. If you want to keep watch over how Windows Server Virtualization is developing, point your newsreader to *http://blogs.technet.com/virtualization/default.aspx.*

Avi's Corner, found at *http://avibm.spaces.live.com/default.aspx?_c02_owner=1*, is a blog by Avi Ben-Menahem, a Program Manager for Active Directory Certificate Services (AD CS).

Blogs by MVPs

Microsoft Most Valuable Professionals (MVPs) are also avid bloggers, generally, and here are two of them who blog frequently about features of Windows Server 2008:

Directory Services/Active Directory is a blog by Ulf B. Simon-Weidner, an MVP who works as a consultant for Microsoft platforms at major companies in Germany. Ulf has a lot of great insights to share, and you can find his blog at *http://msmvps.com/blogs/ulfbsimonweidner/default.aspx.*

Steve Schofield Weblog is a blog by IIS MVP Steve Schofield. You'll find tons of interesting stuff there about IIS 7. The URL for this blog is *http://weblogs.asp.net/steveschofield/default.aspx*.

You can find many more blogs by MVPs at *http://msmvps.com/blogs/Bloggers.aspx*. I'm sure a lot of them deal from time to time with various aspects of Windows Server 2008, but I've gotta get this book finished in time for TechEd, so let's move on.

Channel 9

Channel 9 is a "conversation" between Microsoft and its customers. It has videos, podcasts, screencasts, wikis, forums, and other sources of information you can download, contribute to, or ask questions about. Channel 9 can be found on MSDN at *http://channel9.msdn.com*. There's a lot of good stuff there concerning Windows Server 2008, but it's getting close to suppertime, so I'm going to wind up this chapter now (and the book) with a brief conclusion.

Microsoft Press Books

Finally, Microsoft Press will soon be publishing a whole bunch of top-notch books about Windows Server 2008 and related technologies to complement this one (which I hope you also feel has been top-notch—and fun to read as well). The following is a partial list of titles that are being planned at the time of this writing. You can get a current list of titles at *http://www.microsoft.com/learning/books/windows/longhorn/*.

- *Windows Server 2008 Resource Kit*
- *Windows Server 2008 Virtualization Resource Kit*
- *Windows Server 2008 Security Resource Kit*
- *Windows Administration Resource Kit: Productivity Solutions for IT Professionals*
- *Windows Server 2008 Active Directory Resource Kit*
- *Internet Information Services (IIS) 7.0 Resource Kit*
- *Windows Server 2008 Administrator's Companion*
- *Windows Server 2008 TCP/IP Protocols and Services*
- *Windows Server 2008 Terminal Services*
- *Windows Server 2008 Networking Guide*
- *Understanding IPv6, Second Edition*
- *Microsoft Group Policy Guide, Second Edition*
- *Windows Server 2008 Administrator's Pocket Consultant*
- *Windows Server 2008 Inside Out*
- *Internet Information Services (IIS) 7.0 Administrator's Pocket Consultant*

- *Microsoft Windows PowerShell Step By Step*

- *Windows PowerShell Scripting Guide*

- *Microsoft Windows PowerShell & Command-line Administrator's Pocket Consultant*

If you're like me, you'll probably want to order as many of these titles as your budget will permit, so keep your eyes on the list of new and upcoming Microsoft Press titles at *http://www.microsoft.com/mspress/hop/* so you can preorder these titles as soon as they become available. And while you're at it, why not buy a few extra copies of this book for your colleagues? And some for your friends? And a copy for your boss. And several for your top customers. And don't forget your mother-in-law...

Conclusion

Well, that's it. It's time to wrap things up, as my editor has to do the once-over on this chapter so that we can get the book revised, into pages, and off to the printer in time to get it into your hands at TechEd this June. I hope you've enjoyed reading this book as much as I've enjoyed writing about Windows Server 2008. I welcome your feedback if you want to contact me concerning anything covered in this book. Cheers!

Mitch Tulloch, MVP
Web site: *http://www.mtit.com*
E-mail: *info@mtit.com*

Index

A

ABE (Access Based Enumeration), 272
Acar, Tolga, 7, 409
Access Based Enumeration (ABE), 272
account lockout settings, 169 to 170
action processes, for Identity Lifecycle Manager, 156
Active Directory
  installing role on Windows server core installations, 134
  in Windows 2000 Server, 150 to 151
  in Windows Server 2003, 151 to 153
  in Windows Server 2008, 4, 153 to 154
Active Directory Application Mode (ADAM), 152 to 153, 172. *See also* Active Directory Lightweight Directory Services
Active Directory Certificate Services (AD CS)
  availability, 91
  defined, 10, 73, 154
  enhancements in Windows Server 2008, 176 to 182
  enrollment process, 176 to 177
  formerly Certificate Services, 154
  Network Device Enrollment Service support, 177
  Online Certificate Status Protocol support, 177 to 178
  role services, 73
  Web enrollment changes, 177
Active Directory directory services, 150. *See also* Active Directory Domain Services
Active Directory Domain Controller role service, 73
Active Directory Domain Services (AD DS)
  auditing enhancements, 158 to 163
  availability, 91
  defined, 10, 73, 154
  enhancements in Windows Server 2008, 158 to 172
  formerly Active Directory directory services, 154
  Read-Only Domain Controller, 164 to 165
  restartable, 13, 168 to 169
  role services, 73 to 74
  Started State, 169
  Stopped State, 169

Active Directory Federation Services (AD FS)
  defined, 10, 74, 153, 154
  improved import/export functionality, 183
  limiting deployment using Group Policy, 184
  overview, 182
  role services, 74
  Web Agents, 74
Active Directory Installation Wizard, 165 to 166
Active Directory Lightweight Directory Services (AD LDS)
  availability, 91
  creating instances, 172 to 176
  defined, 74
  formerly Active Directory Application Mode, 154
  overview, 172 to 173
  Setup Wizard, 173 to 176
Active Directory Rights Management Services (AD RMS)
  availability, 91
  defined, 10, 74, 154
  enhancements in Windows Server 2008, 186
  formerly Windows Rights Management Services, 114
  overview, 186
  role services, 74 to 75
Active Server Pages (ASP) role service, 80
AD CS. *See* Active Directory Certificate Services
AD DS. *See* Active Directory Domain Services
AD FS. *See* Active Directory Federation Services
AD FS Web Agents role service, 74
AD LDS. *See* Active Directory Lightweight Directory Services
AD RMS. *See* Active Directory Rights Management Services
ADAM (Active Directory Application Mode), 152 to 153, 172. *See also* Active Directory Lightweight Directory Services
Add Feature Wizard (AFW), 54, 102 to 103
Add Roles Wizard (ARW), 98 to 101
/admin switch, 206 to 207
Administrator Password, changing on Windows server core installations, 118
ADMX/ADML files, 58 to 59
ADSI Edit snap-in, 170, 175

Advanced Encryption Standard (AES), 181
Adventures in Server Land blog, 453
(AES) Advanced Encryption Standard, 181
AFW (Add Feature Wizard), 54, 102 to 103
Antonov, Sergei, 66
AppCmd.exe tool, 354 to 357
Application Development role service, 80 to 81
application pools, 350, 370
Application Server Core role service, 75
Application Server role
    defined, 75
    installing, 372 to 374
    overview, 371 to 373
    PowerShell as multitool for managing, 374
    role services, 75 to 76
applications
    clustering, 15
    deploying to Web, 14
    installing on Windows server core installations,
        135
approval actions, 157
approval processes, for Identity Lifecycle
        Manager, 156
Arunkundram, Rajiv, 6, 34, 35
ARW (Add Roles Wizard), 98 to 101
Ask the Performance Team blog, 452
ASP (Active Server Pages) role service, 80
ASP.NET, integrating with IIS 7.0, 348, 369
ASP.NET role service, 80
Audit Directory Service Access, 158, 161
audit policies, Windows Server 2008
    Detailed Directory Service Replication, 161
    Directory Service Access, 161, 162
    Directory Service Changes, 161, 162, 163
    Directory Service Replication, 161
authentication processes
    for 802.1X NAP enforcement, 337 to 339
    for Identity Lifecycle Manager, 155 to 156
Authorization Manager, 151
authorization policies
    connection, 236
    creating for TS Gateway, 236 to 237
    resource, 236
autoenrollment, defined, 176 to 177
automatic remediation, NAP support for, 288 to
        289
automatic updates, enabling for Windows server
        core installations, 126 to 129, 146

B

Background Intelligent Transfer Service (BITS)
        Server, 88, 91
Balcanquall, Alex, 5
Base Class Library (BCL), 85
Basic Authentication module, 351 to 352
Basic Authentication role service, 81, 346
BDD (Business Desktop Deployment), 11, 431
BDE (BitLocker Drive Encryption)
    availability, 91
    combining RODCs with, 13
    data volume feature, 408
    defined, 88
    EFI support, 408 to 409
    new authenticator, 408
    overview, 407 to 408
    Windows Server 2008 enhancements, 408 to
        409
Behbahani, Aurash, 5, 183, 185
Ben-Menahem, Avi, 5, 453
Beta Central, 421, 445
Bhat, Nitin T., 6
Bisht, Ahmed, 4
BitLocker Drive Encryption (BDE)
    availability, 91
    combining RODCs with, 13
    data volume feature, 408
    defined, 88
    EFI support, 408 to 409
    new authenticator, 408
    overview, 407 to 408
    Windows Server 2008 enhancements, 408 to
        409
BITS (Background Intelligent Transfer Service)
        Server, 88, 91
blogs, 452 to 453
branch offices, Read-Only Domain Controller
        solution, 164 to 165
Brockway, Tad, 7
business continuity, 18 to 19
Business Desktop Deployment (BDD), 11, 431

C

CA (Certification Authority)
    defined, 73
    verifying configuration in NAP IPSec
        environment, 328, 329, 331
    Web Enrollment, 73

CALs. *See* Terminal Services, Client Access Licenses
CAP12 Diagnostics, 179 to 180
CardSpace, 86
CBS (Component Based Servicing), 47, 95 to 96
CertEnroll.dll COM control, 177
certificate revocation lists (CRLs), 177 to 178, 185
Certificate Services, 150 to 151. *See also* Active Directory Certificate Services
certificate templates, 180 to 181
Certificates snap-in, 181
Certification Authority (CA)
   defined, 73
   verifying configuration in NAP IPSec environment, 328, 329, 331
   Web Enrollment, 73
CGI. *See* Common Gateway Interface (CGI) role service; FastCGI applications
Chandwani, Santosh, 6, 404
Channel 9, MSDN, 454
chats, TechNet, 448 to 449
Chiesa, Dino, 5, 374
child partitions
   with enlightened guest, 26 to 27
   with guest running Linux, 28
   with legacy guest, 27
chkdsk.exe tool, 257
Christensen, Elden, 5, 258
Cisco Systems, 287
Claims-Aware Agent, 74
class libraries, .NET Framework, 85
ClearType, 193, 194
CLI (command-line interface). *See* command line; Server Manager, command-line interface
Client Access Licenses. *See* Terminal Services, Client Access Licenses
Client Certificate Mapping Authentication role service, 81
clock, Windows, 146
CLR (common language runtime), 85
CLS (Common Language Specification), 85
Cluster Administration tool, 268
cluster logging, 273 to 278
Cluster Migration tool, 273
Cluster Service, 258, 261
Cluster Service Accounts (CSAs), 261
cluster.exe tool, 271 to 272

clusters and clustering. *See also* Failover Clustering
   applications overview, 15
   best practices, 266
   creating and managing clusters, 267 to 268, 269
   defined, 251
   dynamic disks and, 257
   migrating from Windows Server 2003 to Windows Server 2008, 273
   Network Load Balancing as form of, 252
   new quorum model, 254 to 256
   overview, 251
   providing high availability for file servers, 269 to 273
   server clusters, 252
   storage enhancements in Windows Server 2008, 256 to 257
   troubleshooting, 273 to 274
   validating solutions, 261 to 266
   Windows server core installation support, 146
   Windows Server Virtualization vs. Virtual Server support, 29
CNG (Suite B), 180
color quality, 193
columns, TechNet, 451
COM + Network Access, 75
command line
   advantages of working from, 110
   installing roles and features from, 105 to 107
   installing roles on Windows server core installations from, 131 to 134
   managing Windows server core installations from, 130 to 131
   performing initial Windows server core configuration tasks, 118 to 120
Common Gateway Interface (CGI) role service, 80
Common HTTP Features role service
   defaults, 346
   defined, 80
   subcomponents, 80, 346
common language runtime (CLR), 85
Common Language Specification (CLS), 85
Component Based Servicing (CBS), 47, 95 to 96
configuration APIs, Windows Process Activation Service, 94
Configure Quorum Settings Wizard, 256

Connection Manager Administration Kit, 88
/console switch, 206
Control datetime.cpl file, 120
Control intl.cpl file, 120
Control Panel applet, 119
control panels, in Windows server core
    installations, 120
controls. *See* Identity and Access Management
Create A shared Folder Wizard, 271
CRLs (certificate revocation lists), 177 to 178, 185
Crypto Next Generation (CNG), 409
CSAs (Cluster Service Accounts), 261
Custom Logging role service, 81

D
Date, Amit, 5, 282
Date And Time applet, 119
date, setting on Windows server core
    installations, 119
datetime.cpl file, 120
dcpromo.exe tool, 134, 165 to 166. *See also* Active
    Directory Installation Wizard
Default Document role service, 80
Deily, Eric, 5, 366, 368
deployment
    automating common tasks by using
        ServerManagerCmd.exe, 52 to 53
    Microsoft Solution Accelerator for Business
        Desktop Deployment, 11, 431
    Microsoft Solution Accelerator for Windows
        Server Deployment, 431
    of Web applications and services, 14
    of Windows clients and servers, 11 to 12
Deployment Server role service, 83
desktop composition, 196
Desktop Experience, 88
Detailed Directory Service Replication, 161
device drivers
    microkernelized hypervisor and, 22 to 23, 23 to
        24
    monolithic hypervisor and, 22
    VSP and, 25
    Windows Server 2008 support for display
        drivers, 417 to 419
    for Windows server core installations, 111, 135
Device Redirection Framework, 196 to 198
Device Specific Modules (DSMs), 90, 388 to 389
DFS Namespace role service, 72, 77
DFS Replication role service, 72, 77

DHCP protocol
    deployment considerations, 404
    as NAP enforcement method, 289, 289 to 290,
        302
    Stateless and Stateful Server functionality, 403
        to 404
    support in Windows Server 2008, 402 to 404
DHCP Server, 76, 259
Dickens, Charles, 67
Dickens, Scott, 6, 427
Digest Authentication role service, 81
Directory Browsing role service, 80
Directory Service Access, 161, 162
Directory Service Changes, 161, 162, 163
Directory Service Integration, message queuing,
        90
Directory Service Replication, 161
Directory Services/Active Directory blog, 453
Directory Services Restore Mode, 168, 169
Disk Management
    initializing new disks, 273
    Windows server core installations and, 146
Disk Signature, 258
disk space, for installing Windows server core
        installations, 145
DiskPart.exe command, 257
disks
    pass-through access, 27, 28
    physical vs. virtual, 27
    replacing, 273
    self-healing, 257, 258
display drivers, 417 to 419
displays
    color quality, 193
    configuring resolution on Windows server core
        installations, 129 to 130
    data prioritization, 195
    device driver support, 417 to 419
    spanned monitors, 193
Distributed File System role service, 72, 77
Distributed Transactions, 76
DNS Server
    availability, 91
    configuring networking on Windows server
        core installations, 76
    installation options for RODCs, 166 to 167
    installing on Windows server core installations,
        132 to 134
    Read-Only Domain Controllers and, 166 to 167

domain controllers
  modes when running Windows Server 2008,
    169
  restarting, 13, 168 to 169
Download Center, 442 to 443
drivers. *See* device drivers
DSMs (Device Specific Modules), 90, 388 to 389
Dussart, Nils, 6, 50
dynamic disks, 257

E

EAP (Extensible Authentication Protocol), 291,
    334
EAP-TLS authentication protocol, 291
Easy Print, 199 to 200
ECs (enforcement clients), 298
Edson, Chris, 5, 334, 339
EFI (Extensible Firmware Interface)
  BitLocker Drive Encryption support, 408 to 409
  x64 network boot support, 430
802.1X enforcement
  debugging by using client-side troubleshooting,
    331 to 334
  defined, 291, 332
  failed authentications, 337 to 338
  as NAP enforcement method, 302
  overview, 291
  successful authentications, 338 to 339
  troubleshooting NPS for PEAP-based NAP, 335
    to 339
Einstein, Albert, 67 to 68
Elhajj, Tim, 7, 350
enforcement clients (ECs), 298
enlightened guest operating system, 26 to 27
enrollment agents
  defined, 181
  overview, 181
  restricted, 182
entitlement actions, 157
Equal_Per_Session resource allocation policy,
    246 to 247
Equal_Per_User resource allocation policy, 246,
    246 to 247
Erdogan, Samim, 6
ETW (Event Tracing for Windows), 60
event logs
  cluster logging and, 273 to 278

in Windows server core installations, 112, 136
    to 137
Event Trace Log (.etl) format, 277
Event Tracing for Windows (ETW), 60
Eventing model, 274, 276
events
  in Identity Life Cycle Manager, 157
  NAP client, 322 to 323
Extensible Authentication Protocol (EAP), 291
Extensible Firmware Interface (EFI)
  BitLocker Drive Encryption support, 408 to 409
  x64 network boot support, 430

F

Failover Cluster Management snap-in, 268 to
    269, 270
Failover Clustering
  availability, 91
  best practices, 266
  creating and managing clusters, 267 to 268, 269
  defined, 89
  goals of improvements, 253 to 254
  high-availability enhancements, 15
  list of enhancements in Windows Server 2008,
    252 to 253
  Maintenance Mode, 257
  management tools, 273 to 278
  networking enhancements, 259 to 261
  providing high availability for file servers, 269 to
    273
  role of GeoClusters, 259 to 261
  SCSI bus resets and, 256
  security enhancements, 261
  storage enhancements, 256 to 257
  validating solutions, 261 to 266
Failure Request Tracing, 365 to 368
FastCGI applications, 371
Fax Server
  accounts model, 416 to 417
  availability, 91
  defined, 76
  private mode, 414, 415
  public mode, 414, 415
  Reassign setting, 414, 415
  role enhancements in Windows Server 2008,
    414 to 415

features
  defined, 72
  installing from Initial Configuration Tasks
     screen, 102 to 103
  installing on Windows server core installations,
     134
  removing from Windows server core
     installations, 134
  ways to install, 95
Federation Service, 74
Federation Service Proxy, 74
federation trusts. *See* Active Directory Federation
     Services
Fibre Channel protocol, 15, 266
File Server Resource Manager (FSRM)
  defined, 77
  as File Server role service, 71
  snap-in aspect, 45 to 46, 72
File Server role
  managing in Server Manager, 45 to 46
  role services, 72
  tools for managing, 378 to 380
File Services role
  availability, 91
  defined, 77
  subcomponents, 77
File Transfer Protocol (FTP), 371
File Transfer Protocol (FTP) Management
     Console role service, 82
File Transfer Protocol (FTP) Publishing Service,
     80, 82 to 83
File Transfer Protocol (FTP) Server role service,
     82
The Filing Cabinet blog, 453
Firewall, Windows, 61, 141
Fitzgerald, Eric, 5, 413
Follette, Donovan, 5, 158
font smoothing, 193 to 194
forums, TechNet, 449 to 450
Friedrich, Kurt, 6
FSRM (File Server Resource Manager)
  defined, 77
  as File Server role service, 71
  snap-in aspect, 45 to 46, 72
FTP (File Transfer Protocol), 371
FTP (File Transfer Protocol) Management
     Console role service, 82
FTP (File Transfer Protocol) Server role service,
     82

G
Gajjala, Vijay, 7
GeoClusters, 259 to 261
Goel, Somesh, 6, 194
GPT (GUID Partition Table) disks, 256
granular password policies, 169 to 172
graphic user interface (GUI), Windows server
     core support, 120
Group Policy
  ADMX/ADML files and, 58 to 59
  auditing organizational units, 159 to 161
  Central Store feature, 59
  Comments feature, 58
  enhancements to, 56 to 59
  feature set, 57 to 58
  GPO account lockout settings, 169 to 170
  GPO password policies, 169 to 170
  limiting Federation Service deployment, 184
  for managing Windows server core installations
     remotely, 141 to 142
  relationship to Server Manager, 57
  Search and Filters feature, 57 to 58
  Starter GPOs feature, 58
  Windows server core support, 112
Group Policy Team blog, 452
guest operating systems
  enlightened, 26 to 27
  vs. host operating systems, 19
  legacy, 26, 27
  microkernelized approach, 24
  parent partition and, 25, 25 to 26
GUI, Windows server core support, 120
GUID Partition Table (GPT) disks, 256
Guthrie, Scott, 453

H
Harman, Dan, 5, 53
HBAs (host bus adapters), 400
Health And Diagnostics role service
  defaults, 346
  defined, 81
  subcomponents, 81, 346
health policy validation, NAP support for, 288,
     289
Health Registration Authority (HRA)
  client-side troubleshooting of NAP IPSec
     enforcement, 324 to 326
  defined, 78
  IPSec enforcement and, 292

Health Registration Authority (*continued*)
   role in IPSec enforcement, 292 to 294
   server-side troubleshooting of NAP IPSec
      enforcement, 326 to 330
   setting up, 292
high availability
   ensuring, 14 to 15
   Failover Clustering enhancements, 15
   for file servers, 269 to 273
High Availability Wizard, 270
Hill, Brett, 5, 349, 363
Hill, Tres, 7
Holk, Eric, 5, 198
host bus adapters (HBAs), 400
Host Credential Authorization Protocol, 78
hot-add technologies, Windows Server
     Virtualization vs. Virtual Server, 28, 29
Howard, John, 453
Howard, Michael, 452
HRA Copy Discovery feature, 292
HRA (Health Registration Authority)
   client-side troubleshooting of NAP IPSec
      enforcement, 324 to 326
   defined, 78
   IPSec enforcement and, 292
   role in IPSec enforcement, 292 to 294
   server-side troubleshooting of NAP IPSec
      enforcement, 326 to 330
   setting up, 292
HTTP Activation role service, 75
HTTP Errors role service, 80
HTTP Logging role service, 81
HTTP Redirection role service, 80
HTTP Support, message queuing, 90
HTTPS, 406 to 407
Hui, Wai-O, 7, 326, 331
Hybrid virtualization, 20 to 21
hypervisors
   defined, 21
   microkernelized, 22 to 24
   monolithic, 22
   overview, 21

I

ICT (Initial Configuration Tasks) screen
   illustrated, 40
   installing roles and features from, 97 to 103
   overview, 39 to 42
IDA. *See* Identity and Access Management
Identity and Access Management (IDA)

Active Directory and, 10
   defined, 10
   overview, 149 to 150
   in Windows 2000 Server, 150 to 151
   in Windows Server 2003, 151 to 153
   in Windows Server 2008, 10, 153 to 154
Identity Federation Support role service, 75
Identity Lifecycle Manager (ILM)
   action processes, 156
   approval processes, 156
   attaching processes to events, 157 to 158
   authentication processes, 155 to 156
   overview, 154 to 155
   ways to manage identity, 155 to 158
Identity Management for UNIX, 74
identity selectors, 86
iilreset command, 356 to 357
IIS. *See* Internet Information Services
IIS 6.0 Management Compatibility role service,
   82
IIS 6.0 Management Console role service, 82
IIS 6.0 Metabase Compatibility role service, 82
IIS 6.0 Scripting Tools role service, 82
IIS 6.0 WMI Compatibility role service, 82
IIS Client Certificate Mapping Authentication
   role service, 81
IIS Management Console role service, 82
IIS Management Scripts And Tools role service,
   82
IIS Manager, 351 to 354
ILM. *See* Identity Lifecycle Manager
Incoming Remote Transactions role service, 76
Indexing Service, 77
Initial Configuration Tasks (ICT) screen
   illustrated, 40
   installing roles and features from, 97 to 103
   overview, 39 to 42
inputPath command option, 105 to 106
Internet Information Services (IIS)
   administration tools, 351 to 360
   administration.config file, 361
   anonymous user, 349
   applicationHost.confg file, 360 to 361
   caching modules, 345
   centralized Web farm configuration, 370
   compression modules, 345
   configuration and deployment, 360 to 364
   configuration options, 363
   content modules, 344 to 345

Internet Information Services (IIS) (*continued*)
  defined, 80
  delegated remote administration, 370
  deploying Web applications and services, 14
  diagnostics, 365
  enhanced application pool isolation, 370
  enhancements for Windows Server 2008, 370 to
    371
  evolution, 341
  extensibility, 368 to 369
  Failure Request Tracing, 365 to 368
  FastCGI applications, 371
  HTTP modules, 344
  installing WMI provider in, 359
  integrating ASP.NET with, 348, 369
  IUSR account, 349
  logging and diagnostics modules, 345
  Microsoft Web Administration API, 359 to 360
  modular architecture, 342 to 347
  remote management for, 359
  request processing, 348
  Runtime Status and Control API, 66
  security and patching enhancements, 342 to
    350
  security modules, 344
  server-level configuration files, 364
  URL filtering, 349 to 350
  version 7.0 enhancements overview, 341 to 342
  Web Administration API, 66
  Windows PowerShell and, 66
Internet Printing Client, 89
Internet Server Application Programming
    Interface (ISAPI) Extensions role service,
    81
Internet Server Application Programming
    Interface (ISAPI) Filters role service, 81
Internet Storage Naming Service (iSNS), 89, 401
    to 402
intl.cpl file, 120
IP And Domain Restrictions role service, 81
ipconfig/all command, 121 to 122, 122 to 123
IPSec enforcement
  client-side troubleshooting, 324 to 326
  configuring, 292
  Health Registration Authority and, 292
  how it works, 292
  as NAP enforcement method, 289, 302
  NAP IPSec Clients vs. NAP Servers, 324
  server-side troubleshooting, 326 to 331

IPSec, Windows Server 2008 improvements, 259
ISA Server, combining with TS Gateway, 234 to
    235, 296 to 297
iSCSI Boot Firmware (iBF), 398
iSCSI Initiator. *See* Microsoft iSCSI Initiator
iSCSI protocol, 15, 266, 390 to 391
iSCSI Storage Area Networks (SANs)
  advantages, 392 to 393
  best practices, 394 to 395
  common TCP/IP problems, 395
  inbox support, 391 to 396
  overview, 390 to 391
  performance considerations, 393, 396
  remote boot feature, 397 to 400
  security considerations, 393 to 394
iSNS (Internet Storage Naming Service), 89, 401
    to 402

J
Jain, Kapil, 6, 317
Jain, Samir, 6, 405, 407

K
Kalra, Manish, 6
Kasheff, Zardosht, 7, 200
KDCs (Key Distribution Centers), 164 to 165
Kelnar, Tom, 7, 334
Key Distribution Centers (KDCs), 164 to 165
Key Management Service (KMS), 432, 433, 433 to
    434, 434 to 438
Key Service Providers (KSPs), 180, 181
Krishnan, Amith, 5
KSPs (Key Service Providers), 180, 181
Kumar, Ajay, 4, 239

L
Lake, Claudia, 5, 369
Langworthy, Emily, 5, 390, 397, 400, 402
legacy guest operating systems, 26, 27
Licensing Diagnosis tool, 241 to 243
Licensing Manager
  configuring Terminal Server License Server, 238
    to 239
  Revoke CAL option, 240 to 241
licensing, virtualization, 35
Liebendorfer, Craig, 5
Linux, as guest OS in child partition, 28
Lissoir, Alain, 4, 64

live migration, Windows Server Virtualization vs. Virtual Server, 29
load balancing, third-party, 248. *See also* Network Load Balancing
Local Session Manager (LSM), 202
local terminals, defined, 204
Logging Tools role service, 81
London, Kevin, 6, 231, 232
Lotlikar, Mahesh, 6, 209, 214
Lowe, David, 5
LPR Port Monitor, 89
LSM (Local Session Manager), 202
Lumba, Piyush, 6

M

majority quorum model, 254 to 255
Majumdar, Moon, 6, 167
MAK (Multiple Activation Key), 432, 433
Management Service role service, 82, 359
Management Tools role service
  defaults, 347
  defined, 80, 82
  subcomponents, 82
Mas, Marcelo, 6, 185
Mason, Andrew, 5, 120, 130, 136, 140, 452
Mayfield, Paul, 6
Mehta, Yogesh, 7, 180
Melo, Eduardo, 5, 96, 107
Menzel, George, 5, 419
Message Queuing
  defined, 89
  Message Queuing DCOM Proxy, 90
  Message Queuing Services, 89 to 90
  Message Queuing Triggers, 90
  overview, 89
  subcomponents, 89 to 90
Message Queuing Activation, 75
Metadirectory Services. *See* MMS
Michael Howard's Web log, 452
microkernelized hypervisors, 22 to 24
Microsoft Connect, 422, 443 to 445
Microsoft Developer Network (MSDN), 451 to 452, 454
Microsoft Device Specific Modules (DSMs), 90, 388 to 389
Microsoft Download Center, 442 to 443
Microsoft Identity Integration Server (MIIS), 152
Microsoft Intermediate Language (MIL), 85

Microsoft iSCSI Initiator
  benefits, 391
  configuration, 396
  deployment, 396
  features, 392
  installing, 391
  overview, 390 to 391
Microsoft Metadirectory Services (MMS), 151
Microsoft MPIO. *See* MPIO
Microsoft Online Responder, 178
Microsoft POS for .NET 1.1 device redirection, 199
Microsoft Press books, 454 to 455
Microsoft Simple Certificate Enrollment Protocol, 73
Microsoft Solution Accelerator for Business Desktop Deployment, 11, 431
Microsoft Solution Accelerator for Windows Server Deployment, 431
Microsoft TechNet
  Beta Central, 421
  chats, 448 to 449
  columns, 451
  defined, 445
  Flash newsletter, 451
  forums, 449 to 450
  magazine, 451
  subscription, 421
  URL, 445
  user groups, 450
  webcasts, 446 to 447
Microsoft Visual Studio, 86
Microsoft Web Administration API, 359 to 360
Microsoft Windows Server 2008. *See* Windows Server 2008
Microsoft Windows Server TechCenter, 442
migrating clusters from Windows Server 2003 to Windows Server 2008, 273
MIIS (Microsoft Identity Integration Server), 152
MIL (Microsoft Intermediate Language), 85
MMC snap-ins. *See also* Server Manager
  ADSI Edit, 170, 175
  Certificates, 181
  Disk Management, 146, 273
  Failover Cluster Management, 258, 268 to 269, 270
  File Server Resource Manager, 45 to 46

MMC snap-ins (*continued*)
   NAP Client Configuration, 317 to 318
   Network Policy Server, 307 to 316
   PKIView, 179
   Shared Folders, 46
   Storage Explorer, 384 to 386
   Terminal Services Configuration, 193, 241 to
      243, 244, 247
   tools for administering Windows server core
      installations remotely, 140 to 141
   TS Gateway Management, 236
   TS RemoteApp Manager, 139, 217 to 219
   Virtualization Management Console, 36
   Windows Server Backup, 381 to 382
MMS (Microsoft Metadirectory Services), 151
mobile users, TS support for, 13 to 14
monitors, spanned, 193
monolithic hypervisors, 22
Morello, John, 6, 235, 297, 307
Morgan, Suzanne, 7, 390, 397, 400, 402
MPIO (Multipath I/O), 15, 90, 387 to 390
MSDN (Microsoft Developer Network), 451 to
   452, 454
MSDN subscription, 421
msDS-LockoutDuration attribute, 171
msDS-LockoutObservationWindow attribute,
   171
msDS-LockoutThreshold attribute, 171
msDS-MaximumPasswordAge attribute, 171
msDS-MinimumPasswordAge attribute, 171
msDS-MinimumPasswordLength attribute, 171
msDS-PasswordComplexityEnabled attribute,
   171
msDS-PasswordHistoryLength attribute, 170
msDS-PasswordReversibleEncryptionEnabled
   attribute, 170
msDS-PasswordSettingsPrecedence attribute, 170
msDS-PSOApplied attribute, 171
msDS-PSOAppliesTo attribute, 171
msDS-Resultant PSO attribute, 172
MSMQ Server, 89
.msu files, 136
Multicasting Support, message queuing, 90
Multipath I/O (MPIO), 15, 90, 387 to 390
multipathing, defined, 387
Multiple Activation Key (MAK), 432, 433
Muralidharan, Harini, 5, 294, 326, 331

N
NAC. *See* Network Access Control
Named Pipes Activation, 75
NAP. *See* Network Access Protection
NAP Client Configuration snap-in, 317 to 318
NAP Server, defined, 324
Nath, Satyajit, 6, 410
NDES (Network Device Enrollment Service), 177
.NET Environment, Windows Process Activation
   Service, 93
.NET Extensibility role service, 80
.NET Framework 2.0 extensibility, 86
.NET Framework 3.0
   CardSpace feature, 86
   class libraries, 85
   common language runtime, 85
   defined, 83 to 84
   list of components, 372
   list of subcomponents, 84
   Microsoft Intermediate Language, 85
   overview, 84 to 86
   presentation subsystem, 86
   as Windows Server feature, 72
   Workflow Foundation feature, 86 to 87
.NET Remoting and Enterprise Services, 87
NetBIOS protocol, 259
Network Access Control (NAC)
   defined, 287, 288
   infrastructure support for processes, 288 to 289
   as platform, 287
   port-based, 291
   vendor support, 287
Network Access Protection (NAP)
   architectural overview, 297 to 298
   choosing enforcement methods, 302 to 304
   client layers, 298 to 299
   combining with TS Gateway, 235, 297
   configuring clients, 317 to 318
   configuring NPS, 307 to 317
   defined, 10 to 11
   delayed enforcement, 303
   deploying, 304 to 305
   deploying Windows Server 2008 on, 42
   diagnostic overview, 319 to 323
   enforcement methods, 289 to 292, 304 to 305
   event logging, 322 to 323
   how it works, 299 to 301
   immediate enforcement, 304
   implementing, 301 to 304

Network Access Protection (NAP) (*continued*)
  limiting access to network resources, 288, 289
  managing policy exceptions, 306 to 307
  need for, 286
  overview, 287 to 288
  phased implementation, 303 to 304
  remediation phase, 288 to 289, 303
  Reporting Only phase, 303
  troubleshooting, 319 to 339
  TS Gateway support, 233 to 234
Network Access Quarantine Control, 287
Network Auto Discovery, 25 to 29
Network Device Enrollment Service (NDES), 177
Network Level Authentication (NLA), 191 to 192, 212
Network Load Balancing Manager, 279
Network Load Balancing (NLB)
  adding health monitoring to applications, 280 to 281
  availability, 91
  defined, 90
  enhancements in Windows Server 2008, 15, 247, 278 to 280
  as form of clustering, 252
  IPv6 support for servers, 279
  troubleshooting, 281 to 282
  in Windows Server 2003, 247
Network Policy And Access Services role
  adding Network Policy Server role service, 299
  availability, 91
  defined, 77
  subcomponents, 77 to 78
Network Policy Server (NPS)
  adding when implementing TS Gateway, 235
  configuring by using MMC snap-in, 307 to 316
  defined, 77 to 78
  HRA and, 292
  in NAP architecture, 297, 299
  programmatic configuration, 316 to 317
  subcomponents, 299
networks, Windows Server 2008 improvements, 402 to 407
newsgroups, TechNet, 450
NLA (Network Level Authentication), 191 to 192, 212
NLB (Network Load Balancing)
  adding health monitoring to applications, 280 to 281
  availability, 91

defined, 90
enhancements in Windows Server 2008, 15, 247, 278 to 280
  as form of clustering, 252
  IPv6 support for servers, 279
  troubleshooting, 281 to 282
  in Windows Server 2003, 247
Notepad, on Windows server core installations, 113 to 114
notification actions, 157
NPS. *See* Network Policy Server
Nukala, Chandra, 5, 323, 339

O

OAR (Owner Access Restriction), 410
oclist.exe tool, 131 to 132, 133, 134
ODBC Logging role service, 81
Olson, Jason, 5, 348, 360, 453
Online Certificate Status Protocol (OCSP), 73, 177 to 178
Online Responder, 178
operating systems. *See also* Windows Server 2008
  creating child partitions, 28
  enlightened guest, 26 to 27
  guest vs. host, 19
  legacy guest, 26, 27
  Windows Server Virtualization features, 28
Outgoing Remote Transactions role service, 76
Owner Access Restriction (OAR), 410

P

parent partition, 25 to 26
partitions
  child with enlightened guest, 26 to 27
  child with guest running Linux, 28
  child with legacy guest, 27
  defined, 21
  drivers in, 22 to 23, 23 to 24
  in microkernelized hypervisor, 23, 23 to 24
  parent, 25 to 26
password policies
  granular, 169 to 172
  msDS-LockoutDuration attribute, 171
  msDS-LockoutObservationWindow attribute, 171
  msDS-LockoutThreshold attribute, 171
  msDS-MaximumPasswordAge attribute, 171
  msDS-MinimumPasswordAge attribute, 171
  msDS-MinimumPasswordLength attribute, 171

password policies (*continued*)
   msDS-PasswordComplexityEnabled attribute, 171
   msDS-PasswordHistoryLength attribute, 170
   msDS-PasswordReversibleEncryptionEnabled attribute, 170
   msDS-PasswordSettingsPrecedence attribute, 170
   msDS-PSOApplied attribute, 171
   msDS-PSOAppliesTo attribute, 171
   msDS-Resultant PSO attribute, 172
password settings objects (PSOs), 171
Password Synchronization, 74
patch management, 135 to 136, 145
Patel, Kalpesh, 6
PEAP authentication, 291, 332, 334
PEAP-MS-CHAP authentication protocol, 291
PEAP-TLS authentication protocol, 291
Peer Name Resolution Protocol (PNRP), 90
Performance Monitor, 396
Performance Services role service
   defaults, 347
   defined, 82
   subcomponents, 82
Pierson, Nick, 6, 183, 184, 185
piping commands, 65
PKI (public key interface)
   certificate revocation checking, 177 to 178, 185
   Enterprise PKI tool, 179
   troubleshooting, 179 to 180
PKIView snap-in, 179
Plug And Play (PnP)
   redirecting PnP devices, 196 to 198
   Windows server core installation support, 135
PNRP (Peer Name Resolution Protocol), 90
Point-to-Point Protocol (PPP), 291
port-based network access control, 291
PowerShell. *See* Windows PowerShell
PPP (Point-to-Point Protocol), 291
Prasad, Rahul, 6, 115, 139
presentations. *See* Windows Presentation Foundation
Print Services
   availability, 91
   defined, 78
   role services, 78
printer redirection, 199 to 200
Process Model, Windows Process Activation Service, 93

Provision A Shared Folder Wizard, 15, 380
Provision Storage Wizard, 15, 379
PSOs (password settings objects), 171

Q
quarantine agents (QAs), 298
quarantine server (QS), 299
quorum disks, 254 to 256

R
RADIUS, 253 to 254, 308 to 309
Ralston, Ward, 7
RAM, for Windows server core installations, 145
RDC. *See* Remote Desktop Connection
Read-Only Domain Controllers (RODCs)
   as branch-office solution, 164 to 165
   dcpromo support for, 166
   defined, 13, 164
   installation options for DNS Servers, 166 to 167
   as Key Distribution Centers, 164 to 165
   local administrator role, 165
   Windows server core installation support, 145
redirecting
   PnP devices, 196 to 198
   print jobs, 199 to 200
regedit.exe tool
   configuring display resolution for Windows server core installations, 130
   presence on Windows server core installations, 113
remediation servers, 290
Remote Access Service role service, 78
Remote Application Publishing, 139
Remote Assistance feature, 90
remote booting, 397 to 400
Remote Desktop Connection (RDC)
   connecting to Windows server core installation, 112
   desktop composition, 196
   display data prioritization, 195
   display improvements, 193 to 195
   enabling by using unattended installation, 211
   enabling on Windows server core installations, 112
   enhancements to user's desktop experience, 195 to 196
   font smoothing feature, 193 to 194
   Network Level Authentication support, 191 to 192

Remote Desktop Connection (RDC) (*continued*)
  overview, 191
  Security Layer setting, 212
  Server Authentication support, 192
  support for PnP device redirection, 196 to 197
  in TS Gateway enforcement, 295
  user authentication, 211 to 212
Remote Desktop Protocol (RDP), 212, 230, 231
Remote Installation Services (RIS), 424, 430 to 431
remote management, IIS, 359, 370
Remote Server Administration Tools (RSAT)
  defined, 53 to 54, 91, 140
  feature administration tools, 91
  list of features, 54
  list of roles, 54
  list of tools, 91
  overview, 91
  role administration tools, 91
  Windows server core installation limitations, 145
remote terminals, defined, 204
remoting technologies
  as part of domains, 62
  role of Server Manager CLI, 107
  Windows Remote Management, 12, 107, 142
  in workgroups, 62 to 64
Removable Storage Manager (RSM), 92
request events, 157
Request Filtering role service, 81, 349, 349 to 350
Request Monitor role service, 81
resolution, display, configuring on Windows server core installations, 129 to 130
Restartable Active Directory Domain Services (AD DS), 13, 168 to 169
Rhodes, Kevin, 6, 305
Rights Management Service (RMS), 151 to 152. *See also* Active Directory Rights Management Services
RIS (Remote Installation Services), 424, 430 to 431
RMS (Windows Rights Management Service), 151 to 152. *See also* Active Directory Rights Management Services
Robbins, Thom, 7, 88
RODCs. *See* Read-Only Domain Controllers
role services
  for Active Directory Certificate Services, 73
  for Active Directory Domain Services, 73 to 74

  for Active Directory Federation Services, 74
  for Active Directory Lightweight Directory Services, 74
  for Active Directory Rights Management Services, 74 to 75
  for Application Server, 75 to 76
  available to install on Windows Server 2008, 72 to 83
  defined, 71
  for DHCP Server, 76
  for DNS Server, 76
  examples, 71
  for Fax Server, 76
  for File Server, 72
  for File Services, 77
  installing on server, 95 to 107
  for Network Policy and Access Services, 77 to 78
  for Print Services, 78
  for Terminal Services, 79, 209 to 210
  for UDDI Services, 79
  for Web Server (IIS), 80 to 82
  for Windows Deployment Services, 83
  for Windows SharePoint Services, 83
roles. *See* server roles
Routing and Remote Access blog, 452
Routing and Remote Access Services, 78
Routing role service, 78
Routing Service, message queuing, 90
Roybal, Isaac, 5
RPC Over HTTP Proxy, 92, 235
RSAT. *See* Remote Server Administration Tools
RSM (Removable Storage Manager), 92

S
SACL (system access control list), 159
Sadler, Jez, 5, 431
Sampath, Sriram, 7, 202, 203, 249
SANs. *See* iSCSI Storage Area Networks
SAS protocol, 15
SCEP (Simple Certificate Enrollment Protocol), 177
Schutz, Mike, 6
ScottGu's blog, 453
scregedit.wsf script, 126 to 129, 143 to 144
scripting, Windows Server Virtualization vs. Virtual Server support, 29. *See also* Windows PowerShell
SCSI Inquiry data, 258

SCW (Security Configuration Wizard), 47, 49 to 50

SDO (Server Data Objects) API, 316

Secure Socket Layer (SSL), 406

Secure Socket Tunneling Protocol (SSTP), 404 to 407

security
  enhancements to Internet Information Services, 342 to 350
  ensuring policy compliance, 10 to 11
  improvements in Windows Server 2008, 407 to 413
  weaknesses in monolithic hypervisor model, 22

Security Configuration Wizard (SCW), 47, 49 to 50

Security Services role service
  defaults, 347
  defined, 81
  subcomponents, 81

self-healing disks, 257, 258

Sen, Siddhartha, 6, 281

Server Authentication, 192

server clusters, 15

server consolidation, 18

Server Core blog, 452

Server Data Objects (SDO) API, 316

server draining, 248 to 249

Server for Network Information Service, 74

Server Manager
  Add Feature wizard, 196
  as all-in-one tool, 47
  command-line interface, 107
  command-line version, 50 to 53
  vs. Computer Management, 42, 48
  defined, 12
  handling installer technologies, 96
  home page, 43
  installing roles and features by using, 104
  installing secure-by-default roles, 47
  managing file server, 45 to 46
  managing server roles, 44 to 47
  overview, 42 to 43
  relationship of SCW to, 50
  vs. Security Configuration Wizard, 47
  vs. System Center, 47

Server Message Block (SMB) protocol, 386 to 387

server roles. *See also individual role names*
  Active Directory Certificate Services (AD CS), 73
  Active Directory Domain Services (AD DS), 73 to 74
  Active Directory Federation Services (AD FS), 74
  Active Directory Lightweight Directory Services (AD LDS), 74
  Active Directory Rights Management Services (AD RMS), 74 to 75
  Application Server, 75 to 76
  consolidating multiple roles as separate virtual machines, 18
  defined, 71
  DHCP Server, 76
  DNS Server, 76
  enabling administration, 91
  examples, 71
  Fax Server, 76
  File Services, 77
  installing by using Server Manager, 47
  installing from command line on Windows server core installations, 131 to 134
  installing from Initial Configuration Tasks screen, 97 to 101
  list of those available to install on Windows Server 2008, 72 to 83
  Network Policy and Access Services, 77 to 78
  Print Services, 78
  secure by default, 47
  support for, 71 to 72
  Terminal Services, 79, 209 to 210
  UDDI Services, 79
  ways to install, 95
  Web Server (IIS), 80 to 82
  Windows Deployment Services, 83
  Windows SharePoint Services, 83

Server Side Includes role service, 81

ServerManagerCmd.exe tool
  automating common deployment tasks by using, 52 to 53
  defined, 50
  installing roles and features by using, 105 to 107
  what it can do, 50 to 51
  what it can't do, 51

Service Oriented Architecture (SOA), 87

Services for Network File System (NFS), 77

session 0 isolation, 202 to 203
Session Broker. *See* TS Session Broker
sessions
  administrative, 206 to 209
  console, 205 to 206
  defined, 204
  disconnected, 204 to 205
  overview, 204
  reconnecting, 205
  terminals for, 204 to 205
  user vs. administrative, 207 to 208
Shammugam, Harish Kumar Poongan, 5, 241, 243
Share And Storage Management snap-in, 15, 378 to 379
shared disk quorum model, 254
Shared Folders snap-in, 46
shared storage, 255
SHAs (system health agents), 298
Shastri, Suryanarayana, 7, 415, 417
Shekel, Oded, 6, 177, 178, 181, 182
shells. *See* Windows PowerShell
shimming architecture, 114 to 115
SHVs (system health validators)
  configuring, 312 to 315
  defined, 299
  troubleshooting, 337
Simon-Weidner, Ulf B., 7, 166, 172, 453
Simple Certificate Enrollment Protocol (SCEP), 177
Simple Network Management Protocol (SNMP) Services, 92
Simple SAN Management, 91
Simple TCP/IP Services, 92
Single Instance Store, 77
single sign-on (SSO), 200 to 201
slmgr.vbs script, 125 to 126
Sloss, Joel, 5
SMB (Server Message Block) protocol, 386 to 387
SMfS (Storage Manager for SANs), 92, 384
Smith, Aaron, 4, 439
SMTP Server, 91, 92
SNMP Service, defined, 92
SNMP Services
  defined, 92
  SNMP Service, 92
  SNMP WMI Provider, 92

Snover, Jeffrey, 5, 65, 68
SOA (Service Oriented Architecture), 87
SoftGrid Application Virtualization, 36 to 37
Solution Accelerator for Business Desktop Deployment, 431
Solution Accelerator for Windows Server Deployment, 431
Somendra, Aruna, 5, 246
spanned monitors, 193
Spanning Tree Protocol, 400
SSL (Secure Socket Layer), 406
SSO (single sign-on), 200 to 201
Staples, Bill, 5, 66
Static Content role service, 80
Steve Schofield's Weblog, 454
Storage Area Networks (SANs). *See* iSCSI Storage Area Networks
Storage Explorer, 15, 384 to 386
Storage Manager for SANs (SMfS), 92, 384
storage technologies
  persistent reservations and, 256
  shared, 255
  Windows Server 2008 enhancements, 256 to 257
Subsystem for UNIX-based Applications (SUA), 93
Success auditing, 159, 162
Sullivan, Kevin, 6, 59
system access control list (SACL), 159
System Center products, 31, 47 to 48, 68
System Center Virtual Machine Manager
  overview, 36
  suggested uses, 36
  Web portal, 36
  Windows PowerShell and, 36
  Windows Server Virtualization vs. Virtual Server, 29
system health agents (SHAs), 298
system health validators (SHVs)
  configuring, 312 to 315
  defined, 299
  troubleshooting, 337
System Monitor, 396

T

TAP (Technical Adoption Program), 422
Task Manager
  opening Windows Server Core command
    window, 112
  viewing Desktop Experience results, 224 to 225
TCP Activation, 75
TCP Port Sharing, 75
TechCenter, 442
TechNet. *See* Microsoft TechNet
TechNet Magazine, 451
Technical Adoption Program (TAP), 422
Telnet Client, 93
Telnet Server, 93
Templin, Reagan, 6, 354, 357, 364
Teo, Soo Kuan, 6, 245
Terminal Server License Server, 238 to 239
Terminal Server role service
  defined, 79
  installing, 209
Terminal Services
  availability, 91
  basic enhancements in Windows Server 2008,
    190 to 210
  Client Access Licenses, 238 to 241
  core engine improvements, 202
  desktop enhancements, 195 to 196
  Easy Print, 199 to 200
  font-smoothing feature, 193 to 194
  improvements to, 13 to 14
  installing and managing, 209 to 216
  installing role from command line, 105
  logging off sessions, 139 to 140
  managing sessions by using Server Manager
    console, 215 to 216
  managing sessions from command line, 140
  managing Windows server core installations
    remotely, 137 to 138
  overview, 79
  redirecting PnP devices, 196 to 198
  relationship of Windows System Resource
    Manager to, 246 to 247
  Remote Desktop Connection, 191 to 197
  RemoteApp feature, 14, 216 to 226
  restarting command prompt, 140
  role management tools, 215
  role services, 79
  session 0 isolation, 202 to 203
  session issues, 203 to 209
  single sign-on (SSO), 200 to 201

  unattended setup, 210 to 214
  using with Windows server core, 139 to 140
  Web Access feature, 14
  WMI Provider, 243 to 246
Terminal Services Configuration snap-in, 193,
    241, 244
Terminal Services Team blog, 453
TFTP (Trivial File Transfer Protocol), 93, 427 to
    429
time, setting on Windows server core
    installations, 119
time zone, setting on Windows server core
    installations, 119, 120
Timon, Chuck, 5, 261, 265, 269, 278
Titus, Tobin, 7, 359
Tracing role service, 81
transition events, 157
Transport Server role service, 83
troubleshooting
  802.1X enforcement, 331 to 334
  client-side IPSec enforcement, 324 to 326
  clusters and clustering, 273 to 274
  NAP overview, 319 to 323
  Network Load Balancing, 281 to 282
  Network Policy Server for PEAP-based NAP, 335
    to 339
  PKI (public key interface), 179 to 180
  server-side IPSec enforcement, 326 to 331
  system health validators, 337
  TS Licensing, 241 to 243
trusts, federation. *See* Active Directory Federation
    Services
TS Easy Print, 199 to 200
TS Gateway
  adding role service, 235
  benefits, 237
  best practices, 238
  combining with ISA Server, 234 to 235
  combining with NAP, 235
  configuring clients for SSO, 201
  creating authorization policies for, 236 to 237
  defined, 14, 79, 210, 232
  how it works, 233
  implementing, 235 to 237
  installing, 55
  as NAP enforcement method, 289, 294 to 297
  overview, 232 to 233
  support for NAP, 233 to 234
  vs. VPNs, 232, 234
TS Gateway Management snap-in, 236, 237

TS License Server
    scope of automatic discovery, 213 to 214
    troubleshooting, 242 to 243
TS Licensing
    CAL revocation, 240 to 241
    configuring Terminal Server License Server after
        installation, 238 to 239
    database folder, 214
    defined, 79, 210
    device-based, 238, 240 to 241
    Per-User mode, 238, 240
    purpose, 238
    troubleshooting, 241 to 243
TS Licensing Manager, 214
TS RemoteApp
    benefits, 225 to 226
    best practices, 226
    defined, 14
    integration with TS Web Access, 226 to 227
    relationship to TS Web Access, 227 to 228
TS Session Broker, 79, 210, 247 to 249
TS Web Access
    benefits, 232
    configuring data source, 228 to 230
    creating on non-default Web site, 231 to 232
    defined, 14, 79, 210
    integration with TS Remote App, 226 to 227
    multiple remote desktops for, 230 to 231
    overview, 226 to 230
    relationship to TS RemoteApp, 227 to 228
TS Web Access Web site, 214
TS Web Client Web site, 214
TSG_QEC, 295
Tulloch, Mitch, 2
Turnbull, Scott, 6
Type 1 virtualization
    architecture, 21
    microkernelized, 22 to 24
    monolithic, 22
    overview, 21
Type 2 virtualization, 20

U

UAC (User Account Control), 60, 61, 145
UDDI (Universal Description, Discovery, and
        Integration) Services, 79
Unattend.xml file, 210 to 214
Ureche, Tony, 7, 409
URL Authorization role service, 81

User Account Control (UAC), 60, 61, 145
User-Mode Device Framework, 198

V

V3 certificate templates, 180 to 181
Validate A Configuration Wizard, 262 to 265
Vanniarajan, Kadirvel C., 6, 405, 407
Victor, Nisha, 6
Vidali, Ram, 323
Virtual Labs, 448
Virtual Machine Monitor (VMM), 20 to 21
Virtual Machine Service (VM Service), 26
Virtual Machine Worker Process (VM Service), 26
virtual machines
    consolidating multiple server roles, 18
    guest vs. host operating systems, 19
    managing in Windows Server 2008, 29 to 30
    process vs. system, 21
    Windows Server Virtualization features, 28
    Windows Server Virtualization vs. Virtual
        Server, 29
Virtual PC, 25 to 26
virtual private networks (VPNs)
    enforcement and, 303
    how NAP works, 299 to 301
    as NAP enforcement method, 289, 290 to 291
    new type of tunnel, 404 to 407
    vs. TS Gateway, 232, 234
    as way to provide remote access to clients, 290
        to 291
Virtual Server, 28, 29
virtualization
    background, 9
    consolidating multiple server roles, 18
    consolidation candidates, 33 to 34
    deploying, 31 to 34
    guest vs. host operating systems, 19
    Hybrid model, 20 to 21
    infrastructure planning, 34
    licensing issues, 35
    optimizing placement, 34
    role in ensuring application compatibility, 19
    role in ensuring business continuity, 18 to 19
    role in provisioning workloads, 19 to 20
    role in testing new platforms, 19
    server solution areas, 32 to 33
    sizing environment, 32 to 34
    SoftGrid Application Virtualization, 36 to 37
    System Center Virtual Machine Manager, 36

virtualization (*continued*)
Type 1, 21 to 24
Type 2, 20
in Windows Server 2008, 24 to 28
Virtualization Management Console snap-in, 36
Virtualization Service Client (VSC), 26 to 27
Virtualization Service Provider (VSP), 25 to 26, 27
Vista. *See* Windows Vista
Visual Studio, 86
VL (Volume Licensing), 433
VM Service (Virtual Machine Service), 26
VMBus, 26, 27
VMM (Virtual Machine Monitor), 20 to 21
Volume Activation
defined, 12, 432
deploying in Windows Server 2008, 432 to 439
key management service, 432
multiple activation keys, 432
types of keys, 432
Volume Licensing (VL), 433
Volume Shadow Copy Service (VSS), 28, 257
VPNs (virtual private networks)
enforcement and, 303
how NAP works, 299 to 301
as NAP enforcement method, 289, 290 to 291
new type of tunnel, 404 to 407
vs. TS Gateway, 232, 234
as way to provide remote access to clients, 290 to 291
VSC (Virtualization Service Client), 26 to 27
VSP (Virtualization Service Provider), 25 to 26, 27
VSS (Volume Shadow Copy Service), 28, 257

W

Waxman, Peter, 6
Wbemtest.exe tool, 245
WCF (Windows Communication Foundation), 84, 87 to 88
WDS. *See* Windows Deployment Services
Web Application Development role service, 80 to 81
Web applications and services, deploying, 14
Web enrollment, 177
Web farms, centralized configuration, 370
Web Proxy Cache, Online Responder, 178

Web Server (IIS) role
adding when implementing TS Gateway, 235
availability, 91
default installation, 346 to 347
defined, 80
IIS modular architecture, 342 to 347
installing by using ServerManagerCmd.exe, 105
removing by using ServerManagerCmd.exe, 105
as requirement for running TS Web Access, 227
role services, 80 to 82
Web Server (IIS) Support role service, 75
Web Server role service
defined, 80
Management Tools subcomponent, 80, 82
subcomponents, 80 to 82
Web Services (WS-*), 10, 88
webcasts, TechNet, 446 to 447
wevtutil.exe command, 136 to 137
WF (Windows Workflow Foundation), 86 to 87
WF (Workflow Foundation), 86 to 87
whatif command option, 105
Wilenzick, Mike, 6
Windows 2000 Client Support, message queuing, 90
Windows 2000 Server, 150 to 151
Windows Auditing, 411 to 413
Windows Authentication role service, 81
Windows Automated Installation Kit (Windows AIK), 19 to 20
Windows CardSpace, 86
Windows clock, Windows server core installations and, 146
Windows Communication Foundation (WCF), 84, 87 to 88
Windows Core Networking blog, 453
Windows Deployment Services (WDS)
availability, 91
client components, 424
custom network profiles, 426 to 427
defined, 11, 83
enhancements to RIS, 424, 430 to 431
management components, 424
multicast deployment, 424 to 427
server components, 424
TFTP windowing, 427 to 429
types of components, 423 to 424
using to deploy Windows server core installations, 145
x64 EFI network boot support, 430

Windows Fax Server
  accounts model, 416 to 417
  availability, 91
  defined, 76
  private mode, 414, 415
  public mode, 414, 415
  Reassign setting, 414, 415
Windows Firewall, 61, 141
Windows Installer, 220 to 222
Windows Internal Database, 93
Windows Management Instrumentation (WMI)
  DCOM security, 61
  defined, 59
  enhanced security features, 60
  firewall issues, 61
  improved tracing and logging, 60
  manageable entities and, 62
  namespace security, 60, 61
  remote connection, 60 to 64
  as remoting technology, 107
  on Windows server core installations, 112 to
    113
  Windows Vista enhancements to, 12 to 13, 59 to
    60
Windows Portable Devices, 196
Windows PowerShell
  command consistency, 65
  defined, 12
  for IIS administration, 66, 357 to 359
  as multitool for managing Application Servers,
    374
  overview, 64, 373 to 374
  piping commands, 65
  System Center Virtual Machine Manager and, 36
  uses for, 64
  Windows server core installations and, 131
Windows PowerShell blog, 452
Windows Presentation Foundation (WPF), 86
Windows Process Activation Service Support role
    service, 75
Windows Process Activation Service (WPAS)
  defined, 93
  functionality, 347, 347 to 348
  overview, 93, 347
  as requirement for running TS Web Access, 227
  as requirement for running Web Server (IIS),
    347
  subcomponents, 93 to 94

Windows Remote Management (WinRM)
  defined, 12
  for managing Windows server core installations
    remotely, 142
  as remoting technology, 107
Windows Remote Shell (WinRS), 12, 142, 145 to
    146
Windows Rights Management Service (RMS), 151
    to 152. *See also* Active Directory Rights
    Management Services
Windows Search Service, 77
Windows Server 2003
  Administration Tools Pack, 53
  File Services, 77
  identity and access in, 151 to 153
  migrating clusters to Windows Server 2008, 273
  Remote Administration mode, 208
  Terminal Server mode, 208
Windows Server 2008
  Active Directory and, 4, 149 to 186
  architecture and Windows Server Virtualization,
    24 to 25, 25 to 28
  available features to install, 83 to 94
  Component Based Servicing architecture, 95 to
    96
  core enhancements to Terminal Services, 190 to
    210
  deploying, 421 to 440
  enhancements to Active Directory Certificate
    Services, 176 to 182
  enhancements to Active Directory Rights
    Management Services, 186
  IDA and, 10, 153 to 154
  IIS 7.0 enhancements, 370 to 371
  improved import/export functionality using
    Active Directory Federation Services, 183
  improvements to Terminal Services, 13 to 14
  initial configuration tasks, 39 to 42
  installing, 422 to 423
  installing minimal subset. *See* Windows server
    core
  licensing issues, 35
  managing virtual machines, 29 to 30
  manual installation, 422 to 423
  Microsoft product home Web page, 441
  Microsoft Windows Server TechCenter, 442
  networking improvements, 402 to 407
  new and improved tools, 12 to 13
  new features and feature enhancements, 3 to 4

Windows Server 2008 (*continued*)
    new Group Policy functionality, 56 to 59
    new storage features and enhancements, 15
    obtaining, 421 to 422
    password and account lockout policies, 169 to 172
    pre-release aspect, 1 to 3
    product groups and server editions, 433 to 436
    reasons for deploying, 9 to 16
    Remote Server Administration Tools, 53 to 55
    SCW improvements, 49 to 50
    security improvements, 407 to 413
    storage improvements, 378 to 402
    team members, 4 to 7
    three pillars, 3
    unattended installation, 423
    virtualization in, 24 to 28
    Volume Activation feature, 12, 432 to 439
    Windows Deployment Services, 11, 423 to 431
Windows Server Backup
    command-line utility, 383 to 384
    defined, 94
    MMC snap-in, 381 to 382
    vs. NT Backup, 384
    overview, 381 to 382
Windows server core installation
    activating server, 125
    advantages, 115 to 116
    changing server name, 123
    command-line tools, 112
    configuring display resolution, 129 to 130
    configuring networking, 121 to 123
    defined, 111
    enabling automatic updates, 126 to 129
    enabling Remote Desktop, 112
    GUI support, 120
    included and excluded roles and features, 116 to 117
    initial configuration, 118 to 119
    initial screen, 110
    as installation option, 11, 25, 28, 30 to 31
    installing applications, 135
    joining domain, 124
    managing from command line, 130 to 131
    managing servers remotely by using Terminal Services, 137 to 138
    minimizing disk and servicing footprint, 114 to 115
    opening command window by using Task Manager, 112
    patch management, 135 to 136, 145
    PowerShell and, 131
    rationale, 115 to 116
    servicing, 136
    system requirements, 145
    Terminal Services and, 139 to 140
    tips for running installations, 144 to 146
    ways to manage, 130 to 136
    what is installed, 111 to 114
    what is not installed, 111
    vs. Windows Server 2008, 145
    WMI infrastructure on, 112 to 113
Windows Server Division Weblog, 452
Windows Server Failover Clustering (WSFC). *See* Failover Clustering
Windows Server Update Service (WSUS), 135
Windows Server Virtualization
    features, 28 to 29
    pass-through disk access, 27
    Server Core installation and, 31
    significance, 16
    testing technologies, 24
    vs. Virtual Server, 29
    Windows Server 2008 architecture and, 24 to 25, 25 to 28
Windows SharePoint Services role, 83
    installing by using ServerManagerCmd.exe tool, 106 to 107
Windows System Resource Manager (WSRM)
    availability, 91
    benefits of installing on terminal servers, 246 to 247
    defined, 94, 246
    Windows Server Virtualization support, 28
Windows Token-Based Agent, 74
Windows Virtualization Team blog, 453
Windows Vista, deploying, 19 to 20
Windows Workflow Foundation (WF), 86 to 87
WinRM (Windows Remote Management)
    defined, 12
    for managing Windows server core installations remotely, 142
    as remoting technology, 107
WinRS (Windows Remote Shell), 12, 142, 145 to 146
WINS Server, 91, 94
Wireless Networking, 94

wizards
 Active Directory Installation Wizard, 165 to 166
 Active Directory Lightweight Directory Services
  Setup Wizard (AD LDS), 173 to 176
 Add Feature Wizard, 54, 102 to 103
 Add Roles Wizard, 98 to 101
 Configure Quorum Settings Wizard, 256
 Create A shared Folder Wizard, 271
 High Availability Wizard, 270
 Provision A Shared Folder Wizard, 15, 380
 Provision Storage Wizard, 15, 379
 Security Configuration Wizard, 47, 49 to 50
 Validate A Configuration Wizard, 262 to 265
WMI Provider
 accessing SNMP information, 92
 installing in IIS 7.0, 359
 using to manage Terminal Services, 243 to 246
 using to track Terminal Services licensing, 245
  to 246
 virtualization and, 23, 26
Woersching, Eric, 5
Woolsey, Jeff, 5, 31
Workflow Foundation (WF), 86 to 87
Workflow Runtime, 87
WPAS (Windows Process Activation Service)
 defined, 93
 functionality, 347, 347 to 348

 overview, 93, 347
 as requirement for running TS Web Access, 227
 as requirement for running Web Server (IIS),
  347
 subcomponents, 93 to 94
WS-Atomic Transactions, 76
WS-Management, on Windows server core
  installations, 113
WS-* (Web Services), 10, 88
WSRM. *See* Windows System Resource Manager
wvetutil.exe, 140

X
XCopy deployment, 14, 66
XML Paper Specification (XPS) document viewer,
  84
XML schema, Windows Server 2008, 371
XPS Viewer, 84

Y
Yaqoob, Asad, 5, 429

Z
Zhao, Lu, 6, 183, 184, 185

Mitch Tulloch

Mitch Tulloch was lead author for the *Microsoft Windows Vista Resource Kit* (Microsoft Press, 2007) and is a widely recognized expert on Windows administration, networking, and security. Mitch has published over 200 articles for different IT pro sites and magazines and has written over a dozen books, including the *Microsoft Encyclopedia of Networking* and the *Microsoft Encyclopedia of Security* (both from Microsoft Press), *Windows Server Hacks* (O'Reilly Media, 2004) and *IIS 6 Administration* (McGraw-Hill/Osborne, 2003). Mitch has been the technical reviewer for numerous IT pro titles from Microsoft Press, and he has developed and taught graduate-level courses in Information Security Management (ISM) for the Masters of Business Administration (MBA) program of Jones International University. Mitch also writes a weekly editorial for IT World's iWindows in the Enterprise newsletter, which is read by thousands of IT professionals around the world.

Mitch has been repeatedly awarded Most Valuable Professional (MVP) status by Microsoft for his outstanding contributions in supporting both his local IT pro user group and the larger global community of IT professionals around the world. The Microsoft MVP Program recognizes individuals who share a deep commitment to building community among IT professionals and show a willingness to help others with their questions and problems. You can find out more about Microsoft's MVP Program at *http://mvp.support.microsoft.com.*

Mitch is president of MTIT Enterprises, an IT content-development business based in Winnipeg, Canada. Before starting his own business in 1998, Mitch worked as a Microsoft Certified Trainer (MCT) for Productivity Point. For more information about Mitch, see his Web site at *http://www.mtit.com.* You can also contact Mitch at *info@mtit.com* with your questions and suggestions; just be sure to use the subject "Feedback on Book" so that your message doesn't get routed to his junk mail folder by mistake!

What do you think of this book?

We want to hear from you!

Do you have a few minutes to participate in a brief online survey?

Microsoft is interested in hearing your feedback so we can continually improve our books and learning resources for you.

To participate in our survey, please visit:

www.microsoft.com/learning/booksurvey/

...and enter this book's ISBN-10 number (appears above barcode on back cover*).
As a thank-you to survey participants in the United States and Canada, each month we'll randomly select five respondents to win one of five $100 gift certificates from a leading online merchant. At the conclusion of the survey, you can enter the drawing by providing your e-mail address, which will be used for prize notification only.

Thanks in advance for your input. Your opinion counts!

* Where to find the ISBN-10 on back cover

ISBN-13: 000-0-0000-00000-0
ISBN-10: 0-0000-00000

Example only. Each book has unique ISBN.

Microsoft *Press*